Voting Behaviour in Canada

Voting Behaviour in Canada

Edited by Cameron D. Anderson and
Laura B. Stephenson

UBCPress · Vancouver · Toronto

20 19 18 17 16 15 14 13 12 11 10   5 4 3 2 1

Printed in Canada on FSC-certified ancient-forest-free paper (100% post-consumer recycled) that is processed chlorine- and acid-free.

Library and Archives Canada Cataloguing in Publication

Voting behaviour in Canada / edited by Cameron D. Anderson and Laura B. Stephenson.

Includes index.
ISBN 978-0-7748-1783-7 (bound); 978-0-7748-1784-4 (pbk.)

   1. Voting – Canada. 2. Voting research – Canada.

JL193.V675 2010	324.60971	C2010-900144-3

e-book ISBNs: 978-0-7748-1785-1 (pdf); 978-0-7748-5936-3 (epub)

Canadä

UBC Press gratefully acknowledges the financial support for our publishing program of the Government of Canada (through the Canada Book Fund), the Canada Council for the Arts, and the British Columbia Arts Council.

This book has been published with the help of a grant from the Canadian Federation for the Humanities and Social Sciences, through the Aid to Scholarly Publications Programme, using funds provided by the Social Sciences and Humanities Research Council of Canada.

UBC Press
The University of British Columbia
2029 West Mall
Vancouver, BC V6T 1Z2
www.ubcpress.ca

Contents

Illustrations

Figures

Tables

Preface

All modern democracies operate on the basis of representation. The act of choosing representatives through free and fair elections is fundamental to the exercise of legitimate democratic authority. For many citizens, participation through voting is the single most important (and often the only) political act that they will ever undertake. Given its importance to the practice of legitimate democratic authority, voting behaviour (how and why citizens vote) has long held a central place in the study of politics. The study of voting behaviour, from the original investigations into American elections to the multitude of theories, country studies, and elements that comprise the field today, is fascinating in its diversity. Situated within and contributing to this literature, this book seeks to illuminate the puzzle of individual vote choice by focusing on important factors that influence the electoral decisions of Canadian citizens.

The genesis of this volume is threefold. First, the origins of this book are rooted in our shared curiosity about Canadian and comparative voting behaviour. Each of us was inspired to begin our own studies in this area by an outstanding scholar of electoral behaviour – Elisabeth Gidengil of McGill University (Anderson) and John Aldrich of Duke University (Stephenson). Under the tutelage of these mentors, we individually came to realize that the study of voting behaviour can be enriched and expanded by looking beyond one's own border, incorporating new ideas, and testing boundaries of understanding. We are indebted to them for this pivotal role in our professional development.

Second, as we moved from graduate school to academic positions at the University of Western Ontario, we (individually and collectively) observed the absence of a book-length volume dedicated to voting behaviour in Canada. In particular, we recognized that there was no book examining various aspects of the vote decision, rather than a specific election, in the existing Canadian literature. With this omission in mind, we set out to craft a project that would fill this gap.

Third, the process of developing this book was greatly facilitated by our colleagues and friends in other Canadian universities. We were (and continue to be) inspired by the excellent work on Canadian political and voting behaviour being conducted by junior scholars in Canada. In recent years, many top-notch junior scholars have emerged in this field, and we thought that this project would be a wonderful forum to showcase their research. We were delighted that many agreed to contribute to this volume, and we believe that their work represents the cutting edge of voting behaviour research in Canada.

Acknowledgments

Work on this project officially began in November 2007 at a workshop held in London, Ontario. We wish to thank the following for financial support: the Social Sciences and Humanities Research Council of Canada; the Dean's Office in the Faculty of Social Science and the Office of the Vice-President-Research, both of the University of Western Ontario; and Greg Lyle of Innovative Research Group. The workshop brought together junior faculty and graduate students to discuss the papers that ultimately became chapters in this volume. Having a critical group of scholars who were familiar with each other's work, the main theories in the field, and the data that were being used was a wonderful experience. The comments, discussions, and ideas that emerged over the weekend were of the highest quality and led to significant improvements in the research. We would like to thank, in addition to the contributors to this volume, Blake Andrew, Marc-André Bodet, Fred Cutler, Cristine de Clercy, Caroline Dick, Eugenie Dostie-Goulet, Anna Esselment, Peter Ferguson, Jeffrey Parker, Joanna Quinn, Jason Roy, Daniel Rubenson, Ajay Sharma, Steve White, and Alexandra Wilton for contributing to the weekend. We also extend our gratitude to the staff in the Department of Political Science at the University of Western Ontario who, as always, supported us in this endeavour and helped to facilitate our efforts.

This volume would not have been published without the support of UBC Press. We thank the press for seeing merit in this project early on and throwing its support behind it. Beyond agreeing to publish this book, UBC Press has been an absolutely first-class organization to work with. Our editor, Emily Andrew, has been a model of efficiency, wisdom, patience, and good humour who has expertly guided us through the process virtually from start to finish.

Finally, we would be remiss if we did not recognize those who encourage and energize us every day to pursue our academic interests: our families. Kerry and Sadie Anderson and Jason, Maddie, and Ally McCready are simply the most important people in the world to us. Thank you for your continuing love, support, and patience.

Voting Behaviour in Canada

The Puzzle of Elections and Voting in Canada

Cameron D. Anderson and Laura B. Stephenson

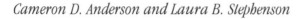

On 23 January 2006, the Canadian electorate voted to remove the Liberal Party from power and replace it with the newly united Conservative Party as Canada's new government. This electoral result signalled the end of over a decade of electoral success for the Liberals, who had won three majority governments and one minority government in succession. Although the defeat in 2006 marked the end of a Liberal dynasty, the result, perhaps more profoundly, conveyed the continued ability of the Canadian electorate to influence the content and character of the federal government. In this sense, the 2006 election outcome reaffirmed that elections are pivotal to the practice and success of democracy.

Beyond the details of specific elections, voting is a critical topic of study in political science because the act of choosing representatives through regular elections is fundamental to the exercise of legitimate democratic authority. For many citizens, the act of electing and/or defeating a government representative is the single most important political act that they will ever undertake. Even though there are many opportunities to get involved in politics (joining a political party, campaigning, signing a petition, and so on), the act of voting is often the only way that most citizens engage with the process and practice of politics. Given the central role, visibility, and importance of voting to democracy, understanding how and why citizens vote has long been a focus of study for many political scientists.

In this chapter, we provide a loose metaphor – that of complex puzzles – for thinking about and understanding elections and voting. Completing a puzzle inevitably involves identifying all the relevant pieces and then organizing them to present a coherent picture. To get a complete picture of voting behaviour, then, the many factors that contribute to an electoral result must be identified.

The metaphor of a puzzle can also be applied to illuminate the nature of electoral choice at the level of the individual voter. Each vote decision is a composite of several factors that explain how and why the person votes the way that he or she does. Viewing electoral choice in this way, a key intention of this book, as well as each of the chapters, is to elaborate some of the factors that can contribute to developing a comprehensive picture of vote decisions. Each chapter discusses a different piece of the puzzle (such as partisanship, economic conditions, and campaign effects) that is known to influence the vote decision among the Canadian electorate and considers how important it is to developing a coherent picture of individual vote choice.

Each of the pieces focused on in this volume has been identified from a rich and lengthy literature on voting decisions in advanced industrial democracies. These pieces form the basis of how political scientists think about and attempt to understand individual vote choice in Canada. Several of the topics engage theories that have also been pursued in other national contexts, such as in the United States or Great Britain, so there is the added interest of comparing Canadian results with those in different countries to uncover any universal or unique aspects of voting behaviour.

The bulk of this introductory chapter is designed to provide a roadmap through the terrain of voting behaviour literature, giving an overview of the theories of vote choice and an understanding of the various factors that are highlighted in each. In the following pages, we begin the journey – starting with the socio-psychological model, moving to refinements, and then embarking on a tour of rational and spatial models. Our exploration of vote models ends with a discussion of the model currently most popular in studies of Canadian voting behaviour. Providing a backdrop for the chapters to come, we then detail the collective understanding of Canadian voting behaviour and how these findings relate to established vote models. We conclude this introductory chapter with an overview of the chapters that follow, and we suggest ways of viewing each topic in light of the many broad voting models.

Approaches to the Study of Voting in Canada

The Socio-psychological Model of Voting
Much of the current understanding of voting behaviour in Canada has its roots in investigations into American elections. The first model of voting emerged out of work done by researchers at Columbia University

(Lazarsfeld, Berelson, and Gaudet 1944; Berelson, Lazarsfeld, and McPhee 1954). Initially, the scholars pursued a "consumer preference" model, in which elections were seen as events through which consumers (voters) were inundated with advertising (campaign materials) to entice them to choose (vote for) one product (candidate) over another (Niemi and Weisberg 1993). However, after analyzing data about voters during the 1940 American election, the authors found that many vote decisions had been made *prior* to the beginning of the campaign. Thus, it was clear that the campaign was not the central mechanism by which vote choice was shaped. The researchers developed a different theory of voting behaviour that focused on social features. They argued that vote choice could be understood as the outcome of three factors: one's socioeconomic status, one's religion, and one's area of residence. Looking at these factors (operationalized as education, income, class, religion, urban or rural residence), the authors put forward two volumes (Lazarsfeld, Berelson, and Gaudet 1944; Berelson, Lazarsfeld, and McPhee 1954) arguing for the need to understand one's background in order to understand one's vote.

However, when their model was applied to the 1948 American election by a team of researchers at the University of Michigan, it did not produce strong results. In fact, it appeared that the theory was wrong; if long-term social characteristics influenced vote choices, then how could *changes* in the vote total be explained, given that social characteristics varied little from the previous election? In response to this challenge, the Michigan scholars set out to understand the role of both long-term and short-term influences on one's vote. Specifically, they argued that there was a "funnel of causality" that began with the social characteristics (ethnicity, race, religion, education, occupation, class, parental partisanship) that had been identified by the Columbia school, which the Michigan scholars conceptualized as influencing an individual's personal attachment to a party (partisanship). In addition, the researchers recognized the importance of factors closer in time to the vote than partisanship: evaluation of candidates, evaluation of issues, campaign effects, and conversations with family and friends. All of these factors together were argued to influence how a voter chose to cast his or her ballot (see Figure 1.1). Although conceptually the Michigan model, as it came to be known, encompassed many variables that spanned a significant amount of time, the researchers themselves focused on partisanship, candidate evaluation, and issue positions in their famous book, *The American Voter* (Campbell et al. 1960). The authors found that partisanship and candidate evaluations

Figure 1.1

The funnel of causality

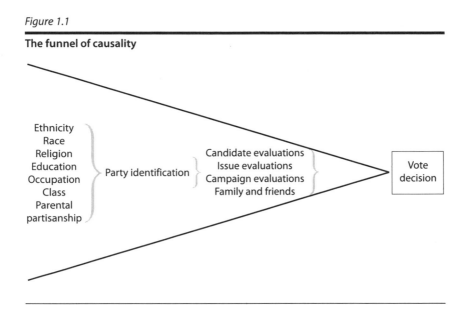

were most influential and that issues had little impact on vote choice in the elections that they studied.

Clarke et al. (2004) developed a modified version of this model in their study *Political Choice in Britain,* in which they present a valence model of voting behaviour. The valence model focuses on the voter's expectations of what the candidates will be able to accomplish in office – in other words, it goes beyond campaign promises and policy stances to consider whether or not the candidate will be able to deliver. It is based on Stokes's (1963, 1992) idea of a valence issue, an issue on which parties agree about what needs to be done. Voters cannot choose between candidates on the basis of their positions on these types of issues, but these issues are still significant in voting decisions since voters consider the ability to deliver the desired outcome in distinguishing between candidates. Clarke et al. (2004) also recognize, explicitly, that voters' opinions of future performances will be biased by their use of cognitive shortcuts, such as leader evaluations and partisanship. In using this model, they move away from the narrow application of the Michigan model found in *The American Voter* to a fuller conceptualization of the many factors that Campbell et al. (1960) included in their description of the "funnel of causality."

Several of the elements of these models have sparked particular attention from scholars. Below we discuss in greater detail two of the pieces in the sociopsychological model of voting.

Issue Voting

Campbell et al.'s (1960) finding that issues were less important than partisanship or candidate evaluations, despite their model's expectations, struck a chord with some researchers. Disagreement (or perhaps disbelief) that issue positions were not relevant for voters led scholars to develop a revisionist school of voting behaviour. This school, while generally accepting of the Michigan model's premises, addressed the limited role of issues. The revisionist project has spawned many interesting adaptations of the findings of the original model. One of the biggest refinements is that issues really can have an impact on elections. Issue voting was found to be significant by several authors, one of the earliest and most prominent being V.O. Key Jr. (1966). He argued that issue voting takes the form of voters voting for (against) a candidate with whom he or she is satisfied (dissatisfied). However, issue voting can occur only if there is a clear difference between the policy positions of the candidates and their parties – if both parties take the identical stance on an issue, then voting for one or the other will do nothing to effect change. Thus, this early finding of issue significance made a case for considering the specific context in which issues might matter. RePass (1971) and Pomper (1972) found similar support in their own research for the importance of issues.

Other scholars refined the idea of issue voting by recognizing the specific characteristics of issues. Carmines and Stimson (1980) extended the argument to take into account the difficulty of the issue. They argued that "easy" issues, ones on which most individuals can form clear opinions, are those that are long-standing, concerned more with policy ends than with means, and are more symbolic than technical. More difficult or "hard" issues, those that are obscure or complex, are less easily comprehended by voters – only a select group of sophisticated (educated) individuals would have the necessary capacity to incorporate their preferences regarding such issues into their vote decisions. Fiorina (1981) advanced the idea of issue voting by considering the past and the future. He discussed the role of retrospective and prospective voting – in one case voting on the basis of how issues were handled in the past and in the other voting on how issues will be handled in the future. In lay terms, retrospective voting is the equivalent of "throwing the rascals out" if one determines that those currently in office are, in fact, rascals. Prospective voting demands more of a voter since he or she must sort through campaign promises and the probability of those promises being fulfilled (similar to the valence model) in order to determine the "right" way to vote on the basis of the issue.

Another extension of the idea of issue voting is issue ownership (Budge and Farlie 1983; Petrocik 1996). Issue ownership means that a party is perceived to be the most competent on a specific issue – whether by reputation, because of past performance, or due to ideological affinity. In other words, the party has a clear reputation as being best suited to handle the issue. In keeping with a valence model of voting (see above), the theory of issue ownership posits that voters cast their ballots for the party that "owns" the issues that are salient and/ or most important to them in the election (Bélanger and Meguid 2008). For parties, then, developing a reputation for issue ownership and attempting to constrain campaign issues to those already "owned" are significant campaign considerations.

Finally, the role of issues in vote choice has also been studied from the angle of economic conditions. As a subset of issue voting, the general premise of economic voting is that economic conditions act as shorthand decision criteria for evaluating the incumbent's performance. If the economy is better (worse) today than when the incumbent came to office or over the past year, then voters will reward (punish) the incumbent with re-election (defeat). The basic formula of economic voting has been tested extensively, and widespread comparative evidence suggests that economic conditions significantly influence vote choice (see, for example, Lewis-Beck and Stegmaier 2000). Thus, it has come to be recognized that issues do have significance under specific circumstances but that the role of issues is complex and nuanced. The focus on partisanship, issues, and leader evaluations in the Michigan model has been justified despite early evidence to the contrary.

Campaign Effects

Less a refinement to the Michigan model than an elaboration, a significant body of work has developed that focuses on the most proximate causes of voting identified in the "funnel of causality" – campaign effects. Recall that the Michigan model did not incorporate these factors directly, although they are included in its overall conception of vote choice. Work in this area has investigated the effects of political campaigns, with mixed results. The prevailing consensus is that campaigns have minimal effects (see the review in Brady, Johnston, and Sides 2006). Especially with the emphasis on partisanship (and thus long-standing predispositions) that emerged from early research into voting, it was generally held that campaigns did (and could) not factor strongly in a voter's evaluation of candidates if he or she decided whom to vote for prior to the campaign. However, the idea that campaigns can have only minimal effects on voter behaviour is no longer uncontested. The consensus has been challenged by a refined definition of what constitutes a campaign effect and the application of new methodologies.

Initially, the minimal effects view of campaigns was supported by evidence that little or no persuasion had occurred: that is, voters had not been swayed to prefer a candidate by the substance of the campaign. However, when researchers changed their focus to consider priming or agenda setting, their findings were significantly different. Returning to the research of the Columbia school, even then it was found that campaign information had the effect of reinforcing weak predispositions of voters, polarizing them toward one candidate over another (see the discussion in Brady, Johnston, and Sides 2006). Essentially, campaigns brought dormant (or weak) ideas and opinions to the forefront and thus contributed to the ultimate vote choice. The search for these kinds of alternative campaign effects was taken up in earnest during the 1980s. Bartels (1987, 1988), for example, found that when partisan predispositions were irrelevant (such as during American primary elections) campaigns became much more important in that events and media coverage impacted perceptions of candidate viability. Franklin (1991) and Alvarez (1997) found similar results in senatorial elections and presidential elections respectively.

The second change to the study of campaign effects deals with methodology. Most voting research has been, and continues to be, conducted with surveys. Typical surveys provide a snapshot of opinions and attitudes held at a single point in time. There are two limitations inherent in this research design. First, surveys depend on the information that a respondent provides. In the case of campaigns, this means that any analysis of campaign effects is necessarily dependent on how accurately and truthfully the respondent reports his or her exposure to campaign materials. Second, campaigns are dynamic events that occur over several days or months – thus, a snapshot of voter attitudes is limited in what it can reveal about a phenomenon. Many national election surveys, such as the Canadian Election Study, the British Election Study, and the American National Election Study, conduct campaign-period and post-election panel surveys, which partially overcome the difficulty of a single-moment snapshot. If it is possible to conduct surveys before and after specific campaign events, such as debates, then a two-part panel survey can reveal the effects of that event. However, the difficulty of planning in advance for the important events in a campaign limits this method. A significant development in survey research methodology that addresses these concerns specifically is the rolling cross-section (RCS) survey. This methodology was first used in the 1984 American National Election Study and, since 1988, has been used for Canadian Election Studies (CES); in 2001 and 2005, it was also employed by the investigators of the British Election Study. The process involves building a data set from individuals surveyed at different points throughout the campaign (each day in the Canadian case), thus allowing researchers to observe changes in attitudes and opinions that occur over the course of the campaign. Using this methodology, significant campaign effects have been observed, such as the impact of a debate on leader evaluations and the importance of rhetoric for setting the agenda for the election (Johnston et al. 1992).

Experimental methodologies have also yielded very interesting findings about campaign effects. Experiments have the advantage of allowing researchers to control, monitor, and verify that campaign materials were in fact received by a subject. Furthermore, in an experimental setting, many other factors that might influence vote choice can be controlled. Of course, what this methodology gains in precision is lost in external validity, as it is very difficult to make an experiment taking place in a lab hold the same meaning as actually going to a voting booth. Nonetheless, this methodology has provided some interesting results. Early research into the question of turnout, for example, found that canvassing, in person and by phone, and paper advertising were able to increase voter turnout (Eldersveld 1956; Bochel and Denver 1971; Gerber and Green 2000). Other studies have analyzed how exposure to different messages and different media affects voters (Ansolabehere and Iyengar 1994; Lodge, Steenbergen, and Brau 1995). Such studies have found that negative information is more powerful than positive information (Iyengar and Simon 2000), that campaigns contribute to the information that a voter has about candidates and parties (Ansolabehere and Iyengar 1994), and that voters adjust their evaluations of candidates in response to campaign materials (Lodge, Steenbergen, and Brau 1995).

Research into priming, agenda setting, and framing has also shown that the messages directed at voters during a campaign can have real effects on vote choice. Priming – that is, making certain considerations more salient (and therefore more important) in one's decision making – has been shown to be a significant influence in election campaigns in Canada and the United States (see, for example, Jenkins 2002 and Druckman 2004). Work on agenda setting has shown that the criteria on which candidates and parties are judged in an election can be influenced by the rhetoric of the campaign (Iyengar and Kinder 1987; Johnston et al. 1992). Soroka (2002) demonstrates the role of the media in determining which issues are prominent on the political agenda. It has also been shown that polls, publicized as pieces of information, can have an impact on perceptions of the candidates' chances and vote choice itself (Blais, Gidengil, and Nevitte 2006). Finally, extensive work on framing has shown that how an issue is "packaged" for public consumption can make a real difference in the opinions that are formed by citizens. Frames can influence opinions by emphasizing specific information (Nelson and Willey 2001) and in turn making specific concerns more salient (Nelson and Oxley 1999) in decision making. In election campaigns, the frames used by the media can have significant effects (Rhee 1997; Trimble and Sampert 2004).

Researchers have also made significant headway in understanding which campaign messages are effective and when. Zaller (1992), for example, suggests that predispositions can act as a buffer between information and beliefs; those who hold opinions weakly, then, are the most apt to be affected by political communication. A person is affected by campaign materials typically through an increase in information, leading to an "enlightened" perspective on the vote choice (Gelman and King 1993). The interaction between messages and prior attitudes can lead to polarization, whereby a person's opinion is reinforced and becomes clearer (Ansolabehere and Iyengar 1994). It has also been found that messages that are consistent with voter expectations tend to be the most effective (Iyengar and Valentino 1999), as are messages delivered by credible sources (Druckman 2001). Finally, it has been shown that there is a "negativity bias," such that negative information tends to be more influential than positive information (Holbrook et al. 2001), although it may also have the effect of depressing turnout (Ansolabehere and Iyengar 1994). Thus, a great deal of scholarship has demonstrated that, despite early research to the contrary, events most proximate to one's vote choice, during the campaign, can have a significant effect on voting behaviour.

Spatial and Rational Models of Vote Choice

Although the sociopsychological approach is prominent in voting studies, a second important approach to the study of vote choice is rooted in work that considers spatial competition (Hotelling 1929). The work of Downs (1957) and Black (1958) brought the idea of spatial competition into the political realm by arguing that it is possible to understand voter behaviour on the basis of preferences and spatial distances from political alternatives (candidates or parties). This strand of literature, also known as proximity voting, assumes that all actors (voters and parties/candidates) are motivated by their own self-interests to develop preferences for their political options. Specifically, the spatial model of voting assumes that a voter's policy preferences can be understood in a dimensional space – each dimension representing a different policy issue (see Figure 1.2). The voter casts a ballot for whichever candidate is located closest to his or her position in that n-dimensional space – a so-called

Figure 1.2

An example of spatial preferences: Two issues

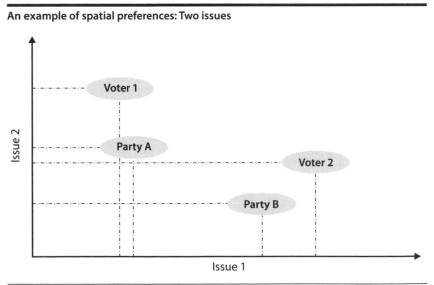

rational vote (Enelow and Hinich 1984). Parties therefore have an incentive to ensure that their policy positions are close to the median of all policy dimensions. Thus, the idea of the median voter dictating policy was born.

The directional theory of voting incorporates ideas from theories of symbolic politics to elaborate on the basic spatial model. Rabinowitz and Macdonald (1989) point out that people react to issues in terms of both the direction of the stance taken and the *intensity* of the stance. Thus, a candidate who takes a more extreme stance in a voter's preferred direction may be preferred over a candidate with a moderate stance: "The candidate who is most appealing to those on his or her side of the issue is the candidate who provides the most stimulation by being intense" (Rabinowitz and Macdonald 1989, 109). A candidate who takes a moderate stance on an issue is not recognized by voters for taking that stance and thus will not accrue votes on the basis of that issue. Macdonald, Listhaug, and Rabinowitz (1991) found that this model was more appropriate than the simple proximity model for evaluating voter behaviour in multiparty systems.

Another strand of rational voting theory also originates in expectations expressed in Downs (1957). Downs recognizes that all party options are not equally likely – even though a party may be very close to one's ideal policy points, it might have no chance of winning either a seat or the election as a whole. In such a scenario, a voter may realize that casting a sincere ballot for his or her most preferred party is unlikely to affect the outcome of the election. A voter is left with two options: cast a strategic vote or abstain from voting altogether.

Strategic voting can be defined as voting for a candidate other than one's first preference, when the chances of one's first preference winning in the election are slight, to prevent another candidate from winning. The idea behind strategic voting is that voters would prefer that a second preference wins rather than a third or lower preference – therefore, they choose to vote strategically (that is, not for their sincere preference) in order to prevent the worst/least preferred outcome from occurring. In the Canadian case, the federal election of 2008 provides an excellent example as there was talk of environmentally conscious voters supporting either the NDP or the Liberal Party candidate, depending on which had the best chance of winning, in order to prevent the Conservative candidate from winning in a riding. This model was stated most clearly by McKelvey and Ordeshook (1972). Studying voting behaviour from this angle has revealed that few voters actually cast strategic ballots – and this informa-tion has opened up a new avenue of research into how voters perceive their political options and how knowledgeable voters are about the real-istic outcomes of electoral contests (Blais and Turgeon 2004; Abramson et al. 2005; Levine 2007; Merolla and Stephenson 2007b).

Under the scenario of a voter's preferred party having little chance of winning, the second option is not to cast a ballot at all. Downs (1957) and others after him (see Riker and Ordeshook 1968) envision the deci-sion to vote as being about not only the benefit to be received by the voter if the preferred candidate wins but also the probability of that oc-curring. Downs argues that a voter will cast his or her ballot for the candidate whose expected utility (probability multiplied by benefit) is highest. If a voter is perfectly indifferent between the candidates, then he or she should abstain from voting.

Downs (1957) also theorizes that a voter with a clear preference may abstain if the expected utility is higher than the costs of voting. A voter's expected utility depends on the probability of a preferred candidate win-ning – but this depends not only on the voter's ballot but also on the ballot of every other voter. Thus, the real question is whether one *specific* ballot can make the difference in whether a candidate wins or loses – in ridings of 125,000 people, the rational expectation is about an 8 in 100,000 chance of casting the deciding ballot. This particular contention has been formalized as the calculus of voting, usually stated as

$$V = pB - C,$$

> where V is casting a ballot,
> p is the probability of the preferred candidate winning,
> B is the benefit expected from the preferred candidate, and
> C is the cost of voting.

This formulation of an individual's vote decision introduces one difficulty – if the costs of voting are never zero, and the chances of casting a win-ning ballot are infinitesimal, then it is never rational for anyone to vote. However, we know that people do vote – regularly – and therefore this has become known as the paradox of voting.

Downs (1957) reconciles this difficulty by acknowledging that there is a danger that, if all voters follow this rational calculus and abstain from voting, democracy will collapse. He argues that, because voters value democracy, they will figure that into their benefits of voting and, as we see empirically, go to the polls. In this revised version of the calculus of voting (stated formally by Riker and Ordeshook 1968), the voting decision is $V = pB - C + D$, where D is a term that encompasses feelings of duty to preserve the democracy.

There are many critics of this theory of voting behaviour (see, for example, Green and Shapiro 1994; Blais 2000). Others have developed different rational theories of voting to overcome reliance on a voter's "duty" to explain voter turnout. Minimax theory (Ferejohn and Fiorina 1974) is one of the most famous. Ferejohn and Fiorina (1974, 528) argue that "the minimax regret criterion specifies that the citizen should choose the act which minimizes his maximum regret." After significant calculation, they conclude that "a citizen following the minimax regret decision rule votes for his preferred candidate rather than abstains if the utility gain from the election of his preferred candidate exceeds four times the utility loss of the voting act" (528).[1] Thus, the spatial model of voting enriched the study of voting behaviour by shedding light on proximity voting, strategic voting, and turnout – each of which is a fascinating aspect of voting behaviour.

The Block Recursive Approach

Finally, there is another broad model of voter behaviour, which has found prominence in the study of Canadian elections especially. Each of the above theories and approaches to voting behaviour highlights a specific series of variables that can be used to explain vote choices. Although such models individually emphasize particular factors, it is often, if not always, the case that these approaches fail to explain the voting decisions of the entire electorate. Some explanatory factors might be more appropriate for some voters than others, and all factors will not or cannot account for every vote decision. In part proceeding from these observations, Miller and Shanks (1996) developed a comprehensive approach to explaining voting behaviour that they entitled the "block recursive model."

This model of vote choice incorporates many if not all of the broad theoretical innovations from the sociopsychological and rational schools of thought. As such, the model includes sociodemographic variables, values and beliefs, partisanship, issues, leadership, and campaign dynamics. Underlying the model is the central premise that some factors known to influence vote choice are closer in time to the vote decision (such as voters' issue positions or leader evaluations), whereas other factors (such as relevant sociodemographics) are more temporally distant from the vote. Those that are distant may have both direct and indirect effects on vote choice by way of their influence on factors that come later in time (closer to the actual vote). For example, partisanship is usually developed before a campaign begins in the "funnel of causality," but it may have a significant effect on how one evaluates candidates in the race. Thus, groups (or "blocks") of factors are included in the model sequentially, so as to use statistical results to reveal the interplay between long-term predispositions and short-term and proximate variables. Largely follow-ing the funnel of causality shown in Figure 1.1, the ordering used in recent Canadian Election Study investigations[2] puts social background characteristics first, followed by underlying beliefs and attitudes, partisan identification, economic evaluations, issue opinions, evaluations of the incumbent's performance, leader evaluations, and finally strategic con-siderations. At each stage, only those variables that are statistically sig-nificant when first introduced into the model are retained. In the end, a researcher using this model is left with a very powerful model of vote choice *and* knowledge of how the various factors interact with each other.

When the block recursive model was first introduced, reviews were quick to praise the innovation as a benchmark for future studies of elec-toral behaviour (Shapiro 1997; Brody 1998; Kapp 1998). However, any explanatory approach as comprehensive as this one purports to be can be criticized on a number of grounds. In the first instance, the block recursive strategy has been criticized for the nature of causal ordering choices. In a review of the original Miller and Shanks model, Shapiro (1997) observes that the selection and ordering of independent variables are not done deductively. Beyond criticisms regarding the selection and ordering of variables, many criticize the inability of the model to capture and incorporate campaign and media effects (Shapiro 1997; Brody 1998). Brody argues that media effects and the actions of politicians and can-didates in election campaigns often form the basis of impression, and ultimately, preference formation, but the block recursive model is largely silent on these important effects. Finally, the model can also be criticized for lacking the ability to differentiate the relative importance of different blocks of independent variables. The presumption underlying the model is that everything matters that is included in the regression, but beyond that there is little theoretical basis to predict or generate expectations regarding the relative effects of different variables in the model.

Canadian Voting Behaviour: Findings and Innovations

Having outlined the main theoretical approaches to the study of voting behaviour, we now turn our attention to how these models have been applied to elucidate the dynamics of voting in Canada. When the socio-psychological voting models were first "exported," researchers such as John Meisel, Philip Converse, Mildred Schwartz, and Maurice Pinard took advantage of the Canadian case as a new testing ground for the theories. Their findings about the Canadian electorate laid the base for the study of voting behaviour in Canada. Based on these initial contributions, work on voting behaviour in Canada has done much to elaborate theoretical understanding of the specific issues of Canadian voting behaviour.[3] Below we delve into the details of this research by considering specific categories of vote choice factors – sociodemographics, values and beliefs, partisanship, leader evaluations, issue attitudes, and campaign effects – relating to the sociopsychological models. Because the block recursive model incorporates most of these factors, all of the findings relate to that model as well. Finally, we consider the evidence for proximity voting, strategic voting, and turnout, relating to the spatial model of vote choice.

Sociodemographics

With respect to the Columbia tradition of voting studies, a great deal of early work on Canadian voting focused on, and found strong results for, social groups as vote determinants (Regenstreif 1965; Meisel 1975). However, not all social groupings had the same effect on vote choice in Canada, as in other contexts. In particular, Alford (1963) argued that Canada was a country where class voting did not occur. His findings encouraged later researchers, such as Ogmundson (1975), Kay (1977), Lambert and Hunter (1979), and Lambert et al. (1987), to investigate further. Despite the use of different theoretical approaches and methodologies, the role of class in Canadian voting was still found to be weak. Other researchers, such as Zipp and Smith (1982), Archer (1985), and Pammett (1987), found that the absence of a class cleavage had significant negative implications for the electoral fortunes of the NDP at the federal level.

The finding of the weakness of class also encouraged some researchers to examine differences across the various regions of the country. An evolutionary model of class voting was hypothesized, whereby class voting should increase as urbanization and industrialization changed the salience of region for voters (see the discussion in Gidengil 1992). Researching the applicability of this model, Jenson (1976) found no evidence to support it – the class cleavage remained weak even in the most industrialized provinces.

In contrast to the nearly non-existent role of class in accounting for Canadians' vote decisions, region of residence has been found consistently to have prominent effects. Blake (1972) found no evidence of a decline in the importance of region to voting outcomes since 1908; thus, the regional feature of Canadian politics provided "context" for voters in which the partisan choices, electoral competitiveness, and underlying dispositions of voters differed. In a later study, Blake (1978) argued that the influence of regionalism could be boiled down to differences in context – such as the distribution of individuals, the party system, and the competitiveness of the parties in those areas. Beyond that explanation, research has also demonstrated the existence of different regional political cultures (Simeon and Elkins 1974, 1980; Henderson 2004), some evidence of which was also found by investigators of the 1974 Canadian National Election Study in terms of voting behaviour (Clarke et al. 1979). Gidengil (1989) took the influence of region on vote behaviour a step further and found that regional context had an impact on the level of class voting observed.

Region remains a relevant sociodemographic factor in Canadian voting studies today. Successive findings from recent Canadian Election Study teams, using the block recursive model, demonstrate the salience of region and regional patterns of voting in Canada (Nevitte et al. 2000; Blais et al. 2002a; Gidengil et al. 2006a). For example, in the 2004 Canadian federal election, Gidengil et al. (2006a) report that the probability of voting for the Conservative Party was fifteen points higher in the western provinces and more than eighteen points lower in the Atlantic provinces (compared to Ontario). In contrast, the probability of voting for the Liberal Party in 2004 was eighteen points lower in the western provinces and almost sixteen points higher in the Atlantic provinces (compared to Ontario).

Some research has been directed toward *why* regional patterns exist and persist. In this vein, Gidengil et al. (1999) explore gaps in Liberal support between Ontario, the Atlantic, and the west and gaps in Reform support between Ontario and the west in the 1997 election. Their findings suggest that these gaps in support reflect true regional differences that cannot be explained by differences in sociodemographic makeup. In particular, they find that regional gaps in voting behaviour are driven by differences in political orientations, beliefs, and basic political priorities. Others, however, such as Clarke, Pammett, and Stewart (2001), contend that regional differences in political attitudes are overstated.

Last, in terms of the effects of region, some work has considered the role of rural, urban, and increasingly suburban residence on voting patterns. Although publications from recent CES teams do not demonstrate consistently strong findings for a rural/urban difference, evidence from the 2004 federal election suggests that the probability of rural residents voting for the Conservative Party was 11.5 points higher than that of urban residents (Gidengil et al. 2006a). In a useful reconceptualization of urban differences in voting, Walks (2005) considers variation in attitudes and voting patterns between urban and suburban residents. Using data from 1965-2000, he finds evidence of change in that urban voters have shifted to the ideological left and vote disproportionately for parties on the left, whereas suburban voters have shifted to the ideological right and tend to be more inclined to vote for parties on that end of the spectrum. Others who have studied this topic include Cutler and Jenkins (2000), Thomas (2001), and Wasko and O'Neill (2007). All find evidence of where one lives influencing attitudes, and thus voting behaviour, although some suggest that these effects can be explained by sociodemographic differences in rural and urban areas.

Outside region and class, religion has been found to be one of the strongest vote determinants in Canada (Gidengil 1992; Blais 2005). Perhaps the defining effect of religion in Canadian voting behaviour is that Catholics tend to vote disproportionately for the Liberal Party.[4] This finding emerged early (Regenstreif 1965) and has been remarkably consistent (Blais 2005), despite the dramatic increase in secularism in the country. Irvine (1974) proposed an explanation for this cleavage (parental transfer and socialization), which was refuted by Johnston (1985). Johnston's own solution (1991) has proven more stable (Bélanger and Eagles 2006), but it does not provide a clear statement of the causal mechanisms at work in perpetuating this cleavage. It has also been shown that, despite its endurance, the religious cleavage can be overcome by the effects of media exposure (Mendelsohn and Nadeau 1997). Despite the many efforts to account for the continued role of religion in Canadian voting patterns, Blais (2005) contends that we still do not know exactly why this relationship persists. In many ways, the issue of religious voting in Canada remains one of the least understood aspects of Canadian voting behaviour.

A few studies have also increased our awareness of another sociodemographic characteristic that influences voting behaviour in Canada: gender. Looking at voting patterns from 1965 to 1997, Erickson and O'Neill (2002) suggest the emergence of a "modern gender gap" (where women vote for left-wing parties and men for right-wing ones) in Canadian voting in the 1990s, in which differences in voting patterns between men and women became evident. They specify that the differences are more pronounced outside Quebec and that the gender gap is contingent on the overall variability in elections, the multiparty system, the salience of brokerage politics, and Canada/Quebec differences. In a study of electoral support for the right-wing Canadian Alliance Party in the 2000 Canadian federal election, Gidengil et al. (2005) find that structural and situational explanations of gender difference do little to account for the gap. Rather, the authors argue that gender differences in support for right-wing parties reflect underlying differences in values and beliefs between men and women (such as the appropriate role of the state and traditional moral values). Gidengil et al. (2006a) also find a gender gap in electoral support in the 2004 Canadian federal election, in which women were 3.9 points less likely to vote for the Conservative Party and 4.2 points more likely to vote for the NDP.

Finally, recent work suggests that marriage is a significant demographic influence. Wilson and Lusztig (2004) find evidence of a "marriage gap," such that married voters are more likely to prefer a conservative party (in their study, either the Reform or the Canadian Alliance Party) and tend to be morally more traditional than unwed voters. Thus, the study of sociodemographic voting factors has revealed some interesting features of the Canadian case: class matters little, region matters much, religion is an important cleavage, and significant gender and marriage gaps exist.

Values and Beliefs

Another category of vote choice factors includes the values and beliefs of voters. Most voters hold fundamental or underlying attitudes about politics that can be important factors in their vote decisions. Examples of such factors are views of the proper role of the state in society and the economy; affective orientations of voters to the political system (including cynicism, trust, and regionalism); and voters' beliefs about the best means of accommodating Quebec and Canada's political and economic integration with the United States. Blais et al. (2002a) suggest that underlying beliefs must be taken into account in any attempt to develop a comprehensive understanding of vote choice in Canada.

In their book on the 1997 Canadian federal election, Nevitte et al. (2000) highlight the role of ideological foundations of vote choice in Canada. They demonstrate the relative ideological coherence of party supporters, with Reform Party supporters (the data are from the 1997 election) closest to the economic and social "right" and NDP supporters closest to the "left." True to their brokerage histories, Nevitte et al. observe that supporters of both the Progressive Conservatives and the Liberals closely mirrored one another on a number of dimensions between the poles of NDP and Reform supporters, echoing earlier findings by Scarrow (1965) that the Progressive Conservative and Liberal Parties were very similar in terms of policy. These findings are reinforced by the results of Scotto, Stephenson, and Kornberg (2004).

Blais et al. (2002a) provide some sense of the magnitude of the effects of values and beliefs in the 2000 Canadian federal election. They observe that including measures of values and beliefs, such as social conservatism, free enterprise, attitudes toward minorities, feminism, religiosity, regional alienation, and cynicism in the model of vote choice contributes 10 percentage points to the explained variance of the model for voters outside Quebec. Within Quebec, the amount of variance explained through values and beliefs jumps 40 percentage points (largely based on the impact of attitudes regarding sovereignty).

Beyond this, a number of other scholarly contributions over the past fifteen years articulate how beliefs and attitudes influence voting. One study considers the role of antiparty attitudes on vote choice (Bélanger 2004). As a type of value orientation toward the political system, Bélanger distinguishes between "specific antipartyism" (rejection of major political parties such as Liberals or Conservatives) and "generalized antiparty" sentiment (rejection of political parties *en masse*). He finds that voters who reject traditional major parties (such as the Liberals or Conservatives) are more likely to vote for a third party (such as the Bloc Québécois or the Reform Party), whereas voters who express generalized antipartyism are more likely to abstain. Building on the role of underlying values and beliefs in third-party vote choice, Bélanger and Nadeau (2005) consider the role of political trust and the effects of its decline among the Canadian electorate. This article demonstrates that, whereas increasing distrust in the Canadian electorate fostered abstention, it had a more significant impact by facilitating third-party support.

Partisanship

One of the most studied aspects of the Michigan tradition of voting research in Canada is partisanship. Early researchers found that partisanship was an important consideration for Canadian vote choice, but the nature of Canadian partisanship has been an issue of significant debate since the 1970s. In the American context, partisanship is considered to be a stable, long-standing attachment that individuals refer to when making political choices (Campbell et al. 1960). However, the institutional context differs significantly between Canada and the United States, making salient the question of whether the concept can be exported. This issue was also raised with respect to partisanship in Britain (Butler and Stokes 1974). Indeed, there are a number of reasons to expect that partisanship might not explain electoral behaviour in the Canadian case as well as it does in the American one. For example, Canada lacks institutional arrangements (such as primaries and multiple ballots) favouring the development of party identification; for decades the two main parties were similar moderate, centrist parties; and there is a lack of symmetry between many of the party systems at federal and provincial levels, which might undermine the development of a consistent attachment to a particular party (Uslaner 1989; Gidengil 1992).

Meisel (1973, 67) sparked significant debate with his observation that "the concept of Party Identification, as used by scholars associated with the Michigan Survey Research Center ... may be almost inapplicable in Canada." Jenson (1975) and Elkins (1978), in this vein, argued that Canadian partisanship was of a different sort – more flexible, less stable, and more tied to vote choice than in the United States. In Jenson's view, partisanship "travelled with the vote" and thus was hard to distinguish as a separate attachment. Sniderman, Forbes, and Melzer (1974) strongly disagreed with this conceptualization of Canadian partisanship and took pains to argue that Canadian and American partisanship are of the same breed. This strand of research produced one of the most interesting amendments to the Michigan model and perhaps the most significant in terms of the study of Canadian voting behaviour.

Harold Clarke, Lawrence LeDuc, Jane Jenson, and Jon Pammett were responsible for conducting the Canadian Election Studies during the 1970s and 1980. Their research produced several volumes, beginning with *Political Choice in Canada* (1979). In it, the authors argue that partisanship in Canada can best be understood as having two variants – a flexible type and a durable type. Durable partisans can be understood, and classified, in the same way as American partisans. That is, their vote choice is strongly influenced by their partisanship, and their partisanship remains a significant identity even between elections. Flexible partisans, on the other hand, are individuals who hold their attachment much less strongly and are more likely to be swayed by the more proximate aspects of a vote decision, such as issues and candidates (the other aspects of the Michigan model). In fact, partisanship can be influenced by the same factors as vote choice; thus, for some, partisanship does indeed "travel with the vote" (Leduc et al. 1984, 478). Clarke and his colleagues used this framework to analyze the elections held between 1974 and 1993 and consistently found that flexible and durable partisans were swayed to differing degrees by vote considerations. LeDuc et al. (1984), for example, demonstrated the volatility and instability of the Canadian electorate using the panel surveys of 1974-1979-1980. These findings were replicated in a later study as well (Clarke, Kornberg, and Wearing 2000).

The finding of instability in Canadian partisanship marks a real departure from the original articulation of the Michigan model, and it is not without critics (see, for example, Schickler and Green 1997; Green, Palmquist, and Schickler 2002; and Gidengil et al. 2006b). Johnston (1992) and Blais et al. (2001a) have made the argument that the question wording used by Clarke et al. (1979) in their panel study may have been flawed. The central problem, according to Johnston (1992) and Blais et al. (2001a), is that the response categories did not allow for the option of not identifying with any of the parties. As a result of being required to choose one party in order to answer the survey question, the incidence of partisan volatility may have been inflated. Thus, Blais and his colleagues argue that the flexible and durable partisan approach to partisanship in Canada "underestimates the number of durable partisans and overstates the flexibility of Canadians' partisan ties" (2002a, 116). Clarke, Kornberg, and Scotto (2007), however, suggest that there is experimental evidence to the contrary. Regardless of this debate, recent findings suggest the ongoing importance of partisanship as a key explanatory factor underlying the stability of Canadians' vote choices (Nevitte et al. 2000; Blais et al. 2002a; Gidengil et al. 2006a). Indeed, Blais et al. (2002a) go so far as to argue that understanding the outcome of the 2000 Canadian federal election is impossible without taking into consideration the role of party identification. Thus, despite the potentially different nature of partisanship in Canada compared with that in the United States, it remains a fundamental factor in understanding Canadian voting behaviour.

Issue Opinions

A central expectation of the Michigan model of voting is that shorter-term factors, such as issues and economic evaluations, have significant effects on the vote decision. Issues can include diverse phenomena such as moral issues (such as abortion or same-sex marriage), fiscal issues (spend/tax more/less), public policy issues (such as health care or the environment), as well as election or government-specific issues (such as the sponsorship scandal). The collective wisdom suggests that issues do matter in Canadian voting (Nevitte et al. 2000; Blais et al. 2002a; Gidengil et al. 2006a). However, depending on the circumstances of the specific election, there might be differences in the sorts of issues that matter to voters and how much they matter. For instance, one of the defining issues in the 2000 federal election campaign was health care and the existence of some ambiguity regarding the Canadian Alliance Party's true intention for the maintenance of public health care. Blais et al. (2002a) observe that favourable views of public health care increased the probability of voting for the incumbent Liberal Party by 2.2 points in the 2000 federal election.[5] In comparison, Gidengil et al. (2006a) observe that views of health care in the 2004 federal election increased the probability of voting for the Liberal Party by two points.[6]

Beyond differences between elections in terms of the importance and nature of issue voting, Fournier et al. (2003) find that the importance that voters place on issues can mediate their impacts on voting. According to this line of research, voters more concerned about a particular issue (for example, health care) assign more weight to their evaluation of government performance on that issue when voting. This also relates to issue ownership. Nadeau et al. (2001) show that perceptions of party competence on specific issues are important factors in one's vote decision in Canada. Bélanger and Meguid (2008) go a step further to identify, in keeping with Fournier et al. (2003), that the salience of an issue is a factor in whether or not issue ownership of that specific issue will guide voters.

Another type of issue voting refers to evaluations of the economy. A number of pieces have been published articulating the relationship between economics and vote choice in Canada. Specific accounts of the 1997, 2000, and 2004 Canadian federal elections suggest a noticeable yet limited effect on vote choice in those elections (Nadeau et al. 2000; Nevitte et al. 2000; Blais et al. 2002a; Gidengil et al. 2006a). Additionally, a range of studies has continued to demonstrate the salient effects of economic conditions (and subjective perceptions of them) on federal incumbent support (Happy 1986, 1989, 1992; Clarke and Kornberg 1992; Nadeau and Blais 1993, 1995; Gélineau and Bélanger 2005; Anderson 2008).[7] Other studies demonstrate how federal economic voting differs by regions of the country (Godbout and Bélanger 2002) and the role of local economic conditions on federal vote choice (Cutler 2002). Further fleshing out the economic bases of party choice in Canada, Perrella (2005) suggests that short-term economic perceptions explain support for "mainstream parties" (Liberals and Conservatives), whereas long-term economic changes (such as unemployment and labour force participation rates) account for some of the support for non-mainstream parties.

A few studies have also considered the role of economic conditions on government support at the provincial level. Tellier (2006) finds that provincial economic conditions have an effect on provincial government popularity and, in particular, that unemployment shapes support for left-wing parties and that the nature of public deficits structures support for centre and right-wing governing parties. Similarly, Anderson (2008) observes that subjective evaluations of provincial economic conditions strongly shape provincial vote choice. In contrast, Gélineau and Bélanger (2005) find little support for the role of provincial economic conditions in provincial incumbent support. Rather, they report that provincial incumbent support tends to be driven by national economic conditions.

A related strand of work considers the relative importance of issues versus the economy. Election-specific findings suggest that, at least in the Canadian case, economic evaluations have a limited impact on vote choice (Nevitte et al. 2000; Blais et al. 2002a; Gidengil et al. 2006a). Beyond this, Blais et al. (2002b) suggest that in the 1997 federal election, issues were decisive in the vote decision for about 9 percent of voters, and the economy was decisive for about 4 percent of the electorate. Comparing Canada with the United Kingdom and the United States, the authors observed similar results: both issues and the economy influenced vote choice, but issues had a greater effect (Blais et al. 2004b).

Candidate Evaluations
The evaluation of candidates is the final major component of the Michigan model, after partisanship and issues. Views of party leaders and their leadership have proven to be an important component in the Canadian

vote calculus. Indicative of CES findings in other years, Gidengil et al. (2006a, 18) observe that "really liking the leader (in the 2004 election) increased the probability of voting for his party by 20 to 28 points." In Clarke et al.'s (1996) assessments of voting in the 1993 election, they also found that leader evaluations were important. Considering the same time period, Brown et al. (1988) apply a schema framework to attempt to understand the organization of leader evaluations in the minds of citizens. They find that leader images are shaped more by perceptions of a prototypical leader than by specific evaluations of individual leaders. The specific characteristics of a party leader also have an effect on vote choice. Cutler (2002) finds a negative relationship between vote choice and voters' increasing sociodemographic dissimilarity with party leaders. With respect to gender specifically, O'Neill (1998) finds that female leaders in the 1993 election attracted women to their parties. Finally, while Johnston (2002, 173) observes that evaluations of leaders' character and competence have an influence on vote choice, he suggests that the effects are a "factor at the margins" of electoral choice. As a result, when an election is close, Johnston suggests that it may be worth focusing on leaders' personalities.

Aside from leaders, voters have also been found to consider the candidates in their own ridings (Cunningham 1971).[8] There is evidence of an incumbency advantage in provincial and federal elections, such that voters are more likely to prefer incumbent candidates than others (Krashinsky and Milne 1983, 1985) even when there are particularly large shifts in voter preferences during the election (Krashinsky and Milne 1986). More generally, Blais et al. (2003a) find that many Canadians form preferences about their local candidates, especially those voters who live in rural ridings and are more politically knowledgeable. These preferences were decisive considerations for 5 percent of voters in the 2000 election. Thus, the research indicates that local candidates do matter for vote choices, although in a limited way.

Campaign Effects
Last but not least, in terms of the sociopsychological model, the funnel of causality recognizes the potential influence of campaigns on vote choice. With few exceptions, the factors chronicled to this point pertain to influences outside of or prior to an election campaign. Although views of issues or leaders might be mobilized during campaigns, the

independent effects of these factors can crystallize electoral decisions for some voters prior to an actual election (as the above discussion of campaign effects makes clear). Indeed, Fournier et al. (2001) find that, in Canada, close to 50 percent of the electorate make up their minds before an election campaign gets under way. Although the relatively high degree of pre-campaign vote deciders introduces a certain degree of vote choice stability during an election campaign, it also suggests that there is a significant proportion of the electorate for whom the campaign can be pivotal in their electoral decision making. Building on the findings that challenge the minimal effects thesis, a number of recent pieces in the literature on Canada look at the effect of campaigns on vote decisions.

Following on their 2001 piece, Fournier et al. (2004) question the extent to which voters are actually influenced by campaign events and media coverage. They find that the vote intentions of campaign deciders are not randomly volatile but reflect specific campaign events and media coverage. Additionally, they confirm that pre-campaign deciders are not influenced by campaign events. These findings nicely complement the work of Johnston et al. (1992), which provides strong evidence that strategic choices by the candidates in terms of which issues to focus on can have significant effects on the outcome of the election. In their book, Johnston et al. chronicle how the choice to campaign on the free trade issue pushed consideration of the Meech Lake issue to the background and made opinions about free trade strong influences on vote choice.

Given the focus on leaders in politics generally but particularly in an election campaign, leadership debates have the potential to fundamentally shift a party's electoral fortunes.[9] That said, evidence from recent Canadian elections suggests that such debates may not always be important. LeDuc (1994), for example, shows that the 1993 debates did little to affect the election outcome, although they did have some effect on voter perceptions of Kim Campbell and Jean Chrétien. Assessing the role of the 1997 Canadian election leaders' debate, Blais et al. (1999) find that, though the debate had a substantial impact on vote intention, this effect was temporary and ultimately negligible in the outcome of the election. In contrast, in the 2000 Canadian election, Blais et al. (2003b) observe that the leaders' debates significantly improved the electoral prospects for the Conservative Party under Joe Clark and hurt those of the Chrétien Liberals.

Proximity Voting

In regard to rational choice models of voting, work within the Canadian case has been limited. The debate over whether the proximity model performs better than the directional model has been taken up by Canadian scholars, although the block recursive and sociopsychological models have received much more attention. Contrary to the work of Macdonald, Listhaug, and Rabinowitz (1991) in the American context, both Johnston, Fournier, and Jenkins (2000) and Blais et al. (2001c) find that the proximity model is more appropriate than the directional model in the Canadian case, using data from the 1993 and 1997 federal elections.

Strategic Voting

Although the proximity and directional models of voting have received limited consideration in the Canadian literature, the application of strategic models of voting has been much more prominent and productive. Canada is a particularly good case study for strategic voting because of the prominence of third parties, especially the longevity of the NDP despite never having formed the government. The earliest study of strategic voting in Canada was conducted by Black (1978), who found evidence in favour of the probability component of the expected utility model (McKelvey and Ordeshook 1972) in the 1968 and 1972 election studies. Merolla and Stephenson (2007b), also using the expected utility model, found evidence of strategic voting in the 1988-2000 elections.

Advances in the study of strategic voting have also emerged from studies of Canada. Blais and Nadeau (1996) propose a two-step procedure for evaluating strategic voting that concentrates on voters who have a clear incentive to vote strategically. Blais et al. (2001b) found that perceptions of the likelihood of the local candidate winning had more influence on strategic behaviour than perceptions of which party was likely to form the government. This finding suggests the importance of local context and competition over national contests when understanding what influences the decision to vote strategically. In another paper, Blais (2002) developed an argument for why third-party supporters might not follow the strategic voting logic, using evidence from the 1988 election. Finally, Blais and Turgeon (2004) argue that strategic voting levels may be low because many voters are ill informed about the chances of the candidates in their ridings, on which their strategic voting decisions may depend.

Thus, though spatial models of voting are less prominent in the Canadian literature, there are some areas in which applying the rational voter model has been used productively.

Turnout

The spatial model of voting also has expectations about the decision to vote in the first place. All of the elaborate theory and sophisticated statistical modelling to unravel the puzzles of electoral decisions would be inconsequential if no one decided to vote. Although not a focus of early voting studies, the issue of turnout has become more prominent in Canada in recent years due to the declining rates of turnout. In the 1988 federal election, about 75 percent of eligible voters turned out to vote, and this was broadly consistent with postwar levels of turnout in Canadian federal elections.[10] However, national turnout declined in each of the next four federal elections; in 2004, just over 60 percent of registered voters turned out.[11] Although turnout rose to 64 percent in 2006, it dropped again in 2008 to 59 percent. In part motivated by these real-world dynamics, a range of work has been published that seeks to understand, in the Canadian case, why turnout has declined. The central finding for declining turnout levels focuses on youth (in particular, those voters born after 1970) and the relatively lower likelihood of youth to turn out (Nevitte et al. 2000; Blais et al. 2002a; Pammett and LeDuc 2003; Blais et al. 2004a). Findings from the 2000 Canadian election suggest that youth may be as much as 27 percent less likely to turn out compared with the oldest cohort of voters (Rubenson et al. 2004), although there is some evidence that youth turnout increased in 2004 (Elections Canada 2005; Johnston, Matthews, and Bittner 2007). Beyond the central observation that youth are less likely to turn out, the question of *why* has also occupied the research agenda in recent years. Blais et al. (2004a) find evidence of period and life cycle effects and argue that the decline is evidence of a cultural change toward lower levels of political interest and democratic duty. Howe (2006) focuses on the importance of political knowledge in turnout, drawing on findings from a comparison of Canadian data and data from the Netherlands. Finally, Johnston, Matthews, and Bittner (2007) argue that turnout decline can be blamed on the decline in the competitiveness of elections. To date, however, no completely satisfactory answer for why turnout has declined in Canada has been reached.

Organization of the Book

As the above review indicates, the study of voting behaviour in Canada has come a long way since the first applications of the Columbia model by Meisel and others. A great deal is known about what matters to Canadians when they decide whom to vote for – and a great deal remains to be understood. What is most obvious, however, is that no single model or explanation is able to provide a comprehensive and complete explanation of how Canadians vote. Indeed, recent work (aside from the books of the CES teams, using the block recursive model) tends to focus on understanding how one factor matters for voting, such as region or gender. In the chapters that follow, this trend is continued. This introductory chapter should be considered background for the upcoming chapters – each takes as its point of departure a theory or regularity of voting behaviour (Canadian or comparative) and examines it in terms of modern Canadian voting behaviour.

This book is divided into three sections. First, we consider the explanatory role of long-standing attachments in modern Canadian elections – those prioritized in the Columbia model of voting. The chapter by Goodyear-Grant looks at the role of gender in Canadian voting behaviour. In particular, she considers who is more likely to vote for female candidates and assesses the reasons that some people are more likely to vote for female candidates than male candidates. Drawing on theories of female political involvement, and using data from a recent election, this chapter makes a novel contribution to the study of gender and politics in Canada by evaluating the applicability of these theories for female Canadian voters.

The chapters by Bilodeau and Kanji and Stephenson address two of the long-observed regularities highlighted by Blais (2005) – that non-European immigrants and Catholics prefer the Liberal Party over all others. Bilodeau and Kanji address the issue of immigrants – specifically the "new" immigrants from non-European countries. Central questions driving their analysis include how strong are immigrants' allegiances to the Liberal Party, and are immigrants more likely to maintain that allegiance than native-born Canadians or immigrants from European countries? Stephenson's chapter considers the enduring bond between Catholics and the Liberal Party. Stephenson assesses the strength of this relationship by considering the impact of issue disagreements (over same-sex marriage and the sponsorship scandal) on the bond in the 2004 and 2006 Canadian federal elections.

Another long-standing attachment, specifically highlighted by the Michigan model of vote choice, is partisanship. As detailed above, the debate over the nature of partisan identification in Canada remains a significant and interesting part of the study of Canadian voting behaviour. The chapter by Bélanger and Stephenson addresses this debate by questioning whether political parties themselves have a role in determining the nature of attachments that voters develop. Specifically, since the entrance of non-brokerage parties (Reform/Alliance, Bloc Québécois) to the party system, has there been a difference in the type of allegiance that partisans hold for the various parties?

The next section of the volume considers shorter-term influences on Canadian voting behaviour, also recognized in the funnel of causality: issues and leader evaluations. Anderson's chapter looks at issue voting in the context of the economy and teases out the relative importance of different types of economic evaluations in recent elections. This is the first time that such issues have been addressed in the Canadian context since the 1980 election (Uslaner 1989). The chapter by Bélanger and Nadeau also looks at the impact of economic conditions on voting behaviour but in the sense of investigating whether prolonged economic hardship leads to an increase in voting for non-traditional, third parties. In this sense, they consider how economic conditions are related to protest voting against the Liberal and Conservative Parties. The chapter by Bittner considers the role that perceptions of a leader's character and competence play in vote considerations. She asks whether Canadians differentiate between leaders, especially leaders of the same party, and whether these evaluations are isolated or related to evaluations of the other candidates.

The final two substantive chapters of the volume consider the most proximate considerations in vote choice – those related to the campaign. Matthews's chapter looks, with surprising results, at the effect of campaign issues on how voters cast their ballots. Despite the logic of the enlightenment theory of political campaigns (Gelman and King 1993), Canadians do not seem to exhibit these effects in recent elections. Pickup's chapter considers the impact of the publication of poll results – specifically how the information provided by polls affects voters' perceptions of the election race. His findings indicate that polls do influence voters, and his demonstration of how poll results can have lasting effects is particularly relevant for understanding the relationship between polls and election outcomes in the 2004 and 2006 elections.

We believe that these chapters (and thus this volume) represent an important step forward in cataloguing what is known about the "puzzle" of Canadian voting behaviour.[12] In the conclusion, we (Anderson and Stephenson) discuss the implications of the individual chapter findings for the collective understanding of how Canadians vote. The research in this volume recognizes that all voters are not the same – and the time for one-size-fits-all voting models, as in the Columbia and Michigan days, might be nearing a close. The factors that the major voting models identify remain important – but to best understand their impacts, we need to look at voters as separate beings who may have very different calculations when they enter the voting booth.

Notes

1   For an in-depth discussion of turnout and rational choice models, see Aldrich (1993).
2   Here we are referring to the research conducted by the principal investigators of the recent Canadian Election Studies; specifically, we are referring to Nevitte et al. (2000); Blais et al. (2002a); and Gidengil et al. (2006a).
3   Two important review articles that chronicle the study of voting behaviour in Canada prior to the 1990s are Elkins and Blake (1975) and Gidengil (1992).
4   Another group that has been identified as disproportionately supporting the Liberal Party is non-European immigrants (Blais 2005). This attachment is discussed further in Chapter 3 of this volume.
5   Based on results reported in Appendix C and among voters outside Quebec (Blais et al. 2002a).
6   Based on results reported in Table 4 and among voters outside Quebec (Gidengil et al. 2006a).
7   Although Carmichael (1990) finds no evidence of economic effects on federal government support, Nadeau and Blais (1993) suggest that this is due to different methodological choices in the modelling of aggregate economic effects.
8   Irvine (1982) presents evidence to the contrary, showing that MPs do not reap the benefits of constituency activities at election time. He argues that the Canadian electoral system does little to encourage a bond between MPs and constituents.
9   Although not considering the effects on vote choice per se, a number of pieces examine the media coverage of leader debates and campaign coverage more generally and the nature of bias introduced in these accounts (see, for example, Gidengil and Everitt 1999, 2003a, 2003b).
10   From the Elections Canada website, http://www.elections.ca/.
11   Ibid.
12   Many of the chapters make use of sophisticated methodologies. For a general introduction to reading statistical results, please consult "Reading Political Behaviour: A Note on Methodology," http://www.politicalscience.uwo.ca/faculty/stephenson.

References

Abramson, Paul R., John H. Aldrich, André Blais, Matthew Diamond, Abraham Diskin, Indridi H. Indridason, Daniel Lee, and Renan Levine. 2005. "Preferences and Choices in FPTP and PR Elections." Paper presented at the annual meeting of the American Political Science Association, Washington, DC, 1 September.

Aldrich, John. 1993. "Rational Choice and Turnout." *American Journal of Political Science* 37, 1: 246-78.

Alford, Robert R. 1963. *Party and Society: The Anglo-American Democracies.* Chicago: Rand McNally.

Alvarez, R. Michael. 1997. *Information and Elections.* Ann Arbor: University of Michigan Press.

Anderson, Cameron D. 2008. "Economic Voting, Multilevel Governance, and Information in Canada." *Canadian Journal of Political Science* 41, 2: 329-54.

Ansolabehere, Stephen, and Shanto Iyengar. 1994. "Riding the Wave and Claiming Ownership over Issues: The Joint Effects of Advertising and News Coverage in Campaigns." *Public Opinion Quarterly* 58, 3: 335-57.

Archer, Keith. 1985. "The Failure of the New Democratic Party: Unions, Unionists, and Politics in Canada." *Canadian Journal of Political Science* 18, 2: 354-66.

Bartels, Larry. 1987. "Candidate Choice and the Dynamics of the Presidential Nomination Process." *American Journal of Political Science* 31, 1: 1-30.

–. 1988. *Presidential Primaries and the Dynamics of Public Choice.* Princeton: Princeton University Press.

Bélanger, Éric. 2004. "The Rise of Third Parties in the 1993 Canadian Federal Election: Pinard Revisited." *Canadian Journal of Political Science* 37, 3: 581-94.

Bélanger, Éric, and Bonnie M. Meguid. 2008. "Issue Salience, Issue Ownership, and Issue-Based Vote Choice." *Electoral Studies* 27, 3: 477-91.

Bélanger, Éric, and Richard Nadeau. 2005. "Political Trust and the Vote in Multiparty Elections: The Canadian Case." *European Journal of Political Research* 44, 1: 121-46.

Bélanger, Paul, and Munroe Eagles. 2006. "The Geography of Class and Religion in Canadian Elections Voting Revisited." *Canadian Journal of Political Science* 39, 3: 591-610.

Berelson, Bernard, Paul F. Lazarsfeld, and William N. McPhee. 1954. *Voting.* Chicago: University of Chicago Press.

Black, Duncan. 1958. *The Theory of Committees and Elections.* Cambridge, UK: Cambridge University Press.

Black, Jerome H. 1978. "The Multicandidate Calculus of Voting: Applications to Canadian Federal Elections." *American Journal of Political Science* 22, 3: 609-38.

Blais, André. 2000. *To Vote or Not to Vote? The Merits and Limits of Rational Choice.* Pittsburgh: University of Pittsburgh Press.

–. 2002. "Why Is There So Little Strategic Voting in Canadian Plurality Rule Elections?" *Political Studies* 50, 3: 445-54.

–. 2005. "Accounting for the Electoral Success of the Liberal Party in Canada." *Canadian Journal of Political Science* 38, 4: 821-40.

Blais, André, Elisabeth Gidengil, Agnieszka Dobrzynska, Neil Nevitte, and Richard Nadeau. 2003a. "Does the Local Candidate Matter? Candidate Effects in the Canadian Election of 2000." *Canadian Journal of Political Science* 36, 3: 657-64.

Blais, André, Elisabeth Gidengil, Richard Nadeau, and Neil Nevitte. 2001a. "Measuring Party Identification: Canada, Britain and the United States." *Political Behaviour* 23, 1: 5-22.

–. 2002a. *Anatomy of a Liberal Victory.* Peterborough: Broadview Press.

–. 2003b. "Campaign Dynamics in the 2000 Canadian Election: How the Leader Debates Salvaged the Conservative Party." *PS: Political Science and Politics* 36, 1: 45-50.

Blais, André, Elisabeth Gidengil, and Neil Nevitte. 2006. "Do Polls Influence the Vote?" In *Capturing Campaign Effects*, ed. Henry E. Brady and Richard Johnston, 263-79. Ann Arbor: University of Michigan Press.

Blais, André, Elisabeth Gidengil, Neil Nevitte, and Richard Nadeau. 2004a. "Where Does Turnout Decline Come From?" *European Journal of Political Research* 43, 2: 221-36.

Blais, André, and Richard Nadeau. 1996. "Measuring Strategic Voting: A Two-Step Procedure." *Electoral Studies* 15, 1: 39-52.

Blais, André, Richard Nadeau, Elisabeth Gidengil, and Neil Nevitte. 1999. "Campaign Dynamics in the 1997 Canadian Election." *Canadian Public Policy* 25, 2: 197-205.

–. 2001b. "Measuring Strategic Voting in Multiparty Plurality Elections." *Electoral Studies* 20, 3: 343-52.

–. 2001c. "The Formation of Party Preferences: Testing the Proximity and Directional Models." *European Journal of Political Research* 40, 5: 81-91.

–. 2002b. "The Impact of Issues and the Economy in the 1997 Canadian Federal Election." *Canadian Journal of Political Science* 35, 2: 409-21.

Blais, André, and Mathieu Turgeon. 2004. "How Good Are Voters at Sorting Out the Weakest Candidate in Their Constituency?" *Electoral Studies* 23, 3: 455-61.

Blais, André, Mathieu Turgeon, Elisabeth Gidengil, Neil Nevitte, and Richard Nadeau. 2004b. "Which Matters Most? Comparing the Impact of Issues and the Economy in American, British, and Canadian Elections." *British Journal of Political Science* 34, 3: 555-63.

Blake, Donald E. 1972. "The Measurement of Regionalism in Canadian Voting Patterns." *Canadian Journal of Political Science* 5, 1: 55-80.

–. 1978. "Constituency Contexts and Canadian Elections: An Exploratory Study." *Canadian Journal of Political Science* 11, 2: 279-305.

Bochel, J.M., and D.T. Denver. 1971. "Canvassing, Turnout, and Party Support: An Experiment." *British Journal of Political Science* 1, 3: 257-69.

Brady, Henry E., Richard Johnston, and John Sides. 2006. "The Study of Political Campaigns." In *Capturing Campaign Effects*, ed. Henry E. Brady and Richard Johnston, 1-26. Ann Arbor: University of Michigan Press.

Brody, Richard. 1998. "Review of the New American Voter." *Party Politics* 4, 2: 261-63.

Brown, Steven D., Ronald D. Lambert, Barry J. Kay, and James E. Curtis. 1988. "In the Eye of the Beholder: Leader Images in Canada." *Canadian Journal of Political Science* 21, 4: 729-55.

Budge, Ian, and Dennis J. Farlie. 1983. *Explaining and Predicting Elections: Issue Effects and Party Strategies in Twenty-Three Democracies.* London: Allen and Unwin.

Butler, David, and Donald Stokes. 1974. *Political Change in Britain: The Evolution of Electoral Choice.* 2nd ed. Basingstoke: Macmillan.

Campbell, Angus, Philip E. Converse, Warren E. Miller, and Donald E. Stokes. 1960. *The American Voter.* New York: Wiley.

Carmichael, Calum. 1990. "Economic Conditions and the Popularity of the Incumbent Party in Canada." *Canadian Journal of Political Science* 23, 4: 713-26

Carmines, Edward, and James Stimson. 1980. "The Two Faces of Issue Voting." *American Political Science Review* 74, 1: 78-91.

Clarke, Harold D., Jane Jenson, Lawrence LeDuc, and Jon H. Pammett. 1979. *Political Choice in Canada.* Toronto: McGraw-Hill Ryerson.

–. 1996. *Absent Mandate.* 3rd ed. Toronto: Gage.

Clarke, Harold D., and Allan Kornberg. 1992. "Support for the Canadian Federal Progressive Conservative Party since 1988: The Impact of Economic Evaluations and Economic Issues." *Canadian Journal of Political Science* 25, 1: 29-53.

Clarke, Harold D., Allan Kornberg, and Thomas Scotto. 2007. "The Valence Politics Model of Electoral Choice in Canada: A Brief History with Thoughts about the Future." Paper presented at the annual meeting of the Canadian Political Science Association, Saskatoon, SK, 30 May-1 June.

Clarke, Harold D., Allan Kornberg, and Peter Wearing. 2000. *A Polity on the Edge.* Peterborough: Broadview.

Clarke, Harold D., Jon H. Pammett, and Marianne C. Stewart. 2001. "The Forest for the Trees: Regional (Dis)Similarities in Canadian Political Culture." In *Regionalism in Canadian Politics,* ed. Lisa Young and Keith Archer, 43-76. Toronto: Oxford University Press.

Clarke, Harold D., David Sanders, Marianne C. Stewart, and Paul Whiteley. 2004. *Political Choice in Britain.* Oxford: Oxford University Press.

Cunningham, Robert. 1971. "The Impact of the Local Candidate in Canadian Federal Elections." *Canadian Journal of Political Science* 4, 2: 287-90.

Cutler, Fred. 2002. "The Simplest Shortcut of All: Sociodemographic Characteristics and Electoral Choice." *Journal of Politics* 64, 2: 466-90.

Cutler, Fred, and Richard Jenkins. 2000. "Where One Lives and What One Thinks: Implications for Rural/Urban Opinion Cleavages for Canadian Federalism." Paper presented at the Transformation of Canadian Political Culture and the State of the Federation Conference, Institute of Intergovernmental Affairs, Queen's University, Kingston, ON, 13-14 October.

Downs, Anthony. 1957. *An Economic Theory of Democracy.* Boston: Addison-Wesley.

Druckman, James N. 2001. "On the Limits of Framing Effects: Who Can Frame?" *Journal of Politics* 63, 4: 1041-66.

–. 2004. "Priming the Vote: Campaign Effects in a U.S. Senate Election." *Political Psychology* 25, 4: 577-94.

Eldersveld, Samuel. 1956. "Experimental Propaganda Techniques and Voting Behavior." *American Political Science Review* 50, 1: 154-65.

Elections Canada. 2005. "Estimation of Voter Turnout by Age Group at the 38th Federal General Election." Final report, December.

Elkins, David. 1978. "Party Identification: A Conceptual Analysis." *Canadian Journal of Political Science* 11, 2: 419-35.

Elkins, David, and Donald Blake. 1975. "Voting Research in Canada: Problems and Prospects." *Canadian Journal of Political Science* 8, 2: 313-25.

Enelow, James M., and Melvin J. Hinich. 1984. *The Spatial Theory of Voting.* New York: Cambridge University Press.

Erickson, Lynda, and Brenda O'Neill. 2002. "The Gender Gap and the Changing Woman Voter in Canada." *International Political Science Review* 23, 4: 373-92.

Ferejohn, John, and Morris P. Fiorina. 1974. "The Paradox of Not Voting: A Decision Theoretic Analysis." *American Political Science Review* 68, 2: 525-36.

Fiorina, Morris. 1981. *Retrospective Voting in American National Elections.* New Haven: Yale University Press.

Fournier, Patrick, André Blais, Richard Nadeau, Elisabeth Gidengil, and Neil Nevitte. 2003. "Issue Importance and Performance Voting." *Political Behavior* 25, 1: 51-67.

Fournier, Patrick, Richard Nadeau, André Blais, Elisabeth Gidengil, and Neil Nevitte. 2001. "Validation of Time-of-Voting-Decision Recall." *Public Opinion Quarterly* 65, 1: 95-107.

–. 2004. "Time-of-Voting Decision and Susceptibility to Campaign Effects." *Electoral Studies* 23, 4: 661-81.

Franklin, Charles H. 1991. "Eschewing Obfuscation? Campaigns and the Perception of U.S. Senate Incumbents." *American Political Science Review* 85, 4: 1193-1214.

Gélineau, François, and Éric Bélanger. 2005. "Electoral Accountability in a Federal System: National and Provincial Economic Voting in Canada." *Publius: The Journal of Federalism* 35, 3: 407-24.

Gelman, Andrew, and Gary King. 1993. "Why Are American Presidential Election Campaign Polls So Variable When Votes Are So Predictable?" *British Journal of Political Science* 23, 4: 409-51.

Gerber, Alan S., and Donald P. Green. 2000. "The Effects of Personal Canvassing, Telephone Calls, and Direct Mail on Voter Turnout: A Field Experiment." *American Political Science Review* 94, 3: 653-64.

Gidengil, Elisabeth. 1989. "Class and Region in Canadian Voting: A Dependency Interpretation." *Canadian Journal of Political Science* 22, 3: 563-87.

–. 1992. "Canada Votes: A Quarter Century of Canadian National Election Studies." *Canadian Journal of Political Science* 25, 2: 219-48.

Gidengil, Elisabeth, André Blais, Joanna Everitt, Patrick Fournier, and Neil Nevitte. 2006a. "Back to the Future? Making Sense of the 2004 Canadian Election Outside Quebec." *Canadian Journal of Political Science* 39, 1: 1-25.

–. 2006b. "Is the Concept of Party Identification Applicable in Canada? A Panel-Based Analysis." Paper presented at the ECPR 34th Joint Sessions of Workshops, Nicosia, Cyprus, 25-30 April.

Gidengil, Elisabeth, André Blais, Neil Nevitte, and Richard Nadeau. 1999. "Making Sense of Regional Voting in the 1997 Federal Election: Liberal and Reform Support Outside Quebec." *Canadian Journal of Political Science* 32, 2: 247-72.

Gidengil, Elisabeth, and Joanna Everitt. 1999. "Metaphors and Misrepresentation: Gendered Mediation in News Coverage of the 1993 Canadian Leaders' Debates." *Harvard International Journal of Press/Politics* 4, 1: 48-65.

–. 2003a. "Conventional Coverage/Unconventional Politicians: Gender and Media Coverage of Canadian Leaders' Debates, 1993, 1997, 2000." *Canadian Journal of Political Science* 36, 3: 559-77.

–. 2003b. "Talking Tough: Gender and Reported Speech in Campaign News Coverage." *Political Communication* 20, 3: 209-32.

Gidengil, Elisabeth, Matthew Hennigar, André Blais, and Neil Nevitte. 2005. "Explaining the Gender Gap in Support for the New Right: The Case of Canada." *Comparative Political Studies* 38, 10: 1171-95.

Godbout, Jean-François, and Éric Bélanger. 2002. "La dimension régionale du vote économique canadien aux élections fédérales de 1988 à 2000." *Canadian Journal of Political Science* 35, 3: 567-88.

Green, Donald, Bradley Palmquist, and Eric Schickler. 2002. *Partisan Hearts and Minds.* New Haven: Yale University Press.

Green, Donald P., and Ian Shapiro. 1994. *Pathologies of Rational Choice Theory.* New Haven: Yale University Press.

Happy, J. 1986. "Voter Sensitivity to Economic Conditions: A Canadian-American Comparison." *Comparative Politics* 19, 1: 45-56.

–. 1989. "Economic Performance and Retrospective Voting in Canadian Federal Elections." *Canadian Journal of Political Science* 22, 2: 377-87.

–. 1992. "The Effects of Economic and Fiscal Performance on Incumbency Voting: The Canadian Case." *British Journal of Political Science* 22, 1: 117-30.

Henderson, Ailsa. 2004. "Regional Political Cultures in Canada." *Canadian Journal of Political Science* 37, 3: 595-615.

Holbrook, Allyson, Jon A. Krosnick, Penny S. Visser, Wendi L. Gardner, and John T. Cacioppo. 2001. "Attitudes toward Presidential Candidates and Political Parties: Initial Optimism, Inertial First Impressions, and a Focus on Flaws." *American Journal of Political Science* 45, 4: 930-50.

Hotelling, Harold. 1929. "Stability and Competition." *Economic Journal* 39, 1: 41-57.

Howe, Paul. 2006. "Political Knowledge and Electoral Participation in the Netherlands: Comparisons with the Canadian Case." *International Political Science Review* 27, 2: 137-66.

Irvine, William P. 1974. "Explaining the Religious Basis of the Canadian Partisan Identity: Success on the Third Try." *Canadian Journal of Political Science* 7, 3: 560-63.

–. 1982. "Does the Candidate Make a Difference? The Macro-Politics and Micro-Politics of Getting Elected." *Canadian Journal of Political Science* 15, 4: 755-82.

Iyengar, Shanto, and Donald Kinder. 1987. *News that Matters: Television and Public Opinion.* Chicago: University of Chicago Press.

Iyengar, Shanto, and Adam F. Simon. 2000. "New Perspectives and Evidence on Political Communication and Campaign Effects." *Annual Review of Psychology* 51: 149-69.

Iyengar, Shanto, and Nicholas A. Valentino. 1999. "Who Says What? Source Credibility as a Mediator of Campaign Advertising." In *Elements of Reason,* ed. Arthur Lupia, Mathew D. McCubbins, and Samuel Popkin, 108-29. New York: Cambridge University Press.

Jenkins, Richard W. 2002. "How Campaigns Matter in Canada: Priming and Learning as Explanations for the Reform Party's 1993 Campaign Success." *Canadian Journal of Political Science* 35, 2: 383-408.

Jenson, Jane. 1975. "Party Loyalty in Canada: The Question of Party Identification." *Canadian Journal of Political Science* 8, 4: 543-53.

–. 1976. "Party Systems." In *The Provincial Political Systems: Comparative Essays,* ed. David J. Bellamy, Jon H. Pammett, and Donald C. Rowat, 118-31. Toronto: Methuen.

Johnston, Richard. 1985. "The Reproduction of the Religion Cleavage in Canadian Elections." *Canadian Journal of Political Science* 18, 1: 99-113.

–. 1991. "The Geography of Class and Religion in Canadian Elections." In *The Ballot and Its Message*, ed. Joseph Wearing, 108-35. Toronto: Copp, Clarke, Pitman.

–. 1992. "Party Identification Measures in the Anglo-American Democracies: A National Survey Experiment." *American Journal of Political Science* 36, 2: 542-59.

–. 2002. "Prime Ministerial Contenders in Canada." In *Leaders' Personalities and the Outcome of Democratic Elections*, ed. Anthony King, 158-83. New York: Oxford University Press.

Johnston, Richard, André Blais, Henry E. Brady, and Jean Crête. 1992. *Letting the People Decide*. Montreal : McGill-Queen's University Press.

Johnston, Richard, Patrick Fournier, and Richard Jenkins. 2000. "Party Location and Party Support: Unpacking Competing Models." *Journal of Politics* 62, 4: 1145-60.

Johnston, Richard, J. Scott Matthews, and Amanda Bittner. 2007. "Turnout and the Party System in Canada, 1988-2004." *Electoral Studies* 26, 4: 735-45.

Kapp, Lawrence. 1998. "Book Review of *The New American Voter*." *Perspective on Political Science* 21, 1: 31.

Kay, Barry J. 1977. "An Examination of Class and Left-Right Party Images in Canadian Voting." *Canadian Journal of Political Science* 10, 1: 127-43.

Key, V.O. Jr. 1966. *The Responsible Electorate*. Cambridge, MA: Belknap Press.

Krashinsky, Michael, and William J. Milne. 1983. "Some Evidence on the Effect of Incumbency in Ontario Provincial Elections." *Canadian Journal of Political Science* 16, 3: 489-500.

–. 1985. "Additional Evidence on the Effect of Incumbency in Canadian Elections." *Canadian Journal of Political Science* 18, 1: 155-65.

–. 1986. "The Effect of Incumbency in the 1984 Federal and 1985 Ontario Elections." *Canadian Journal of Political Science* 19, 2: 337-43.

Lambert, Ronald D., James E. Curtis, Steven D. Brown, and Barry J. Kay. 1987. "Social Class, Left/Right Political Orientations, and Subjective Class Voting in Provincial and Federal Elections." *Canadian Review of Sociology and Anthropology* 24, 4: 526-49.

Lambert, Ronald, and Alfred A. Hunter. 1979. "Social Stratification, Voting Behaviour, and the Images of Canadian Federal Political Parties." *Canadian Review of Sociology and Anthropology* 16, 3: 287-304.

Lazarsfeld, Paul F., Bernard Berelson, and Hazel Gaudet. 1944. *The People's Choice*. New York: Duell, Sloan, and Pearce.

LeDuc, Lawrence. 1994. "The Leaders' Debates: Critical Event or Non-Event?" In *The Canadian General Election of 1993*, ed. Alan Frizzell, Jon H. Pammett, and Anthony Westell, 127-41. Ottawa: Carleton University Press.

LeDuc, Lawrence, Harold D. Clarke, Jane Jenson, and Jon H. Pammett. 1984. "Partisan Instability in Canada: Evidence from a New Panel Study." *American Political Science Review* 78, 2: 470-84.

Levine, Renan. 2007. "Sources of Bias in Voter Expectations under Proportional Representation." *Journal of Elections, Public Opinion, and Parties* 17, 3: 215-34.

Lewis-Beck, M., and M. Stegmaier. 2000. "Economic Determinants of Electoral Outcomes." *Annual Review of Political Science* 3: 183-219.

Lodge, Milton, Marco R. Steenbergen, and Shawn Brau. 1995. "The Responsive Voter: Campaign Information and the Dynamics of Candidate Evaluation." *American Political Science Review* 89, 2: 309-26.

Macdonald, Stuart Elaine, Ola Listhaug, and George Rabinowitz. 1991. "Issues and Party Support in Multiparty Systems." *American Political Science Review* 85, 4: 1107-31.

McKelvey, Richard D., and Peter C. Ordeshook. 1972. "A General Theory of the Calculus of Voting." In *Mathematical Applications in Political Science*, vol. 6, ed. James F. Herndon and Joseph L. Bernd, 32-78. Charlottesville: University of Virginia Press.

Meisel, John. 1973. *Working Papers on Canadian Politics.* Enlarged ed. Montreal: McGill-Queen's University Press.

–. 1975. *Working Papers on Canadian Politics.* 2nd ed. Montreal: McGill-Queen's University Press.

Mendelsohn, Matthew, and Richard Nadeau. 1997. "The Religious Cleavage and the Media in Canada." *Canadian Journal of Political Science* 30, 1: 129-46.

Merolla, Jennifer L., and Laura B. Stephenson. 2007a. "Behind the Scenes: Understanding What Influences the Determinants of Strategic Voting." Paper presented at the annual meeting of the American Political Science Association, Chicago, IL, 30 August-2 September.

–. 2007b. "Strategic Voting in Canada: A Cross-Time Analysis." *Electoral Studies* 26, 2: 235-46.

Miller, Warren E., and J. Merrill Shanks. 1996. *The New American Voter.* Cambridge, MA: Harvard University Press.

Nadeau, Richard, and André Blais. 1993. "Explaining Election Outcomes in Canada: Economy and Politics." *Canadian Journal of Political Science* 26, 4: 775-90.

–. 1995. "Economic Conditions, Leader Evaluations, and Election Outcomes in Canada." *Canadian Public Policy* 21, 2: 212-19.

Nadeau, Richard, André Blais, Elisabeth Gidengil, and Neil Nevitte. 2000. "It's Unemployment, Stupid! Why Perceptions about the Job Situation Hurt the Liberals in the 1997 Election." *Canadian Public Policy* 26, 1: 77-93.

–. 2001. "Perceptions of Party Competence in the 1997 Election." In *Party Politics in Canada.* 8th ed., ed. Hugh G. Thorburn and Alan Whitehorn, 413-30. Toronto: Prentice-Hall.

Nelson, Thomas E., and Zoe M. Oxley. 1999. "Issue Framing Effects on Belief Importance and Opinion." *Journal of Politics* 61, 4: 1040-67.

Nelson, Thomas E., and Elaine Willey. 2001. "Issue Frames That Strike a Value Balance: A Political Psychology Perspective." In *Framing Public Life: Perspectives on Media and Our Understanding of the Social World*, ed. Stephen D. Reese, Oscar H. Gandy, and August E. Grant, 245-67. Mahwah, NJ: Lawrence Erlbaum Associates.

Nevitte, Neil, André Blais, Elisabeth Gidengil, and Richard Nadeau. 2000. *Unsteady State: The 1997 Canadian Federal Election.* Don Mills: Oxford University Press.

Niemi, Richard G., and Herbert F. Weisberg. 1993. "The Classics of Voting Behavior." In *Classics in Voting Behavior*, ed. Richard G. Niemi and Herbert F. Weisberg, 1-12. Washington, DC: CQ Press.

Ogmundson, Rick. 1975. "Party Class Images and Class Voting in Canada." *American Sociological Review* 40, 4: 506-12.

O'Neill, Brenda. 1998. "The Relevance of Leader Gender to Voting in the 1993 Canadian National Election." *International Journal of Canadian Studies* 17: 105-30.

Pammett, Jon H. 1987. "Class Voting and Class Consciousness in Canada." *Canadian Review of Sociology and Anthropology* 24, 2: 269-89.

Pammett, Jon, and Lawrence LeDuc. 2003. *Explaining the Turnout Decline in Canadian Federal Elections.* Ottawa: Elections Canada.

Perrella, Andrea M.L. 2005. "Long-Term Economic Hardship and Non-Mainstream Voting in Canada." *Canadian Journal of Political Science* 38, 2: 335-57.

Petrocik, John R. 1996. "Issue Ownership in Presidential Elections, with a 1980 Case Study." *American Journal of Political Science* 40, 3: 825-50.

Pomper, Gerald M. 1972. "From Confusion to Clarity: Issues and American Voters, 1956-1968." *American Political Science Review* 66, 2: 415-28.

Rabinowitz, George, and Stuart Elaine Macdonald. 1989. "A Directional Theory of Voting." *American Political Science Review* 83, 1: 93-121.

Regenstreif, Peter. 1965. *The Diefenbaker Interlude.* Don Mills: Longman.

RePass, David E. 1971. "Issue Salience and Party Choice." *American Political Science Review* 65, 2: 389-400.

Rhee, June Woong. 1997. "Strategy and Issue Frames in Election Campaign Coverage." *Journal of Communication* 47, 3: 26-48.

Riker, William H., and Peter C. Ordeshook. 1968. "A Theory of the Calculus of Voting." *American Political Science Review* 62, 1: 24-42.

Rubenson, Daniel, André Blais, Patrick Fournier, Elisabeth Gidengil, and Neil Nevitte. 2004. "Accounting for the Age Gap in Turnout." *Acta Politica* 39, 4: 407-21.

Scarrow, Howard A. 1965. "Distinguishing between Political Parties: The Case of Canada." *Midwest Journal of Political Science* 9, 1: 61-76.

Schickler, Eric, and Donald Philip Green. 1997. "The Stability of Party Identification in Western Democracies: Results from Eight Panel Surveys." *Comparative Political Studies* 30, 4: 450-83.

Scotto, Thomas J., Laura B. Stephenson, and Allan Kornberg. 2004. "From a Two-Party-Plus to a One-Party-Plus? Ideology, Vote Choice, and Prospects for a Competitive Party System in Canada." *Electoral Studies* 23, 3: 463-83.

Shapiro, Robert. 1997. "Review of *The New American Voter.*" *Political Science Quarterly* 112, 2: 313-14.

Simeon, Richard, and David J. Elkins. 1974. "Regional Political Cultures in Canada." *Canadian Journal of Political Science* 7, 3: 397-437.

–. 1980. *Small Worlds: Provinces and Parties in Canadian Political Life.* Toronto: Methuen.

Sniderman, Paul M., H.D. Forbes, and Ian Melzer. 1974. "Party Loyalty and Electoral Volatility: A Study of the Canadian Party System." *Canadian Journal of Political Science* 7, 2: 268-88.

Soroka, Stuart. 2002. *Agenda-Setting Dynamics in Canada.* Vancouver: UBC Press.

Stokes, Donald E. 1963. "Spatial Models of Party Competition." *American Political Science Review* 57, 2: 368-77.

–. 1992. "Valence Politics." In *Electoral Politics,* ed. Dennis Kavanagh, 141-64. Oxford: Clarendon Press.

Tellier, Geneviève. 2006. "Effect of Economic Conditions on Government Popularity: The Canadian Provincial Case." *Canadian Journal of Political Science* 39, 1: 27-51.

Thomas, Timothy L. 2001. "An Emerging Party Cleavage: Metropolis vs. the Rest." In *Party Politics in Canada*. 8th ed., ed. Hugh G. Thorburn and Alan Whitehorn, 431-42. Toronto: Prentice-Hall.

Trimble, Linda, and Shannon Sampert. 2004. "Who's in the Game? The Framing of the Canadian Election 2000 by the *Globe and Mail* and the *National Post*." *Canadian Journal of Political Science* 37, 1: 51-71.

Uslaner, Eric M. 1989. "Looking Forward and Looking Backward: Prospective and Retrospective Voting in the 1980 Federal Election in Canada." *British Journal of Political Science* 19, 4: 495-513.

Walks, R. Alan. 2005. "The City-Suburban Cleavage in Canadian Federal Politics." *Canadian Journal of Political Science* 38, 2: 383-413.

Wasko, Kevin, and Brenda O'Neill. 2007. "The Urban/Suburban/Rural Cleavage in Canadian Political Opinion." Paper presented at the annual meeting of the Canadian Political Science Association, Saskatoon, SK, 30 May-1 June.

Wilson, J. Matthew, and Michael Lusztig. 2004. "The Spouse in the House: What Explains the Marriage Gap in Canada?" *Canadian Journal of Political Science* 37, 4: 979-96.

Zaller, John. 1992. *The Nature and Origins of Mass Opinion*. New York: Cambridge University Press.

Zipp, John F., and Joel Smith. 1982. "A Structural Analysis of Class Voting." *Social Forces* 60, 3: 738-59.

Part 1

Long-Standing Attachments and Voting

Who Votes for Women Candidates and Why? Evidence from Recent Canadian Elections

Elizabeth Goodyear-Grant

Gender has been an important consideration in the Canadian voting behaviour literature at least since the 1990s. Scholars have produced important findings on the partisan gender gap (Gidengil 1995; Erickson and O'Neill 2002; Gidengil et al. 2005) and other topics. There is consistent evidence of gender gaps in voters' preferences and political decisions across a wide range of contexts, yet many interesting questions remain. One of these questions is how men and women in the electorate react to the opportunity to vote for women candidates,[1] a question that has received relatively little attention in Canada.

There is a simple answer to the question "who votes for women candidates?" Everybody. At the same time, there is evidence that certain types of voters are especially attracted to female candidates, and much of the existing work focuses on results indicating that female voters are more likely than their male counterparts to vote for women candidates, a phenomenon often referred to as a gender affinity effect. In Canada, existing work focuses on affinities between women party leaders and voters (O'Neill 1998; Banducci and Karp 2000; Cutler 2002; Bashevkin 2009).

This chapter looks for evidence of a straightforward gender affinity effect between Canadian voters and candidates with the help of data from the 2004 and 2006 Canadian Election Studies (CES), and it finds none on both counts. In both the 2004 and the 2006 federal elections, male voters were more likely than female voters to cast ballots for women candidates. Following this finding, the chapter assesses whether in the 2004 federal election certain *types* of men and/or women, who hold specific political attitudes or social locations theorized as significant, were more likely than others to vote for women.

Taking a step back from the voting behaviour literature, this chapter ties in with important questions about gender and representation, particularly women's chronic underrepresentation in legislatures and politics more generally. Globally, women's representation in national legislatures is disproportionately low compared to women's population numbers. In Canada, women's proportion of seats in the House of Commons has stalled at just over 20 percent for over a decade. There has been virtually no progress in women's representation at the federal level since the 1997 federal election. The 30 percent threshold commonly thought necessary to establish a "critical mass" of women legislators has remained out of reach, leaving aside the issue of parity in representation (Dahlerup 1988).

One question that arises when considering women's political representation is whether women voters constitute a natural constituency for women candidates. In other words, are women particularly drawn to candidates of the same sex, and what undergirds such a relationship? More crucially for women's representation, if women voters are not a natural constituency, then why not? Do women voters prioritize their gender identities over other sources of social and political identity? Do women legislators, once elected, prioritize their own gender identities (or those of their electoral "cores") in their legislative work? These are some of the broader issues that surround this chapter, for it implicitly raises questions, about the role of gender identity in political representation, which are fundamental to an understanding of voting behaviour, legislative politics, and our society more generally.

Theory

Who Votes for Women and Why?

Voters are not systematically biased against female candidates. In Canada, there is evidence that women candidates fare slightly better in the aggregate than their male counterparts, when other factors are equal (Black and Erickson 2003). Consequently, "the question regarding women candidates has shifted from whether people will vote for them to which voters are most likely to do so" (Dolan 2006, 36).

Voters appear to have "baseline gender preferences" (Sanbonmatsu 2002, 20) for candidates of one sex or the other (Zipp and Plutzer 1985; Paolino 1995; Dolan 1998, 2004; Sanbonmatsu 2002; Brians 2005). Dolan (2004, 101) reports that women were 9 percentage points more likely than men to vote for women candidates in US House elections from 1990 to 2000. Like much of the work on voting behaviour generally, literature examining who votes for women and under what conditions has developed primarily out of the American context, particularly in response to the congressional elections of 1992, the so-called Year of the Woman.

Although the 1992 US elections were groundbreaking in their attention to gender issues and the unprecedented election of women candidates, other US elections have been different. In some elections, candidates' sex mattered little to vote choices, and in others, the gender affinity hypothesis was turned on its head, with males voting in greater proportions than females for female candidates (Dolan 2004). Clearly, results are not consistent or conclusive regarding the effects of candidates' sex on the vote, because "context is a crucial mediator in creating gender differences in voting" (Sapiro and Conover 1997, 501). The idiosyncrasies of an electoral environment might play a fundamental role in determining when, how, and for whom candidates' sex matters.

Turning to specific hypotheses, the literature provides a variety of explanations for why and under what conditions female candidates may be preferred. Some of the theories are particular to women voters, and some apply to voters of both sexes. One of the strongest predictors of voting for women candidates, and a factor that affects women voters only, is gender consciousness. Women candidates enjoy an edge among women voters because women voters implicitly believe that shared gender is akin to shared experiences or issue concerns (Tolleson-Rinehart 1992). Gender consciousness motivates women voters to support women candidates not simply because they are of the same gender but also because their shared gender has political implications. Gender consciousness acts as the critical link connecting women voters' gender identities with the sex of candidates.[2] Implicit in much of the gender consciousness literature is the belief that women's gender consciousness is feminist (Gurin 1985), but recent work demonstrates the existence of a conservative women's gender consciousness (Schreiber 2002), which has important implications for how we conceptualize and empirically analyze questions about women voting for women. The idea that gender consciousness can be liberal or conservative – feminist or more traditional – means that women voters of all partisan and ideological stripes may be motivated to vote for women in larger numbers than male voters; it also suggests that scholars must analytically separate "gender consciousness" from "feminist consciousness" when evaluating gender gaps in political behaviour.

A second factor underlying support for women candidates is voters' attitudes toward women's political underrepresentation. The idea is that voters of either sex who view women's underrepresentation as problematic are more likely to vote for women candidates than are those who view underrepresentation as unproblematic. This explanation can apply to voters of either sex, for many men hold principled critiques of women's underrepresentation (Gidengil 1996).

Another explanation often highlighted in the literature is that voters of either sex who oppose welfare state retrenchment are more likely to vote for women candidates than voters who are not opposed to such retrenchment (Dolan 2004). For women voters, the desire to protect the welfare state might be motivated by self-interest. Due to the feminization of poverty, occupational segregation, the gender-wage gap, and the tendency for women to head lone-parent families, females are more likely than males to be both clients and providers of welfare state services (Newman and White 2006). A consistent consideration in work on the partisan gender gap, the relative economic vulnerability of women voters might lead them to vote for women as an effort to protect their material interests.

The key to understanding this explanation is the idea that voters of both sexes tend to view women candidates as special protectors of the welfare state. The belief that women candidates are such protectors might stem from women candidates' own policy priorities and track records – factors that likely have less importance in Canada than in the United States, because in Canada party discipline is strict, and campaigns tend to be centrally controlled and leader dominated, resulting in comparatively little room for women candidates to carve out distinct policy agendas. At the same time, a belief that women candidates are welfare state protectors, if it exists, might also stem from factors such as the gendered division of political labour within governments and legislatures. For example, there is a global tendency for women ministers to be located within a particular subset of cabinet posts, including health, education, social welfare, women's issues, and other "soft" portfolios (Davis 1997), and evidence in Canada has been abundant (Cochrane 1979; Trimble 1992; Studlar and Moncrief 1999). Since Canadian voters have long seen women ministers concentrated in "soft" portfolios, it would not be surprising if voters have come to the conclusion that women MPs are special protectors of the welfare state.

A fourth factor that might encourage voting for female candidates is the political climate itself. In contexts where political corruption and scandal are particularly relevant, voters of both sexes seem to turn to female candidates (Dolan 1998). Like its immediate predecessor, this explanation is also embedded in the social psychology literature on stereotyping. During times of political scandal or corruption, voters might be particularly drawn to women candidates because of "fairer sex" perceptions rooted in gender stereotypes that characterize women as more ethical, honest, and trustworthy than men (Huddy and Terkildsen 1993). Women candidates might be seen as better suited or more willing to "clean up" government.

A fifth explanation highlights voters' experience with female candidates or politicians. When a jurisdiction has experience with a female politician, there might be less apprehension about voting for women among citizens of both sexes. Women candidates have "proven" that they can do the job, and citizens will be more likely to vote for women. This effect will be distinct from any general incumbency advantage enjoyed by candidates generally, male and female alike. Although many of the other explanations focus on attitudinal factors, this explanation speaks to the importance of contextual factors on vote choice. Such factors structure the vote in the sense that they define the electoral environment, whereas attitudinal factors affect how individuals respond to the environment. This explanation also addresses questions about the effects of female candidates on the political system, whereas the dominant focus in the gender and representation literature, including the voting behaviour literature, is on how the political system affects women candidates (Dolan 2006).

A final explanation sees candidates' sex as a potential heuristic or low-information shortcut (Popkin 1991, chapter three) that allows voters to cast "correct" vote choices when faced with information deficits. There is compelling evidence that less knowledgeable voters are more likely to rely on candidates' characteristics, particularly readily visible cues such as gender and race, to make vote choices (Lau and Redlawsk 2001). Sex can act as a heuristic in a variety of ways. A candidate's sex can provide a basis for voters to make inferences about his or her issue agendas, issue positions, ideologies, or traits, as noted above. On a simpler level, "obvious social or demographic similarity" can be used by itself to make the vote choice (Cutler 2002, 467), a process that Cutler calls the "decision criterion of last resort" (466).

To summarize, this chapter tests seven hypotheses about the types of voters who are more likely to support women candidates, and these hypotheses are all derived from the existing literature.

1   H_1 – *gender affinity effect:* females are more likely than males to vote for female candidates.

2   H_2 – *female gender consciousness:* women voters who are gender conscious are more likely than other women voters to cast ballots for women candidates. This hypothesis applies to women voters only.

3   H_3 – *conscious desire for descriptive representation:* voters of either sex who view women's underrepresentation as problematic are more likely to vote for women candidates than those who view underrepresentation as unproblematic.

4   H_4 – *protection of the welfare state:* voters of either sex who oppose welfare state retrenchment are more likely to vote for women candidates than voters who are ambivalent about the welfare state or who support retrenchment.

5   H_5 – *clean up government:* voters of either sex who are concerned about political corruption will be more likely than voters who are unconcerned about it to vote for female candidates.

6   H_6 – *tried and tested:* when a riding has experience with a female politician, there is less apprehension about voting for women among citizens of both sexes.

7   H_7 – *candidate's sex as heuristic:* voters who lack party affiliations and political knowledge should be more likely to vote for candidates of their same sex than voters who do have partisan identities and/or adequate levels of political knowledge.

The hypotheses should not necessarily be seen as disparate or competing. In fact, they overlap in all sorts of ways. The best way to distinguish the hypotheses is to think of them as differing in the factors that they *emphasize* as important to citizens' decisions to vote for women candidates.

Before proceeding, I should underscore the importance of context given that the chapter must grapple with how well hypotheses derived primarily from work on American voters travel to the Canadian setting. Institutional, historical, and cultural differences between the two jurisdictions must be considered in light of how they affect the hypotheses and the interpretation of results as well as how we think about gender affinity effects across systems more generally. There are obvious differences that relate directly to the questions at hand. First, Canada's is a parliamentary system characterized by strict party discipline and centrally controlled, leader-dominated election campaigns. In the United States, candidates are not similarly bound in their policy priorities and positions, and campaigns are candidate centred; for both reasons, candidates play a more central role in Americans' vote choices compared with those of Canadians. Stated differently, candidates' sex might be comparatively less important to women's and men's vote choices in Canada because institutional and political cultural factors that encourage the centrality of candidate considerations in the case of US voters are absent or muted in the Canadian setting. Recent work on local candidates in Canada suggests that their influence on vote choice may be on the upswing (Carty and Eagles 1999, 2005), or perhaps we have simply understated it in past work on Canadian campaigns. The implication is that candidates are not irrelevant to vote choice in Canada but simply less central than candidates in other settings.

Another important difference between the two jurisdictions is the number of parties in the party system. The United States is a two-party system, suggesting that vote choice is comparatively straightforward. Canada is a multiparty system, although this is not quite accurate as a general statement given that some parties do not have an electoral presence across the country (the BQ), some parties are uncompetitive in entire provinces or regions (the NDP in Quebec), and at the constituency level there are instances where one of the so-called mainline parties, the Liberals and Conservatives, is uncompetitive. The result is significant variation in the number of parties that play a role in voters' ballot choices, especially for those voters without firm partisan attachments, who must, in theory, weigh all the plausible options. This type of complexity suggests that the candidate-sex-as-heuristic hypothesis will play an important role for some Canadian voters who cannot or will not sort through multiple partisan options. Although this chapter does not empirically assess the effect of the number of parties on the hypotheses, the issue of party system complexity has been raised here as a flag, for it is an important system difference between the United States and Canada that should play a role in future work on gender affinity effects.

Another issue related to parties is the centrality of partisanship to the vote, as the chapters in this volume by Bilodeau and Kanji and by Bélanger and Stephenson point out. Obviously, this consideration is not jurisdiction specific. Partisanship tends to complicate examinations of gender affinity effects, both in cases where women voters cast ballots for women candidates and in cases where they do not. There are many citizens who vote for whatever local candidate their preferred party nominates in the riding or district, regardless of who the candidate is. In other words, for some voters, it does not matter whether the candidate is male or female, young or old, rich or poor, and in these cases a vote for a female candidate is often the result of coincidence, not design. In jurisdictions where women candidates tend to run disproportionately for liberal parties and where women are more likely than men to vote for the same parties, apparent gender affinity effects might be artificially magnified or even spurious. These issues must be considered given the strong impact of partisanship on the vote, and the quantitative analyses presented later in the chapter attempt to do that.

The complication works the other way too. In any election, there will be women voters who might prefer women candidates but who are not presented with an opportunity to vote for women because their party did not nominate a woman locally. In ridings where there are simply no women candidates, the option of defecting temporarily to other parties in order to support women candidates is not available, and even if it were many voters would not defect from their party of choice. These are difficult factors to account for and build into analyses of gender affinity effects. Quantitative analyses assessing whether certain types of men and women are more likely than others to vote for women are presented later in this chapter, and ridings that did not have at least one female candidate running for one of the major parties in the 2004 federal election were excluded from the analyses. So the chapter does address the second complication. However, for voters whose party ran a male candidate, but whose constituency did have at least one woman candidate (from another party or parties), this issue is not addressed. In such cases, women voters might have temporarily defected from their standing party of choice in order to vote for women, and in other cases, partisan identities would have trumped the desire to vote for a woman, leading voters to cast sincere votes.

Additional Considerations

Naturally, additional considerations arise for analyses of who votes for women because the role of candidates' sex has a "more complex and nuanced impact on voters than we may have imagined" (Dolan 2004,

154). First, of particular importance is the idiosyncratic context of each election. In this vein, the 2004 and 2006 Canadian federal elections might be particularly good contexts for testing hypotheses about who votes for women. Looking specifically at the 2004 election, the party leaders in the race were less well known than were those in elections of the recent past. Three of the four major parties had new leaders in 2004: Paul Martin (Liberal), Stephen Harper (Conservative), and Jack Layton (NDP). Voters likely had less firm opinions about the three new leaders than they would have had about long-standing leaders, providing openings for other factors, such as local candidates (Blais et al. 2003) and by extension the sex of local candidates, to have an impact on vote choice. Second, in the 2004 federal election, not one of the major parties had a female leader at its helm – the first time that this had happened since 1988 – and the same was true of the 2006 election. Both elections were free of sex-of-leader effects on the vote. Testing the chapter's hypotheses in other recent elections, such as those of 1997 and 2000, would be more difficult because of the necessary but challenging task of separating known sex-of-leader effects (O'Neill 1998; Banducci and Karp 2000) from possible sex-of-candidate effects.

The 2004 and 2006 federal elections were also contexts in which we might expect to find higher support for female candidates generally because scandal was at the top of the political agenda, particularly in 2006. In the 2004 race, the sponsorship scandal had been a prominent issue in the media for some time before the June vote, and the opposition parties made it a focal point of their campaigns. In 2006, the sponsorship scandal and governance more generally were central issues in the campaign. As discussed above, women candidates can benefit electorally when corruption becomes a campaign issue (Burrell 1994) due to "fairer sex" stereotypes about women.

Data and Methodology

The data sets used are the 2004 and 2006 Canadian Election Studies, to which has been added constituency-level information on the candidates who ran for the four major parties (the Liberals, the Conservatives, the NDP, and the BQ).[3] The dependent variable is whether respondents voted for a woman candidate (or, perhaps more accurately for some voters, for a party that ran a woman candidate in the respondent's constituency).[4] The chapter tests the gender affinity effect hypothesis for both the 2004 and the 2006 federal elections, and it then proceeds to test the remaining hypotheses about which types of voters are more likely to vote for women, using 2004 election data.

In the 2004 federal election, there were 1,685 candidates, 391 women and 1,294 men. Overall, women represented 23 percent of all candidates. There was at least one woman candidate in 236 of the 308 federal ridings, but in only 172 ridings was there at least one woman from one of the four major parties, which represents 56 percent of ridings. In the 2006 federal election, there were 1,634 candidates, 380 women and 1,254 men. Women again represented 23 percent of candidates. At least one woman candidate was present in 241 of the 308 federal ridings, but only in 182 ridings was there at least one woman from one of the four major parties (59 percent, an increase of 3 percent from the previous election). Ridings where there were no women candidates for any of the four major parties are excluded from the analyses, as there was no opportunity in these cases to vote for a woman. Additionally, CES respondents who abstained, who voted for parties/candidates other than the four major parties, and whose federal ridings were indeterminable are likewise excluded.[5]

The four major parties were by no means equal in terms of the number of female faces on their slates. The NDP led the pack in both elections (31 percent in 2004, 45 percent in 2006), followed by the BQ (24 percent in 2004, 31 percent in 2006), the Liberals (24 percent in 2004, 26 percent in 2006), and the Conservatives (12 percent in 2004, 12 percent in 2006).

In addition to the primary hypothesis about gender affinity effects, this chapter tests six hypotheses on whether certain types of women or certain types of men were more likely to vote for women in 2004. In this sense, the chapter examines two overarching questions. First, are findings in the United States that women are more likely to vote for women also observed in Canada? Second, what characteristics do supporters of women candidates share?

To test the female gender consciousness hypothesis (H_2), models include a variable that measures women respondents' sense that women are disadvantaged as a group because of their shared group characteristic (being female) and that something should be done collectively to correct the situation.[6] Models also include a variable that ranks women respondents' attitudes toward feminists from most negative to most positive. This variable helps to assess whether it is a gender consciousness or a specifically feminist consciousness that increases women voters' support for women candidates.

To test the desire for descriptive representation hypothesis (H_3), models include a variable that measures the extent to which respondents agree that the underrepresentation of women in the House of Commons is problematic.

To test the protection of the welfare state hypothesis (H_4), models include a variable that asks whether government should spend more, less, or the same as now on welfare.

To test the clean up government hypothesis (H_5), models include a variable coded 1 for respondents who thought that government corruption was the most important issue of the 2004 election and 0 for those who prioritized all other issues.

To assess the tried and tested hypothesis (H_6), analyses include a variable coded 1 for respondents who lived in ridings that had female incumbents in 2004 and 0 for those who did not. In addition to this female incumbent variable, analyses include a similar variable for male incumbency in order to control for the general incumbency advantage.[7]

To test whether voters use candidates' sex as a heuristic (H_7), models include a variable that interacts a lack of knowledge (measured by whether the respondent knew the 2004 leaders, a dummy variable) with a lack of partisan affiliation to determine whether voters who did not have access to two of the most important bases of vote choice (leadership and party identity; Cutler 2002) were more likely to use voter-candidate similarity based on sex as a shortcut to the vote.

Finally, a variable is included that is coded 1 for respondents whose preferred party (if they had one)[8] ran female candidates locally in 2004 and 0 if not. This variable attempts to recognize the fact that partisanship structures the vote, as explained above, rendering considerations about candidates' sex secondary or even irrelevant for some voters.

After conducting tabular analysis of gender and voting for women candidates to evaluate H_1, I use multivariate analysis to evaluate the remaining six hypotheses, using data from the 2004 federal election. Logistic regression models (with coefficients reported as odds ratios) were estimated separately for male and female CES respondents, a common practice in the literature on gender gaps in partisanship and public opinion (Gilens 1988; Gidengil 1995; Sapiro and Conover 1997; Chaney, Alvarez, and Nagler 1998; Kaufmann and Petrocik 1999; Clarke et al. 2004). Separating respondents by sex permits assessment of whether the effect of individual variables on voting (or not) for female candidates is different for women than for men. For example, men and women voters might have not only different attitudes toward women's underrepresentation in the House of Commons – with one sex viewing it as a major problem and the other sex viewing it predominantly as a minor problem, for example – but men and women might assign women's underrepresentation different weight in the decision to vote for a woman candidate. As Gilens (1988, 21) points out, estimating models separately for men and women allows research on gender differences in political decision making to estimate both gender differences in the relationships between independent and dependent variables and differences in the distributions of men and women among the categories of the independent variables. In the literature, this strategy was adopted first to account for the fact that men and women often have different issue positions and issue saliencies, for both affect vote choice as well as other political decisions. It is well known at this point that men and women assign different priorities to welfare spending (May and Stephenson 1994; Richardson and Freeman 2003), to give one example. More broadly, this strategy conforms to the notion that heterogeneous modelling is often appropriate for heterogeneous voters (Bartle 2005).

Results

Starting with the first hypothesis, the results indicate that women voters were *not* more likely than men to cast ballots for women candidates in the 2004 and 2006 federal elections. This finding might be consistent with previous work demonstrating that the impact of voters' sex on voting for women candidates is not direct (Matland and King 2002). As Table 2.1 indicates, among the respondents who voted and who lived in ridings where at least one major party candidate was a woman, 23 percent of men cast ballots for female candidates in 2004 compared with 19 percent of women. Put simply, male voters were statistically more likely than female voters to vote for women candidates in 2004. The story was slightly different in 2006, as Table 2.2 illustrates, for there were no statistically significant differences between male and female voters' likelihood of casting ballots for women candidates, but the hypothesis is again disconfirmed. Interestingly, comparing the two tables demonstrates that voters of both sexes were more likely to cast ballots for women candidates in 2006 than in 2004 (4 percent more men and 6 percent more women), and this is in light of the fact that women's proportion of candidacies remained the same from 2004 to 2006 (23 percent).

Table 2.1

Votes cast for candidates in the 2004 federal election, by sex of candidate

	Male voters (%)		Female voters (%)		Totals (%)	
Male candidates	710	(77.3)	900	(80.7)	1,610	(79.2)
Female candidates	208	(22.7)	216	(19.3)	424	(20.9)
Total	918	(100.0)	1,116	(100.0)	2,034	(100.0)

Pearson chi^2 = 3.3305; Pr = 0.068

Source: 2004 CES, 2004 candidate data.

Table 2.2

Votes cast for candidates in the 2006 federal election, by sex of candidate

	Male voters (%)		Female voters (%)		Total (%)	
Male candidates	763	(73.2)	870	(74.5)	1,633	(79.2)
Female candidates	279	(26.8)	298	(25.5)	577	(20.9)
Total	1,042	(100.0)	1,168	(100.0)	2,210	(100.0)

Pearson chi^2 = .4544; Pr = .500

Source: 2006 CES, 2006 candidate data.

Overall, though these results disconfirm the gender affinity hypothesis, they tell us only that women were not more likely than men to vote for women candidates. As mentioned above, this finding could simply indicate that the preferred parties of many men fielded women candidates or, conversely, the preferred parties of many women did not field women candidates. Furthermore, there is no indication of why the female candidates were comparatively preferred by men in the case of the 2004 election.

I turn next to multivariate analyses using data from the 2004 election. Although women were not generally more likely than men to vote for female candidates in 2004, certain types of women and certain types of men were. There are important similarities across the two models (labelled "Male Voters" and "Female Voters"), as Table 2.3 illustrates. For both sexes, by far the most important factor that influenced the decision to choose a female candidate in this election was simply whether one's preferred party had a woman candidate in the riding. This relationship is powerful but not unexpected, as discussed above. Put simply, many Canadians cast their ballots primarily on the basis of partisan identity,

Table 2.3

Logistic regressions of vote for a female candidate in 2004

	Male voters		Female voters	
	OR	SE	OR	SE
Woman candidate for preferred party	38.67***	12.21	51.04***	16.06
More should be done for women		1.26	0.56	
High affect toward feminists		0.59	0.28	
Underrepresentation of women a problem	0.47**	0.13	1.69*	0.44
Maintain welfare spending	1.46	0.38	1.04	0.31
Corruption most important issue	1.13	0.28	0.65	0.21
Female incumbent in riding	1.52***	0.43	2.70**	0.91
Male incumbent in riding	0.45**	0.12	1.13	0.35
No party ID	1.16	0.52	1.81	0.95
Low leader knowledge	0.24*	0.13	0.60	0.34
No party ID*/low leader knowledge	5.08	4.61	3.45	2.94
N	612		636	
Pseudo-R^2	33.06		37.88	

Odds ratios (OR) reported in first column of each model, standard errors (SE) reported in second column.
* $p < .05$; ** $p < .01$; *** $p < .001$
Source: 2004 CES; 2004 candidate data.

and the characteristics of the local candidate might be immaterial or secondary. Although these respondents cast votes for female candidates, their personal feelings about female candidates in general or the female candidate who ran under their preferred party's banner in 2004 might have had no role in vote choice. Some voters might have been pleased for a variety of reasons that their preferred parties nominated women candidates in 2004, but these voters would not have defected from their preferred parties en masse had a male candidate been nominated instead. American scholars have made similar conclusions, noting that partisan identity and incumbency are the primary determinants of vote choice in all elections (Dolan 2004, 2006).

Another similarity between the two models is the positive effect of experience with a female candidate, as the tried and tested hypothesis predicts. Both men and women were significantly more likely to cast ballots for female candidates when there was a female incumbent in the riding in 2004 (50 of the 308 ridings had female incumbents), and this is distinct from a general incumbency advantage, which is accounted for, given that the model includes a male incumbent variable. There are two interesting points to be made about the effects of incumbency across the two models. First, experience with a female politician had a stronger positive effect on women voters' support for women candidates than on male voters' support (odds ratio of 2.70 versus 1.52).[9] Second, in ridings that had male incumbents in 2004, male voters were significantly less likely to vote for women (odds ratio of 0.45), whereas the same effect did not hold true for female voters. Seemingly, male voters had a general preference for incumbents in 2004, whereas female voters had a specific preference for female incumbents. It is not immediately clear why this might be the case.

Although there are similarities across the two models, there is also one notable difference. The only attitudinal variable that significantly affected the likelihood of voting for female candidates was the attitude toward the underrepresentation of women. Men and women voters had opposite reactions on this front. Among women voters, those who regarded the underrepresentation of women as problematic were much more likely to vote for women candidates than women who did not regard it as problematic, a finding in line with the desire for descriptive representation hypothesis. This finding provides initial evidence that when women voters view women's political underrepresentation critically – particularly women's numerical underrepresentation, which is more visible than substantive underrepresentation – women are more likely to cast ballots for female candidates.

Among male voters, on the other hand, criticism of the underrepresentation of women was negatively correlated with voting for women. Men who saw women's underrepresentation as problematic were more likely than those who were indifferent to it to vote for male candidates (not female candidates). This finding is contrary to that predicted by the hypothesis. Speculating on this finding, I would say that women's underrepresentation might not be a primary or even a salient factor in men's vote calculus, even among men who believe that women's underrepresentation is problematic. That their underrepresentation does not carry significant weight in men's vote choices might be natural, given that the issue does not generally have personal consequences for men, who are themselves adequately represented in legislatures.

The rest of the variables essentially produce null findings. There was no support for the remaining hypotheses about the types of men and the types of women who would be particularly likely to vote for women candidates. Gender consciousness – either general or the specifically feminist variety – had no effect on women voters in 2004. For voters of both sexes, attitudes toward welfare spending had no effect on voting for women candidates, even though voters often stereotype women candidates as welfare state protectors. The salience of corruption appears to have had no impact on support for women candidates, despite past evidence that they benefit from gender stereotypes in such climates and the fact that political corruption and governance more generally were important campaign issues in 2004. Finally, candidates' sex did not act as a "decision criteria of last resort" (Cutler 2002, 466) for voters who had no party attachments and were unable to identify the major party leaders. The interaction term of low leader knowledge and no party identification was insignificant in both models.

Conclusion

This chapter represents a first cut through not only these particular data but also questions about whether and under what conditions people vote for women candidates in Canada. The primary finding is that, on the whole, women were not more likely than men to vote for female candidates in 2004 and 2006. In fact, men were slightly more likely to vote for women candidates in 2004, a finding consistent with several US studies on the issue, such as work on the 1994 US Senate races (Dolan 2004). Although scholars, media, and politicians themselves often make implicit and explicit assumptions that women voters constitute a natural constituency for women candidates, such beliefs can be misleading. In certain elections, such as Canada's 2004 federal election, female voters have been less likely than male voters to vote for female candidates. Paired with work on partisan gender gaps – which finds more variability in vote choice among women than between men and women (Erickson and O'Neill 2002) – the preceding analyses (and mixed findings from the American context) caution against viewing women as a cohesive bloc.

The findings in this chapter also emphasize the fact that low levels of female representation are not the result of bias among voters. Contemporary voters are not systematically biased against women candidates (also found by Black and Erickson 2003). When women run, women win, as the success rates of men and women candidates over time attest. From 1968 to 1980, women candidates' success rates were in the single digits. Women were run disproportionately in lost-cause ridings (Brodie 1985), and their very low success rates over the period were partly the result. Changes have occurred over the past two decades, however. As a group, women candidates perform at the ballot box nearly as well as (and in the 1993 Canadian federal election, better than) their male counterparts.[10] Two points are important here. First, for most of the past two decades, the rate at which women candidates win elections has grown in absolute terms. Second, after 1988, women's electoral success rate has been nearly on par with that of male candidates and was actually higher in 1993. At this stage, then, one of the keys to increasing women's representation appears to be in growing women's proportion of candidates. Women's share of candidacies has increased over the past two decades – from 19 percent in 1988 to 23 percent in 2006 (and 2008) – though by no means at the pace needed to achieve a legislative critical mass.

Additionally, it is important to keep in mind that gender is one among a host of variables that can influence vote choice, as discussed in the first chapter of this volume. It would be folly to assume that women voters prioritize gender identity in vote choice or that the majority of women voters even have politically salient gender identities that structure electoral decision making. Party identification plays a predominant role in vote choice for a large portion of voters, as noted above, more so perhaps than gender and other attitudinal factors (Thompson and Steckenrider 1997; Dolan 2004). Even when women voters are gender conscious, gender consciousness is not automatically a salient consideration in the vote calculus. Naturally, this point about the saliency of gender consciousness raises important questions about *when* gender identities are mobilized, what role candidates play in cuing or priming the role of gender identities in the vote choice, and how.

What do the results obtained from the preceding analyses mean? First, the coincidence of female candidacy and partisan identity has a predictably strong influence on voting for women. For many voters, it simply does not matter who the local candidate is; party is the primary determinant of vote choice. This is a truism of Canadian voting behaviour, as it is in other countries. Certainly, there is room for the local candidate to matter (Carty and Eagles 1999, 2005; Blais et al. 2003), but this room is comparatively limited, especially as considered against the dynamics of candidate-centred systems. Interestingly, American scholars have drawn the same conclusions about the primacy of other factors in the vote choice – particularly partisanship and incumbency – so this represents a similarity across the two jurisdictions, even though US elections are thought to be relatively candidate centred.

On the influence of local candidates, if partisan dealignment is on the rise (Nevitte 1996) and local candidates are becoming more prominent in Canadian politics (Carty and Eagles 1999, 2005; Blais et al. 2003), then local candidates and their personal traits might become more important to vote choice in the future. In fact, candidates' sex is only one factor that may matter. Similar hypotheses about race or ethnicity affinity effects may become topics of study in Canadian voting behaviour. Like gender, race and ethnicity are politically relevant characteristics, and candidates' race/ethnicity can often be visible to voters, raising the possibility of affinity effects for voters of the same backgrounds. Thus, race/ethnicity may be revealed as a basis of vote choice in some contexts if research similar to that presented in this chapter were undertaken.

Another conclusion coming directly from my analyses is that experience with a female politician in the past matters for voters of both sexes. Pioneers lay the groundwork that enables the success of subsequent candidates, and voting for women appears to be no different. We know that women politicians are sometimes viewed as novel or alien to politics partly because the archetypical politician is decidedly male in both traits and issue concerns. Put simply, male politicians have long been the norm, and there are lingering doubts in the minds of some voters, news makers, and other politicians that women have what it takes to do the job (Huddy and Terkildsen 1993; Lawless 2004). Considering the wider political environment, then, it is no surprise that voters respond positively to proof that women can run, win, and legislate as well as men, and this positive response is in the form of voting for women candidates.

In the meantime, to get a better handle on how the sex of the local candidate affects the vote, two types of research might prove particularly fruitful. First, we need to conduct surveys that do a more thorough job of examining the extent to which voters know, have feelings about, and take into consideration the local candidates in their vote decisions. The CES has questions about local candidates, but these questions are too few and too general to test hypotheses about voting for female candidates. Second, research on the reasons for vote switching – crossing party lines to cast a ballot for a rival party – may be particularly revealing, as would research on non-partisan or "floating" voters. Indeed, examining instances in which men and women defect from their preferred parties or how non-partisans make vote choices might give additional insight into the effect of local candidates' characteristics on the vote in Canada, including the conditions under which candidates' sex matters.

Notes

1 I use the term "candidate" in this chapter to refer to candidates for office in the context of their local campaigns in constituencies. I use the term "leader" to refer to party leaders *as leaders*. In parliamentary systems, party leaders play a dual role in elections because they are also candidates for office in their own constituencies.

2 "Gender consciousness" is conceptually distinct from "gender identity" (or, in broader terms, "group consciousness" is distinct from "group identity"). Gender identity is simpler, denoting identity with women as a group. Gender consciousness, on the other hand, "requires that an individual believe that members of the group are disadvantaged by social, political, or economic structures, and that this disadvantage comes from systematic discrimination, not from individual failures" (Bruce and Wilcox 2000, 19).

3 None of the other parties in our current party system has ever won a seat federally. I thank Ilana Ludwin for her research assistance in collecting these data.

4 If a respondent voted Liberal, and the riding's Liberal candidate was female, then that respondent received a score of 1 for the dependent variable. If a respondent in the same federal riding voted Conservative, and the Conservative candidate was male, then that respondent received a score of 0.

5 These cases are respondents who either refused to provide their postal code to the CES or provided a wrong or incomplete postal code.

6 For greater detail on coding of variables and original variables used for recoding, please contact the author.

7 The operationalization of this variable has limitations. Among them is the fact that experience with female candidates and/or elected MPs prior to the 2000 federal election is not taken into account. Certainly, there are ridings in the data set that did not have female incumbents in 2004 (and for which a code of 0 is entered) but that have had female MPs in the past. The decision to define experience with female MPs restrictively was motivated in part by the greater assurance that voters would remember that a woman had held the seat.

8 With this variable, I only code strong or moderate partisans as having a party identification. Weak identifiers and "leaners" are coded as having no party identification. This is how I treat party identification throughout the chapter.

9 See http://www.ats.ucla.edu/stat/stata/faq/oratio.htm for information on interpreting an odds ratio.

10 In 1988, male candidates' success rate was 19 percent compared with 12.9 percent for women; in 1993, it was 14 percent compared with 15.2 percent; in 2000, it was 18.8 percent compared with 16.6 percent; in 2004, the figures were the same; and in 2006, it was 19.3 percent compared with 16.8 percent.

References

Banducci, Susan A., and Jeffrey A. Karp. 2000. "Gender, Leadership, and Choice in Multiparty Systems." *Political Research Quarterly* 53, 4: 815-48.

Bartle, John. 2005. "Homogeneous Models and Heterogeneous Voters." *Political Studies* 53, 4: 653-75.

Bashevkin, Sylvia, ed. 2009. *Opening Doors Wider: Women's Political Engagement in Canada.* Vancouver: UBC Press.

Black, Jerome, and Lynda Erickson. 2003. "Women Candidates and Voter Bias: Do Women Politicians Need to Be Better?" *Electoral Studies* 22, 1: 81-100.

Blais, André, Elisabeth Gidengil, Agnieszka Dobrzynska, Neil Nevitte, and Richard Nadeau. 2003. "Does the Local Candidate Matter? Candidate Effects in the Canadian Election of 2000." *Canadian Journal of Political Science* 36, 3: 657-64.

Brians, Craig L. 2005. "Women for Women? Gender and Party Bias in Voting for Female Candidates." *American Politics Research* 33, 3: 357-75.

Brodie, Janine. 1985. *Women and Politics in Canada*. Toronto: McGraw-Hill Ryerson.

Bruce, John M., and Clyde Wilcox. 2000. "The Structure of Feminist Consciousness among Women and Men: A Latent Structural Analysis." Paper presented at the annual meeting of the American Political Science Association, Washington, DC, 1 September.

Burrell, Barbara. 1994. *A Woman's Place Is in the House: Campaigning for Congress in the Feminist Era*. Ann Arbor: University of Michigan Press.

Carty, R. Kenneth, and Munroe Eagles. 1999. "Do Local Campaigns Matter? Campaign Spending, the Local Canvass, and Party Support in Canada." *Electoral Studies* 18, 1: 69-87.

–. 2005. *Politics Is Local: National Politics at the Grassroots*. Toronto: Oxford University Press.

Chaney, Carol K., R. Michael Alvarez, and Jonathan Nagler. 1998. "Explaining the Gender Gap in US Presidential Elections, 1980-1992." *Political Research Quarterly* 51, 2: 311-39.

Clarke, Harold D., Marianne C. Stewart, Mike Ault, and Euel Elliott. 2004. "Men, Women, and the Dynamics of Presidential Approval." *British Journal of Political Science* 35, 1: 31-51.

Cochrane, Jean. 1979. *Women in Canadian Politics*. Toronto: Fitzhenry and Whiteside.

Cutler, Fred. 2002. "The Simplest Shortcut of All: Sociodemographic Characteristics and Electoral Choice." *Journal of Politics* 64, 2: 466-90.

Dahlerup, Drude. 1988. "From a Small to a Large Minority: Women in Scandinavian Politics." *Scandinavian Political Studies* 11, 4: 275-97.

Davis, Rebecca Howard. 1997. *Women and Power in Parliamentary Democracies: Cabinet Appointments in Western Europe, 1968-1992*. Lincoln: University of Nebraska Press.

Dolan, Kathleen A. 1998. "Voting for Women in the 'Year of the Woman.'" *American Journal of Political Science* 42, 1: 272-93.

–. 2004. *Voting for Women: How the Public Evaluates Women Candidates*. Boulder, CO: Westview Press.

–. 2006. "Women Candidates in American Politics: What We Know, What We Want to Know." Paper presented at the meeting of the Midwest Political Science Association, Chicago, IL, 20-23 April.

Erickson, Lynda, and Brenda O'Neill. 2002. "The Gender Gap and the Changing Woman Voter in Canada." *International Political Science Review* 23, 4: 373-93.

Gidengil, Elisabeth. 1995. "Economic Man – Social Woman? The Case of the Gender Gap in Support for the Canada-US Free Trade Agreement." *Comparative Political Studies* 28, 3: 384-408.

–. 1996. "Gender and Attitudes toward Quotas for Women Candidates in Canada." *Women and Politics* 16, 4: 21-44.

Gidengil, Elisabeth, Matthew Hennigar, André Blais, and Neil Nevitte. 2005. "Explaining the Gender Gap in Support for the New Right: The Case of Canada." *Comparative Political Studies* 38, 10: 1171-95.

Gilens, M. 1988. "Gender and Support for Reagan: A Comprehensive Model of Presidential Support." *American Journal of Political Science* 32, 1: 19-49.

Gurin, Patricia. 1985. "Women's Gender Consciousness." *Public Opinion Quarterly* 49, 2: 143-63.

Huddy, Leonie, and Nayda Terkildsen. 1993. "Gender Stereotypes and the Perception of Male and Female Candidates." *American Journal of Political Science* 37, 1: 119-47.

Kaufmann, Karen M., and John R. Petrocik. 1999. "The Changing Politics of American Men: Understanding the Sources of the Gender Gap." *American Journal of Political Science* 43, 3: 864-87.

Lau, Richard, and David P. Redlawsk. 2001. "Advantages and Disadvantages of Cognitive Heuristics in Political Decision Making." *American Journal of Political Science* 45, 4: 951-71.

Lawless, Jennifer L. 2004. "Women, War, and Winning Elections: Gender Stereotyping in the Post-September 11th Era." *Political Research Quarterly* 57, 3: 479-90.

Matland, Richard E., and David C. King. 2002. "Women as Candidates in Congressional Elections." In *Women Transforming Congress*, ed. Cindy Simon Rosenthal, 119-45. Norman: University of Oklahoma Press.

May, Ann Mari, and Kurt Stephenson. 1994. "Women and the Great Retrenchment: The Political Economy of Gender in the 1980s." *Journal of Economic Issues* 28, 2: 533-42.

Nevitte, Neil. 1996. *The Decline of Deference: Canadian Value Change in Cross-National Perspective.* Peterborough, ON: Broadview.

Newman, Jacquetta, and Linda A. White. 2006. *Women, Politics, and Public Policy: The Political Struggles of Canadian Women.* Toronto: Oxford University Press.

O'Neill, Brenda. 1998. "The Relevance of Leader Gender to Voting in the 1993 Canadian National Election." *International Journal of Canadian Studies* 17, 2: 105-30.

Paolino, Phillip. 1995. "Group-Salient Issues and Group Representation: Support for Women Candidates in the 1992 Senate Elections." *American Journal of Political Science* 39, 2: 294-313.

Popkin, Samuel L. 1991. *The Reasoning Voter: Communication and Persuasion in Presidential Campaigns.* Chicago: University of Chicago Press.

Richardson, Lilliard E. Jr., and Patricia K. Freeman. 2003. "Issue Salience and Gender Differences in Congressional Elections, 1994-1998." *Social Science Journal* 40, 3: 401-17.

Sanbonmatsu, Kira. 2002. "Gender Stereotypes and Vote Choice." *American Journal of Political Science* 46, 1: 20-34.

Sapiro, Virginia, and Pamela Johnston Conover. 1997. "The Variable Gender Basis of Electoral Politics: Gender and Context in the 1992 US Election." *British Journal of Political Science* 27, 4: 497-523.

Schreiber, Ronnee. 2002. "Injecting a Woman's Voice: Conservative Women's Organizations, Gender Consciousness, and the Expression of Women's Policy Preferences." *Sex Roles* 47, 7-8: 331-42.

Studlar, Donley T., and Gary F. Moncrief. 1999. "Women's Work? The Distribution and Prestige of Portfolios in the Canadian Provinces." *Governance: An International Journal of Policy and Administration* 12, 4: 379-95.

Thompson, Seth, and Janie Steckenrider. 1997. "The Relative Irrelevance of Candidate Sex." *Women and Politics* 17, 4: 71-92.

Tolleson-Rinehart, Sue. 1992. *Gender Consciousness and Politics.* New York: Routledge.

Trimble, Linda. 1992. "The Politics of Gender in Modern Alberta." In *Government and Politics in Alberta,* ed. Allen Tupper and Roger Gibbins, 219-46. Edmonton: University of Alberta Press.

Zipp, John F., and Eric Plutzer. 1985. "Gender Differences in Voting for Female Candidates: Evidence from the 1982 Election." *Public Opinion Quarterly* 49, 2: 179-97.

The New Immigrant Voter, 1965-2004: The Emergence of a New Liberal Partisan?

Antoine Bilodeau and Mebs Kanji

Since the 1960s, the origin of new immigrants in Canada has shifted gradually from the United Kingdom and northern, western, and southern Europe to Asia, eastern Europe, the Middle East, Latin America, and Africa. The proportion of immigrants from "non-traditional source countries" has skyrocketed from about 20 percent in 1965 to more than 80 percent of all new immigrants settling in Canada every year. The demographic weight of these new Canadians has grown continuously since 1965 and is expected to continue to increase in the years to come. This demographic change has led to the emergence of a new group of voters: what we call "new immigrant voters."[1] In this chapter, we investigate the consequences of the arrival of these voters for electoral dynamics in Canada.

To date, there have been few thorough attempts to investigate the electoral habits of the new immigrant voter. We know that Canadians of non-European ethnic background (part of the new immigrant voter category) have been more inclined to support the Liberal Party of Canada than other segments of the population (Blais 2005). Other than this, however, there is little information that is based on systematic analysis.[2] Do the findings of André Blais suggest that the new immigrant voter is a stable Liberal partisan/voter? In this analysis, we pick up from where Blais left off in his presidential address to the Canadian Political Science Association in 2005. Our objective is to start drawing a more detailed portrait of the new immigrant voter in Canada and to evaluate the consequences that the arrival of new immigrant voters has had on the Canadian political landscape. In so doing, our chapter offers an additional perspective on the study of partisanship in Canada.[3]

Two broad questions structure our analysis. First, what are the consequences of this influx of new immigrant voters for the Liberal Party? Nevitte et al. (2000) and Blais et al. (2002) contend that the Liberal Party partly owed its 1997 and 2000 victories to its relatively larger stock of loyal partisan voters. To what extent has the influx of new immigrants from non-traditional source countries contributed to the electoral success of the Liberal Party in the past four decades?

Second, what are the potential consequences of this entry of new immigrant voters for the broader Canadian party system? Scholars have suggested that voting patterns and the structure of party systems in Western democracies over the past decades have shifted. Accumulated evidence points to increased signs of volatility, a drop in the predictability of voting behaviour, and increased fragmentation in party systems (Dalton and Wattenberg 2000; Dalton 2006). Even though historically the Canadian voter has been described by some as being a "flexible" partisan (Clarke et al. 1996),[4] there is systematic evidence to suggest that at least some of the trends observed in other Western democracies may also be taking place in Canada. For example, the proportion of party identifiers in Canada has dropped significantly between 1965 and today (Dalton 2000). Also, voter volatility and the proportion of citizens taking longer to make their electoral decisions have increased (Dalton, McAllister, and Wattenberg 2000). Even though not all of the above changes necessarily imply that voters nowadays are more sophisticated than they were before, there is evidence that voters are increasingly likely to make up their minds based on policy preferences, performance judgments, and candidate images rather than on strong and stable partisanship. In other words, the classic partisan voter may slowly be replaced by a different and maybe more sophisticated voter. In the conclusion to this chapter, we speculate, based on our findings, about how the growing influx of new immigrants from non-traditional source countries may add to the dynamics of such trends, particularly in terms of support for the Liberal Party.

Theory

To assess the consequences of the new immigrant voter both for the Canadian party system and for the Liberal Party specifically, we need to evaluate the electoral character of the new immigrant voter. Does the new immigrant voter behave more like a classic partisan voter who makes up his or her mind based on strong partisan preferences or like a new

sophisticated voter who makes up his or her mind based on policy preferences, performance judgments, and candidate images?

According to the classic partisan voter perspective, partisan attachments
are thought to be social-psychological anchors resulting from early life
socialization in the family environment, where children more or less
inherit their parents' partisan attachments (Campbell et al. 1960; Sears
1993, 120). Because of the origins and nature of partisan attachments
as conceived by the social-psychological perspective, it seems unlikely
that the new immigrant voter could behave like a classic partisan voter.
If partisan attachments are developed out of early family socialization,
then new immigrant voters are unlikely to have developed such a bond
with any Canadian party because their early socialization happened in
a different country. Only through a long process of resocialization can
we imagine that new immigrant voters would develop such a social-
psychological type of partisan attachment in Canada.

Of course, it is plausible that immigrants might turn to their pre-
migration party identifications and ideological orientations to help them
build new partisan attachments in the host country. Immigrants might
rely on pre-migration partisan attachments as an information shortcut
to rapidly develop new partisan attachments in the host country. Finifter
and Finifter (1989) have observed such an adaptation mechanism in
their study of American immigrants in Australia. However, the case of
American immigrants in a highly similar political system is far different
from that of the new immigrant voter who often comes to Canada from
a distinct cultural environment. In fact, McAllister and Makkai's study
(1991) tends to indicate that immigrants moving to a highly dissimilar
political system struggle more in developing partisan attachments in the
host country. Their study demonstrates that immigrants in Australia who
come from non-English-speaking countries are less likely to hold a partisan attachment than other immigrants. Therefore, because new immigrant voters in Canada have not experienced early family socialization
in the Canadian political system, and because of the significant cultural
and political differences between Canada and their countries of origin,
we would not expect new immigrant voters to behave like classic partisan
voters.

Is this to suggest, then, that new immigrant voters might behave more
like new sophisticated voters? The emerging politically sophisticated
voter is typically characterized in the literature as being more volatile

(Dalton and Wattenberg, 2000; Dalton 2006). Such voters are deemed to be flexible partisans because they are capable of orienting their voting choices according to policy preferences, performance judgments, and candidate images as opposed to relying heavily on partisan attachments. On these grounds, it is also difficult to conceive of the new immigrant voter as being a member of this particular breed of cognitively sophisticated and volatile voters. Their relatively short-lived experiences in the new political system are likely to provide only limited guidance to new immigrant voters in understanding the Canadian political system, its parties, political figures, and political norms.

Following from the above discussion, it appears unlikely that the new immigrant voter would behave like either the classic partisan voter or the new sophisticated voter. What are we to expect, then, from this new immigrant voter? What will characterize his or her electoral behaviour? Two sets of considerations must be taken into account to answer this question. First, even though new immigrant voters are likely to struggle to acquire, understand, and internalize the information necessary to comprehend all of the political dynamics of the host country, they will likely develop the minimal skills necessary to comprehend the basic political dynamics. That populations in most Western democracies have a low level of political knowledge has been well documented (Delli Carpini and Keeter 1996), and more recent research now emphasizes the mechanisms and information shortcuts on which people rely to make sensible political decisions in spite of their lack of knowledge (Lupia 1994; Lupia and McCubbins 1998). Based on the evidence regarding the role of information shortcuts, it is plausible to expect that the new immigrant voter might become cognitively competent enough to identify which party would be most likely to represent and defend his or her interests and, once chosen, to remain with that party.

Second, this political choice, initially made on low information and with the use of information shortcuts, could evolve into a more stable partisan attachment. In contrast to the social-psychological perspective conceiving of partisan attachments as originating from early family socialization, another perspective conceives of partisan attachments as emerging out of a "running tally" of evaluations about parties' capacities to represent and defend one's interests (Fiorina 1981). If partisan attachments emerge out of a running tally of continuously updated evaluations, then new immigrant voters' initial political preferences could evolve over time into more stable partisan attachments that would lead these voters to resemble the classic partisan voter. In fact, McAllister and Makkai (1991) present evidence consistent with this interpretation by demonstrating that immigrants' partisan loyalties in Australia most often emerge out of economic self-interest. This conclusion is further supported by Cain, Kiewiet, and Uhlaner (1991), who argue that, the longer Latino immigrants reside in the United States, the more likely they are to identify as Democrats and to become stronger Democrat identifiers because of the persistent reputation of the Democrats as being best suited to defend immigrants' interests.

Therefore, although the new immigrant voter is unlikely to have acquired a partisan attachment early in life from family socialization in Canada, it appears plausible to expect the new immigrant voter to develop a partisan attachment from a self-interested cognitive process of repeated positive experiences with a given party. It is then also plausible to expect the new immigrant voter, over time, to come to resemble the classic partisan voter, with a stable and enduring partisan attachment.

However, most of the considerations and arguments presented above are derived from limited evidence and theoretical models that have yet to be tested specifically and systematically on the immigrant population. Therefore, the analyses that follow are explorative and aim first and foremost to document in a detailed and systematic way the electoral habits of this new immigrant voter in Canada in order to help us gradually develop a theoretical framework for this voter.

Methodology

This chapter limits its investigations to the relationship that the new immigrant voter entertains with the Liberal Party of Canada. Three sets of factors justify our decision. First, we chose the Liberal Party over any other party because, as mentioned, Canadians of non-European origins have been known to rally behind that party in large proportions (Blais 2005); it thus seems to us a natural point of focus for our analyses. Second, focusing on the Liberal Party simplifies and shortens the presentation of findings. Taking all parties into account at once might hide specific tendencies and patterns, and discussing each party separately would be a long and tedious task well beyond the scope of this chapter. Looking at the Liberal Party is thus the first step in understanding new immigrant voting behaviour, with further steps to follow in later research projects. Third, and most important, we chose the Liberal Party because it was one of the most successful parties in Western democracies in the latter part of the twentieth century (Blais 2005, 821). If we are to search for a possible connection between the arrival of the new immigrant voter and electoral changes in Canada, we must examine support for the "natural governing party" (Carty 2006, 826) or the centrepiece of the party system in Canada since 1867.

Our analytical approach is to compare the new immigrant voter with the Canadian-born voter to assess which one most resembles the classic partisan voter and which one most resembles the new sophisticated voter. This being said, the classic partisan voter and the new sophisticated voter are merely two conceptual points of reference, and therefore we do not expect to find that the Canadian-born voter or the new immigrant voter perfectly resembles either of these two "types." They idealize reality and present theoretical guidelines for understanding empirical evidence. Perhaps the new immigrant voter and the Canadian-born voter will exhibit characteristics of both types of voters.

Furthermore, we focus on the new immigrant voter and the Canadian-born voter as if they form homogeneous groups. Such a decision allows us to generalize and simplify the analysis. By making this decision, however, we are likely to overlook more refined patterns of behaviour found within each group. Canadian-born voters and immigrant voters do not constitute homogeneous groups (Blais et al. 2002). The group of new immigrant voters includes immigrants from various origins, socio-economic backgrounds, and lengths of residence in Canada. Some immigrants will have been in the country for only a few years, whereas others will have been here for a few decades already. Therefore, by making this choice to focus on the group rather than on the individual, we necessarily leave for later research other important intragroup or individual-level considerations (such as the impact that an immigrant's length of residence or age at migration might have on his or her electoral behaviour).

To assess the impact of the arrival of the new immigrant voter on the Liberal Party of Canada and the broader Canadian party system, we examine and compare the new immigrant voter and the Canadian-born voter on three dimensions. First, is there any cross-time evidence to suggest that the new immigrant voter selects the Liberal Party more consistently than the Canadian-born voter? Second, does the new immigrant voter exhibit signs of being a stable or volatile Liberal voter across elections? And third, is the new immigrant voter a strong or weak Liberal partisan identifier? We explore these questions by conducting a cross-time examination of the new immigrant voter's electoral habits between 1965 and 2004 using the Canadian Election Studies (CES).[5]

Results

The New Immigrant Voter: A Liberal Voter?

We begin by examining the distribution of Liberal voting among new immigrant voters and Canadian-born voters between 1965 and 2004.[6] Not surprisingly, the evidence reported in Figure 3.1 indicates that support for the Liberal Party among both groups has varied over time. During the past forty years or so, Liberal support has oscillated from lows of 31 percent and 24 percent in 1984 for new immigrant voters and Canadian-born voters, respectively, to highs of 67 percent and 55 percent in the 1960s.[7] What these findings clearly indicate is that even the Liberal Party, sometimes referred to as the "natural governing party" of Canada, has not been entirely immune from ebbs and flows of voter support. The findings also show that, among Canadian-born voters, the contemporary

Figure 3.1

Liberal voting among the new immigrant voter and the Canadian-born voter (1965-2004)

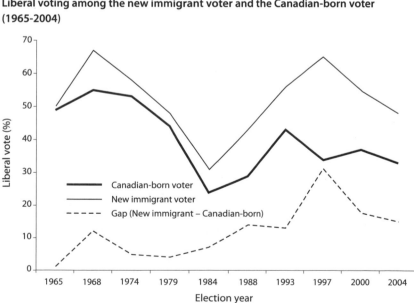

Source: 1965-2004 Canadian Election Studies

Liberal Party has never been as popular as it was during the early Trudeau era (so-called Trudeaumania). At the same time, notice also that immigrants from non-traditional source countries have consistently supported the Liberal Party in greater proportions than the Canadian-born population. Moreover, unlike the Canadian-born population, the cross-time evidence pertaining to Liberal support among new immigrant voters suggests that the Chrétien Liberals were at one point virtually as popular as the Trudeau Liberals.

Furthermore, support for the Liberal Party among new immigrant voters and Canadian-born voters appears to be diverging over time. The dashed line in Figure 3.1 reports the percentage gap in Liberal support between new immigrant voters and Canadian-born voters. The results in this case clearly indicate that the gap in Liberal support was gradually increasing between 1965 and 2004. The gap fluctuated from year to year but on the whole increased from 1 percentage point in 1965 to about 15 percentage points in 2004.[8] Thus, not only is the new immigrant voter more supportive of the Liberal Party than the Canadian-born voter, but also (according to our evidence) this difference in voting preference has been steadily increasing since 1965. During his presidential address, Blais (2005, 830) indicated that the post-1990s gap in Liberal Party support between those of non-European ethnicity and others was larger than the pre-1990s gap. Our findings add to that understanding by demonstrating that Liberal Party support among new immigrant voters and Canadian-born voters has been increasingly diverging over time.

Further analyses (results not shown) indicate that the share of Liberal Party support that comes from new immigrants from non-traditional source countries now exceeds the proportion of support derived from immigrants who come from more traditional source countries. In 1965, only 3.6 percent of Liberal voters in the sample of the Canadian Election Study were immigrants from non-traditional source countries. That proportion, however, has steadily increased to approximately 10 percent, as indicated by the evidence in the 2004 CES. At the same time, the proportion of Liberal Party support derived from immigrants from traditional source countries fell from 15 percent in 1965-68 to about 7 percent in 2004. Thus, not only are new immigrants from non-traditional source countries increasingly more inclined than the Canadian-born population to support the Liberal Party, but they now also account for a greater share of Liberal Party support than immigrants from traditional source countries.

Figure 3.2

Proportion who voted Liberal two elections in a row (among Liberal voters only*)

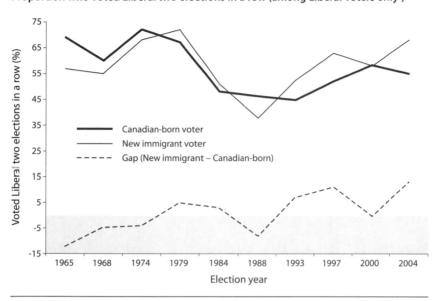

Source: 1965-2004 Canadian Election Studies

* Respondents who have never voted Liberal (in the current or the previous elections) are not included in this analysis.

The New Immigrant Voter: A Volatile or Stable Liberal Voter?

The preceding analysis suggests that the new immigrant voter might be increasingly relevant to the future success of the Liberal Party. But how reliable is this new immigrant voter? How likely is he or she to continue supporting the Liberal Party over the long term? Figure 3.2 reports the proportion of new immigrants and members of the Canadian-born population who voted for the Liberal Party in two consecutive federal elections over the past four decades. As part of every CES, respondents are asked to indicate which party they voted for in the current and past elections. To assess the stability of Liberal support, we look at whether respondents reported a vote for the Liberal Party for both the current and previous elections.[9] People had to report a vote for the Liberal Party in either the current or the previous election to be included in this section of the analysis. Not surprisingly, the proportion of stable Liberal voters varies considerably from one election to another. However, some clear trends emerge. For instance, the evidence indicates that Canadian-born voters were more stable supporters of the Liberal Party prior to 1980 than they have been since then. Moreover, whereas new immigrant voters were once more volatile than Canadian-born voters in their support for the Liberal Party, the more recent evidence suggests that new immigrant voters are now more stable supporters of the Liberals than their Canadian-born counterparts.

Furthermore, the evidence in Figure 3.2 indicates that between 1965 and 2004, the gap between immigrants from non-traditional source countries and the Canadian-born population in terms of stable Liberal voters gradually increased.[10] The gap shifted from –12 in 1965 to +13 in 2004, a 25-point reversal. According to the preceding analysis, therefore, it appears that over the years, the new immigrant voter shifted from being a volatile to a stable Liberal voter, whereas the Canadian-born voter appears to be becoming more volatile in terms of his or her support for the Liberal Party.

The New Immigrant Voter: A Partisan Liberal Identifier?

The inclination to support a party over two consecutive elections indicates a pattern of voter stability, but it says very little about the new immigrant voter's propensity to remain committed to the Liberal Party over the long term. For this purpose, we turn now to an examination of partisanship. Has the new immigrant voter begun to establish a partisan bond with the Liberal Party? If so, how intense is this connection? And what does the cross-time evidence suggest about the trajectory of this relationship over the long term?

During every election, the Canadian Election Study asks respondents to indicate whether they usually identify with any of the main political parties.[11] Figure 3.3 reports the percentage of immigrants from non-traditional source countries and members of the Canadian-born population who report thinking of themselves as Liberals.[12] Because intensity of partisanship can vary, it is not surprising to find that attachments to the Liberal Party among both immigrants and the Canadian-born population have fluctuated across elections, although not as dramatically as the actual vote (see Figure 3.1). Note too that the proportion of Liberal identifiers among both immigrants from non-traditional source countries and the Canadian-born population has declined since the Trudeau era. Still, what is particularly remarkable about these findings is that they almost consistently indicate that immigrants from non-traditional source countries identify more with the Liberal Party than their Canadian-born counterparts. The only two exceptions are 1965, when the latter were

Figure 3.3

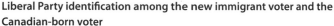

Liberal Party identification among the new immigrant voter and the Canadian-born voter

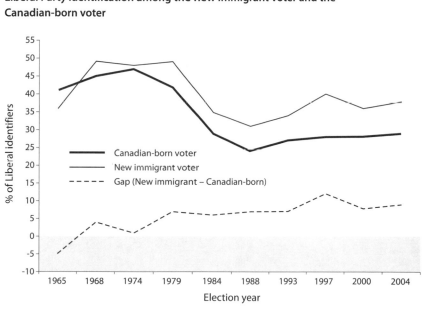

Source: 1965-2004 Canadian Election Studies

more inclined to identify with the party than the former, and 1974, when both groups were about equally likely to hold a Liberal partisan identification. Ever since then, the new immigrant voter has consistently and increasingly been more likely than the Canadian-born voter to be a Liberal partisan.

Indeed, the dashed line in Figure 3.3 indicates that the gap in Liberal party identification between the new immigrant voter and the Canadian-born voter has grown considerably. In 1965, the new immigrant voter was slightly less likely to identify with the Liberal Party than the Canadian-born voter. Since the 1960s, that trend has been gradually reversed, and the new immigrant voter is now much more likely to be a Liberal identifier than the Canadian-born voter (from –5 to +9, a 14-point reversal). The Liberal Party's greater capacity to attract the new immigrant voter than the Canadian-born voter, then, is not limited to voting but also extends, and increasingly so, to the feeling of partisanship.

Beyond this quantitative increase in the proportion of immigrants identifying with the Liberal Party lies a qualitative change in the nature

Figure 3.4

Intensity of Liberal Party identification among the new immigrant voter and the Canadian-born voter*

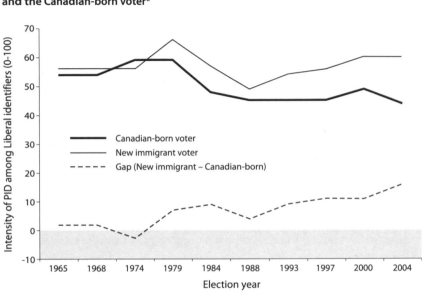

Source: 1965-2004 Canadian Election Studies

*   Respondents who do not identify with the Liberal Party are not included in this analysis.

of partisanship. After being asked whether they thought of themselves as Liberals, respondents were also asked whether they felt very strongly (100), fairly strongly (50), or not strongly (0) about the Liberal Party.[13] Figure 3.4 reports the cross-time evidence pertaining to the strength of party attachment among Liberal identifiers. The intensity of Liberal partisanship among Canadian-born voters clearly weakened between 1965 and 2004. The average strength of attachment among Liberal identifiers in the Canadian-born population plummeted from 54 in 1965 (on a 0-100 scale) to 44 in 2004. Conversely, the intensity of Liberal partisanship among new immigrants from non-traditional source countries increased slightly from 56 in 1965 to about 60 in 2004, with a marked increase from 49 to 60 between 1988 and 2004.

Moreover, similar to what we observed in the preceding analyses, the evidence suggests that the intensity of Liberal partisanship for these two groups may also be diverging. The dashed line in Figure 3.4 demonstrates that the gap in the strength of Liberal partisan attachment between the new immigrant voter and the Canadian-born voter increased substantially from a 2-point gap in 1965 to a 16-point gap in 2004. These findings indicate that not only is the new immigrant voter becoming more attached to the Liberal Party, but also the intensity of that attachment has increased over time. Whereas in 1965 the new immigrant voter and the Canadian-born voter were more or less equally attached to the Liberal Party, in terms of both expressing a Liberal partisanship and the intensity of that partisanship, over the past four decades, the new immigrant voter has grown into a more frequent and intense Liberal partisan than the Canadian-born voter.

Conclusion

Over the past four decades, Canada's new immigrant population from non-traditional source countries has expanded significantly in both size and importance. In his 2005 presidential address to the Canadian Political Science Association, André Blais emphasized how little we know about the electoral habits of these new Canadians of non-European origins and how essential it is to deepen our knowledge about these new immigrants, especially when it comes to their tendency to support the Liberal Party. In this chapter, we have begun to paint a systematic cross-time portrait of the new immigrant voter and to assess the consequences of the continuing influx of these new citizens for the long-term fortunes of the Liberal Party and the broader Canadian party system.

Several conclusions might be drawn from our analysis. First, the evidence in this chapter demonstrates that new immigrant voters support the Liberal Party more than Canadian-born voters and that this gap has been expanding over the years. Second, this analysis shows that new immigrant voters exhibit signs of being stable voters for the Liberals over consecutive elections and that they are increasingly more inclined to do so than Canadian-born voters. Third, our evidence indicates that new immigrant voters have been slowly growing more attached to the Liberal Party and that the intensity of this attachment has increased. Compared with their Canadian-born counterparts, therefore, who seem to be gradually shedding their traditional Liberal partisan ties, new immigrant voters appear to be becoming more committed Liberal partisans.[14] In the 1960s, fewer than one in twenty Liberal voters was an immigrant from a non-traditional source country. This proportion has now increased to more than one in ten.[15] Currently, the new immigrant voter still represents a limited proportion of Liberal support, but we might speculate based on past demographic trends that the continued influx of immigrants from non-traditional source countries could have important implications for the long-term fortunes of the Liberal Party and the future dynamics of the Canadian party system.[16]

As mentioned earlier, Nevitte et al. (2000) and Blais et al. (2002) concluded that the Liberal Party partly owed its 1997 and 2000 victories to its larger stock of loyal partisan voters. Based on the results of our analysis, we might add to the argument the growing relevance of the new immigrant voter for the Liberal Party's future success. The cross-time evidence indicates that in the past, when support for the Liberal Party declined, the new immigrant voter remained more loyal to the Liberal Party than the Canadian-born voter; when support for the Liberal Party went up, new immigrant voters rallied behind the party in larger numbers than Canadian-born voters. During the past four decades at least, the new immigrant voter has played an increasing role in helping to maintain the Liberal Party's significance on the Canadian political landscape. And if past demographic trends remain consistent, then the influence of the new immigrant voter on the future of the Liberal Party is only likely to increase. In a context of increased electoral volatility and partisan instability, this may prove to be a distinct competitive advantage. This new influx of voters and partisan supporters also represents for the Liberal Party somewhat reassuring news that could counterbalance the evidence of Bélanger and Stephenson (this volume), showing that Liberal partisans in the general population tend to be less loyal than those of other parties.

As for the influence that the new immigrant voter might have on the broader Canadian party system, the preliminary findings from our analysis indicate that the new immigrant voter tends to resemble the partisan voter type that we developed earlier more than the Canadian-born voter, at least when it comes to relating to the Liberal Party. The new immigrant voter is a more stable voter and a stronger partisan voter than the Canadian-born voter. These results suggest that continued immigration of this sort may gradually work to counter partisan dealignment and contribute to stabilizing the current Canadian party system.

That the new immigrant voter seems to behave like a partisan voter might be somewhat surprising at first sight. After all, immigrants from non-traditional source countries are unlikely to have developed a partisan attachment early in life through a process of family socialization consistent with the social-psychological perspective. The immigrant voter nevertheless appears to have developed a Liberal partisan attachment that makes him or her resemble the classic partisan voter. We cannot further explore here the process by which new immigrant voters come to develop Liberal partisan attachment. However, given the impossibility of the family socialization origin of their attachment, we speculate that the bond between new immigrant voters and the Liberal Party likely emerges from a self-interested cognitive process of repeated positive experiences with the party; this process would be consistent with Fiorina's (1981) perspective on partisan attachments as resulting from a "running-tally" of continuously updated evaluations of a party's capacity to represent one's interests.[17]

The above discussion on the nature of the attachment of the new immigrant voter to the Liberal Party is also helpful in proposing new avenues for understanding the specific reason that immigrants have become attached to the Liberal Party as opposed to any other party. Blais (2005) briefly considered, without much success, whether socioeconomic characteristics of Canadians of non-European origin and their policy preferences could explain why they support the Liberal Party more than any other party. Our speculation about the nature of the bond between the new immigrant voter and the Liberal Party (the "running-tally" perspective) suggests that the Liberal Party might have been successful in attracting the new immigrant voter's support specifically because it has been perceived by immigrants as being best able and willing to defend their interests and to address their preoccupations. Such a perspective would be consistent with what others have observed in the United States (Cain, Kiewiet, and Uhlaner 1991) and in Australia (McAllister and Makkai 1991), as explained in our theoretical section.

This alternative explanation resembles the "issue ownership" theory (Petrocik 1996). The argument is that the Liberal Party has gained the vote and loyalty of the new immigrant voter because it has offered gestures and adopted major policies to protect and help immigrants and ethnic minorities. This issue ownership could have emerged out of two major symbolic policies adopted by the Liberals. It was a Liberal prime minister, Trudeau, who oversaw the adoption of the policy of multiculturalism in 1971. It was also Trudeau who oversaw the 1982 adoption of the Charter of Rights and Freedoms that protects, among other things, the multicultural character of Canada and minorities against discrimination, two founding blocks of Canadian multiculturalism.[18]

This issue ownership explanation, however, might look somewhat less compelling if one considers recent years only. The Liberals under Chrétien started to take a much harder stance on immigration and multicultural-ism after they were elected in 1993, a stance well illustrated by their deci-sion to disband the Department of Multiculturalism and Citizenship and make it a subpart of Canadian Heritage (Abu-Laban and Gabriel 2002). Since 1993, the Liberals appear to have lost somewhat their ownership over multiculturalism and immigration issues. But it is also possible that in relative terms, the Liberals actually preserved their stra-tegic pro-immigration positioning. After 1993, even if the Liberal Party was less pro-immigrant, the Reform Party and the Canadian Alliance were proposing (or were perceived to be proposing) more stringent im-migration policies, and the Bloc Québécois was simply focused on an issue that has never been appealing to most immigrants: namely, Quebec sovereignty. Under these conditions, even if the Liberal Party was relatively less willing to defend immigrants' and ethnic minorities' interests than it had been before, it was probably still perceived to be the most willing to do so compared with the other parties.

Regardless of how accurate this issue ownership explanation might seem, we are navigating here in the realm of speculation, and unfortu-nately it would be difficult at this stage, if not impossible, to verify this argument across time using the Canadian Election Studies. New ques-tions in the CES asking respondents which party and leader are best suited to handle issues such as immigration, minority rights, and multi-culturalism would help in testing the relevance of the issue ownership explanation and in understanding the relationship between the new immigrant voter and the Liberal Party. In the same vein, asking a special sample of immigrant voters, as part of the CES, more specific questions relating to immigrants' situations, preferences, and behaviours would also help in drawing the portrait of this new immigrant voter and under-standing the consequences of his or her arrival on the Canadian political landscape. Furthermore, beyond studies investigating the political be-haviour of immigrants, it would be helpful to engage in studies system-atically documenting and analyzing the policies, mechanisms, and gestures made by parties to gain the support and loyalty of immigrants and other Canadian citizens.

Finally, if the new immigrant voter stands as an emerging Liberal par-tisan in this era of growing partisan dealignment, then the portrait of the

Table 3.1

Proportion of new and old immigrant voters by election year

	Immigrants				Canadian-
	New (%)		Old (%)		Total (100%)	born
1965	72	(20)	290	(80)	362	1,756
1968	116	(23)	386	(77)	502	2,264
1974	101	(25)	307	(75)	408	2,154
1979	116	(30)	266	(70)	382	2,336
1984	157	(35)	290	(65)	447	2,929
1988	180	(41)	261	(59)	441	3,114
1993	145	(48)	157	(52)	302	2,028
1997	210	(43)	284	(57)	494	3,405
2000	327	(65)	173	(34)	500	3,133
2004	297	(50)	297	(50)	594	3,701

new immigrant voter is far from complete. In this chapter, we have discussed the partisan preferences of the new immigrant voter, but only partly so. To present a more complete picture, we need to expand our investigation to the relationship between the new immigrant voter and the other parties. We also need to investigate the relationship between length of residence in Canada and partisan outlook. Not all new immigrant voters are "brand" new; some have been residing in Canada for many years, and it is possible that the new immigrant voter converges with the Canadian-born voter the longer he or she resides in Canada (see Table 3.1). Furthermore, we need to consider the portrait of the new immigrant voter with regard to his or her non-partisan outlook. Is the new immigrant voter interested in and knowledgeable about politics, efficacious, cynical, and/or active in the political system? Answering these questions would help us to understand not only the new immigrant voter but also, likely, the relationship between this voter and the Liberal Party of Canada.

Acknowledgments
We would like to thank Nada Fadol and Nicki Doyle for their research assistance in this project.

Notes

1 Traditional source countries include northern, western, and southern Europe as well as Anglo-American democracies. Non-traditional source countries include all other countries.
2 Canada is not unique in this situation; to our knowledge, there has been no systematic investigation of the immigrant voter in other Western democracies.
3 For a more traditional discussion of partisanship in Canada, see Bélanger and Stephenson (this volume).
4 See Anderson and Stephenson (this volume) for a discussion of this finding.
5 Our analyses focus solely on the first generation of immigrants: that is, those born outside Canada.
6 Although Blais (2005) looked at ethnicity, our focus here is on immigrants only (people born outside Canada); we prefer to avoid the more subjective question of ethnicity. Furthermore, our classification of "immigrants from non-traditional backgrounds" includes some immigrants of European origin (especially recent immigrants from eastern Europe).
7 The vote was coded 1 if the respondent reported a vote for the Liberal Party in the current election and 0 otherwise.
8 The progression from 1965 to 2004 in the Liberal voting gap between the new immigrant voter and the Canadian-born voter grew steadily. The 1997 election, however, appears almost as a special case, not because it went counter to the 1965-2004 trend but because it was the year for which we measured the largest gap in Liberal voting and the year for which immigrant voting in absolute terms was at its peak (right behind 1968). It is hard to explain this fact. A brief review of the 1997 campaign does not allow us to identify any major event that at first sight would be a plausible explanation for this great polarization. Blais et al. (1999) identify that the leaders' debate and a negative ad produced by the Reform Party against the federal party leaders from Quebec had an impact on voting intentions. It is hard, however, to link either of these events to our gap in Liberal voting between the new immigrant voter and the Canadian-born voter, and in any case, Blais et al. claim that the impact of these events was only temporary. Another possibility is that during the 1997 election campaign, new immigrant voters perceived the Reform Party as too extreme with regard to immigration issues, which might have led them to rally in greater proportions behind the Liberal Party. Nevitte et al. (2000, 93) clearly indicate that a large proportion of Canadians who wanted to do more for ethnic minorities and admit more immigrants to Canada expressed the opinion that the Reform Party was too extreme. It is possible, then, that immigrants were simply more likely to find the Reform Party too extreme. We briefly investigated this possibility, but it is not possible to reach any conclusion. Although a larger proportion of immigrants from non-traditional source countries than Canadian-born voters perceived the Reform Party as too extreme (37 percent versus 30 percent), the gap is relatively small, and we simply do not know whether this gap was larger in 1997 than in 1993 (the 1993 CES does not provide information on this matter). The specific reason for the 1997 election gap in Liberal voting between the new immigrant voter and the Canadian-born voter would need to be investigated further in a detailed analysis of the election.
9 These are not panel data; respondents are asked to recall how they voted in the previous election. There is a possibility of overestimating the stability of people's

votes either because of their desire to report consistency or because of their deficient recollections of their previous behaviours (see Himmelweit, Jaeger Biberian, and Stockdale 1978). Nevertheless, because our focus is comparative (new immigrant voter and Canadian-born voter and across time), we see no reason that the bias should differ for each group of respondents or vary across time. In other words, if there is bias, we presume that it is constant across groups and across time.

10 We also performed the analysis using an overall measure of stability that includes all parties. The pattern is not as pronounced when we use this specification, but the same general trend is replicated, even considering that we overestimated stability by qualifying a stable voter as everybody who voted for the Progressive Conservative, Reform, Canadian Alliance, or Conservative Party across elections (results not presented).

11 The question asks respondents, "in federal politics, do you usually think of yourself as a (names of parties)?" Respondents were coded 1 if they expressed thinking of themselves as Liberals and 0 otherwise.

12 We consider here only whether or not respondents think of themselves as Liberals regardless of how strong this identification is.

13 The question asks respondents, "how strongly (Liberal) do you feel, very strongly, fairly strongly, or not very strongly?" Respondents were coded as 100 when they felt very strongly, 50 when they felt fairly strongly, and 0 when they felt not very strongly. Only respondents who identified with the Liberal Party are included in this section of the analysis.

14 The differences between the new immigrant voter and the Canadian-born voter might be explained by factors such as sociodemographics and region. To ensure that the differences observed are not caused by demographic differences, we performed some multivariate analyses controlling for these factors. The results of these additional analyses demonstrate that controlling for age, sex, education, income, employment status, and region does not alter the conclusions of our findings. Most of the differences observed between the new immigrant voter and the Canadian-born voter remain the same size. It is also possible that our category of immigrants from non-traditional source countries masks the variation that exists within this group of respondents. Immigrants from non-traditional source countries certainly do not form a homogeneous group, and it would have been interesting to pursue more detailed explorations of immigrants' partisan preferences by unpacking this group of respondents. Unfortunately, this is not possible given our small immigrant sample for every election year.

15 These estimates are based on the proportion of Liberal voters comprised of immigrants from non-traditional source countries as reported by the respondents' votes in the Canadian Election Studies.

16 One important consideration in determining whether immigrants from non-traditional source countries will have a significant impact on the future of the Liberal Party is the extent to which they will pass on their Liberal preferences to their children. Unfortunately, we do not have specific information about the partisan preferences of the second generation of immigrants. Nevertheless, should the motivations of immigrants in supporting the Liberal Party be associated with the party's commitment to defending immigrants' and ethnic minorities' interests, we would have good reason to believe that immigrants' Liberal preferences would be passed on to the second generation. Indeed, studies in the United States have

shown that the "ethnic awareness" of immigrants, or the perception of their distance from the host society and the sense of their marginalization, is often greater with the passage of time in the host country and among the second generation (Portes 1984). Based on such conclusions, we can expect the second generation to be even more supportive of the party perceived as the best suited to defend ethnic minorities' interests.

17   One important consideration in determining the type of voter whom the new immigrant voter constitutes is length of residence. Investigating the impact of length of residence on immigrants' partisan support would allow us to determine whether immigrants' preferences change and how they change the longer the immigrants reside in Canada. It is difficult, however, to conduct reliable investigations of this matter within the scope and orientation of this cross-time project. Alternatively, the partisan orientation of the governments when immigrants arrived in Canada could also be a significant factor (whether Liberals or Conservatives were in power). Indeed, since the Liberal Party has formed the government for most of the years covered in this chapter, it is possible that immigrants from non-traditional source countries have been more likely to support that party simply because they are "loyal" to the government that first "hosted" them in Canada. Blais (2005, 831) examined such a possibility and found that it provided only a limited explanation of partisan preferences among Canadians of non-European origin.

18   Immigrants from non-traditional source countries qualify in vast majority as visible minorities in Canada. We can speculate that this characteristic is potentially what "unites" them and is part of the explanation of their support for the Liberal Party. Visible minorities, immigrants and non-immigrants, are often victims of discrimination and marginalization and thus are most likely to benefit from policies promoting a multicultural agenda and protection of ethnic minorities. This "visible minority" status differentiates immigrants from non-traditional source countries from those from traditional source countries, and this could explain why support for the Liberal Party has increased significantly among immigrants from the former countries but not among those from the latter countries. The multicultural agenda and the protection of ethnic minorities were issues that appealed to "visible minority" immigrants only.

References

Abu-Laban, Yasmeen, and Christina Gabriel. 2002. *Selling Diversity: Immigration, Multiculturalism, Employment Equity, and Globalization.* Peterborough, ON: Broadview Press.

Blais, André. 2005. "Accounting for the Electoral Success of the Liberal Party in Canada." *Canadian Journal of Political Science* 38, 4: 821-40.

Blais, André, Elisabeth Gidengil, Richard Nadeau, and Neil Nevitte. 2002. *Anatomy of a Liberal Victory.* Mississauga, ON: Broadview Press.

Blais, André, Richard Nadeau, Elisabeth Gidengil, and Neil Nevitte. 1999. "Canadian Dynamics in the 1997 Election." *Canadian Public Policy* 25, 2: 197-205.

Cain, Bruce E., D. Roderick Kiewiet, and Carole J. Uhlaner. 1991. "The Acquisition of Partisanship by Latinos and Asian Americans." *American Journal of Political Science* 35, 2: 390-422.

Campbell, Angus, Philip E. Converse, Warren E. Miller, and Donald E. Stokes. 1960. *The American Voter.* Chicago: University of Chicago Press.

Carty, R. Kenneth. 2006. "Political Turbulence in a Dominant Party System." *PS: Political Science and Politics* 39, 4: 825-27.

Clarke, Harold D., Jane Jenson, Lawrence LeDuc, and Jon H. Pammett. 1996. *Absent Mandate: Canadian Electoral Politics in an Era of Restructuring.* 3rd ed. Toronto: GAGE.

Dalton, Russell J. 2000. "The Decline of Party Identification." In *Parties without Partisans: Political Change in Advanced Industrial Democracies,* ed. Russell J. Dalton and Martin P. Wattenberg, 19-36. New York: Oxford University Press.

Dalton, Russell J. 2006. *Citizen Politics: Public Opinion and Political Parties in Advanced Industrial Democracies.* Washington, DC: CQ Press.

Dalton, Russell J., Ian McAllister, and Martin P. Wattenberg. 2000. "The Consequences of Partisan Dealignment." In *Parties without Partisans: Political Change in Advanced Industrial Democracies,* ed. Russell J. Dalton and Martin P. Wattenberg, 37-63. New York: Oxford University Press.

Dalton, Russell J., and Martin P. Wattenberg. 2000. "Partisan Change and the Democratic Process." In *Parties without Partisans: Political Change in Advanced Industrial Democracies,* ed. Russell J. Dalton and Martin P. Wattenberg, 261-85. New York: Oxford University Press.

Delli Carpini, Michael X., and Scott Keeter. 1996. *What Americans Know about Politics and Why It Matters.* New Haven: Yale University Press.

Finifter, Ada W., and Bernard M. Finifter. 1989. "Party Identification and Political Adaptation of American Migrants in Australia." *Journal of Politics* 51, 3: 599-630.

Fiorina, Morris P. 1981. *Retrospective Voting in American Elections.* New Haven: Yale University Press.

Himmelweit, Hilde H., Marianne Jaeger Biberian, and Janet Stockdale. 1978. "Memory for Past Vote: Implications of a Study of Bias in Recall." *British Journal of Political Science* 8, 3: 365-75.

Lupia, Arthur. 1994. "Shortcuts versus Encyclopaedias: Information and Voting Behaviour in California Insurance Reform Elections." *American Political Science Review* 88, 1: 63-76.

Lupia, Arthur, and Mathew D. McCubbins. 1998. *The Democratic Dilemma: Can Citizens Learn What They Need to Know?* New York: Cambridge University Press.

McAllister, Ian, and Toni Makkai. 1991. "The Formation and Development of Party Loyalties: Patterns among Australian Immigrants." *Australian and New Zealand Journal of Sociology* 27, 2: 195-217.

Nevitte, Neil, André Blais, Elisabeth Gidengil, and Richard Nadeau. 2000. *Unsteady State: The 1997 Canadian Federal Election.* Don Mills, ON: Oxford University Press.

Petrocik, John R. 1996. "Issue Ownership in Presidential Elections, with a 1980 Case Study." *American Journal of Political Science* 40, 3: 825-50.

Portes, Alejandro. 1984. "The Rise of Ethnicity: Determinants of Ethnic Perceptions among Cuban Exiles in Miami." *American Sociological Review* 49, 3: 383-97.

Sears, David O. 1993. "Symbolic Politics: A Socio-Psychological Theory." In *Explorations in Political Psychology,* ed. Shanto Iyengar and William J. McGuire, 113-49. Durham, NC: Duke University Press.

The Catholic-Liberal Connection: A Test of Strength

Laura B. Stephenson

Religion has long been a significant factor in voting behaviour in Canada. Since the study of election surveys began, three party-religion links have been evident – Catholics vote for the Liberal Party, Protestants vote for the major conservative party of the day (Progressive Conservative, Canadian Alliance, or Conservative), and non-religious individuals vote for the NDP (see, for example, Meisel 1956; Schwartz 1974; Johnston et al. 1992; and Blais 2005). These relationships continue to be found in modern analyses of the most recent elections (see, for example, Gidengil et al. 2006).

That religion has played and continues to play a role in Canadian voting behaviour is noteworthy given that religion does not have a prominent place in Canadian politics. Canadian politicians rarely are photographed attending worship services, and campaigns do not focus on the denominations (or personal beliefs) of the leaders. The relationship is also curious given social trends *away* from religion and *toward* secularism. Nevitte (1996), for example, notes that there is a movement worldwide toward less religiosity and increased moral permissiveness. On the other hand, Dalton (2002) finds that, despite these social changes, the influence of religion on voting behaviour continues to be significant, declining far less than that of class. Blais (2005, 822), too, argues that researchers must not forget the importance of social characteristics when understanding vote choice – though many may believe "that social background characteristics are no longer very relevant to vote choice ... we miss a crucial part of the story ... if we choose not to examine its social bases."

Among the religion-party links, the Catholic-Liberal relationship is of particular interest. First, its stability has been evident since the 1940s, whereas the other relationships have either faltered (see Clarke et al.

1980 regarding the Protestant-Conservative relationship) or been weaker (the NDP-no religion connection). Blais's (2005) tour-de-force analysis of the voting connection between Catholics and the Liberal Party shows that the connection did not fade in Canadian Election Studies (CES) data from 1965 to 2004. Even though the number of people claiming no religious affiliation increased from 4 percent in 1971 to 16 percent in 2001,[1] the change in religiosity appears not to have affected the Liberals' advantage among Catholics, which only disappeared in 2006 and even then not at all when Quebec is excluded from the analysis (see Figure 4.1; 2006 data without Quebec not shown). Second, Catholic support of the Liberal Party has been a significant (and possibly sustaining) factor in the party's success (Blais et al. 2002), giving it particular relevance in Canadian politics. Third, although several have tried, no researcher has been able to determine exactly *why* this voting regularity continues (Irvine 1974; Johnston 1991; Blais 2005; Fairie 2007; Stephenson 2007).

The purpose of this chapter is to better understand the limits of the ties connecting religion and vote choice in Canada outside Quebec by investigating whether the predisposition of a religious group to vote for a

Figure 4.1

Vote for Liberal Party, Catholic, and Non-Catholic (%)

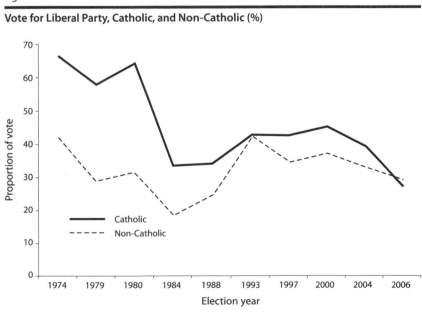

Source: Data compiled by author from Canadian Election Studies, various years

specific party is affected by issue disagreement. I focus here on the most studied religious connection – between Catholics and Liberals – and test whether the tendency of Catholics to vote for the Liberal Party is strong enough to withstand issue disagreement or whether Catholics are vulnerable to being persuaded away from their long-standing religious attachment to the party by their issue stances. In particular, I question how the debate over same-sex marriage, which saw the Liberal Party and Catholics on opposite sides of the issue and has obvious moral salience, and the well-publicized sponsorship scandal, which angered Liberals and Catholics alike (not to mention other Canadians), affected the relationship between the two groups. Drawing on literature indicating that sophistication plays a role in the impact of issues on vote choice, I also consider whether the effect of Catholic identity on voting differed by this characteristic. Data from the 2004 and 2006 Canadian federal elections, when both of these issues emerged prominently during the campaigns, are used for the analysis.

The results in this chapter accomplish two things. First, they shed some light on the strength and nature of the long-standing attachment of Catholics to the Liberal Party, a bond that has never been fully explained. Second, they support the claims of Dalton (2002) and Blais (2005) that sociodemographic factors cannot be ignored when understanding vote choice. No matter how improbable or unlikely they may seem, such voting relationships can be surprisingly tenacious.

Theory

A Long History of Religion and Politics

Given that many react with disbelief when told that the bond between Catholics and the Liberal Party exists, it is worthwhile first to consider the existing evidence of the role that religion plays in voting. Scholars of voting behaviour have long been aware that religion is an important factor in vote choice. For example, it has been established that the evolution of many party systems was influenced by the religious cleavages in societies (Lipset and Rokkan 1967). Certain denominations remain effectively tied to certain parties – in many countries, Catholics support right-wing parties, although in Canada (and elsewhere) a different alignment exists (see Fairie 2007 for a discussion). Recently, the issue of religion and politics has received renewed attention from scholars interested in understanding the implications of an old cleavage for modern society

(Guth and Fraser 2001; Layman 1997; Kotler-Berkowitz 2001; O'Neill 2001, 2004; Malloy 2005).

Evidence of the importance of the religious cleavage to Canadian voting behaviour in particular is considerable and long standing. Laponce's 1972 study of the elections from 1949 to 1968, for instance, noted the significance of Catholic support for the Liberal Party. For the elections between 1957 and 1968, his analysis of the Liberal Party's support showed that religion "is the variable which, in all years, discriminates most" (280). Also writing about this time period, Alford (1963) noted the existence of Catholic-Liberal and Protestant-Conservative ties, although he found that Protestants were more likely also to consider class in their vote than Catholics. Many other studies confirm these results and emphasize especially the strength of the Catholic-Liberal connection, which emerges most consistently (Meisel 1956, 1973; Anderson 1966; Grayson 1973; Lijphart 1979; Clarke et al. 1980, 1996; Guth and Fraser 2001; Johnston et al. 1992; Nevitte et al. 2000; Blais et al. 2002; Gidengil et al. 2006). Blais et al. (2002, 96) state that it would be "impossible to understand the Liberals' victory in the 2000 election without recognizing the extent to which their strength outside Quebec hinges on the support of Catholics and Canadians of non-European origins," and Gidengil et al. (2006, 7) note that "Catholics remained a key source of Liberal support, as they have through all the changes in Canada's electoral landscape over the past five decades."

Although a fairly stable and significant relationship, the tie between Protestants and conservative parties is less well documented than the Catholic-Liberal connection. However, evidence indicates that it has gained strength in recent years. In the 1974 election, Clarke et al. (1980) found that the Protestant-Conservative bond had weakened to the point where Protestant support was divided equally between the Liberals and Conservatives. After the Reform Party (later the Canadian Alliance) was formed in 1987, its strong moral conservative stances resonated with evangelical Christians, with the effect of pulling their support away from the Progressive Conservatives (Lusztig and Wilson 2005). The same moral conservatism activated the evangelical community to the benefit of the new Conservative Party (created from a merger of the Canadian Alliance and Progressive Conservative Parties in 2003) when the issue of same-sex marriage became salient. More recently, Blais et al. (2002) and Gidengil et al. (2006) found that Protestant fundamentalists[2] were more likely to vote for the Canadian Alliance (by 8 points) and for the Conservative

Party (by 15.6 points) in the 2000 and 2004 elections, respectively, suggesting that the current effect of the connection is considerable.

The relationship between the NDP and those without a religious identity has also become clearer and more prominent in recent elections. A hint of such a relationship was initially found in Meisel's (1973) study of the 1968 election, where the NDP was found to draw support from non-Catholics. Clarke et al. (1980), analyzing the elections in the 1970s, found that the NDP got more support from those with no affiliation than those with a religious affiliation. Similarly, Johnston et al. (1992) found that the NDP in the 1988 election enjoyed their greatest support from non-religionists, who were nearly twice as likely as Protestants or Catholics to support that party. In the 2004 election, the effect was strong enough to increase the probability of someone with no religious affiliation voting for the NDP by 9.5 points (Gidengil et al. 2006). Thus, there is ample evidence that religious affiliation (and non-affiliation) have mattered and continue to matter in Canadian society.

Can the Religious Cleavage Be Overcome?

As mentioned above, the persistence of the religious cleavage in Canada, especially the loyalty of Catholics to the Liberal Party, is a puzzle that has engaged the efforts of many researchers. Much research has tried to understand the basis of the Catholic-Liberal connection, particularly since the historic battles that involved religion (denominational schooling, for example) are long since over (Johnston 1985; Gidengil 1992), and Canadian political parties do not and have not historically embraced religious issues or groups as their own (Engelmann and Schwartz 1975).[3] A new research angle, pursued in this chapter, is to try to understand the effect of religious identity on voting by treating it like any other long-standing attachment. Instead of considering *why* the attachments exist, perhaps we should consider under which conditions they do *not*. Thus, the objective of this chapter is to consider whether the stability of the Catholic-Liberal connection, the most stable of the denomination-party bonds, is vulnerable to issue disagreement.

The literature on issue voting is obviously relevant to this research approach. In the introduction to this volume, the concept of the funnel of causality was presented, noting that issues are more proximate causes of vote choice than long-standing predispositions (such as religion). Several scholars in the revisionist school took pains to demonstrate that issues mattered (for example, Carmines and Stimson [1980]), after initial findings from the sociopsychological model of voting suggested otherwise (Campbell et al. 1960). It has also been shown that issue positions make a difference for Canadian voters. Johnston et al. (1992) found that the free-trade issue was especially important in the 1988 election, and Clarke et al. (1996) found that issues were important factors in vote choice, especially for voters with flexible partisanship.[4] More recent work has also demonstrated that voters consider their issue positions, on issues such as defence spending, the economy, and health care, when deciding how to vote (Nevitte et al. 2000; Blais et al. 2002; Gidengil et al. 2006). Furthermore, findings indicate that proximity voting, or voting for the party that is closest on issues, is an appropriate model to use in the Canadian case (Blais et al. 2001; Johnston et al. 2000); it has also been shown that the influence of issues increases with their salience and importance to the voter (RePass 1971).

There is also some evidence that, when issues are salient, long-standing religious predispositions have less effect on voters. Research by Mendelsohn and Nadeau (1997) suggests that issue preferences, when made salient through media exposure, can overcome the predisposition of Catholics to vote Liberal. They suggest that media exposure is a form of priming that causes voters to focus on secular considerations in their vote decisions. Thus, their work is an indirect but suggestive test of the potential for issues to overwhelm the tendency to vote along religious lines. In this chapter, I undertake a more direct test of the role of issues by focusing on specific issue stances that could contradict a religious connection.

When evaluating the potential for issues to overwhelm religion-based voting preferences, it is important to consider whether the effects of issue disagreement might differ by political sophistication. Work by Bittner (2007) and Roy (2009) has shown that political information can lead to the diminishing of many socioeconomic cleavages as vote factors in Canada. Bittner finds that, as Catholics become more informed, they are less likely to differ from other Canadians, and Roy's findings indicate that low-information voters are influenced by Catholic identity, whereas high-information voters are not. It is thus possible that the issue disagreement between Catholics and the Liberal Party might influence the role of religion in voting only for more sophisticated Catholics.

Political sophistication is also relevant from the standpoint of issue voting. Researchers have found that one's political sophistication, or knowledge of politics, plays a role in whether issues are considered in voting (Goren 1997). This finding addresses some of the concerns about the cognitive requirements of issue voting; in *The American Voter*, Campbell et al. (1960) argued that the influence of issues was hindered by the fact that many voters were unaware of the issues, were not interested enough to recognize the issues, and were cognitively unable to connect issue stances with party policy. Converse's (1964) finding that opinion coherence was rare supported this stance in that, to use issues to choose a candidate, as the spatial model expects, a voter needs to be able to compare issue preferences with party stances and political choices. The work of Macdonald, Rabinowitz, and Listhaug (1995) shows that sophistication does make voters more likely to use issues in decision making, even if the spatial model is not the best representation of voter behaviour.

This chapter addresses the influence of religious identity and issues on vote choice through two specific hypotheses. First, given their proximity to the vote choice, one might expect that a religious attachment would be vulnerable to issue disagreement. Is the traditional voting behaviour of Catholics altered when the Liberal Party's positions conflict with personal issue stances? Second, in line with the research on sophistication and issue voting, are more sophisticated individuals more likely to be swayed by contrary issue stances to abandon their religious attachment to a political party? The answers to these questions reveal the potential for issue disagreement to overcome the long-standing predisposition between Catholics and the Liberal Party.

The Issues

Because it is unclear exactly why Catholics prefer the Liberal Party, I consider here the effects of two different issues – one that goes against an issue stance of the Catholic Church (which should be important if one's Catholic *beliefs* create a preference for the Liberal Party), and one that has less religious foundation but high secular salience. The results of Mendelsohn and Nadeau (1997) suggest that the secular issue should be able to overcome the religious attachment. The expected effect of moral issue disagreement is less clear – though it might not increase the importance of secular considerations, such disagreement could affect whether a Catholic believes that the Liberal Party is in line with his or her preferences. Depending on the results, this investigation could indicate a weakness in the relationship, which could decrease the effect of religion on voting in Canada. Additionally, by analyzing the Catholic-Liberal relationship specifically in terms of its potential vulnerability, we might gain greater insight into the source of its strength.

The first issue that I consider is same-sex marriage. Before 2003, modern incidents of conflicting issue stances and predispositions were not common for Catholic Liberal supporters. Beginning in that year, however, the same-sex marriage issue introduced conflict into the relationship in the form of moral disagreement. When Prime Minister Jean Chrétien announced that he would ask the Supreme Court of Canada to rule on the constitutionality of legislation to permit same-sex marriage, he opened himself (and his party) to a barrage of criticism.[5] The Catholic Church, in a statement approved by Pope John Paul II, called on Catholic politicians to oppose such a policy. Although both Chrétien and his successor, Paul Martin, are Catholic, neither stated that he was inclined to bend to the will of the Church. This issue enraged people of many different religions, but it presented a key challenge to the Liberal-Catholic relationship,[6] as 39 percent and 40 percent of Catholic respondents to the Canadian Election Study (outside Quebec) in 2004 and 2006, respectively, opposed same-sex marriage.[7] If the preference of Catholics for the Liberal Party is at all related to sympathetic issue positions,[8] then the emergence of this issue, and its clear moral implications for Catholics, could have caused many Catholics to rethink their voting behaviour.

The second issue is the sponsorship scandal, which emerged as an important political issue in 2004. The Liberal Party was found to have directed $100 million to "friendly" advertising firms under the guise of a fund intended to promote the image of Canada in Quebec. This issue does not address morality or the specific nature of Catholic ties to the Liberal Party, but it angered many Liberal supporters (including Catholics) and was highly salient not only in the 2004 election (see Gidengil et al. 2006) but also in the 2006 election. Outside Quebec, 72.2 percent of Liberal supporters in the CES indicated that they were somewhat or very angry in 2004; in 2006, 74.6 percent indicated the same. The data also indicate that Catholic respondents (outside Quebec) were even angrier than the average Liberal supporter – 79 percent in both 2004 and 2006 indicated that they were somewhat or very angry. Again, the question of interest here is how Catholics who were angry over this issue dealt with the conflicting pressures of their predisposition to vote Liberal and their issue-based desire to vote for a different party. Was such conflict strong enough to erode the Catholic voting tendency? Comparing the results for this issue with those for same-sex marriage might also give us some insight into the nature of the attachment between Catholics and Liberals, as which kind of issue disagreement had the most influence on the vote relationship might provide information about the source of the attachment.

Methodology

To test whether issue stances caused Catholics to rethink their long-standing vote tendencies in 2004 and 2006, I used individual-level vote data from the 2004 and 2006 Canadian Election Studies. Quebec is excluded from the study, in keeping with other research (Johnston 1985; Mendelsohn and Nadeau 1997) and to avoid conflating the effects of the variables with other significant voting influences (such as region or language). Along with a dependent variable of voting for the Liberal Party (coded 0 for no and 1 for yes), there are five key independent variables. Because studies have found that religiosity can make a difference in the strength of the religious cleavage,[9] the Catholic identity variable was created from both self-identified religious denomination as well as the importance of religion for the respondent. Only Catholics who indicated that religion was very or somewhat important were classified as Catholic in the coding. Those who held opposing issue stances to the Liberal Party were identified in two issue variables: a dummy variable to indicate opposition to same-sex marriage, and a variable to indicate how angry the respondent was about the sponsorship scandal. To account for the salience of the latter for citizens, the variable was created by multiplying one's level of anger (ranging from 0 to 3, with higher values indicating more anger) by an indicator of whether the respondent noted corruption as the most or second most important issue in the election. The final variable ranges from 0 to 9. Two interaction variables were also created to indicate Catholics who held issue opinions about same-sex marriage and the sponsorship scandal that contradicted those of the Liberal Party. Several control variables are included in the analyses (age, gender, university education, and residence in the western provinces[10]) as well as two other variables related to Liberal voting preferences (non-European immigrant, French as a mother tongue[11]). To consider the effects of political sophistication, scales (0 to 1) were created for the 2004 and 2006 data sets, using a battery of four knowledge questions from each survey.[12] A dummy variable for high sophisticates was created by identifying respondents that answered three or four questions correctly.

Results

The hypotheses considered in this chapter question whether issue disagreement is enough to overcome the predisposition of Catholics to support the Liberal Party. Before addressing the hypotheses, I ran simple logit models for Liberal vote choice to confirm that the Catholic variable was in fact significant with the 2004 and 2006 data. As expected, it was positive and significant in both years (odds ratio = 1.48 [p = 0.002] and 1.61 [p = 0.000] respectively; full results available on request). These results, though not surprising, provide a baseline by which to measure the results for the Catholic variable in the other analyses – Catholicism was a significant vote factor in 2004 and 2006, prior to controlling for issue disagreement.

The first set of analyses considers the impact of disagreement over the same-sex marriage issue on the tendency for Catholics to vote Liberal. Table 4.1 reports the results of models that include the same-sex marriage opposition variable and the interaction of that variable and Catholic identity. To simplify the interpretation of the logit results, odds ratios are reported; an odds ratio greater than 1 indicates a positive effect, whereas an odds ratio less than 1 indicates a negative effect. It is important to remember that the odds ratio for the Catholic dummy variable shows the effect of Catholic identity on Liberal voting conditional on the value of another (in this case, when the voter did not oppose same-sex marriage).[13] The interaction term odds ratio is the unique effect of Catholic identity on voting Liberal when one *disagrees* with the party about same-sex marriage and thus is of particular interest. If issue disagreement overwhelms the tendency to support the party, then the value will be negative.

In 2004, the Catholic dummy variable (representing all Catholics who supported same-sex marriage) was positive (greater than 1) but not significant. The interaction variable, however, was also positive and significant. The direction of the effect suggests that opposition to same-sex marriage did not prevent Catholics from supporting the Liberal Party. In 2006, both the Catholic dummy variable and the Catholic oppose same-sex marriage interaction were positive and significant. Again, the vote choices of those affected by issue disagreement with the party were influenced differently than the choices of those who agreed with the party (because the interaction term was significant), but the effect was positive, *toward* supporting the Liberal Party – clearly, moral disagreement did little to change the voting preferences of Catholics.

Table 4.1

The impact of opposition to same-sex marriage on the tendency of Catholics to vote for the Liberal Party

Dependent Variable = Vote Liberal	2004		2006	
	Odds ratio	Robust standard error	Odds ratio	Robust standard error
Age	1.015***	0.004	1.013***	0.004
Male	1.113	0.119	1.034	0.111
University education	1.489***	0.165	1.157	0.131
West	0.581***	0.064	0.521***	0.057
Non-European ethnicity	2.872***	0.645	2.270***	0.517
French mother language	1.145	0.279	1.360	0.326
Catholic	1.254	0.082	1.366*	0.204
Oppose same-sex marriage	0.613***	0.082	0.465***	0.067
Interaction: Catholic who opposes same-sex marriage	1.592*	0.392	1.769*	0.448
N	3,197		2,983	
Pseudo-R^2	0.0445		0.0506	

* $p \le .1$; ** $p \le .01$; *** $p \le .001$

To further clarify the impact of issue disagreement for Catholics, I calculated the predicted probability of voting Liberal when one did and did not agree with the stance of the party.[14] The decrease in predicted probability due to issue disagreement – in other words, the extent to which issue disagreement diminished the Catholic-Liberal connection – is graphed in Figure 4.2. In 2004, if the voter was a Catholic, then the probability of voting for the Liberal Party if he or she opposed same-sex marriage was 0.227 (on a 0-1 scale), whereas the probability if one did not oppose same-sex marriage was 0.231, a significant ($p \le .001$) but insubstantial difference (0.004). For those who were not Catholic, the predicted probability of voting Liberal was 0.131 if one opposed same-sex marriage and 0.195 if one did not, a difference of 0.064.[15] The issue of same-sex marriage appears to have done little to interfere with the tendency of Catholics to prefer the Liberal Party, although there is a slight decrease in the probability of voting Liberal when one disagrees with the party. In 2006, the same-sex marriage issue had more impact on the voting behaviour of Catholics, as those opposed were about 4 points (0.039) less likely to vote for the party. However, the effect of issue disagreement

Figure 4.2

Decrease in predicted probability of Liberal support due to issue disagreement over same-sex marriage

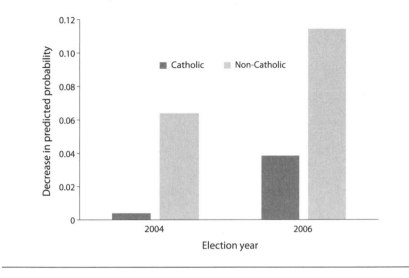

among non-Catholics was much greater, over 11 points (0.115). One should not forget that the same-sex marriage issue is a moral issue, one on which the Catholic Church was absolutely clear about its stance and one that should have caused conflict for all Catholics who were torn between following the teaching of their Church and their political leanings. That such an issue did not significantly erode the vote relationship between Catholics and the Liberal Party suggests that the bond between Catholics and Liberals might not be as religious in nature as one might expect.

If moral issue disagreement did not pull Catholics away from their tendency to vote Liberal, perhaps a more secular (and potentially salient) issue did. Consider now the effect of the sponsorship scandal issue. Table 4.2 shows the results for the logit models for 2004 and 2006. In 2004, as expected, the Catholic dummy variable was significant and positive, whereas the anger variable was significant and negative. The interaction was negatively signed, as one might expect if issue disagreement caused Catholics to turn away from the party, but the effect was insignificant. This suggests that anger over the sponsorship scandal was not enough to diminish the likelihood of Catholics voting for the Liberal Party above and beyond the initial effect of the predisposition. In 2006, the pattern

Table 4.2

The impact of the sponsorship scandal on the tendency of Catholics to vote for the Liberal Party

	2004		2006	
Dependent Variable = Vote Liberal	Odds ratio	Robust standard error	Odds ratio	Robust standard error
Age	1.018***	0.003	1.014***	0.004
Male	1.162	0.127	1.022	0.111
University education	1.672***	0.188	1.293*	0.147
West	0.612***	0.068	0.537***	0.060
Non-European ethnicity	2.379***	0.529	1.957**	0.453
French mother language	1.038	0.257	1.278	0.320
Catholic	1.586*	0.329	1.514*	0.315
Anger over sponsorship scandal	0.769***	0.030	0.779***	0.028
Interaction: Catholic who is angry over sponsorship scandal	0.967	0.072	1.017	0.066
N	3,197		2,983	
Pseudo-R^2	0.0664		0.0660	

*$p \le .1$; ** $p \le .01$; *** $p \le .001$

was mostly replicated, although the interaction term was slightly positive (but still insignificant). The values for the interaction terms in both of these regressions indicate that, while both Catholicism and anger over the sponsorship scandal influenced voting for the Liberal Party, anger felt by *Catholics* did not affect their vote choice uniquely. Thus, anger over the sponsorship scandal (disagreement with the Liberal Party) did not override voting predisposition in 2004 or 2006.

Accounting for Sophistication

The above analyses consider the entire Canadian population outside Quebec. As mentioned earlier, however, one's level of political sophistication can make a difference in whether or not he or she incorporates the issues into the vote calculus and how important issues are to the vote decision. It has also been found that sophistication can decrease the impact of Catholicism. These findings create the expectation that high sophisticates should be more affected by issue disagreement than low sophisticates and that the tendency to vote Liberal may be overcome among high-sophisticate Catholics. To test this hypothesis, I divided the data according to the high-sophistication dummy variable, creating subsamples of low sophisticates and high sophisticates. The models used for the analyses by sophistication are the same as for the whole sample.

Table 4.3 shows the results for both issues and for both levels of sophistication. For ease of presentation, only the key independent variables of interest are reported.[16] The results for the same-sex marriage issue show that the interaction terms for low sophisticates in both years were positive (odds ratio greater than 1) and significant. This finding indicates that the relationship between less sophisticated Catholics who opposed same-sex marriage and the Liberal Party remained positive even with issue disagreement, but the finding can also reflect the fact that low sophisticates were not cognizant of the disagreement between their issue stance and their voting preference. Among high sophisticates, for whom the conflict should have been clearer, the interaction terms were insignificant in both years and positive once again in 2006. It appears that Catholics with higher levels of sophistication were not more likely to incorporate the contradiction between their religion and the Liberal Party's stances into their vote decisions, although those who supported same-sex marriage (in agreement with the party's stance) were significantly more likely to vote Liberal.

For the sponsorship scandal issue, one interaction term had a value greater than 1, and one had a value less than 1, in each sophistication subsample. However, only in one case (for high sophisticates in 2004) was the interaction term significant and negative, as expected. There does not appear to have been any systematic effect of sophistication on the likelihood of Catholics incorporating anger over the sponsorship scandal into their support (or lack thereof) of the Liberal Party, although it is clear that anger itself was a significant vote factor in both years, for all sophistication levels. It is also interesting to note that the three insignificant interaction terms were very close to having no substantive effect – that is, the odds ratio was very close to 1. Thus, it appears that Catholic support for the Liberal Party was not specifically affected by the sponsorship scandal in 2006 or for low sophisticates in 2004. However, the scandal did have a negative impact on the predisposition of Catholics to vote Liberal in at least one case, which is more than the clearly moral and Church-directed issue of same-sex marriage. It appears that the secular sponsorship scandal had a greater potential to sway at least more sophisticated Catholics away from their traditional predisposition to support the Liberal Party than the moral issue of same-sex marriage.

Table 4.3

The impact of political sophistication on the impact of issue positions and Catholic identity on the tendency to vote for the Liberal Party

	2004		2006	
	Odds	Robust standard	Odds	Robust standard
Dependent Variable = Vote Liberal	ratio	error	ratio	error
Same-sex marriage, low sophistication				
Catholic	0.999	0.204	1.301	0.326
Oppose same-sex marriage	0.550***	0.096	0.574*	0.138
Catholic* oppose same-sex marriage	2.508**	0.782	1.967*	0.778
N		2,133		1,164
Pseudo-R^2		0.0397		0.0406
Same-sex marriage, high sophistication				
Catholic	1.901**	0.469	1.469*	0.278
Oppose same-sex marriage	0.738	0.153	0.424***	0.076
Catholic* oppose same-sex marriage	0.729	0.296	1.557	0.519
N		1,064		1,819
Pseudo-R^2		0.0605		0.0584
Sponsorship scandal, low sophistication				
Catholic	1.419	0.362	1.706*	0.539
Anger over sponsorship scandal	0.798***	0.041	0.844**	0.055
Catholic* anger	1.008	0.096	0.988	0.102
N		2,133		1,164
Pseudo-R^2		0.0491		0.0480
Sponsorship scandal, high sophistication				
Catholic	2.728**	1.133	1.477	0.433
Anger over sponsorship scandal	0.686***	0.045	0.726***	0.033
Catholic* anger	0.788*	0.114	1.027	0.090
N		1,064		1,819
Pseudo-R^2		0.1155		0.0852

Note: Other variables included in the models are age, male, education, residence in western provinces, non-European ethnicity, and French mother language.

* $p \leq .1$; ** $p \leq .01$; *** $p \leq .001$

Conclusion

The results reported above suggest that the connection between the Liberal Party and Catholic Canadians (outside Quebec) is remarkably resilient – so resilient that it was not consistently vulnerable to direct issue disagreement in the analyses. Both the same-sex marriage issue and the sponsorship scandal, although pitting some Catholics against the Liberal Party on the basis of issues, were mostly unable to overcome the tendency of Catholics to support the Liberals. The same-sex marriage issue seems to have had fewer negative consequences than anger over the sponsorship scandal, despite the clear religious implications of the former.

Political sophistication appears to do little to increase the likelihood of issue disagreement overcoming the Catholic-Liberal connection, with the sponsorship scandal issue in 2004 being the only exception. This finding hints that the Catholic-Liberal connection might be vulnerable only among high sophisticates on secular issues that speak directly to how the Liberal Party governs. Overall, however, the results reinforce just how strong the long-standing tendency of Catholics to vote Liberal continues to be. Not only has the relationship withstood secularization and the end of political debate over religion, but it has also withstood clear issue disagreement for most people. The relationship remains a true puzzle of Canadian voting behaviour.

The findings in this chapter have two important implications for our understanding of the role of religion in Canadian voting behaviour. The first implication, with respect to the debate over why Catholics vote for the Liberal Party, is that the apparent insignificance of the same-sex marriage issue to the Catholic-Liberal connection implies that the relationship might have little to do with religion itself. If Catholics prefer the Liberal Party because it promotes issue positions that are sympathetic to their religious beliefs, then the same-sex marriage issue should have put a significant strain on that connection. Instead, it was the sponsorship scandal, a decidedly secular issue, that seems to have had more potential to erode the voting tendency (although no consistent substantial effect was observed).

In the future, scholars would do well to consider which factors, other than religious issue stances, might make Catholics prefer the Liberal Party. Several suggestions have been entertained. One of the most interesting explanations is that a Catholic ethos, or political orientation, underlies the political preferences of Catholics. The argument is that these preferences lead Canadian Catholics to vote for the Liberal Party as the party that best expresses their values. Johnston (1985, 128) first proposed the existence of such an ethos, writing that "a full and proper exploration of the institutional and ideological characteristics of Canadian Catholics may well reveal them to be a distinct subcommunity, even if Catholics are not often that much more conscious than are non-Catholics of their corporate character." He thought that the ethos might be related to an understanding of the ethnic character of Canada – "to those schooled in the company of other Catholics, Canada will seem perhaps more French and almost certainly less British" (112) – but that definition was proven inadequate by Blais (2005) to explain Catholic voting behaviour. Gidengil (1992, 229) suggested an alternative formulation of the ethos, that of enduring values related to ideas about state authority and individual responsibility: "Different religions are associated with very different ideas about questions of individual responsibility, submission to state authority, hierarchy, the organization of society and the extent of the temporal sphere – giving rise to values which can endure even when the religious beliefs themselves have become less salient." Testing this characterization of the ethos was attempted in Stephenson (2007), but the results were weak, likely due to the absence of appropriate questions to measure Catholic attitudes about individual responsibility, social organization, and the state. This avenue of research remains promising, however, especially as the results in this chapter indicate that specific religious issues do not inform the bond between Catholics and the Liberal Party.

The second implication of the findings in this chapter is that the importance of religious identity for understanding voting behaviour cannot be rationalized away. The most consistent religious relationship, between Liberals and Catholics, was not significantly affected by issue disagreement on either a moral issue or a salient secular issue. Despite the closer proximity of issues to the vote choice, it appears that some demographic influences remain extremely powerful and important. Research into the ties between the NDP and non-religionists and the Conservative Party and Protestants would do well to test whether those connections are similarly impervious to issue disagreement. Are all of the religious voting relationships equally tenacious? Or, as previous research suggests, is the Catholic-Liberal connection particularly strong? Further research into the parameters of religion as a voting factor in Canadian politics is required.

The intention of this chapter was to consider whether the traditional predisposition of Catholics to vote for the Liberal Party was vulnerable to issue disagreement in the 2004 and 2006 Canadian elections. The results suggest, somewhat surprisingly, that it was not. Furthermore, the results caution that this long-standing religious predisposition might not be as tenuous, or as easy to "show the door," as one might expect. Although some voters do consider issues, especially those with high cognitive capacity (Goren 1997) and those for whom the issues are particularly salient (RePass 1971), it does not appear that Catholics were particularly bothered when the Liberal Party took an issue stance that contradicted Church teachings. Sophisticated Catholics were found to be more swayed by anger over the sponsorship scandal, at least in 2004. Thus, whereas the Catholic-Liberal connection is strong, it is not completely impenetrable. It appears that only those who have more cognitive ability are vulnerable to the influences of contradictory issue stances – but even then not enough to overcome their long-standing voting predisposition. Therefore, as Blais (2005) suggests, consideration of the religious cleavage should not be eliminated in studies of voting behaviour any time soon.

Acknowledgments

I would like to thank Steve White and the anonymous reviewers for their useful and constructive comments on this project.

Notes

1 Statistics Canada, Table 075-0016, "Historical Statistics, Principal Religious Denominations of the Population, Every 10 Years (Persons) (Table), CANSIM (Database), Using E-STAT (Distributor)," http://estat.statcan.ca; and Statistics Canada, *2001 Census: Analysis Series, Religions in Canada*, 2003, http://www12.statcan.ca.

2 Protestant fundamentalists are a narrower segment of the population than evangelical Christians. The criteria used to indicate fundamentalism in Blais et al. (2002) and Gidengil et al. (2006) are specific beliefs, such as the Bible being the literal word of God. Many evangelicals also hold such beliefs, and thus the finding about fundamentalists can be considered an indication of the voting relationship between evangelicals and the Conservative Party as well.

3 Some of the proposed explanations for this puzzling aspect of Canadian voter behaviour include coincidental socialization (Irvine 1974), the concentration of Catholics in an area (Johnston 1991; Bélanger and Eagles 2006), and the religion of candidates (Blais 2005). Although some of these solutions have found support (Johnston 1991; Bélanger and Eagles 2006), none has been able to explain, definitively, why Catholics continue to prefer the Liberal Party. All that is known with confidence is that the connection is a long-standing attachment for many Canadians.

4 For a discussion of the idea of flexible partisanship, see Bélanger and Stephenson (this volume).

5 Chrétien did this in response to a ruling of the Ontario Court of Appeal to allow same-sex marriages. He sent three questions to the Supreme Court for non-binding opinions: can the federal government change the definition of marriage, does the Charter of Rights and Freedoms protect religious groups from having to perform same-sex marriages, and is the proposed definition of marriage (to permit such unions) constitutional? When Paul Martin became prime minister, he added a

fourth question: is the traditional definition of marriage (between a man and a woman) constitutional? The court's opinion was that the government did have the right to pass the legislation, that it would be constitutional, that religious groups would have the constitutional right to refuse to officiate over same-sex marriages, and that the government had already indicated that this was its position by opting not to appeal the rulings of lower courts on the issue.

6   See Dostie-Goulet (2006) for a statement of the importance of the issue in the 2004 federal election.

7   Data from 2004 and 2006 Canadian Election Studies (see Blais et al. 2004, 2006).

8   There appears to be only minor support for the idea that Catholics vote Liberal because of issue positions. See Grayson (1973) and Blais (2005) for a review of the evidence.

9   See Anderson (1966) and the discussion in Mendelsohn and Nadeau (1997).

10   For a discussion of the reasoning behind these controls, see Mendelsohn and Nadeau (1997).

11   See Blais (2005) for a discussion of these considerations.

12   Alpha = 0.62 for each of the scales.

13   For more information on the use of interaction terms, see Friedrich (1982) and Brambor, Clark, and Golder (2006).

14   The predict command in Stata was used to calculate the predicted probabilities.

15   These predicted probabilities, like all the pairs calculated for different issue stances, differ significantly from each other.

16   Full results are available from the author on request.

References

Alford, Robert R. 1963. *Party and Society: The Anglo-American Democracies.* Chicago: Rand McNally.

Anderson, Grace M. 1966. "Voting Behaviour and the Ethnic-Religious Variable: A Study of a Federal Election in Hamilton, Ontario." *Canadian Journal of Economics and Political Science* 32, 1: 27-37.

Bartels, Larry. 1987. "Candidate Choice and the Dynamics of the Presidential Nomination Process." *American Journal of Political Science* 31, 1: 1-30.

Bélanger, Paul, and Munroe Eagles. 2006. "The Geography of Class and Religion in Canadian Elections Voting Revisited." *Canadian Journal of Political Science* 39, 3: 591-610.

Blais, André. 2005. "Accounting for the Electoral Success of the Liberal Party in Canada." *Canadian Journal of Political Science* 38, 4: 821-40.

Blais, André, Richard Nadeau, Elisabeth Gidengil, and Neil Nevitte. 2001. "The Formation of Party Preferences: Testing the Proximity and Directional Models." *European Journal of Political Research* 40, 5: 81-91.

Blais, André, Elisabeth Gidengil, Richard Nadeau, and Neil Nevitte. 2002. *Anatomy of a Liberal Victory.* Peterborough, ON: Broadview Press.

Blais, André, Elisabeth Gidengil, Neil Nevitte, Patrick Fournier, and Joanna Everitt [principal investigators]. *Canadian Election Study, 2004* [computer file]. Montréal: Département de science politique, Université de Montréal [producer and distributor].

–. *Canadian Election Study, 2006* [computer file]. Montréal: Département de science politique, Université de Montréal [producer and distributor].

Bittner, Amanda. 2007. "The Effects of Information and Social Cleavages: Explaining Issue Attitudes and Vote Choice in Canada." *Canadian Journal of Political Science* 40, 4: 935-68.

Brambor, Thomas, William Roberts Clark, and Matt Golder. 2006. "Understanding Interaction Models: Improving Empirical Analyses." *Political Analysis* 14, 1: 63-82.

Campbell, Angus, Philip E. Converse, Warren E. Miller, and Donald E. Stokes. 1960. *The American Voter.* Chicago: University of Chicago Press.

Carmines, Edward, and James Stimson. 1980. "The Two Faces of Issue Voting." *American Political Science Review* 74, 1: 78-91.

Clarke, Harold D., Jane Jenson, Lawrence LeDuc, and Jon. H. Pammett. 1980. *Political Choice in Canada.* Abridged ed. Toronto: McGraw-Hill Ryerson.

–. 1996. *Absent Mandate.* 3rd ed. Toronto: Gage.

Converse, Philip E. 1964. "The Nature of Belief Systems in Mass Publics." In *Ideology and Discontent,* ed. David Apter, 206-61. New York: The Free Press of Glencoe.

Dalton, Russell J. 2002. *Citizen Politics.* 3rd ed. New York: Chatham House Publishers.

Dostie-Goulet, Eugénie. 2006. "Le mariage homosexuel et le vote au Canada." *Politique et Sociétés* 25, 1: 129-44.

Engelmann, F.C., and M.A. Schwartz. 1975. *Canadian Political Parties: Origin, Character, Impact.* Scarborough: Prentice-Hall.

Fairie, Paul. 2007. "God Only Knows: The Canadian Catholic Voter in a Comparative Context." Poster presented at the annual meeting of the Canadian Political Science Association, Saskatoon, SK, 30 May-1 June.

Friedrich, Robert J. 1982. "In Defense of Multiplicative Terms in Multiple Regression Equations." *American Journal of Political Science* 26, 4: 797-833.

Gidengil, Elisabeth. 1992. "Canada Votes: A Quarter Century of Canadian National Election Studies." *Canadian Journal of Political Science* 25, 2: 219-48.

Gidengil, Elisabeth, André Blais, Joanna Everitt, Patrick Fournier, and Neil Nevitte. 2006. "Back to the Future? Making Sense of the 2004 Canadian Election Outside Quebec." *Canadian Journal of Political Science* 39, 1: 1-25.

Goren, Paul. 1997. "Political Expertise and Issue Voting in Presidential Elections." *Political Research Quarterly* 50, 2: 387-412.

Grayson, J. Paul. 1973. "Social Position and Interest Recognition: The Voter in Broadview, or Are Voters Fools?" *Canadian Journal of Political Science* 6, 1: 131-39.

Guth, James L., and Cleveland R. Fraser. 2001. "Religion and Partisanship in Canada." *Journal for the Scientific Study of Religion* 40, 1: 51-64.

Irvine, William P. 1974. "Explaining the Religious Basis of the Canadian Partisan Identity: Success on the Third Try." *Canadian Journal of Political Science* 7, 3: 560-63.

Johnston, Richard. 1985. "The Reproduction of the Religion Cleavage in Canadian Elections." *Canadian Journal of Political Science* 18, 1: 99-113.

–. 1991. "The Geography of Class and Religion in Canadian Elections." In *The Ballot and Its Message,* ed. Joseph Wearing, 108-35. Toronto: Copp, Clarke, Pitman.

Johnston, Richard, André Blais, Henry E. Brady, and Jean Crête. 1992. *Letting the People Decide: Dynamics of a Canadian Election.* Montreal: McGill-Queen's University Press.

Johnston, Richard, Patrick Fournier, and Richard Jenkins. 2000. "Party Location and Party Support: Unpacking Competing Models." *Journal of Politics* 62, 4: 1145-60.

Kotler-Berkowitz, Laurence A. 2001. "Religion and Voting Behaviour in Great Britain: A Reassessment." *British Journal of Political Science* 31, 3: 523-54.

Laponce, J.A. 1972. "Post-Dicting Electoral Cleavages in Canadian Federal Elections, 1949-68: Material for a Footnote." *Canadian Journal of Political Science* 5, 2: 270-86.

Layman, Geoffrey C. 1997. "Religion and Political Behaviour in the United States: The Impact of Beliefs, Affiliations, and Commitment from 1980 to 1994." *Public Opinion Quarterly* 61, 2: 288-316.

Lijphart, Arend. 1979. "Religious vs. Linguistic vs. Class Voting: The 'Crucial Experiment' of Comparing Belgium, Canada, South Africa, and Switzerland." *American Political Science Review* 73, 2: 442-58.

Lipset, Seymour Martin, and Stein Rokkan. 1967. *Party Systems and Voter Alignments.* New York: Free Press.

Lusztig, Michael, and Matthew J. Wilson. 2005. "A New Right? Moral Issues and Partisan Change in Canada." *Social Science Quarterly* 86, 1: 109-28.

Macdonald, Stuart Elaine, George Rabinowitz, and Ola Listhaug. 1995. "Political Sophistication and Models of Issue Voting." *British Journal of Political Science* 25, 4: 453-83.

Malloy, Jonathon. 2005. "Why the Political Influence of Canadian Evangelical Christians Is Both Overstated *and* Underestimated." Paper presented at the annual meeting of the Canadian Political Science Association, London, ON, 2-4 June.

Meisel, John. 1956. "Religious Affiliation and Electoral Behaviour: A Case Study." *Canadian Journal of Economics and Political Science* 22, 4: 481-96.

–. 1973. *Working Papers on Canadian Politics.* Enlarged ed. Montreal: McGill-Queen's University Press.

Mendelsohn, Matthew, and Richard Nadeau. 1997. "The Religious Cleavage and the Media in Canada." *Canadian Journal of Political Science* 30, 1: 129-46.

Nevitte, Neil. 1996. *The Decline of Deference.* Peterborough, ON: Broadview Press.

Nevitte, Neil, André Blais, Elisabeth Gidengil, and Richard Nadeau. 2000. *Unsteady State: The 1997 Canadian Federal Election.* Don Mills, ON: Oxford University Press.

O'Neill, Brenda. 2001. "A Simple Difference of Opinion? Religious Beliefs and Gender Gaps in Public Opinion in Canada." *Canadian Journal of Political Science* 34, 2: 275-98.

–. 2004. "Gender, Religion, Social Capital, and Political Participation." Paper presented at the annual meeting of the American Political Science Association, Chicago, 2-5 September.

RePass, David E. 1971. "Issue Salience and Party Choice." *American Political Science Review* 65, 2: 389-400.

Roy, Jason. 2009. "Voter Heterogeneity: Informational Differences and Voting." *Canadian Journal of Political Science* 42, 1: 117-38.

Schwartz, Mildred A. 1974. "Canadian Voting Behaviour." In *Electoral Behaviour: A Comparative Handbook,* ed. Richard Rose, 543-618. New York: Free Press.

Stephenson, Laura. 2007. "The Catholic-Liberal Connection: A Modern Appraisal." Paper presented at the annual meeting of the Midwest Political Science Association conference, Chicago, 12-15 April.

Parties and Partisans: The Influence of Ideology and Brokerage on the Durability of Partisanship in Canada

Éric Bélanger and Laura B. Stephenson

The topic of partisan identification in Canada has occupied the minds of researchers for decades. One of the main issues that has engaged scholars is the nature of Canadian partisanship. In the United States, partisanship is commonly seen as "a psychological identification, which can persist without legal recognition or evidence of formal membership and even without a consistent record of party support"; the concept is central to studies of US voting, as "the strength and direction of party identification are facts of central importance in accounting for attitude and behaviour" (Campbell et al. 1960, 121). Work on Canadian partisanship, however, provides conflicting accounts of how well the concept travels north of the border. Early studies argued that the concept of partisanship acknowledged in the United States does not apply in Canada. Meisel (1973, 67) stated that "the concept of party identification, as used by scholars associated with the Michigan Survey Research Center has proven to be exceptionally rewarding ... Our two surveys suggest, however, that it may be almost inapplicable in Canada ... We have found that party identification seems to be as volatile in Canada as the vote itself." This strong statement spurred much research and began a debate about whether partisan identification in Canada was similar to the type of attachment held by Americans (for two sides of the debate, see Sniderman, Forbes, and Melzer 1974 and Jenson 1975). Later studies refined the understanding of Canadian partisanship, arguing that it is both similar and different. Clarke et al. (1979) developed the concept of *flexible partisanship* to characterize the differences in the Canadian context. Still, the debate continues regarding *how* different, or similar, Canadian partisanship is to the ideal of the American model (for one of the most recent statements, see Gidengil et al. 2006). As Anderson and Stephenson have already highlighted in their introduction to this volume, it remains one of the enduring research questions facing scholars of Canadian voting behaviour.

Throughout this debate, the role of political parties in influencing the nature of their partisans has been only modestly studied.[1] This question is of particular interest given the changes that occurred in the Canadian party system between 1993 and 2006. Prior to 1993, the party system was sometimes characterized as having "two and a half" parties (Siaroff 2003), recognizing the long-standing dominance of the Liberal Party and the Progressive Conservative (PC) Party and the minor, though stable, role of the New Democratic Party (NDP). Since that time, regional parties emerged (Bloc Québécois [BQ], Reform Party), old parties disappeared (PC), and a merger united right-wing voters into a new national party (the Conservative Party of Canada). Not only do the current parties vary in age, reputation, and focus, but they also differ in terms of their ideological intensity; thus, the party system of today differs from the party system on which initial studies of Canadian partisanship were based.

Have these recent party system developments impacted the nature of partisanship in Canada? And if so, how? This chapter addresses the characteristics of partisanship in the various parties of the Canadian federal party system since the early 1990s. Is Canadian partisanship uniform, or does it vary by party? Are certain partisans more loyal, more intense, and more stable in their attachments? Do these characteristics vary systematically by party? This chapter tackles these questions using data from the Canadian Election Studies (CES) of 1993-2006.

Theory

Party identification is generally conceptualized as a long-term social-psychological anchor that guides individuals in their vote choices. The concept originated in the United States, where some nuances exist in its interpretation. The dominant view is that partisanship is a form of social identification that develops very early in adulthood. It is thus impervious to short-term influences and mostly works as a "perceptual screen" that systematically filters out new information about the parties' policies and performance (for proponents of this view, see Campbell et al. 1960 and Green, Palmquist, and Schickler 2002). Others have claimed, however, that partisanship can be partly based on evaluations of the parties' current performance and policy positions. For proponents of this view (see Downs 1957 and Fiorina 1981), partisan identification acts as a "running tally" of information about the parties' capacity to govern. Despite these differences in viewpoint, it is agreed, with minimal controversy, that partisanship is a key determinant of voting behaviour in the United States: both the Republican and the Democratic parties can rely on a significant and relatively stable reservoir of partisans when competing for (re-)election. The debate in the scholarly literature has more to do with the applicability of the concept outside the American polity (see, for instance, Budge, Crewe, and Farlie 1976; Dalton, Flanagan, and Beck 1984; Franklin, Mackie, and Valen 1992; and Bartle and Bellucci 2009).

Prior to the work of Harold Clarke and his colleagues, the applicability of the partisanship concept in Canada was agreed, by many, to be weak. Meisel's (1973) pronouncement about the inappropriateness of the concept for use in Canada was taken seriously, with the notable exception of Sniderman, Forbes, and Melzer (1974). They were the most vocal in arguing that the concept was the same – that Canadians received their partisanship through parental transfer, that it was stable throughout differing vote commitments, and that it was as long-standing as the Michigan school originally theorized. They also found that supporters of both major and minor parties were equally loyal despite the significant differences in the clarity of their positions. In their view, "it is possible to have strong loyalties to political parties even though these parties are not clearly differentiated in economic policy or ideology" (Sniderman, Forbes, and Melzer 1974, 286). However, their work was not uniformly well received (for one of the immediate responses, see Jenson 1975).

Much of this debate was quelled with the work of Clarke and his colleagues. In their book *Political Choice in Canada* (1979), they made the case for distinguishing between flexible and durable partisans on the basis of their volatility between elections, the intensity of the attachment, and the consistency of identification across levels of government. In several articles and books (see, for example, LeDuc et al. 1984; Clarke et al. 1984, 1991, 1996), the concept was shown to differentiate between those Canadian partisans who acted like American ones (the durable partisans) and those Canadian partisans who were, indeed, much more flexible and therefore increasingly swayed by short-term forces. In essence, Clarke and his colleagues argued that the Michigan model of voting, which highlights the role of partisanship, needs to be differentially applied in Canada. According to them, the importance of issues and candidates in vote choice varies considerably according to the nature of one's partisanship: flexible partisans are much more likely to base their vote decisions on short-term factors, such as issues and leadership, than are durable partisans.

Numerous explanations have been offered for why partisanship is generally considered to be weaker in Canada (but see Schickler and Green 1997 and Gidengil et al. 2006 for different opinions). One explanation is that the electoral institutions in Canada do not reinforce partisanship and thus strengthen the attachment. Unlike in the American system, where voters are faced with partisan candidates for almost every office (of which there are many), and where candidates for president are chosen through a primary process that involves citizens rather than a party convention with member delegates (Gidengil 1992), Canadians are asked to vote only periodically, and partisan labels are generally relevant only at the federal and provincial levels.[2] In addition, the parties are not consistent across levels of government; a Liberal Party at the provincial level need not necessarily be related, ideologically or otherwise, to the federal Liberal Party. Thus, voters can hold different partisan identifications at different levels of government; this variance makes partisanship a much less useful cue for voters and therefore a less significant attachment for Canadians (Clarke and Stewart 1987; Stewart and Clarke 1998).

A second explanation, which concerns us more directly here, implicates the parties themselves. It is based on the understanding that Canadian political parties have traditionally followed a "brokerage" model of behaviour in that they develop policies according to what would attract the most support in the short term and what would be attractive to the various regions and regional interests in the country (Clarke et al. 1991). In the federal party system's first incarnation, at the time of Confederation in 1867, the brokerage parties concentrated on bridging the linguistic and religious cleavages between Ontario and Quebec (Johnston et al. 1992); since then, the brokerage parties have expanded to encompass western alienation and the regional interests of the Atlantic provinces as well as the interests of central Canada and the specific nationalist claims of Quebec. Thus, the very nature of brokerage parties prevents them from establishing a strong ideological program that a party label could represent for voters.

This argument has been made most forcefully about the Liberals and Progressive Conservatives. Scarrow (1965, 76) writes that the brokerage style is one of the unique features of Canadian politics: "What distinguishes Canada is that there is no 'cause' to which either of the parties is pledged, and that each party is potentially capable of recruiting to its side the successful vote-getting intermediary." This argument is substantiated in the findings of Engelmann and Schwartz (1975) and Zipp (1978). It is also evident in the more recent studies of Nevitte et al. (2000), Blais et al. (2002), and Scotto, Stephenson, and Kornberg (2004), in which analyses of voter attitudes led to the conclusion that the Liberals and then-existent PCs were largely indistinguishable, both occupying the centre of the spectrum and often alternating positions (leaning to the left or right). Thus, it is possible that the nature of brokerage parties discourages the type of voter commitment that ideological clarity would attract (Stevenson 1987; Clarke et al. 1991; Johnston et al. 1992).

Despite these explanations, the debate has not ended and is in need of updating. When Clarke and his colleagues first began theorizing about Canadian voters as flexible and durable, the party system could reasonably be characterized as "two-party-plus" (Epstein 1964). Much has changed since the end of the 1980s (for a review, see Bickerton, Gagnon, and Smith 1999; Carty, Cross, and Young 2000; and Clarke, Kornberg, and Wearing 2000). The dramatic events of the 1993 federal election saw the decline of two established parties (PC and NDP) and the emergence of two new parties (BQ and Reform). The study of Canadian parties since that time is particularly interesting because the new parties that emerged (the BQ, Reform, and Alliance Parties) did not conform to the traditional brokerage model. In this new party system, sometimes referred to as the fourth party system, the Liberals and Progressive Conservatives (before the PC Party's demise) were confronted with competitors who were "essentially ideological parties" (Carty, Cross, and Young 2000, 36). These parties were neither national nor brokerage in nature, but each had enough voter support to become the official opposition once in the 1990s.

From the perspective of partisanship, the current party system is also interesting because one of the explanations for weak partisanship in Canada depends on brokerage parties being the ones competing for votes. As noted above, because brokerage parties are less ideological than most other political parties, they provide little incentive (or programmatic reasons) for voters to develop attachments. Do the new parties, then, have more committed partisans? Has the nature of Canadian partisanship changed since 1993? With the new configuration of the party system, it is time to update our understanding of partisanship in Canada.

Given the changes to the party system, one might expect to find variation in the types of partisans who belong to each party. More specifically, the brokerage parties might still attract/encourage weaker partisan attachments, whereas the BQ and Reform/Alliance, because they provide (or used to provide) strong ideological statements for voters, might encourage (or have encouraged) stronger partisans, more in keeping with the Michigan model's conception of partisan identification. The study of partisanship by party has not, to date, been the focus of the extant literature. Although many authors have disaggregated their analyses by party, most have not considered the importance of any variation between the parties;[3] furthermore, not much work has been done on partisanship in the fourth party system.[4] This chapter attempts to fill in this gap by evaluating the nature of the partisanship of supporters of each of the main parties between 1993 and 2006.

Methodology

We use individual-level survey data from the 1993-2006 Canadian Election Studies to examine recent trends in Canadian partisanship, with an eye to the potential differences between the parties during that time period. In these CES surveys, party identification is measured using the following question: "In federal politics, do you usually think of yourself as [list of parties], or none of these?"[5] Follow-up questions that measure the strength of partisanship are also asked in each survey:

> *If party identified:* "How strongly [party] do you feel: very strongly, fairly strongly, or not very strongly?"
> *If no party identified:* "Do you generally think of yourself as being a little closer to one of the federal parties than the others?" *If yes:* "Which party is that?"

In the study of partisanship, there is a long-standing debate about how to measure partisanship. Much of the debate centres on the proper way to word the question so as to identify true supporters in a way that is comparable to measures used in other countries (see Johnston 1992, 2006, and Blais et al. 2001 for perspectives on this issue). One of the ways that this has been dealt with is to specify that only those who respond that their partisanship is "very strong" or "fairly strong" be recognized as partisans (Blais et al. 2002). We do not follow that strategy in this chapter, however, because we believe that those who respond with a partisan identification and later classify it as "not very strong" should not be ignored. Acknowledging an identification, when first asked, should be taken as an indication that the identity does in fact mean something to the individual, notwithstanding its intrinsic strength. Thus, in the analysis that follows, the measure of partisanship used is the most basic – those who responded to the first question about partisanship with an identity are considered to be partisans. We conceptualize strength, or intensity, of self-identification as one dimension (among others) of partisanship that should be considered separately from the definition of whether an individual identifies himself or herself as a partisan or not.

To evaluate the nature of the partisans of each party, we consider three different dimensions of attachment: intensity, loyalty, and stability. Intensity refers to one's self-evaluated strength of partisanship (very strong, fairly strong, or not very strong, based on the follow-up questions presented above). Loyalty refers to consistency between one's partisanship and one's vote choice within the same election campaign. Stability refers to consistency in partisanship as measured before and after election day.

Our empirical measures of intensity and loyalty are relatively straightforward since the two concepts are somewhat self-explanatory. Our operationalization of stability, however, requires some explanation. Many studies of partisanship, including the work of Clarke and his colleagues (1979, 1984, 1991, 1996; LeDuc et al. 1984) and Gidengil et al. (2006), have utilized panel survey data in order to track the stability of partisanship over time. The only panel that exists for the period examined in this chapter is the 2004-6 CES panel. Although we do make use of that panel for assessing stability, we also rely on an alternative measure of stability based on shorter time spans: whether or not an individual was swayed, over the course of the campaign, to change his or her partisanship (that is, stability within elections). Only the weakest of partisans are expected to shift their partisanship from before to after the vote.[6] However, if party identification really does "travel with the vote," as argued early in the study of Canadian partisanship, then significant change would be observed. Any change at all is more likely during particularly heated election campaigns, as measuring stability this way looks for those who report one type of partisanship before voting and then report a different identification a month later. This measure does not take into account vote choice as an intervening variable. To be clear, this measure reports short-term stability, which should be high; however, any partisans who do switch over such a short time span provide an indication of which parties have the least committed partisans.

These three dimensions of partisanship (stability, intensity, loyalty) are similar to those used by Clarke and his colleagues in their various studies.[7] One difference in this chapter is that the issue of consistency across levels of government is not addressed. In keeping with the work of others, such as Blake (1982), Gidengil (1992), and Blais et al. (2002), the strength of one's partisanship is not evaluated on the basis of whether or not he or she is consistent at the federal and provincial levels, as there are provinces in which this is not even an option. As mentioned earlier, not only do provincial parties often differ from their federal counterparts (consider the Mike Harris PCs in Ontario compared with the Joe Clark federal PCs of 2000), but some systems do not even have parties of the same name (for example, the Saskatchewan Party is that province's conservative option). Furthermore, there are very different jurisdictions of responsibility for each government, so the issues on which they campaign, and on which voters judge them, are very different. Therefore, as argued by Blake (1982), it can be a rational response of a voter to hold two different partisan identities.

Each of the dimensions of partisanship (stability, intensity, and loyalty) analyzed in this chapter can be treated as qualifiers of partisanship that help to evaluate the level of an individual's commitment to a political party. There might well be a majority of citizens who are ready to declare themselves partisans of a party, but we cannot expect all of them to be attached to their party to the same degree, nor can we expect that being a partisan means the same thing to all voters. This seems to be especially true in Canada, if we are to believe the picture of Canadian partisanship drawn by many of the previous studies on the topic. The three characteristics that we examine here should be seen as contributing, in one way or another, to holding a "type" of partisanship – defined here as either "weak" or "strong" partisanship. If someone is a weak (or flexible) partisan, then he or she is more likely to switch his or her preference over the course of an election campaign and certainly over time; is less likely to state a strong preference; and is less likely to vote according to partisanship. Strong partisans, on the other hand, are expected to maintain their partisanship longer and express more intensity in their identification. Their loyalty, though expected to be stronger on average, might vary with the circumstances of an election, as issues and/or candidates lead them to prefer to vote a different way. The key difference between weak and strong partisans is that the latter, even if they do vote for a different party, should be less likely to change their partisanship at the same time.

As we measure the strength of one's partisanship by stability, intensity, and loyalty, we are explicitly focusing on the behavioural aspects of one's partisanship – whether it carries over time, whether the preference is strongly felt, and how closely it relates to vote choice. Essentially, we are evaluating how influential and important partisanship is for an individual. Even new parties, those that have not formed the government or contested multiple elections, can have strong partisans (even if they are few in numbers) given this operationalization, just as partisans of long-standing parties can be weak (even if they are numerous).

In the following section, these characteristics of partisanship are investigated by party. The expectations for each group of partisans are based on an understanding of the nature of the party itself. The two major traditional parties (Liberal and former Progressive Conservative) are considered brokerage parties because they have a history of adapting their own positions and policies to attract the maximum number of votes from across the country – at times even alternating policy stances (Carty, Cross, and Young 2000). Given this history, partisans of these parties are expected to be among the weakest and most flexible in Canada in the elections they contested. Both of the explanations for weak partisanship discussed above clearly apply to these two parties. The NDP, on the other hand, in keeping with the tradition of smaller Canadian parties, has maintained a clearer ideological basis (Clarke, Kornberg, and Wearing 2000). It adopted a brokerage format to create national appeal during the 1970s (Carty, Cross, and Young 2000, 106), but it remains significantly different from the Liberals and the former PCs. It has always been considered a minor party (the "plus" in the "two-party-plus" system), has never controlled the government, and has espoused a fairly clear ideological vision throughout its history, likely due to its union and socialist ties. Thus, it is expected that the NDP should encourage stronger partisanship from its supporters than the older parties.

Turning to the newer parties, the BQ is not, and the Reform and Alliance Parties were not, brokerage parties; and strong ideological components are/were present in each case. Instead of trying to straddle cleavages and include as many groups as possible, the parties opt(ed) for focused appeals based on strong ideological stances. The partisans of these parties are expected to be the strongest of all in each election they contest.

Finally, the analyses also include the new Conservative Party. The expectations for this party are much less obvious in that the party is a merger of both strong ideological (Alliance) and brokerage (PC) elements (see Bélanger and Godbout 2010). The party contested both the 2004 and 2006 elections as a national party, which sets it apart from the BQ and Reform. However, the party's identification with the ideas of the former Alliance Party is still strong (especially with Stephen Harper as leader), so the expectation is that its followers are likely to be stronger partisans than those of the older brokerage parties. However, the expectation of how Conservative supporters compare with NDP supporters is uncertain.[8]

In addition to looking at the stability, intensity, and loyalty of Canadian partisans, we examine the role of ideology in shaping these characteristics. Because one of the reasons given for weak partisans is that there is no ideological connection with the parties, whether ideological preferences influence the type of partisanship that one holds is of great interest. In their study of political party members, Cross and Young (2002) find evidence of real differences between the members of the new and old parties. Their analyses show that members of the BQ and Alliance, as well as NDP members, were more likely to consider agreement with the party's policies a "very important" reason for joining the party, significantly more than Liberal or PC members at the time. Furthermore, they find significant differences in the attitudes of the party members in terms of social tolerance, economics, provincial powers, and populism, although more so for the BQ and Alliance than the NDP or traditional brokerage parties. In terms of partisanship, then, it is logical to expect that there might be differences that arise because of this ideological variation. The expectations for the analyses in this chapter are that the influence of ideological preferences will be strongest on partisanship for the BQ and Reform/Alliance, almost negligible for brokerage parties, and moderate for the NDP. Again, given the mixed pedigree of the Conservative Party, the expectations for its partisans are uncertain.

Results

Stability
We concentrate first on the dimension of stability as measured by change in partisan identification from the campaign period to the post-election

Figure 5.1

Stability within elections

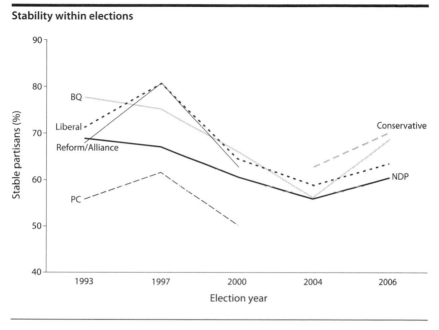

wave of each CES survey (that is, stability within elections). Figure 5.1 shows, for each party in each of the elections from 1993 to 2006, how many individuals maintained the same identification. In 1993, BQ partisans were the most stable over the course of the election (78 percent). Not surprisingly, given that the election results stripped the party of official party status, PC partisans abandoned their party the most, with only 56 percent of campaign-period identifiers continuing to identify with the party after the election. Supporters of the other three parties, Liberal, NDP, and Reform, all had about 70 percent stability. In 1997, the Liberal, PC, and Reform parties benefited from an increase in partisan stability, whereas BQ and NDP supporters reported less stability than their 1993 levels. The substantial stability of BQ and Reform voters is in keeping with our expectations, as the parties are/were more ideological than brokerage. However, the stability of Liberal supporters, especially in 1997, runs counter to expectations; in this case, it might reflect the fact that there was no other viable governing alternative in 1997, and thus there might not have been a party for Liberal supporters, accustomed to supporting a governing party, to defect to at the time. Regardless of any explanation, Liberal supporters were as stable as those of the most clearly defined, ideological parties, despite the brokerage nature of their own party, in 1993 and 1997.

In 2000, all of the parties' partisans were less stable in absolute terms, but PC supporters again stand out as less stable than the others. Only 50 percent of those who said that they identified with the PC Party before the vote also identified with it after. This finding suggests that, over the course of the election, the greatest number of PC supporters "jumped ship" to an alternative party. In terms of our expectations, the stability of BQ and Reform/Alliance partisans in 2000 suggests that these parties' supporters held their partisanship strongly, as expected. The stability of NDP partisans, on the other hand, was lower than that of all others except PC supporters. In 2004, the stability of all supporters kept falling, to around 60 percent. Particularly interesting is that supporters of the new Conservative Party were the most stable in 2004 and 2006, as those elections were particularly competitive (and resulted in minority governments). This pattern is more similar to that of former Alliance Party supporters than previous Progressive Conservative Party supporters and does not follow the expectations for brokerage party supporters. This finding suggests that it might be appropriate to consider the Conservative Party more similar to an ideological party than a brokerage party. Also notable is that Liberal supporters were again more stable than either BQ or NDP supporters; this finding is surprising and interesting given that, in theory, the centrist position of the Liberal Party would likely provide disillusioned supporters with options on either side of the ideological spectrum. In 2006, this latter trend reversed itself, as BQ supporters showed much higher stability, such that the stability of Liberal supporters was lower. All parties, however, showed an increase in the stability of their supporters in that election.

In two election years, 1997 and 2004, a follow-up question about partisanship was asked in the mailed survey conducted several months after the post-election interviews. In each year, the respondents were asked whether there was a party that they felt "a little closer to." This question provides an indication of whether the respondent's allegiance shifted once the election campaign was long over.[9] Figure 5.2 shows the percentage of respondents in 1997 and 2004 who maintained the same allegiance through the campaign period, post-election, and mailed waves of the election study.

Figure 5.2

Stable PID over three waves of election study

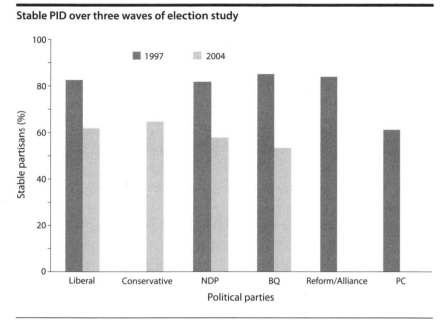

Because the people most likely to answer a mailed questionnaire are the ones who are likely to be the most interested and politically informed, and because they are the ones most likely to be active partisans (see Gidengil et al. 2004), the relative percentages of stable partisans, across parties, is more important than the absolute percentage of stable partisans. As is clear in Figure 5.2, in 1997 almost all of the parties reported similar stability across the three survey waves except for the PC Party, which held on to about 20 percent *fewer* partisans than the other parties. In 2004, a considerably more volatile election, both the NDP and the BQ had fewer stable partisans than either the Liberal or Conservative parties, somewhat against expectations given that the parties were expected to attract more stable partisans than a brokerage party. The stability of the Conservative partisans, which was the highest of all the parties, is in keeping with the results shown in Figure 5.1.

These results, while including some suggestive evidence that Reform, Alliance, and Conservative supporters held or hold more stable partisanship, do not show strong support for the party-specific expectations outlined above. The stability of Liberal supporters is much higher than would be expected given the party's brokerage nature. The low stability

Figure 5.3

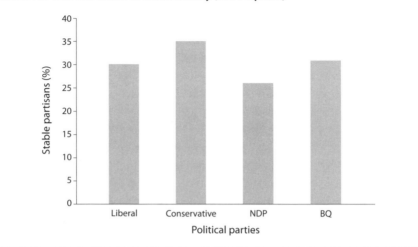

Stable PID over five waves of election study (2004-6 panel)

of NDP supporters, as well, suggests that the ideological content of the party is not enough to encourage the type of stability found for the Reform, Alliance, and Conservative Parties. In particular, the almost uniform stability levels for all parties since 2000 (except the PCs) suggest that this is one dimension on which supporters vary little. What is even more striking, however, is that the stability levels were not higher given the short time span of this measure. Since 2000, at least 30 percent of identifiers for each party reported a different partisanship after the election than before.

Figure 5.3 presents the results from the only panel data available for the period under study: namely, the 2004-6 CES panel. In this panel study, the question on partisan identification was asked a total of five times. In Figure 5.3, we report the level of stability in partisanship for each of the four parties, measured as the proportion of people holding an identification in the 2004 campaign-period wave of the panel who kept the same identification until the 2006 post-election wave. Stability levels were much lower here given that the time elapsed between the first interview and the fifth interview was considerable (almost two full years). Nonetheless, a comparison across parties continues to reveal that the Conservatives are the party with the most stable partisans, followed by the BQ, the Liberals, and the NDP.

Table 5.1

Percentage of identifiers indicating strength of partisan attachment

		1993	1997	2000	2004	2006
Liberal	Very strong	19	18	27	19	22
	Fairly strong	53	55	48	53	53
	Not very strong	28	26	24	27	24
PC	Very strong	12	23	18		
	Fairly strong	52	56	53		
	Not very strong	36	20	28		
Reform/Alliance	Very strong	33	36	34		
	Fairly strong	53	53	52		
	Not very strong	13	11	9		
Conservative	Very strong				28	31
	Fairly strong				55	56
	Not very strong				16	13
NDP	Very strong	20	31	22	32	31
	Fairly strong	50	51	59	58	58
	Not very strong	30	17	18	10	11
BQ	Very strong	25	12	29	13	38
	Fairly strong	59	57	56	65	44
	Not very strong	16	30	14	22	13

Intensity

In each election study, respondents who indicated a partisan identification were asked how strongly they held that identification. In this section, partisanship is examined in terms of the intensity of the attachment held by supporters of each party. Looking at Table 5.1, it is clear that the majority of partisan identifiers indicated that they feel "fairly strongly" about their party. No less than 44 percent and no more than 65 percent of identifiers, for any party, in any year, responded as such. On the other hand, the percentage of individuals willing to respond "very strongly" was much lower and varied significantly by party. "Very strong" identifiers ranged from 18 to 27 percent of Liberal supporters, 12 to 23 percent of PC supporters, 33 to 36 percent of Reform/Alliance supporters, 28 to 31 percent of Conservative supporters, 20 to 32 percent of NDP supporters, and 12 to 38 percent of BQ supporters. Consistently, more Reform/ Alliance and Conservative supporters indicated very strong allegiance. The pattern for the other parties is more variable. Liberal supporters in

2000 expressed more intensity (27 percent) than in any other year. The number of very strong PC supporters also fluctuated around 20 percent, except in 1993, when only 12 percent identified strongly with the party. NDP supporters and BQ supporters were less consistent, changing by 10 percent or more between some elections. In fact, BQ support varied the most in intensity – from a high of 38 percent "very strong" support in 2006 to a low of 12 percent in 1997.

These results suggest that the traditional brokerage parties attract fewer "very strong" partisans than the other parties and that the Reform/ Alliance and Conservative Parties were/are the best at consistently attracting such intense support. Given the ideological background of the Reform and Alliance Parties, this result is commensurate with expectations. The findings for the Conservative Party echo the results for stability found in the previous section in suggesting that it might be inappropriate to look at Conservative Party supporters as similar to supporters of the Liberal Party.

Somewhat surprisingly, BQ supporters, who were expected to be strong supporters because of the party's ideological nature, seem to be mercurial in their intensity. This fluctuation could relate to the salience of separatist sentiments in Quebec (see Nevitte et al. 2000 for such an interpretation). It is interesting that NDP supporters also follow this pattern, although to lesser extremes. In some years the "very strong" NDP support is similar to the support of the other long-standing brokerage parties, whereas in other years the "very strong" supporters are more numerous. This might be an indication of the salience of the ideological elements in the party. Particularly interesting is the upswing in 2004 and 2006 of "very strong" support; in those two elections, the NDP not only came out as a strong (although perhaps unlikely) contender for office but also differentiated itself from the Liberals and Conservatives. It is possible that, in this context, the party's ideological position attracted more ardent supporters because of its difference from the other national parties.

As a whole, these results show that the partisans of the various parties differ in their propensity to strongly identify. This difference somewhat conforms to expectations, in that the Liberal and PC Parties have/had weaker supporters and the Reform/Alliance Party had the strongest supporters, but also raises questions about the importance of election-specific events impacting the intensity of partisanship. The fluctuations in support for the NDP and BQ suggest that the type of electoral appeals made by each party might influence their partisans. In the larger context of partisanship studies, these findings suggest that the difference in patterns of intensity might relate to the ideological clarity of a party itself.

Loyalty

The last dimension on which to evaluate the partisans of each party is loyalty. If Canadian partisanship is, as early researchers believed, "as volatile as the vote itself" (Meisel 1973, 67), then voter loyalty would be nearly absolute. However, that has been proven not to be the case, so the degree to which each party encourages loyalty from its partisans is of interest. Are all parties the same? One argument reviewed earlier, that brokerage partisans attract weak support, suggests that this should not be the case; brokerage parties are likely to have less loyal partisans. Conversely, the ideological nature of the BQ and Reform/Alliance should encourage loyal partisans.

One difficulty in assessing loyalty is the complication of Canada's single-member plurality electoral system ("first past the post") and strategic voting. It has long been theorized, since the work of Duverger (1954), that a first-past-the-post system should support only two parties, as the "winner-take-all" format creates incentives for supporters of minor parties to vote strategically for a party that does have a chance of winning in order to prevent the least-preferred party from winning a plurality of votes. The divide between major and minor parties has been found to be salient in Canadian politics, to the point of being more important for understanding partisan support than left/right ideological placement (Zipp 1978; Bélanger 2007). From this logic, it is expected that minor party supporters should be, *ceteris paribus,* less loyal to their parties than major party supporters. However, research on strategic voting in Canada suggests that the phenomenon is not very prominent (see Merolla and Stephenson 2007). Blais (2002) argues that one reason for the low level of strategic voting is that minor party supporters (in his study, mainly NDP) do not have realistic perceptions of the electoral chances of their preferred party. The major/minor dichotomy refers to the national context, not the local riding, which may be irrelevant for the voter. Another reason offered by Blais is that minor party supporters often feel more strongly toward their party because of their ideological connection. Thus, whereas strategic voting would decrease the loyalty of minor party supporters, it has been shown to be less common than logically expected. In terms of this analysis, then, the expectation is that the minor parties will have relatively fewer loyal supporters than they would if they were

Figure 5.4

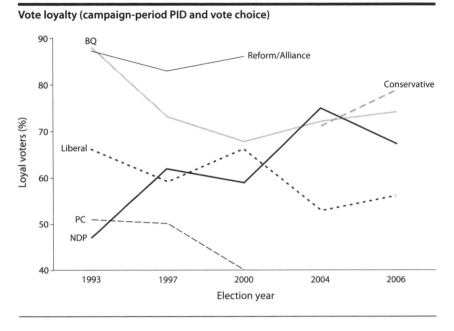

Vote loyalty (campaign-period PID and vote choice)

major parties with the same degree of ideological coherence, although the difference might not be terribly large given the evidence of strategic voting. This is certainly to be expected of the NDP, which, despite being minor, remains first and foremost a national party. However, this expectation might be less relevant for the BQ and Reform/Alliance Parties, given their strong regional support (Bélanger 2004). Because of these regional ties, we might expect partisans of those two parties to be less influenced by strategic considerations and more loyal than NDP partisans.

Figure 5.4 shows the percentage of individuals who indicated a partisan identification and corresponding intended vote choice in the campaign-period survey of each election study. In 1993, the two new ideological parties, the BQ and Reform, had very loyal partisans (88 percent and 87 percent respectively), whereas the PC and NDP supporters were much less loyal (51 percent and 47 percent). The Liberal supporters were moderately loyal at 66 percent. In 1997, the pattern changed only in that the loyalty of BQ supporters fell and that of NDP supporters rose. The most variation in loyalty occurred in 2000, when the PC Party enjoyed vote support from only 40 percent of its partisans, whereas the Alliance had the support of 86 percent. The Liberals, NDP, and BQ all had between

59 and 70 percent partisan loyalty. In 2004, the loyalty of Liberal supporters fell sharply (possibly due to the sponsorship scandal), whereas the NDP, BQ, and Conservatives enjoyed the support of over 70 percent of their partisans. In 2006, the latter three groups of partisans slightly differentiated themselves from each other, as Conservative supporters were more loyal, BQ supporters stayed about the same, and NDP supporters were less loyal. However, all were still more loyal than the Liberal supporters, again possibly a consequence of the sponsorship scandal.

In terms of expectations, the ideological BQ and Reform had the most loyal supporters prior to 2004. Also as expected, the PC and Liberal Parties had less loyal supporters. NDP supporters seem to vary in their loyalty, although in general the trend has been increasing since 1993. In 2004, NDP supporters were actually the most loyal. As expected, the party's followers were generally less loyal than the ideological parties' supporters, but in 2000 they were even less loyal than Liberal supporters – who, although part of a major party, have fewer ideological reasons for supporting their party.

Intensity and Loyalty

Given the striking variation in partisan intensity between the supporters of the various parties, it is interesting to consider whether loyalty is influenced by the intensity of partisanship. In other words, are all "very strong" partisans equally loyal? Or is there party-specific variation among intense supporters that may further explain their expressed loyalty? To address this question, we ran simple vote choice logit models for each party. Dummy variables were created to indicate whether someone was a "very strong," "fairly strong," or "not very strong" partisan for each party. An additional dummy variable was created for those who indicated that they were "a little closer to" the party – individuals who did not reveal a partisan identification in the initial question but, when probed, stated a preference. These individuals are referred to below as "leaners." For the dependent variables, vote choice dummy variables were created for each party, with 1 indicating a vote for and 0 indicating anything else. The results are shown in Table 5.2.

In 1993, the odds ratio for "very strong" Liberal and PC identifiers voting for their parties was about 60, but for the other three parties the odds ratio of voting according to partisanship was dramatically higher, with "very strong" identification. There was a significant drop in the odds ratios for "fairly strong" identifiers of each party and a further drop for "not

Table 5.2

Logit results for vote models (odds ratios reported)

	Liberal	PC	NDP	Reform	BQ**	Conservative
1993						
Very strong	61.62	60.63	222.85	223.78	462.71	
Fairly strong	26.36	31.76	76.57	103.28	41.81	
Not very strong	8.37	9.24	21.57	28.18	37.18	
A little closer to	11.04	11.93	14.86	24.86	17.17	
N	3,775	3,775	3,775	3,775	1,007	
Pseudo-R^2	0.32	0.31	0.40	0.29	0.42	
1997						
Very strong	67.78	53.07	217.66	334.44	1,030.35	
Fairly strong	22.45	22.36	58.58	74.25	91.65	
Not very strong	7.08	7.28	32.02	33.44	39.08	
A little closer to	6.14	10.14	36.28	22.53	37.88	
N	3,949	3,949	3,949	3,949	1,034	
Pseudo-R^2	0.31	0.28	0.42	0.39	0.51	
2000						
Very strong	46.24	132.24	214.37	180.74	73.26	
Fairly strong	24.19	39.84	82.44	96.06	26.52	
Not very strong	9.20	15.03	66.53	27.38	19.04	
A little closer to	7.51	15.82	14.26	27.38	*	
N	3,651	3,651	3,651	3,651	1,250	
Pseudo-R^2	0.32	0.32	0.40	0.40	0.38	
2004						
Very strong	56.34		107.41		52.89	72.62
Fairly strong	22.78		51.76		35	31.31
Not very strong	6.81		44.20		13.26	8.09
A little closer to	7.59		16.52		9.58	17.76
N	4,323		4,323		1,048	4,323
Pseudo-R^2	0.30		0.35		0.36	0.35
2006						
Very strong	107.28		95.35		115.22	121.58
Fairly strong	29.57		42.18		108.58	52.28
Not very strong	6.77		17.24		30.50	15.86
A little closer to	11.11		19.62		7.63	18.61
N	4,058		4,058		1,013	4,058
Pseudo-R^2	0.37		0.35		0.51	0.43

Note: Odds ratios reported. All are statistically significant at $p \leq .001$.

* Dropped because predicted zero outcome perfectly.

** BQ regressions run on Quebec sample only.

very strong" identifiers. "Fairly strong" NDP and Reform identifiers were more likely to vote for their party than the strongest Liberal and PC identifiers. For "a little closer to" voters, the pattern is interesting – the odds ratio was actually higher than that for "not very strong" Liberal and PC identifiers but lower (as would be logically expected) than that for those who at least identified with the other parties. However, the difference was not very strong in the case of the Reform Party. The pattern for the brokerage parties was in keeping with the results of Blais et al. (2001). Most of this pattern was repeated in 1997 – very strong Liberal and PC identifiers were far less likely to be loyal to their parties than supporters of the NDP, Reform, and BQ. The expected pattern for "not very strong" and "a little closer to" identifiers was strong only for Reform supporters.

In 2000, the Liberal "very strong" identifiers were once again least likely to support their party relative to all partisans of that intensity. They were even less likely to vote Liberal than the "not very strong" NDP identifiers were to vote NDP. Interestingly, the intensity of the "very strong" BQ supporters appears to have waned, and they became the second least likely group to support their party. The increased likelihood of PC supporters' loyalty is also notable, perhaps because by 2000, those who identified with the PCs "very strongly" were likely to be intense and aware of their party's uncertain future. In 2004, NDP supporters continued to be the most likely to be loyal voters for every level of identification other than "a little closer to." The pattern of leaners being more loyal than "not very strong identifiers" appeared again for the Liberals and new Conservative Party. One possible explanation is that leaners are those who plan on voting for the party in that election specifically and whose partisanship is indeed travelling with their vote. In 2006, there was an increase in the odds of loyalty for most levels of identification, for every party other than the NDP – perhaps because of the closeness of that particular election. Most interesting is the increase in the loyalty of very strong Liberals and Conservatives, as compared to the decline for the NDP.

The pattern of results shown above indicates a clear difference between parties in the loyalty of their identifiers. The majority of identifiers in Canada are "fairly strong" identifiers, and the relative percentages of "very strong" identifiers usually favour the ideological parties. NDP supporters have been more loyal to their party than either Liberal or PC identifiers, perhaps in recognition of the clearer ideological statement that it provides for voters. The new party identifiers (BQ and Reform/Alliance) seem to be much more loyal overall, especially at the most intense level of partisanship. This loyalty implies that there are characteristics of those parties, possibly ideological intensity, that encourage a stronger attachment from their identifiers.

The Influence of Ideology: Testing the Roots of Interparty Variation

The above discussion has revealed that there are real differences between the parties in terms of the stability, intensity, and loyalty of their supporters. In keeping with expectations, the most ideological parties (the BQ and Reform/Alliance) seem to have (or have had) the most ardent supporters, although BQ supporters are weaker than Reform/Alliance supporters were, NDP supporters are stronger than the other brokerage parties' supporters, and the new Conservative Party's supporters are similar to former Reform/Alliance supporters. Clearly, Canadian partisanship is not uniform across parties.

One of the obvious possible explanations for this variation is the difference in ideological consistency in each party. As argued above, the brokerage parties that existed prior to 1993 provided little in the way of a consistent program to attract loyal supporters, preferring to reconfigure their coalition of support for each election. In this section, we test this hypothesis by looking at whether an ideological link between voters and a party can explain some of the variation in the intensity of partisanship held (which, as seen above, can lead to the most loyal support). Questions about ideology are asked in only three years of the Canadian Election Studies since 1993 (1997, 2000, and 2004), and two different question formats were used. The results for each question are presented separately.

In 2000, respondents in the campaign-period survey of the CES were asked to indicate whether they would place themselves on the left, on the right, or in the centre of the ideological spectrum. They were then asked where they would place each of the parties. Dummy variables were created to indicate whether respondents placed themselves and a party at the same point on the spectrum. These measures of "ideological match" were then tested as independent variables for explaining two separate dependent variables: whether one accepted a partisan identification with that party and the intensity of one's identification. In other words, the analysis looks to see whether placing oneself at the same point on the spectrum as a party (that is, ideological similarity) is a factor in identifying with that party and the strength of identification. Table 5.3 indicates the regression coefficients and their significance from these tests.[10]

Table 5.3

Coefficients for ideological match with party, PID, and strength of identity, 2000

	Partisan identity	Strength of identity
Liberal	1.3130***	0.2982*
PC	1.2082***	-0.0618
NDP	2.5127***	0.3794
Alliance	2.5500***	0.2428
BQ	1.7682***	0.4834*

$* p \leq .1; ** p \leq .01; *** p \leq .001$

All of the relationships between ideological similarity and partisan identity are significant. The coefficients for ideological matching when NDP and Alliance identification are the dependent variables are the largest in magnitude; given that these parties are quite ideological in nature, this is not surprising. Turning to the strength of identity, the coefficients are only significant for Liberal and BQ supporters. This finding indicates that partisan intensity was not strongly affected by ideological similarity in 2000. Contrary to expectations derived from the findings about intensity and loyalty, based on evidence from the 2000 election, ideology does not appear to be the basis of strong partisanship, nor does the relationship seem to differ in keeping with the ideological strength of the parties.

In 1997 and 2004, questions about ideology were asked in a different format. Respondents were asked to place themselves on a left-right scale, from 0 to 10. They were then asked to place each of the parties on a similar scale. These questions provide more information about citizens' ideological views, their intensity, and the nuances of the perceptions of the parties. To conduct an analysis similar to the one above, variables that indicate the absolute distance between one's self-placement and the placement of each party were created. If ideological similarity is part of the reason for identifying with a party, then there should be a negative relationship between stating an identification and the distance from that party ideologically. Similarly, ideological distance should be related to less intense partisanship.

The results confirm these expectations (see Table 5.4). Each relationship between identity and ideological distance from that party is significant and negative. In keeping with the results for 2000, the results also indicate no consistent relationship between the strength of one's

Table 5.4

Coefficients for ideological distance from party and PID, 1997 and 2004

	Partisan identity		Strength of identity	
	1997	2004	1997	2004
Liberal	-0.3918***	-0.4362***	-0.1587*	-0.0593
PC	-0.4505***		-0.1917*	
NDP	-0.5597***	-0.5334***	-0.1073	-0.1771
Reform	-0.5979***		-0.1631	
BQ	-0.7618***	-0.5220***	-0.1034	0.0010
Con		-0.5631***		0.0158

* $p \le .1$; ** $p \le .01$; *** $p \le .001$

partisanship and the ideological distance from a political party. In 1997, the relationship was significant (and appropriate in direction) only for Liberal and PC supporters. In 2004, no relationship was significant. Thus, understanding strength of partisanship in terms of ideological proximity to the party is inappropriate for most Canadian parties most of the time. Ideological similarity does not seem to lie at the root of intensity of partisanship, nor does it differ much according to the ideological nature of the party in question.

Conclusion

The results presented in this chapter provide a picture of the nature of partisanship for each Canadian federal party since 1993. Using CES data, we have analyzed partisanship in terms of stability, intensity, loyalty, and ideology. The results show that there are some real differences between supporters of each of the parties, mostly in terms of intensity and loyalty. These differences are summarized in Table 5.5, which allows us to make some key observations. Not unexpectedly, the traditional brokerage parties, the Liberals and PCs, have (or had, in the case of the PCs) some of the least intense and least loyal supporters. The NDP, although also a national party, does not fit this mould – its supporters are more intense and seem to have become increasingly loyal since 1993. Supporters of the former Reform and Alliance Parties and of the BQ appear to be different from those of the other parties. As one might expect, given their ideological, non-brokerage nature, those supporters were/are more intense and more loyal, although the BQ has recently experienced variation in partisan intensity. The new Conservative Party seems to be encouraging

Table 5.5

Summary of characteristics of partisans, for each party

	Stability	Loyalty	Intensity
Liberal	✓		
PC			
NDP	(✓)	(✓)	(✓)
BQ	(✓)	✓	(✓)
Reform/Alliance	✓	✓	✓
Conservative	✓	✓	✓

Note: ✓ = relatively consistent across the period
    (✓) = varies from one election to the next

the same types of partisans that its Reform/Alliance parent did. Finally, the PCs had, and the NDP has, the least stable partisans, as we would expect from national brokerage parties. The Liberals do not conform to this expectation, however, as they can rely on a stable core of partisans (even though they are neither intense nor loyal).

Given these results, the understanding of Canadian partisans as uniformly weaker than their American counterparts is problematic. Canadian partisans might in fact hold weaker attachments – this chapter does not look at the results comparatively – but partisanship across the different parties is not uniform. The Conservative, Reform, and Alliance parties have (and had) some of the most loyal supporters and the most intense partisans as well. The intensity and stability of BQ supporters seem to vary by election despite the clear ideological nature of the party. NDP supporters also have a variable relationship with their party. What seems to be clear, however, is that these parties are somehow different from the Liberals and the former PCs in the eyes of their supporters, at least until 2006. Ideological parties not only have more intense partisans, but those partisans are also more loyal. This finding suggests that the Liberals' success between 1993 and 2000 might have had a lot to do with the sheer (and stable) number of their supporters at the time – moderate support from many outweighs intense support from some – but this does not bode well for the future of the party if the weakest Liberal partisans consider supporting other parties. Strong partisanship drives and sustains political support. Political parties would do well to attempt to cultivate a large base of strong partisans since the probability of their loyalty is much higher. The parties need to be aware, though, that ideological commitment, which seems to attract strong partisans, often comes at the price of broad appeal – there might be a real trade-off between brokerage and ideological politics in terms of the strength and number of partisans that a party can attract.

In this chapter, we have looked at partisans only. In a recent study of partisanship in Canada, LeDuc (2007) shows that their number has declined steadily over the past two decades, thus reinforcing the "partisan dealignment" account of Canadian partisanship. The decreasing levels of partisans certainly constitute one aspect of the story of the fourth party system in Canada. But, as we have shown here, focusing mainly on those who continue to identify with a party allows us to shed light on another important feature of that system: namely, that Canadian political parties now differ in terms of the nature of their partisanship. In recent years, some of the federal parties have been able to foster stronger and more durable attachments with partisans, a phenomenon that clearly distinguishes the current party system from its more brokerage-oriented predecessors. In 2004, and especially in 2006, the party system seems to have been recovering, solidifying itself in terms of the stability, intensity, and loyalty of partisans, and this situation can be mostly attributed to the NDP, the BQ, and the new Conservative Party.

The variation in intensity and loyalty in accordance with ideology that is highlighted by our study seems to suggest that ideological similarity to a party might be at the root of stronger partisanship. The results presented in this chapter, however, provide no such evidence. Similar ideological self-placement is significantly related to identifying with a party but not to the strength of the attachment. Thus, the "very strong" identifiers, who are considerably more loyal to their parties than less intense partisans, are not also more ideologically connected to their parties. This somewhat counterintuitive finding hints at the need for a more complete investigation of Canadian partisanship to define what it is and what it is not. The results presented in this chapter, which show that there is variation in the stability, intensity, and loyalty of Canadian partisans by party, indicate a need for further study of the connections between parties and the types of partisans they attract.

Acknowledgments
We thank the anonymous reviewers as well as the workshop participants, especially Amanda Bittner, for their useful comments.

Notes

1 As discussed below, an argument was made that the partisanship of Canadians was influenced by the brokerage strategies of the Liberals and Progressive Conservatives (see, for example, Stevenson 1987; Clarke et al. 1991; and Johnston et al. 1992).

2 There are a few cities where partisan labels are used at the municipal level (such as Vancouver), but most cities do not engage in partisan politics.

3 For partial exceptions, see Sniderman, Forbes, and Melzer (1974); Bowler and Lanoue (1996); and Stephenson, Scotto, and Kornberg (2004).

4 With the exception of LeDuc (2007), whose findings we address in our conclusion.

5 Since 2000, the CES used a split-sample partisanship question. They ask the traditional question of one half of the sample and a new question of the other half. The new question aims at measuring more explicitly the absence of partisanship, and its wording is as follows: "Generally speaking, in federal politics, do you usually think of yourself as a [list of parties], or do you usually think of yourself as not having a general preference?" We verified whether the two halves of the samples behaved the same way in those years in terms of loyalty and intensity of partisanship. Although some minor differences are apparent, the patterns of results are the same for people who answered each question. An additional reason that the experiment in question wording is of limited relevance to our study pertains to the fact that we are primarily interested in variation *between* parties. Since the experiments are random, there should be an equal number of partisans in each party who are asked each question.

6 Stability might be higher for individuals whose campaign-period partisanship was recorded later in the campaign. We did conduct some alternative analyses looking at those who were interviewed in the first and second halves of the campaign separately. We found mixed results. In 1993, the stability of all of the parties' pre-post partisanship increased; in 1997, it declined. In 2000, 2004, and 2006, the results were mixed – declines for some (the PCs and NDP in 2000; the Liberals, Conservatives, and NDP in 2004; the Conservatives, NDP, and BQ in 2006) and increases for others. We also looked at vote intention and reported vote (evidence of loyalty) and found similarly mixed patterns. These patterns suggest that whatever forces are operating on individuals to push/pull them to/from a particular party are not uniform and may have much to do with the specific campaign, as there appears to be no consistent pattern between brokerage and ideological parties. We do not address this issue here, although we do think that it is worthy of future study.

7 We are not the first to examine the characteristics of recent Canadian partisans. Stephenson, Scotto, and Kornberg (2004) found that Canadian partisans differed from American partisans between 1984 and 2000 in terms of loyalty (they were weaker) and that intensity mattered for the loyalty shown by partisans of the Liberals, PCs, and NDP. However, the focus of this chapter, comparing characteristics of partisans from each party, is a novel extension to the literature.

8 We recognize that this characterization of the parties divides them the same way that they would be divided if length of time that they have been contesting elections were considered. The brokerage parties have existed the longest and are

expected to have the weakest partisans, whereas the ideological parties are the newest and are expected to have stronger partisans. Differences between parties could perhaps be attributed to the number of voters who might have adopted partisanship through socialization instead of through active choice (which would coincide with the age of the party). We recognize that this is an interesting avenue of further research for understanding differences between parties, but we focus in this chapter on comparing the nature of partisans in each party.

9 Kornberg and Clarke (1992) show that partisanship levels decline significantly between elections.

10 Logit coefficients are reported for partisan identity, and ordered logit coefficients are reported for intensity.

References

Bartle, John, and Paolo Bellucci, eds. 2009. *Political Parties and Partisanship: Social Identity and Individual Attitudes.* London: Routledge.

Bélanger, Éric. 2004. "The Rise of Third Parties in the 1993 Canadian Federal Election: Pinard Revisited." *Canadian Journal of Political Science* 37, 3: 581-94.

–. 2007. "Third Party Success in Canada." In *Canadian Parties in Transition.* 3rd ed., ed. Alain-G. Gagnon and A. Brian Tanguay, 83-109. Peterborough, ON: Broadview Press.

Bélanger, Éric, and Jean-François Godbout. 2010. "Why Do Parties Merge? The Case of the Conservative Party of Canada." *Parliamentary Affairs* 63, 1: 41-65.

Bickerton, James, Alain-G. Gagnon, and Patrick J. Smith. 1999. *Ties that Bind: Parties and Voters in Canada.* Don Mills, ON: Oxford University Press.

Blais, André. 2002. "Why Is There So Little Strategic Voting in Canadian Plurality Rule Elections?" *Political Studies* 50, 3: 445-54.

Blais, André, Elisabeth Gidengil, Richard Nadeau, and Neil Nevitte. 2001. "Measuring Party Identification: Britain, Canada, and the United States." *Political Behavior* 23, 1: 5-22.

–. 2002. *Anatomy of a Liberal Victory.* Peterborough, ON: Broadview Press.

Blake, Donald E. 1982. "The Consistency of Inconsistency: Party Identification in Federal and Provincial Politics." *Canadian Journal of Political Science* 15, 4: 691-710.

Bowler, Shaun, and David J. Lanoue. 1996. "New Party Challenges and Partisan Change: The Effects of Party Competition on Party Loyalty." *Political Behavior* 18, 4: 327-43.

Budge, Ian, Ivor Crewe, and Dennis Farlie, eds. 1976. *Party Identification and Beyond: Representations of Voting and Party Competition.* London: Wiley.

Campbell, Angus, Philip E. Converse, Warren E. Miller, and Donald E. Stokes. 1960. *The American Voter.* New York: Wiley.

Carty, R. Kenneth, William Cross, and Lisa Young. 2000. *Rebuilding Canadian Party Politics.* Vancouver: UBC Press.

Clarke, Harold D., Jane Jenson, Lawrence LeDuc, and Jon H. Pammett. 1979. *Political Choice in Canada.* Toronto: McGraw-Hill Ryerson.

–. 1984. *Absent Mandate: The Politics of Discontent in Canada.* Toronto: Gage.

–. 1991. *Absent Mandate: Interpreting Change in Canadian Elections.* 2nd ed. Toronto: Gage.

–. 1996. *Absent Mandate: Canadian Electoral Politics in an Era of Restructuring.* 3rd ed. Toronto: Gage.

Clarke, Harold D., Allan Kornberg, and Peter Wearing. 2000. *A Polity on the Edge.* Peterborough, ON: Broadview Press.

Clarke, Harold D., and Marianne C. Stewart. 1987. "Partisan Inconsistency and Partisan Change in Federal States: The Case of Canada." *American Journal of Political Science* 31, 2: 383-407.

Cross, William, and Lisa Young. 2002. "Policy Attitudes of Party Members in Canada: Evidence of Ideological Politics." *Canadian Journal of Political Science* 35, 4: 859-80.

Dalton, Russell J., Scott Flanagan, and Paul Allen Beck, eds. 1984. *Electoral Change in Advanced Industrial Democracies: Realignment or Dealignment?* Princeton: Princeton University Press.

Downs, Anthony. 1957. *An Economic Theory of Democracy.* Boston: Addison-Wesley.

Duverger, Maurice. 1954. *Political Parties.* London: Lowe and Brydone.

Engelmann, Frederick C., and Mildred A. Schwartz. 1975. *Canadian Political Parties: Origin, Character, Impact.* Scarborough, ON: Prentice-Hall.

Epstein, Leon D. 1964. "A Comparative Study of Canadian Parties." *American Political Science Review* 58, 1: 46-59.

Fiorina, Morris P. 1981. *Retrospective Voting in American National Elections.* New Haven: Yale University Press.

Franklin, Mark N., Thomas T. Mackie, and Henry Valen, eds. 1992. *Electoral Change: Responses to Evolving Social and Attitudinal Structures in Western Countries.* Cambridge, UK: Cambridge University Press.

Gidengil, Elisabeth. 1992. "Canada Votes: A Quarter Century of Canadian National Election Studies." *Canadian Journal of Political Science* 25, 2: 219-48.

Gidengil, Elisabeth, André Blais, Joanna Everitt, Patrick Fournier, and Neil Nevitte. 2006. "Is the Concept of Party Identification Applicable in Canada? A Panel-Based Analysis." Paper presented at the ECPR 34th Joint Sessions of Workshops, Nicosia, Cyprus, 25-30 April.

Gidengil, Elisabeth, André Blais, Neil Nevitte, and Richard Nadeau. 2004. *Citizens.* Vancouver: UBC Press.

Green, Donald, Bradley Palmquist, and Eric Schickler. 2002. *Partisan Hearts and Minds: Political Parties and the Social Identities of Voters.* New Haven: Yale University Press.

Jenson, Jane. 1975. "Party Loyalty in Canada: The Question of Party Identification." *Canadian Journal of Political Science* 8, 4: 543-53.

Johnston, Richard. 1992. "Party Identification Measures in the Anglo-American Democracies: A National Survey Experiment." *American Journal of Political Science* 36, 2: 542-59.

–. 2006. "Party Identification: Unmoved Mover or Sum of Preferences?" *Annual Review of Political Science* 9: 329-51.

Johnston, Richard, André Blais, Henry E. Brady, and Jean Crête. 1992. *Letting the People Decide.* Montreal: McGill-Queen's University Press.

Kornberg, Allan, and Harold D. Clarke. 1992. *Citizens and Community: Political Support in a Representative Democracy.* New York: Cambridge University Press.

LeDuc, Lawrence. 2007. "Realignment and Dealignment in Canadian Federal Politics." In *Canadian Parties in Transition*, 3rd ed., ed. Alain-G. Gagnon and A. Brian Tanguay, 163-77. Peterborough, ON: Broadview Press.

LeDuc, Lawrence, Harold D. Clarke, Jane Jenson, and Jon H. Pammett. 1984. "Partisan Instability in Canada: Evidence from a New Panel Study." *American Political Science Review* 78, 2: 470-84.

Meisel, John. 1973. *Working Papers on Canadian Politics*. Enlarged ed. Montreal: McGill-Queen's University Press.

Merolla, Jennifer L., and Laura B. Stephenson. 2007. "Strategic Voting in Canada: A Cross-Time Analysis." *Electoral Studies* 26, 2: 235-46.

Nevitte, Neil, André Blais, Elisabeth Gidengil, and Richard Nadeau. 2000. *Unsteady State*. Don Mills, ON: Oxford University Press.

Scarrow, Howard A. 1965. "Distinguishing between Political Parties: The Case of Canada." *Midwest Journal of Political Science* 9, 1: 61-76.

Schickler, Eric, and Donald Philip Green. 1997. "The Stability of Party Identification in Western Democracies: Results from Eight Panel Surveys." *Comparative Political Studies* 30, 4: 450-83.

Scotto, Thomas J., Laura B. Stephenson, and Allan Kornberg. 2004. "From a Two-Party-Plus to a One-Party-Plus? Ideology, Vote Choice, and Prospects for a Competitive Party System in Canada." *Electoral Studies* 23, 3: 463-83.

Siaroff, Alan. 2003. "Two-and-a-Half-Party Systems and the Comparative Role of the 'Half.'" *Party Politics* 9, 3: 267-90.

Sniderman, Paul M., H.D. Forbes, and Ian Melzer. 1974. "Party Loyalty and Electoral Volatility: A Study of the Canadian Party System." *Canadian Journal of Political Science* 7, 2: 268-88.

Stephenson, Laura B., Thomas J. Scotto, and Allan Kornberg. 2004. "Slip, Sliding Away or Le Plus Ça Change ... : Canadian and American Partisanship in Comparative Perspective." *American Review of Canadian Studies* 34, 2: 283-312.

Stevenson, H. Michael. 1987. "Ideology and Unstable Party Identification in Canada: Limited Rationality in a Brokerage Party System." *Canadian Journal of Political Science* 20, 4: 813-50.

Stewart, Marianne C., and Harold D. Clarke. 1998. "The Dynamics of Party Identification in Federal Systems: The Canadian Case." *American Journal of Political Science* 42, 1: 97-116.

Zipp, John F. 1978. "Left-Right Dimensions of Canadian Federal Party Identification: A Discriminant Analysis." *Canadian Journal of Political Science* 11, 2: 251-77.

Part 2
Short-Term Influences on Voting Behaviour

Economic Voting in Canada: Assessing the Effects of Subjective Perceptions and Electoral Context

Cameron D. Anderson

> If democracy works at all, economic conditions ought to shape election results. Modern governments have assumed broad responsibility for the economic welfare of citizens. Governing parties and leaders should thus be rewarded or punished at the polls according to how well they manage the economy.
>
> – Jacobson (1991, 33)

The above quotation makes a fairly strong case about the connection between economic conditions and electoral outcomes. It suggests, in the first instance, that the practice of electoral democracy is (or should be) closely linked with the state of the economy. The basis for this claim is that in the postwar period, governments of advanced industrial democracies (such as Canada) have sought to exercise influence in managing economic outcomes. Governments might seek to control runaway inflation, as was done in the 1970s, when the Canadian federal government introduced wage and price control legislation. Governments might also try to stimulate economic growth within their borders through selective taxation or spending programs designed to facilitate the creation or expansion of business opportunities. Of course, the continued public funding of post-secondary education is seen by many as a long-term government investment to foster a stable, educated, and competitive workforce. For those citizens in need of forms of economic assistance, modern welfare states have massively grown since 1945 to provide an array of programs and services designed to maintain the economic welfare of all citizens.

With this brief summary of the many possible means of government involvement in Canada's economy and the lives of its citizens, it becomes evident that the government has assumed some responsibility for economic conditions and economic livelihoods in Canada.[1] If we take government involvement in the economy seriously, and if we take sincerely the decisions the government makes that have economic implications (for the country as a whole as well as individual citizens), then it becomes evident that the condition of the economy can be a basis for evaluating government performance. This is the core idea in economic voting: evaluating government performance on the basis of economic management and observed economic conditions.

It is well-established that governing parties in democratic countries are in some way and to some extent evaluated on the basis of how they perform in managing the economy (Lewis-Beck 1988; Norpoth, Lewis-Beck, and Lafay 1991; Anderson 1995; Duch and Stevenson 2008). In the most basic formulation of the economic voting model, elections provide voters with the opportunity to hold incumbents accountable for economic performance. When the economy is performing well, the electorate is more likely to vote for the incumbent. When the economy is going badly, voters are less likely to vote for the governing party. Although Bélanger and Nadeau's chapter (this volume) considers how third parties' support is influenced by long-term economic performance, this chapter's focus is squarely on government performance in managing the economy.

Building on the core model of economic voting, this chapter assesses the insights to be gained from whether and how voters use economic conditions as a means of shaping perceptions of past incumbent performance in the Canadian case. It starts by outlining the central theoretical debates within the literature on economic voting. Building on this discussion, the chapter then analyzes an empirical relationship between macroeconomic conditions (national unemployment) and federal incumbent vote share. Finally, having established the central models of economic voting and having tested them with real-world economic data, the chapter shifts to consider the applicability of the economic voting model, using subjective perceptions of economic conditions in federal incumbent support from 1988 to 2006.

Theoretical Debates in Economic Voting
Since initial statements regarding the relationship between economic

conditions and electoral choice first established the theory of economic voting, two central debates have served to form the basis of much of the literature. The first is a temporal debate in which the central question focuses on whether voters draw primarily on past experience or future expectations in their evaluations of incumbents and partisan options at election time. The second considers whether voters' electoral decisions are centrally motivated by their personal economic situations or their perceptions of the state of the national economy. I will consider these debates in turn.

In the first instance, past work on economic voting reflects disagreement over the temporal basis of vote decisions and the relative role of past versus future evaluations. At one pole in this debate are scholars who suggest that voters primarily use elections as a means of sanctioning incumbents for past performance (Key 1964). In a famous formulation, Key (568) suggests that voters are "rational gods of vengeance and of reward" who base vote choices on an analysis of incumbent performance over the previous term. If a voter deems the incumbent to have performed well, then he or she is more likely to support or reward the incumbent with a vote and presumably another term in office. However, if the incumbent has not performed well, the model suggests, then the voter will vote against the incumbent and hope to "throw the rascals out."

The retrospective economic voting model suggests that voters draw on past economic conditions to inform their evaluations of incumbent performance. If the economy has been good/bad, then they choose to vote for/against the incumbent. Underlying this relationship is the presumption that the state of the economy to some degree reflects the management of it by the incumbent. As the epigraph from Jacobson (1991) suggests, modern governments are prominent actors in the economy, and their ability to manage the economy should form a basis for evaluating their performance. A large body of evidence from advanced industrial democracies (including Canada) demonstrates the significant role of retrospective evaluations of past economic conditions in incumbent support (Kramer 1971; Lewis-Beck and Paldam 2000).[2]

On the other side of the debate, many theorize the vote decision as centrally a future-oriented or prospective one. Perhaps the most pivotal statement on the role of prospective evaluations comes from Downs (1957) and his depiction of voters as rational utility seekers. In this understanding of electoral motivation, voters are theorized to consider the available party alternatives and to select whom they believe to be best able to maximize their future utility. Therefore, from the prospective standpoint, the central question that voters ask themselves is this: "Given my current expectations about the future, which party should I vote for to maximize future benefit?"

In the context of the economy and economic voting, the prospective model suggests that voters will evaluate partisan options at election time on the basis of whom they think will best manage the economy in the future, given their expectations of future economic conditions. Some criticize the notion of prospective economic voting as expecting too much of voters to assess future governing performance by parties (Key 1966), on the one hand, and to form accurate expectations of economic conditions, on the other (Conover, Feldman, and Knight 1987). However, as Lockerbie (1991, 281) suggests in his work on prospective economic voting, "all we are assuming is that [voters] be able to discern which party ... would be better able to solve [future economic] problems or aid their personal finances." As such, this approach suggests that voters evaluate electoral choices on the basis of whom they believe will best manage the economy in the future.

A number of studies demonstrate the important role of prospective economic evaluations in shaping government support or approval (Chappell and Keech 1985, 1991; Lockerbie 1991, 1992; MacKuen, Erikson, and Stimson 1992; Erikson, MacKuen, and Stimson 2000; Sanders 2000). In a study of US presidential approval, MacKuen, Erikson, and Stimson (1992) developed the conceptual metaphor of "bankers" versus "peasants." Within this metaphor, peasants are thought of as voters who draw on the relatively naive and myopic dimension of recent economic experience (retrospective) to evaluate the government. In contrast, the banker model suggests sophisticated and far-sighted voters who judge incumbents on the basis of an expected economic future. Their findings supported the notion of voters as bankers who are prospectively oriented in their use of economic conditions to evaluate government competence.

Of course, there are compromise positions regarding this debate. One such position suggests that voters tend to base their decisions on retrospective economic evaluations because they help them to develop an accurate prospective account of likely future economic outcomes resulting from the incumbent's policies of economic management (Downs 1957; Fiorina 1978, 1981). Not surprisingly, there are others who find that both retrospective and prospective dimensions of economic evaluations have a substantial impact on incumbent support (Clarke and Stewart 1994). Although conflicting perspectives on this central temporal debate exist, cumulative findings in the literature on economic voting tend to suggest that retrospective evaluations have a stronger impact on incumbent support than do prospective evaluations (Lewis-Beck and Paldam 2000; Lewis-Beck and Stegmaier 2000).

The second distinction centres on the level of aggregation or context that informs the notion of economic conditions. This debate focuses on how voters conceptualize the economy. Is the electorate primarily concerned with personal or household economic situations? Or are voters mainly concerned with the state of the national economy? As such, the main parameters of the contextual debate contrast the relevant economies: national (or business) economic conditions with household (or personal) economic conditions (Lewis-Beck and Stegmaier 2000). In the parlance of the literature on economic voting, national economic conditions are typically referred to as "sociotropic," whereas the term "egocentric" denotes household or personal economic conditions.

Some readings of Downs's (1957) work might suggest that voters are primarily motivated by egocentric economic evaluations in the utility calculations underlying their vote decisions (see Lacy and Christenson 2007). In this articulation of electoral motivation, voters might be assumed to vote in ways that reflect their immediate material self-interests. A slightly different interpretation of egocentric economic voting suggests that voters form an evaluation of the general state of the economy on the basis of the economic situation of the immediate family (Campbell et al. 1960). As Campbell and his colleagues suggest, "the possibility that what happens to some may not happen to others in the same way seems too differentiated a view of society or politics to have much role in the evaluation process" (240).

In contrast, many suggest that voters draw primarily on perceptions of a sociotropic or national economy to form their economic evaluations (Kinder and Kiewiet 1979, 1981; Feldman 1982). This model presumes not that voters need detailed information about the national economy but that they develop "rough evaluations of national economic conditions" (Kinder and Kiewiet 1981, 132). Furthermore, scholars suggest that these national economic evaluations are at least partially independent from their own personal circumstances (Markus 1988). Finally, as Kinder and Kiewiet (1981) suggest, the use of sociotropic evaluations does not inherently imply altruistic motivations because a good national economy will most likely benefit individual economic situations in the long term.

Most work on economic voting finds that the evaluation of sociotropic economic conditions has a greater influence on incumbent support than egocentric evaluations (Lewis-Beck and Paldam 2000).[3] Because initial studies found that sociotropic conditions mattered more in the United States (Kinder and Kiewiet 1979), some posited that this was a cultural phenomenon in which an "ethic of self-reliance" predominated in the American electorate (Sniderman and Brody 1977; Feldman and Conley 1991). However, as Lewis-Beck (1988) observed in a comparative study, in select European countries, sociotropic conditions exhibited a greater effect on incumbent support than egocentric ones. Although some continue to point to the prominent role of egocentric evaluations (see Nannestad and Paldam 1994), the weight of evidence suggests that sociotropic evaluations tend to matter more than egocentric evaluations in shaping incumbent support (Lewis-Beck and Paldam 2000; Lewis-Beck and Stegmaier 2000).[4]

The amalgamation of these two dimensions of subjective evaluation leads to four logical combinations: sociotropic retrospective, sociotropic prospective, egocentric retrospective, and egocentric prospective. As Lacy and Christenson (2007) note, most analyses of economic voting consider the relative strength of retrospective and prospective evaluations or egocentric and sociotropic evaluations, and very few consider the relative effects on vote choice of all of them. As a result, a central purpose of the analyses in this chapter is to estimate a comprehensive model of economic voting that considers the relative effects of retrospective and prospective as well as sociotropic and egocentric economic evaluations on vote choice in Canada.

Economic Voting in Canada

Does the model of economic voting help to solve the puzzle of voting behaviour in Canada? Although a significant body of research indicates the general reliability of the economic voting model, there are conflicting findings that undermine the universal applicability of the model to all political contexts and situations (Paldam 1991). One response to the observed instability (and consequently the applicability) of economic voting in Canada deals with the clarity of responsibility hypothesis. This response contends that the phenomenon of economic voting will be most prominent in political contexts where responsibility for the economy and/or economic policy can be most clearly attributed to the incumbent government (Powell 1987). Powell and Whitten (1993) demonstrate that the comparative strength of economic voting is conditioned by contextual political factors that affect the clarity of responsibility, such as the presence and governing party control of a politically significant second chamber, the number of government parties, the presence of a minority government, the strength of party cohesion, and the ideological leanings of the incumbents. Powell and Whitten found that economic effects are weakest in those contexts where policy-making responsibility is blurred and "strong and consistent" where it is more focused (410).

Applicable to the case of Canada, recent work extends the clarity of responsibility argument by demonstrating how multilevel or federal institutions can undermine clarity of responsibility within a political system (Anderson 2006). The logic underlying these more recent findings suggests that the existence of more than one significantly empowered level of government makes it harder for voters to attribute responsibility for economic conditions. There are three factors to account for why attribution of responsibility is more difficult in multilevel or federal states. First, the actions of other levels of government might also have effects on economic conditions; second, increased information demands are placed on voters when governance spans multiple levels, and these information requirements are likely to undermine the ability of voters accurately to attribute credit and blame for economic conditions; and third, incentives are created for government actors to engage actively and passively in blame shifting and credit taking.

Although these findings suggest that the presence of multiple orders of government might serve to undermine the ease of attributing economic responsibility, the results do not rule out economic voting writ large. In the context of a highly decentralized, multilevel state such as Canada, a range of previous work finds important economic effects in the vote calculus. In three separate studies of economic voting in Canadian federal elections, Happy (1986, 1989, 1992) finds significant effects on incumbent vote share of aggregate economic conditions such as unemployment, inflation, and income. Confirming these findings, Canadian federal vote functions constructed by Nadeau and Blais (1993, 1995) demonstrate the significant effects of rising unemployment on vote shares for the federal Liberal Party. In contrast, Carmichael (1990) finds that, between 1945 and 1972, bad economic conditions (such as rising unemployment or inflation) benefited the incumbent governing party in federal elections. For federal elections after this period, Carmichael finds no significant effects of economic conditions on federal incumbent support. On this basis, he concludes that the general model of economic voting as developed in the American context might not have universal applicability. However, as Nadeau and Blais (1993) note, one reason for these conflicting findings likely stems from different methodological choices made in the specification of these aggregate models.[5] Finally, the most recent work on federal elections between 1953 and 2001 suggests that national unemployment influences federal incumbent support (Gelineau and Bélanger 2005).

Using individual-level data, one can establish (tepid) evidence of economic effects on votes for the federal incumbent. On the one hand, Clarke and Kornberg (1992) make a strong case for the effects of economic conditions on Conservative support throughout the 1980s and early 1990s. They contend that the conventional wisdom that the Conservatives lost support because of unpopular domestic policy initiatives (such as the failed Meech Lake Accord, the introduction of a new federal tax called the Goods and Services Tax [GST], and the Canada-US Free Trade Agreement) is wrong. Rather, they demonstrate that the Canadian electorate blamed the governing Conservatives for declining economic conditions throughout this period, and these negative effects on Conservative support were stronger than the effects of unpopular policy choices. On the other hand, Blais and his colleagues (2002b) suggest that economic voting in Canada might not be as important as conventional wisdom suggests. Indeed, though they find some evidence of economic voting in the 1997 federal election, they argue that it did not exert a prominent impact on vote choice or affect the outcome of the election. In the 2000 federal election, the same authors find greater evidence of economic voting at the federal level but suggest that the impact of the economy was limited (Blais et al. 2002a). Finally, considering the relative influence of federal and provincial economic conditions on federal vote choice, Anderson (2008) finds that evaluations of national but not provincial economic conditions have significant influences on federal incumbent support.

Beyond such general findings, past studies of federal economic voting consider the effects of variation within the Canadian electorate. For instance, Guérin and Nadeau (1998) consider the impact of the linguistic cleavage on federal economic voting. They find that, contrary to voters in other Canadian provinces, those in Quebec did not vote according to their evaluations of economic conditions. The authors contend that these findings suggest a different electoral rationality for minorities in long-established democracies. Godbout and Bélanger (2002) consider whether regional patterns of partisan competition and the structure of regional economies shape the effects of economic perceptions on federal vote choice. They find that the presence of a strong regional party weakens economic voting and that economic effects in strong ("have") regional economies are typically sociotropic, whereas egocentric evaluations are more prominent among respondents in weak ("have not") regional economies.[6]

Assessing Economic Voting in Canada: A Vote Function

In general, there are two central means through which to assess the relationship between economic conditions and electoral outcomes. One method involves considering this relationship using objective indicators of the national economy. These kinds of measures are always sociotropic and retrospective. The second method uses survey data and assesses the relationships between subjective perceptions of economic conditions and the likelihood of support for the governing party. Subjective measures can be made up of all four combinations of the economic evaluations previously discussed. Although this chapter draws on both types of data to consider the relationship between economic conditions and electoral outcomes in Canada, I will take up the objective measures first.

In the field of economic voting, when one seeks to consider the empirical relationship between actual economic conditions and electoral support, a "vote function" is estimated. Usual economic measures can include unemployment, inflation, as well as economic growth rates. According to the economic voting model, as the economy improves (as measured by any of these indicators), incumbent support at election time should increase. For instance, if national unemployment rates are up (that is, the economy worsens), it is expected that the current federal incumbent will be blamed for these worsening conditions and lose vote support in the subsequent election. In contrast, if the federal government has governed competently during a period of prolonged economic growth, then it is expected that the incumbent party will do well in the next federal election.

Clearly, there are a number of macroeconomic conditions (such as economic growth or inflation) that could be drawn on to assess the effects of economic conditions on federal incumbent vote share. The national unemployment rate is chosen because it tends to be a widely reported figure in news media, and as a result voters can be expected to have some idea of the national unemployment rate and whether it is relatively high or low. Additionally, and perhaps equally important, unemployment is likely an economic condition that has a high degree of salience in the minds of voters. If unemployment is high and getting higher, then voters might be concerned about their job security and/or that of friends and family. If unemployment is low, then this is a good indicator that the economy is performing well in creating jobs, and voters can live without worry for their immediate job prospects or those of their family and friends.

The core relationship between national economic conditions and incumbent support in Canada is demonstrated in Figure 6.1. The graph presents a scatterplot of federal incumbent vote shares for each election

Figure 6.1

Unemployment and federal incumbent vote, 1968-2006

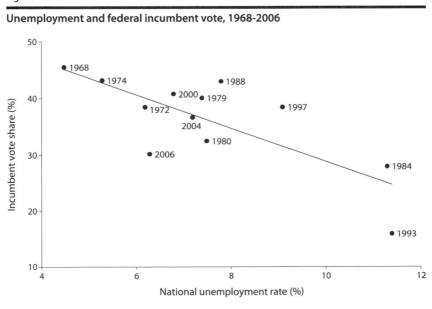

from 1968 to 2006 (plotted along the vertical axis). These vote shares are considered against national unemployment figures for each election year (plotted along the horizontal axis).[7] To aid in presenting the economy-vote relationship, a regression line (or "line of best fit") has been added and demonstrates the expected incumbent vote share as the national unemployment rate increases. In short, the story told by Figure 6.1 is that federal incumbent support is relatively closely aligned with the national unemployment rate. The slope of the regression line is −2.95.[8] This slope indicates that, on average, for each 1 percentage point increase in the national unemployment rate, federal incumbent vote share decreases by almost 3 percentage points. This slope coefficient is significant at $p < .005$.

Although the effect of unemployment is relatively consistent, some federal elections (such as those of 1988 and 2006) are clearly outliers. Outliers to the general trend are best viewed in the context of election-specific dynamics. For instance, though the unemployment rate in the 1988 federal election would have predicted an incumbent vote share of about 35 percent, the incumbent Progressive Conservatives won about 44 percent. This was an election in which current economic conditions were possibly less salient as the election was fought largely on one issue (the Free Trade Agreement with the United States). Similarly, given the national unemployment rate at the time of the 2006 election, one would have expected the Paul Martin-led Liberals to win approximately 40 percent of the popular vote. That they received about 10 percent less than expected can perhaps be understood in the context of voters rejecting an incumbent party mired in the sponsorship scandal.

This is an extremely parsimonious presentation of the effects of economic conditions on electoral outcomes. Indeed, the analysis thus far does not allow for the possibility that there might be regional differences in this relationship or that partisanship might also have profound influences on voters' electoral decisions.[9] However, the overall results clearly suggest that the prospect of federal incumbents' re-election is tied to the state of the economy as measured by indicators such as the national unemployment rate.

Assessing Economic Voting in Canada: Economic Evaluations and Incumbent Support (1988-2006)

This section of the chapter assesses a comprehensive model of economic voting by considering the relative effects of retrospective and prospective and sociotropic and egocentric economic perceptions on incumbent support over the past six federal elections. Because most analyses of economic voting in Canada consider the effects of only one or two dimensions on vote choice, the central contribution of the following analysis and discussion is an assessment of the relative effects of all four types of economic evaluation. Before engaging in this analysis, though, it might be useful to consider the correlations between the subjective economic evaluations.

As mentioned in the earlier discussion of retrospective and prospective models of voting, Fiorina (1981) suggests that, to develop a prospective impression of the economy, voters tend to draw on retrospective economic evaluations. So, for instance, if voters believe that the economy improved over the past year, then they might also be more likely to think that it will improve or continue to be strong in the future. Similarly, Clarke and Kornberg (1992) argue that voters use their personal economic situations (egocentric) to form impressions about the state of the national economy (sociotropic). Applying this logic, where voters feel comfortable about their household economic situations, they might tend to infer that the national economy is similarly strong. In both instances, voters are theorized to use more readily available information (the past and/or their own situation) to inform impressions about economic conditions about which they presumably have less information. This discussion provides some expectations regarding how these economic evaluations might be correlated.

Considering the results in Table 6.1, there appears to be some evidence for the dynamics suggested. In the first instance, it appears that similarities on one dimension of evaluation tend to be more strongly related compared with those correlation coefficients that are different on both dimensions. For example, both types of retrospective economic evaluations exhibit a correlation coefficient of 0.25, and both prospective measures are correlated to a similar degree (0.24). Following the interpretation put forward by Clarke and Kornberg (1992), these correlations suggest that, if one believes that his or her personal situation has improved over the past year, then he or she is also more likely to think that the national economy has done well in the past. Similarly, where a voter believes that his or her personal economic situation will be better in the future, he or she is also more likely to think that the national economy will improve. In sum, this might be evidence of the theorized dynamic that voters draw

Table 6.1

Correlations between subjective economic evaluations (1988-2006)

	Sociotropic retrospective	Egotropic retrospective	Sociotropic prospective	Egotropic prospective
Sociotropic retrospective	1.00	–	–	–
Egotropic retrospective	.25	1.00	–	–
Sociotropic prospective	.31	.13	1.00	–
Egotropic prospective	.16	.27	.24	1.00

Note: All correlation coefficients are statistically significant at $p < .001$.

on more readily available information (personal conditions) to inform perceptions of national economic conditions.

Similarly, there are reasonably strong correlations between retrospective and prospective evaluations at the same level of economic aggregation. For instance, the highest correlation observed is between retrospective and prospective sociotropic (or national) economic evaluations (0.31). Additionally, retrospective and prospective egocentric (or personal) economic conditions are reasonably correlated at 0.27. These findings might be suggestive of Fiorina's (1981) theorized dynamic that voters draw on the more readily available evaluations of the past to inform their expectations of what is likely to happen in the future.

These interpretations are made stronger with the findings that the weakest correlations occur where voters are unable to draw on at least one similar dimension (either temporally or contextually) to inform their economic evaluations. The correlation coefficients for evaluations that differ on both dimensions are 0.14 and 0.16 respectively. The smaller sizes of these coefficients relative to the earlier ones are likely evidence that voters draw on readily available information to reach perceptions about conditions for which they have less information.

Moving beyond the relationships between the various dimensions of subjective economic evaluations, what effect does each kind of economic evaluation have on incumbent support? A logistic regression was estimated using a pooled data set of each Canadian federal election from 1988 to 2006. The model includes controls for sociodemographics (gender, age, income, religion, education, and ethnicity), region, incumbent and opposition party identification (with only fairly and very strong identifiers considered), and election year.[10] The dependent variable in

Table 6.2

The effect of economic evaluations on incumbent support (1988-2006)

	Model 1		
Economic evaluations	Logit coefficients	Robust standard errors	Odds ratios
Sociotropic retrospective	0.20	(0.05)***	1.22
Egocentric retrospective	0.14	(0.05)***	1.15
Sociotropic prospective	0.27	(0.05)***	1.30
Egocentric prospective	0.12	(0.06)**	1.13
	Pseudo R^2 = 0.33		
	N = 8,718		

Note: Not shown but included in the model are sociodemographic, region, election year, and party identification variables.

* $p < .1$; ** $p < .05$; *** $p < .01$

the pooled analysis is voting for the incumbent. This means that, in 1988 and 1993, the incumbent was the Progressive Conservative Party, and for each election thereafter the incumbent was the Liberal Party. As presented in Table 6.2, only the effects of economic evaluations on vote choice are reported and discussed.[11]

Based on results presented in Table 6.2, one can say that each of the four dimensions of economic evaluation has an independent and a statistically significant effect on incumbent support (controlling for all variables in the model) throughout this period of Canadian federal elections. To gain a clearer picture of how economic evaluations influenced incumbent voting over this period, I will consider in some detail each of the economic variables.

In the first instance, the positive coefficient of sociotropic retrospective economic evaluations suggests that evaluations of how the Canadian economy has been doing over the previous year have a positive effect on incumbent support. For each one-unit increase in the sociotropic retrospective economic evaluations (from worse to same over the past year, for instance), the likelihood of voting for the federal incumbent increased by 22 percent (based on the odds ratio). This effect can be clarified by considering the predicted probability of voting for the federal incumbent at different values of the sociotropic retrospective variable.[12] Following this method, if all respondents thought that the national economy had deteriorated over the previous year, then the predicted probability of

Table 6.3

Predicted probability of incumbent vote (1988-2006)

	Change	Incumbent
Baseline vote		.336
Sociotropic retrospective	Worse	.291
	Same	.318
	Better	.345
Egocentric retrospective	Worse	.299
	Same	.318
	Better	.337
Sociotropic prospective	Worse	.281
	Same	.318
	Better	.356
Egocentric prospective	Worse	.300
	Same	.318
	Better	.335

Note: All differences in the predicted probabilities of incumbent vote between different categories of economic evaluations (e.g., worse to same) are statistically significant at the $p < .001$ level.

federal incumbent support would be 29.1 percent (see Table 6.3). In contrast, if all respondents believed that the national economy had improved over the previous year, then the predicted probability of an incumbent vote would be 34.5 percent. This increase in predicted support of 5 percent is statistically significant ($p < .001$).

The other form of retrospective evaluation (egocentric) has a similar effect on federal incumbent support. The predicted probability of incumbent support when the respondent believes that his or her personal economic situation has worsened over the past year (egocentric retrospective evaluation) is 29.9 percent. In contrast, if all respondents believe that the economy has improved over the previous year, then the predicted probability of an incumbent vote jumps to 33.7 percent. This difference is statistically significant ($p < .001$).

Taken together, these findings suggest strong support for the notion of retrospective voting in the Canadian case. Whether in the context of the national economy or that of the economic situation of the individual respondent, believing that economic conditions have improved/worsened significantly increases the likelihood of voting for/against the federal incumbent party. To the extent that economic conditions can be used by voters to reward and punish the government for past performance, these findings strongly suggest that Canadian voters engage in some degree of retrospective sanctioning of the federal incumbent.

Although these results clearly suggest the applicability of the retrospective model of voting among Canadian voters, the results also suggest that a future-oriented or prospective dimension is also prevalent in the vote calculus of the Canadian electorate. Of the four economic variables included in the pooled analysis, prospective evaluations of the Canadian economy have the greatest impact on incumbent voting. Based on a one-unit increase in expectations of the state of the Canadian economy (from staying the same to getting better in the next year, for instance), the likelihood of supporting the federal incumbent jumps by over thirty points, all else being equal (based on the odds ratio). An increase of over seven points in the predicted probability of incumbent support is observed when comparing the probability of incumbent support if all respondents thought that the economy was going to get worse (28.1 percent) with that of all respondents who believed that the national economy was expected to improve over the next year (35.6 percent). This difference is statistically significant at $p < .001$.

The effects on incumbent support of egocentric prospective economic evaluations are the smallest of the four economic variables, but they achieve statistical significance ($p < .05$). The results suggest that, for each one-unit improvement in expectations for the status of one's personal economic situation, the likelihood of supporting the incumbent increases by thirteen points, based on the odds ratio.

Considering these trends as a whole, the central questions of the analysis can be restated. Are Canadian voters prone to retrospective judgments that punish and reward incumbents for past economic performance? Or does the Canadian electorate act according to the expectations of the prospective model of economic voting? Additionally, are voters' electoral decisions primarily motivated by evaluations of sociotropic or national economic conditions? Or do egocentric or pocketbook conditions provide the pivotal inspiration for incumbent support? The answers to these questions appear to be yes on all accounts. However, there are interesting permutations in the trends established that require some further discussion and explication.

The findings of this analysis suggest that sociotropic or national economic conditions tend to have the greatest impact on incumbent vote choice throughout this period. This observation does not exclude the role of egocentric or pocketbook voting but indicates that sociotropic economic evaluations have a greater effect on incumbent voting than egocentric ones. This finding is consistent with most prior comparative work on economic voting (Lewis-Beck and Paldam 2000; Lewis-Beck and Stegmaier 2000). However, the relative strength of prospective evaluations (sociotropic prospective in particular) over that of retrospective evaluations poses an intriguing contradiction to the generally accepted conclusions regarding which form of economic evaluation has the most consistent effect on incumbent support. In short, as mentioned earlier in the chapter, most work on economic voting finds that retrospective evaluations, in the classic reward/punish model, tend to have the greatest effects on incumbent vote choice. If the comparative work finds this to be the case, then what explains the disjuncture of the Canadian results during this period?

In the first instance, the presence of new leaders taking incumbent parties into elections could contribute to this result. During this period of Canadian electoral history, there were two elections in which the governing party was led by a new prime minister (Kim Campbell leading the Progressive Conservatives in 1993 and Paul Martin heading the Liberal Party in 2004). Previous work (Nadeau and Lewis-Beck 2001) on economic voting suggests that, when a new leader takes the incumbent party into an election, voter expectations about future performance under the new leader might be more influential than past performance for incumbent support. This change in leadership effect is likely because past performance and economic management are attributed by voters to the previous leader and not to the new one. As a result, the new leader and the party's past governing performance are not evaluated as strongly on the basis of management of past economic conditions as on expectations about how well the new leader and party will govern in the future (that is, a prospective vote). Based on the results presented in Table 6.4, this account might have some traction at least for the 2004 election. In that year, sociotropic prospective evaluations were the sole economic evaluation to have an effect on incumbent support. This result might indicate voters' future confidence in the economy and Martin's ability to manage it.

A second reason for the relative weakness of retrospective voting throughout this period might centre on the deeply fragmented nature of the federal opposition parties. Previous work on economic voting finds that the clarity of available alternatives to the governing party can influence the strength of retrospective economic effects on incumbent support

Table 6.4

Comparison of economic effects by election year

	Sociotropic retrospective	Egocentric retrospective	Sociotropic prospective	Egocentric prospective
1988	–	–	**	–
1993	–	*	–	–
1997	**	–	*	–
2000	–	**	–	**
2004	–	–	***	–
2006	***	–	**	–

Notes: These results are based on the models estimated in Table 6.2. For each election year, cells indicate the level of statistically significant effect for each economic evaluation. Where – appears, then that economic evaluation was not statistically significant in that year.
$* p < .1; ** p < .05; *** p < .01$

(Anderson 1995). In the 1997 and 2000 (and, to some extent, 2004) federal elections, there was no single opposition party able to form a clear alternative to the governing Liberal Party.[13] Entering the 1997 election, federal opposition parties were deeply divided along regional lines, with the Bloc Québécois dominating in Quebec and the Reform Party having established a stronghold in the western provinces. At the same time, traditional national parties such as the New Democratic Party or the Progressive Conservatives had relatively few seats in the House of Commons and were not nearly strong enough in public opinion polls to provide a realistic "government in waiting" for voters. The nature of the opposition parties in the 2000 federal election looked much the same except for the fact that the Reform Party was now competing under a new name (Canadian Alliance). As a result, voters might have been less likely to sanction the incumbent Liberal Party for its economic management because there was no option waiting in the wings. Results from Table 6.4 provide some support for this assertion given the absence of sociotropic retrospective voting in both the 2000 and the 2004 federal elections. These results suggest that, at least in the domain of the economy, retrospective sanctions of the incumbent were not prevalent in either the 2000 or the 2004 federal election.

Finally, the strength of retrospective evaluations of the Liberal Party's economic management in the 2006 federal election might have been weakened because the Liberals were governing in a minority Parliament. Following work on the clarity of government responsibility, one could argue that voters were less likely to vote on the basis of a retrospective sanction because the minority context acted to blur the extent to which responsibility for past economic conditions could be attributed to the Liberal government (Whitten and Palmer 1999). However, based on the strength of sociotropic retrospective economic evaluations in 2006, it is doubtful that the minority Parliament had any real effect in muting retrospective evaluations of the governing Liberal Party.[14]

Considering these three factors together, it appears that new incumbent leaders and the lack of a viable opposition party (or government in waiting) account for why retrospective evaluations did not figure more prominently in voting decisions over this period of Canadian electoral history.

Conclusion

This chapter has sought to outline the main parameters of the economic voting model and to consider the applicability of the approach to understanding vote decisions in the Canadian case. After articulating the theoretical grounds of the measures of economic conditions and considering prior literature in Canada, the chapter assessed the role of the economy in federal elections. Using an objective economic indicator, findings from the chapter suggest that macroeconomic conditions such as the national unemployment rate were closely aligned with federal incumbent support over a forty-year period (1968-2006). Indeed, based on this selection of federal elections, there is a decent fit between observed national unemployment rates and federal incumbent vote shares.

Using individual-level survey data from federal elections between 1988 and 2006, findings indicate that all four forms of subjective economic perceptions influence federal incumbent support. However, there are interesting and theoretically important variations in the strength and statistical significance of these economic evaluations. In particular, sociotropic prospective evaluations tended to have the strongest and most consistent effects on incumbent vote choice through this era of federal elections. Based on the application of comparative work on economic voting outside Canada, this finding can be understood as reflecting differences in the political context of the specific election.

Consistent with the vast majority of literature on economic voting, this chapter has focused solely on assessing the role of economic evaluations in incumbent support. One novel avenue for future work on economic voting in Canada would be to consider the theoretical possibility that economic evaluations might also influence electoral choice of (some) opposition parties as well. To date, work on economic voting in Canada has not adequately considered the possible ways in which economic conditions might also shape support for non-incumbent parties. Although retrospective evaluations influence the likelihood of supporting the incumbent (that is, the government did a good/bad job managing the economy), once a voter decides to vote for an opposition party retrospective evaluations provide very little indication of which party to vote for. In contrast, the use of prospective evaluations might afford a more solid basis on which to discern between competing opposition parties. This hypothesis has yet to be tested but is likely to be a fruitful avenue of research.

To close, in the 1992 US presidential election campaign, it was widely reported that Democratic nominee Bill Clinton's campaign headquarters had a sign on the wall that read "it's the economy, stupid!" Findings at both the aggregate and the individual levels suggest that Canadian voters get this. Economic management is an important basis on which to evaluate incumbent performance, and more often than not, Canadian voters act on these kinds of evaluations.

Acknowledgments

I would like to thank the anonymous reviewers as well as Laura Stephenson and Jason Roy for comments on this chapter.

Notes

Epigraph: The epigraph to this chapter is drawn from Jacobson, Gary, "The Economy in U.S. House Elections," in *Economics and Politics: The Calculus of Support,* ed. Helmut Norpoth, Michael Lewis-Beck, and Jean-Dominique Lafay, 33-48 (Ann Arbor: University of Michigan Press, 1991).

1 At any one point in time, economic conditions in a country might reflect other determinants than solely the economic management of the current government. Indeed, the health of a country's economy might be affected by international economic pressures, lagged effects of economic policy decisions made by previous governments, or other factors exogenous to the current incumbent. However, given the range of possible influences on the economy, one of the major factors will no doubt be the actions and decisions of the current government.

2 Recent work on economic voting also suggests the prevalence of these mechanisms of vote choice in newly democratized and economically developing countries (Anderson, Lewis-Beck, and Stegmaier 2003; Remmer and Gelineau 2003).

3 Egocentric economic evaluations are also referred to as "pocketbook" evaluations.

4 Clarke and Kornberg (1992) suggest that egocentric economic evaluations shape sociotropic evaluations and that, when both types are included in the same model, the egocentric effects are washed out.

5 The use of aggregate modelling can be highly sensitive to subtle changes in specification, and this is one of the reasons that aggregate findings should also be tested at the individual level.

6 The designation "have" refers to provinces with economies that perform above the national average, whereas "have not" denotes provinces and regions with comparatively poorer economies.

7 Although the literature on economic voting finds that past economic conditions (t-1) influence support or vote share at the current time (t), it also finds that voters are relatively myopic and draw on economic conditions from the recent past (previous quarter or two) more than the distant past (Lewis-Beck and Stegmaier 2000). As a result, the use of national unemployment rates from the election year assumes that voters draw on economic conditions relatively proximate to the election. To use economic conditions from the previous year would extend beyond the demonstrated nature of voter myopia. For instance, in the case of a federal election in the month of November, using economic conditions from the previous year assumes that voters draw on economic conditions up to seven quarters previous. The literature suggests that voters are more myopic than that. Regardless, analyses (not shown) using economic data from the year before produce similar results.

8 The adjusted R^2 for this bivariate regression is a surprisingly high 0.53, which suggests that about 53 percent of the variation in incumbent vote share over this period can be accounted for by the national unemployment rate.

9 Further analyses (not shown) consider the effect of inflation on incumbent support for the same time period. In short, there is no statistically significant effect of inflation on federal incumbent support.

10 Coding for sociodemographic control variables was gender: female = 1, male = 0; age in years; religion: Catholic = 1, all others = 0; education: university graduate = 1, less than university = 0; ethnicity: northern European = 0, all others = 1; income in deciles. A fairly strong or strong identification with the incumbent party = 1 and all others = 0. A fairly strong or strong identification with an opposition party = 1 and all others = 0. This coding leaves non-identifiers as the reference group. Economic evaluations were coded for each dimension: better = 1, stayed the same = 0, worse = –1.

11 Full results are available from the author on request.

12 All predicted probabilities presented in this chapter are generated using the "predict" command in Stata. The values generated indicate the predicted probability of incumbent support at different values of the independent variable in question while holding all non-economic variables in the model at their original values. To assess more clearly the impact of each dimension of economic evaluations, the economic variables were held at "stay the same" (= 0) when the predicted probability of incumbent support at different values of the economic variable of interest (for instance, sociotropic retrospective) was calculated.

13 None of the federal opposition parties was able to compete seriously for government with the Liberals in both 1997 and 2000. In 2004, though the federal Conservative Party was newly united, it is arguable that voters did not yet see it as a viable alternative to the incumbent Liberal Party.

14 Indeed, the strength of sociotropic retrospective evaluations in 2006 might have been a function of how minority Parliaments in Canada operate – with the

governing party not sharing power in a coalition and operating as if holding a majority.

References

Anderson, Cameron D. 2006. "Economic Voting and Multilevel Governance: A Comparative Individual-Level Analysis." *American Journal of Political Science* 50, 2: 449-63.

–. 2008. "Economic Voting, Multilevel Governance, and Information in Canada." *Canadian Journal of Political Science* 41, 2: 329-54.

Anderson, Christopher J. 1995. *Blaming the Government: Citizens and the Economy in Five European Democracies.* Armonk, NY: Sharpe.

Anderson, L., M. Lewis-Beck, and M. Stegmaier. 2003. "Post Socialist Democratization: A Comparative Political Economic Model of the Vote for Hungary and Nicaragua." *Electoral Studies* 22, 3: 469-84.

Blais, André, Richard Nadeau, Elisabeth Gidengil, and Neil Nevitte. 2002a. *Anatomy of a Liberal Victory.* Peterborough, ON: Broadview Press.

–. 2002b. "The Impact of Issues and the Economy in the 1997 Canadian Federal Election." *Canadian Journal of Political Science* 35, 2: 409-21.

Campbell, Angus, Philip Converse, Warren Miller, and Donald Stokes. 1960. *The American Voter.* New York: Wiley and Sons.

Carmichael, Calum M. 1990. "Economic Conditions and the Popularity of the Incumbent Party in Canada." *Canadian Journal of Political Science* 23, 4: 713-60.

Chappell, Henry, and William Keech. 1985. "A New View of Political Accountability of Economic Performance." *American Political Science Review* 79, 1: 10-27.

–. 1991. "Explaining Aggregate Evaluations of Economic Performance." In *Economics and Politics: The Calculus of Support,* ed. Helmut Norpoth, Michael Lewis-Beck, Jean-Dominique Lafay, 207-20. Ann Arbor: University of Michigan Press.

Clarke, Harold, and Allan Kornberg. 1992. "Support for the Canadian Federal Progressive Conservative Party since 1988: The Impact of Economic Evaluations and Economic Issues." *Canadian Journal of Political Science* 25, 1: 29-53.

Clarke, Harold, and Marianne Stewart. 1994. "Prospections, Retrospections, and Rationality: The 'Bankers' Model of Presidential Approval." *American Journal of Political Science* 38, 1: 104-23.

Conover, Pamela, Stanley Feldman, and Kathleen Knight. 1987. "The Personal and Political Underpinnings of Economic Forecasts." *American Journal of Political Science* 31, 3: 559-83.

Downs, Anthony. 1957. *An Economic Theory of Democracy.* New York: Harper and Row.

Duch, Raymond, and Randolph Stevenson. 2008. *The Economic Vote: How Political and Economic Institutions Condition Election Results.* New York: Cambridge University Press.

Erikson, R., M. MacKuen, and J. Stimson. 2000. "Bankers or Peasants Revisited: Economic Expectations and Presidential Approval." *Electoral Studies* 19, 2: 295-312.

Feldman, Stanley. 1982. "Economic Self-Interest and Political Behaviour." *American Journal of Political Science* 26, 3: 446-66.

Feldman, Stanley, and Pamela Conley. 1991. "Explaining Explanations of Changing Economic Conditions." In *Economics and Politics: The Calculus of Support,* ed.

Helmut Norpoth, Michael Lewis-Beck, and Jean-Dominique Lafay, 185-206. Ann Arbor: University of Michigan Press.

Fiorina, Morris. 1978. "Economic Retrospective Voting in American National Elections: A Micro-Analysis." *American Journal of Political Science* 22, 2: 426-43.

–. 1981. *Retrospective Voting in American National Elections.* New Haven: Yale University Press.

Gelineau, François, and Eric Bélanger. 2005. "Electoral Accountability in a Federal State: National and Provincial Economic Voting in Canada." *Publius* 35, 3: 407-26.

Godbout, Jean-François, and Eric Bélanger. 2002. "La Dimension régionale du vote économique canadien aux élections fédérale de 1988 a 2000." *Canadian Journal of Political Science* 35, 3: 567-88.

Guérin, Daniel, and Richard Nadeau. 1998. "Clivage linguistique et économique vote au Canada" *Canadian Journal of Political Science* 31, 3: 557-72.

Happy, J.R. 1986. "Voter Sensitivity to Economic Conditions: A Canadian-American Comparison." *Comparative Politics* 19, 1: 45-56.

–. 1989. "Economic Performance and Retrospective Voting in Canadian Federal Elections." *Canadian Journal of Political Science* 22, 2: 377-87.

–. 1992. "The Effects of Economic and Fiscal Performance on Incumbency Voting: The Canadian Case." *British Journal of Political Science* 22, 1: 117-30.

Jacobson, Gary. 1991. "The Economy in U.S. House Elections." In *Economics and Politics: The Calculus of Support,* ed. Helmut Norpoth, Michael Lewis-Beck, and Jean-Dominique Lafay, 33-48. Ann Arbor: University of Michigan Press.

Key, V.O. 1964. *Politics, Parties, and Pressure Groups.* 5th ed. New York: Thomas Y. Crowell.

Kinder, Donald, and D. Roderick Kiewiet. 1979. "Economic Discontent and Political Behaviour: The Role of Personal Grievances and Collective Economic Judgements in Congressional Voting." *American Journal of Political Science* 23, 3: 495-527.

–. 1981. "Sociotropic Politics: The American Case." *British Journal of Political Science* 11, 2: 129-61.

Kramer, Gerald. 1971. "Short-Term Fluctuations in U.S. Voting Behaviour, 1896-1964." *American Political Science Review* 65, 1: 131-43.

Lacy, Dean, and Dino Christenson. 2007. "The Effect of Information on Economic Voting." Paper presented at the annual meeting of the American Political Science Association, Chicago, 30 August-2 September.

Lewis-Beck, Michael. 1988. *Economics and Elections: The Major Western Democracies.* Ann Arbor: University of Michigan Press.

Lewis-Beck, Michael, and Martin Paldam. 2000. "Economic Voting: An Introduction." *Electoral Studies* 19, 2: 113-22.

Lewis-Beck, Michael, and Mary Stegmaier. 2000. "Economic Determinants of Electoral Outcomes." *Annual Review of Political Science* 3: 183-219.

Lockerbie, Brad. 1991. "The Temporal Pattern of Economic Evaluations and Vote Choice in Senate Elections." *Public Choice* 69, 3: 279-94.

–. 1992. "Prospective Voting in Presidential Elections, 1956-1988." *American Politics Quarterly* 20, 3: 308-25.

MacKuen, Michael, Robert Erikson, and James Stimson. 1992. "Peasants or Bankers? The American Electorate and the US Economy." *American Political Science Review* 86, 3: 597-611.

Markus, Gregory. 1988. "The Impact of Personal and National Economic Conditions on the Presidential Vote: A Pooled Cross-Sectional Analysis." *American Journal of Political Science* 32, 1: 137-54.

Nadeau, Richard, and André Blais. 1993. "Explaining Election Outcomes in Canada: Economy and Politics." *Canadian Journal of Political Science* 26, 4: 775-90.

–. 1995. "Economic Conditions, Leader Evaluations, and Election Outcomes in Canada." *Canadian Public Policy* 21, 2: 212-18.

Nadeau, Richard, and Michael Lewis-Beck. 2001. "National Economic Voting in U.S. Presidential Elections." *Journal of Politics* 63, 1: 159-81.

Nannestad, Peter, and Martin Paldam. 1994. "The VP Function: A Survey of the Literature on Vote and Popularity Functions after 25 Years," *Public Choice* 79, 3-4: 213-45.

Norpoth, Helmut, Michael Lewis-Beck, and Jean-Dominique Lafay, eds. 1991. *Economics and Politics: The Calculus of Support.* Ann Arbor: University of Michigan Press.

Paldam, Martin. 1991. "How Robust Is the Vote Function?" In *Economics and Politics: The Calculus of Support,* ed. Helmut Norpoth, Michael Lewis-Beck, and Jean-Dominique Lafay, 9-31. Ann Arbor: University of Michigan Press.

Powell, G. Bingham Jr. 1987. "Comparative Voting Behaviour: Cleavages, Partisanship, and Accountability." *Research in Micropolitics* 2: 233-64.

Powell, G. Bingham Jr., and Guy Whitten. 1993. "A Cross-National Analysis of Economic Voting: Taking Account of Political Context." *American Journal of Political Science* 37, 2: 391-414.

Remmer, Karen, and François Gelineau. 2003. "Subnational Electoral Choice: Economic and Referendum Voting in Argentina, 1983-1999." *Comparative Political Studies* 36, 7: 801-21.

Sanders, David. 2000. "The Real Economy and the Perceived Economy in Popularity Functions: How Much Do Voters Need to Know? A Study of British Data, 1974-97." *Electoral Studies* 19, 2: 275-94.

Sniderman, Paul, and Richard Brody. 1977. "Coping: The Ethic of Self-Reliance." *American Journal of Political Science* 21, 3: 501-21.

Whitten, Guy, and Harvey Palmer. 1999. "Cross-National Analyses of Economic Voting." *Electoral Studies* 18, 1: 49-67.

Third-Party Support in Canadian Elections: The Role of the Economy

Éric Bélanger and Richard Nadeau

Two key characteristics of Canadian federal politics are the diversity and durability of "third parties" (Lipset 1990).[1] This situation is intriguing given that the Canadian institutional context offers several barriers to new party entry (Harmel and Robertson 1985). For instance, the single-member plurality electoral system used in the country introduces important distortions between the number of votes and the number of legislative seats, which usually penalize small parties (Cairns 1968). In spite of this situation, numerous third parties have experienced significant electoral breakthroughs in Canada over the past decades, and there has rarely been an election in which only the major parties have competed for voter support (for a detailed review, see Bélanger 2007). One of the significant puzzles of Canadian voting behaviour has thus been why does a sizable proportion of the Canadian electorate regularly choose to abandon the two major parties at the polling booth in favour of third parties?

Here we define a third party "as any non-traditional party which has not yet been in power. It thus remains in the eyes of the voters as an untried alternative" (Pinard 1973, 455). These are parties that are not considered as natural (or traditional) governing alternatives because they are either new or have been unable to form a government (Bélanger 2007, 84). Third parties are sometimes referred to as "non-mainstream" (Perrella 2005), a label that is conceptually close to the definition that we adopt here.

Transposed to the case of federal-level Canadian party politics, which concerns us directly in this chapter, this definition implies that any federal party other than the Liberal Party or the (Progressive) Conservative Party is to be considered a third party. Federal third parties thus include formations such as the New Democratic Party (NDP), Social Credit, and more

Figure 7.1

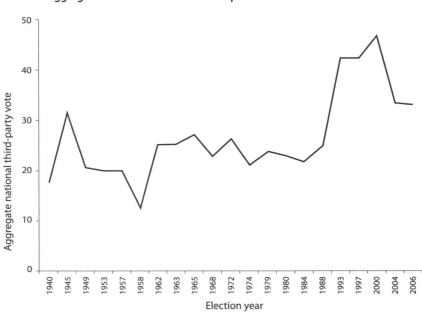

National aggregate vote share of federal third parties

recently the Reform Party, the Bloc Québécois, and the Green Party. Figure 7.1 depicts the level of national support obtained by all third parties in any one federal election held in Canada since 1940. As can be seen, the lowest level of aggregate support garnered by third parties during that period has been 12.8 percent (in 1958), and the highest level has been 47 percent (in 2000). Mean third-party vote during the period was 27 percent, meaning that about one Canadian voter in four typically votes for a federal third party come election time. The level of third-party support was slightly higher during the 1990s, mainly due to the dramatic emergence of the Reform Party/Canadian Alliance and the Bloc Québécois. But even before the 1993 watershed, the mean vote share received by Canadian federal third parties was 23 percent: still about one voter in four. Not surprisingly, this relative stability in third-party voting at the national level somewhat conceals important variations at the provincial level. The two main regions where federal third parties have particularly flourished are Quebec and the western provinces, but third-party support has sometimes been high in the other provinces as well, one recent case being the NDP surge in the Atlantic provinces during the late 1990s.

How can we account for these ups and downs in third-party voting? Several explanations exist, but here we wish to focus on one factor that we think has been insufficiently explored so far: namely, macroeconomic conditions. We are interested in assessing whether economic grievances account for variations in third-party voting in Canadian federal elections. To do so, we rely on a hitherto neglected macroeconomic indicator, disposable income per capita, and test for whether variations in national or provincial income levels provide a reliable prediction of aggregate third-party voting in Canada since the Second World War. Indeed, another quick look at Figure 7.1 suggests that its evolution over time might have roughly corresponded to that of the economy. The Canadian economy was booming in the decade that followed the war, before stabilizing during the 1960s and 1970s. Then Canada experienced two consecutive economic recessions in the 1980s and 1990s, followed by a return to good economic times in the 2000s. Looking at the figure, we can see that, overall, during periods when the economy is on the rise, third-party support is on the decline (and vice versa). But we need to investigate this relationship more deeply and systematically before concluding anything concrete about this phenomenon.

Theory
A number of explanatory factors have been proposed in the literature to account for the electoral success of third parties in Canada and other advanced industrial democracies. Institutional variables constitute a first set. The presence of subnational offices, or multilevel governance, is one such factor. Minor parties in federal systems are said to have less difficulty in garnering support at the national level because they have access to subnational representative positions, and thus to governmental experience, which allows them to become more credible contenders in national contests (Blais and Carty 1991; Gaines 1999; Gerring 2005). Parliamentary systems are also expected to provide a more favourable electoral environment for third parties than presidential systems (Hauss and Rayside 1978; Gerring 2005). Another potential factor that has been investigated in the literature is party ballot access (Harmel and Robertson 1985; Hirano and Snyder 2007). In some countries, such as the United States, ballot access rules (for instance, direct primaries, Australian ballot,

antifusion laws) can be strict to the point of discouraging small parties from presenting candidates and competing in elections.

Probably the most well-known institutional factor is the electoral system. According to what is now referred to as "Duverger's Law," the single-member plurality (or SMP, "first-past-the-post") electoral system favours a two-party system (Duverger 1951, 247). This is partly due to the psychological effect of this system: as only one candidate can win the district seat with only a simple plurality of the votes, a third-party vote is somewhat wasted. In other words, SMP leads to strategic voting behaviour that systematically penalizes less competitive, smaller parties (Blais and Nadeau 1996; Cox 1997, 98). Duverger also proposed the hypothesis that proportional representation (PR) systems favour multi-partyism (1951, 269). Recent tests of this hypothesis have provided evidence of such a tendency toward multipartyism in PR systems by showing that strategic voting decreases as district magnitude increases (Cox 1997; Willey 1998). Although all these institutional factors are certainly important to consider in a cross-national analytical context, they are all constant in the specific case of the postwar Canadian federal system. In fact, that federal third parties have been able to garner significant electoral support despite the use of SMP is evidence enough that other factors are likely at play behind their varying levels of success (Cairns 1968).

In addition to institutional variables, the extant literature has highlighted a series of non-institutional factors that might partly explain the ebbs and flows in third-party voting. Some authors have argued that the emergence of new issues, such as immigration and the environment, accounts for the rise of new (either green or radical right) political parties, especially in European countries, since the 1980s (Kitschelt 1995; Inglehart 1998; Golder 2003). Value change, often associated with declining public trust and rising discontent toward governing institutions, has also been identified as a determinant of third-party success in recent decades (Peterson and Wrighton 1998; Hetherington 1999; Bélanger 2004a; Bélanger and Nadeau 2005; Bélanger and Aarts 2006). Yet other scholars have emphasized the role of party strategies and rhetoric in explaining the success of minor parties (Jenkins 2002; Mair, Müeller, and Plasser 2004), including the substantial role of mainstream party behaviour in this dynamic (Meguid 2008; Hirano and Snyder 2007). Party organization and charismatic leadership have also been proposed as key variables of third-party success (Gagnon 1981; Bell 1993).

In the more specific case of Canada, some scholars have focused on the role of regional political cultures in determining vote patterns (Blais 1973; Simeon and Elkins 1974; Brym 1979; Wiseman 1981; Gidengil 1990; Leuprecht 2003). It has been argued that people living in the Atlantic provinces are more traditional and tend to support mainstream parties more, whereas people in the western provinces have always been more sensitive to populism and have had a greater tendency to support non-mainstream populist parties.

Yet another important body of Canadian literature has focused on the impact of various structural conditions on third-party support. The main condition that has been examined has to do with the economy. An early study by Macpherson (1953) emphasized the role of social class and economic structures in accounting for the emergence of non-traditional radical parties such as the United Farmers of Alberta and the Social Credit Party in the 1920s and 1930s. According to Macpherson, the first of two main conditions for the rise of these parties was the quasi-colonial relationship between Alberta and the country's eastern region at the beginning of the twentieth century, when Alberta was mostly treated as a simple peripheral economic region. This relationship engendered a long-term feeling of alienation toward the Liberal and Conservative Parties of Alberta, which were seen, especially by the farmers, as political instruments of power controlled by Ontario's and Quebec's manufacturing and financial elites. The second condition was the relative class homogeneity among the group of Alberta farmers that started this protest movement and formed those new political parties. Because they shared similar economic interests, this "petty bourgeois" class of agricultural producers was easily able to organize itself politically and to defend its interests against the menace of imperialism.

The work of Pinard (1971) has also looked at economic grievances and the party system's lack of competitiveness as determinants of the rise of Social Credit in Quebec in the 1960s. Of particular importance to our discussion is the presence of specific grievances held against the government among some segments of the electorate. Such grievances are often economic in nature, but they can also be political, ethnic, linguistic, class, regional, or something else. What is important is that these grievances result from "gaps created between a group's expectations and its actual conditions" (Pinard 1971, 119), thus creating readiness among dissatisfied voters to vote against the government in an attempt to improve their conditions. According to Pinard, this is exactly what happened in 1962 in Quebec, where the rural population experienced serious economic hardship and massively voted for Social Credit instead of the traditional federal parties. Pinard's theoretical framework has often been criticized in the past, but it is worth noting that these criticisms were mainly targeted at his claim regarding the impact of one-party dominance (Blais 1973; White 1973). Only Michaud (1999) and Bélanger (2004b) have somewhat questioned his other main argument about the relevance of economic grievances in accounting for the rise of third parties (this criticism will be addressed in the conclusion to this chapter).

According to both Macpherson (1953) and Pinard (1971), then, economic deterioration in a province can sometimes act as a powerful mobilizing factor against the system's mainstream parties (see also Rosenstone, Behr, and Lazarus 1996 for a similar US-based account). Although these authors' respective works have received significant attention from scholars, few studies have actually attempted to confirm, generalize, or update their findings. A recent noteworthy attempt is by Perrella (2005). In his study, which covers the period 1979-2000, he finds that federal third parties benefit from long-term economic hardship. He interprets this phenomenon as evidence in support of Lipset's (1959) claim that generalized affluence (a healthy economy) is a key determinant of government stability and legitimacy in worldwide democracies. More precisely, from a voter's point of view, not benefiting enough from overall economic development and thus being somewhat "left out" of society over the long term are expected to lead to frustration and protest and a search for an alternative that could change the political system. Hence, third parties become attractive options to economically discontented voters because of their "non-mainstream" status: these parties hold the promise of doing things differently because they are outsiders to the current governing elite and system.

Perrella (2005) illustrates this dynamic of discontent by highlighting the impact of long-term (as opposed to short-term) economic hardship on non-mainstream party support. It is important to note that the hypothesized effect of economics on third-party voting is not simply economic voting theory in reverse. As explained more at length in Anderson's chapter (this volume), the literature on economic voting expects that the incumbent party is sanctioned or rewarded for short-term economic conditions. The time horizon of traditional economic voting studies is thus relatively short, typically a year or a full government mandate at the most. If we enlarge this perspective and consider both a longer time horizon (that is, the long-term evolution of economic conditions) and support for parties other than simply the incumbent party, then a different sort of dynamic should be observed. A protest vote for non-mainstream parties that would be associated with bad economic conditions has to be grounded mainly in the perception of being enduringly disadvantaged compared with the wealthier portion of the population and of being systematically penalized by the society's current economic structure (for example, globalization and free trade affecting specific working areas). If such is the case, then we would expect the electoral fate of third parties to hinge more on long-term than on short-term economic decline.

Thus, what the above stream of research suggests is that long-term economic grievances lead some voters to turn toward non-mainstream party alternatives, mainly because they are distrustful of the ability of the mainstream opposition to improve the situation significantly. The long period is crucial in that discontented voters have had the time to try other, more mainstream, party alternatives before finally deciding to abandon the latter completely and try their chances with non-mainstream parties. In keeping with this literature, our main theoretical expectation in this chapter is thus that, as economic conditions deteriorate (improve) over the long term, support for third parties increases (decreases) in Canada.

In further examining the relationship between macroeconomic conditions and third-party support, we improve on past efforts in a number of ways. First, we wish to extend the time period previously examined in the Canadian literature. Perrella (2005), referring to work done by Teixeira and Rogers (2000), argues that the 1980s and 1990s were decades during which class divides were particularly salient following the economic crisis and restructuring of the 1970s. Hence, it is during these two decades that we should observe increased economic grievances and voter resentment. Yet both Macpherson (1953) and Pinard (1971) documented similar dynamics between economic grievances and third-party votes in earlier parts of the twentieth century, so we can expect Perrella's findings to hold for a longer time period. Second, to extend that period, we need to rely on an empirical indicator of macroeconomic conditions that is different from the ones used so far – mostly the unemployment and labour force participation rates. Disposable income might be such an alternative measure, as we will see. Third, previous studies have focused entirely on local (provincial) economic conditions. We currently do not know whether national-level economics also exert a significant pull on third-party support, nor do we know which level (national or provincial) exerts the strongest influence on the vote. Light needs to be shed on these questions, especially given that recent work on Canadian economic voting has indicated that federal incumbents appear to be judged more on their national economic performance than on the provincial state of the economy (Gélineau and Bélanger 2005).

Methodology

Our data analyses use a pooled cross-sectional time-series design. To fully investigate the impact of economic conditions on third-party voting, we need to analyze it over a long period of time. Hence, we examine trends in third-party support in Canada over a period of sixty-six consecutive years (1940-2006). The analysis is performed on a data set that includes for each province the results of all twenty-one federal elections held in Canada between 1940 and 2006.

The use of provincially pooled federal voting data has three distinct advantages. From a statistical standpoint, it allows for more degrees of freedom in the model estimation. In addition, it allows us to evaluate the extent to which provincial economic performance has an effect on the federal vote in each province. Finally, it faithfully reproduces Perrella's (2005, 345) own research design.

The dependent variable is the total (aggregate) percentage of the vote received by federal third parties in each province. This operationalization of the dependent variable is similar to that adopted by Perrella (2005) and by Rosenstone, Behr, and Lazarus (1996) in their longitudinal study of third-party support in the United States. We prefer it to an alternative that would use the percentage of support for each third party individually in each election (Harmel and Robertson 1985; Willey 1998) because we are mainly interested in the *global* impact of macroeconomic conditions on third-party voting *in general*. Political parties are classified as "mainstream" or "third" according to the definition of third party that we adopted at the outset of the chapter: that is, the third-party vote is the total number of votes not going to either the Liberal Party or the (Progressive) Conservative Party.[2] For the purposes of comparison, we also use the provincial percentage of the vote received by the incumbent party as an additional dependent variable. All provincial-level federal election data were compiled from Gagnon and Tanguay (2007, 526-46).

The main independent variables are aggregate measures of interelection economic performance at both the national and the provincial levels. Our indicator of macroeconomic condition is the annual percentage change in real personal disposable income per capita.[3] Given that quarterly or monthly time-series provincial data for this indicator are available on a systematic basis only for the post-1960s period, we decided to rely on annual data instead. By doing so, we can extend our time-series as far back as the mid-1920s. For Canada, income is by far the longest macroeconomic time-series available, as other indicators such as unemployment are available only for the post-Second World War period. The income data were obtained from Statistics Canada.

To compute the change in disposable income for the year prior to the election – our variable of *short-term* income change – we weighted the annual income data for the month in which the specific federal election occurred.[4] The choice of 1940 as the starting year for our analyses is determined by the need also to estimate the impact of *long-term* income change on third-party support. We measure long-term economic change over a ten-year period (current year minus ten years prior).[5] Since disposable income is the economic indicator that we adopt in this chapter, and since this indicator is available in Canada starting only in 1926, we cannot start our analysis before the first federal election held after 1936 – hence the 1940 election as our starting point. In comparison, Perrella's indicator of labour force participation rate is available only starting in 1966. Using income instead of the latter effectively allows us to triple the number of observations previously examined by Perrella.

In addition to these indicators of macroeconomic conditions, all of our models include three regional dichotomous (or dummy) variables: one for the Atlantic provinces, one for the western provinces, and one for Quebec.[6] These variables allow us to test for regional differences in political cultures that might partly account for third-party voting, as some of the literature reviewed above has suggested. Two other dummy variables are also added to the models: one for the 1945 election and another for the 1993 election. These variables aim to capture the impact of specific political events on federal election outcomes. The first event is the conscription crisis of 1944; the second event is the demise of the Meech Lake constitutional accord in the early 1990s. These two "national crises" created a favourable climate for the expression of political grievances in the 1945 and 1993 federal elections, especially in Quebec but in some other provinces as well.

Table 7.1

Combined effects of short-term and long-term income change on federal incumbent and third-party vote (1979-2000)

	Incumbent		Third parties		Incumbent		Third parties	
Provincial income								
Short term	1.74*	(0.69)	-0.83	(0.84)				
Long term	0.03	(0.05)	-0.32***	(0.07)				
National income								
Short term					2.26*	(0.99)	-1.58	(1.20)
Long term					0.05	(0.06)	-0.41***	(0.07)
Atlantic	0.12	(3.19)	-5.32*	(2.08)	0.46	(3.26)	-8.89***	(2.51)
Quebec	-0.68	(6.35)	7.89	(4.90)	-0.24	(6.29)	5.00	(4.83)
West	-9.50**	(3.52)	19.47***	(2.54)	-9.51**	(3.69)	17.66***	(2.84)
Meech	-12.14***	(3.27)	-0.63	(4.14)	-8.98*	(4.38)	-4.28	(5.25)
Constant	35.26***	(3.46)	33.98***	(2.35)	33.06***	(4.26)	39.60***	(3.85)
R^2	0.47		0.64		0.44		0.64	
N	70		70		70		70	

Note: Entries are unstandardized OLS coefficients with panel-corrected standard errors in parentheses.
* $p \leq .1$; ** $p \leq .01$; *** $p \leq .001$

Results

All of our statistical analyses rely on ordinary least squares (OLS) regressions with panel-corrected standard errors to address potential problems of heteroskedasticity.[7] In a first step, to assess whether income is as valid an indicator of macroeconomic conditions as unemployment or labour force participation rate, we reproduce Perrella's (2005) findings by looking at the impact of income change over the shorter period 1979-2000, the same time period examined by Perrella. Table 7.1 presents these results, testing for the joint effects of short- and long-term income change on support for the incumbent party and for third parties separately, using national- and provincial-level measures in turn. One might be concerned that including two different measures of the same indicator might introduce multicollinearity problems in the regression estimation, but such is not the case here: our short- and long-term measures of income change only correlate at .29 (at the national level) and .34 (at the provincial level), not enough to create estimation problems.

These first results broadly confirm Perrella's (2005) conclusions. Short-term income change significantly affects support for the incumbent party, whereas long-term income change (that is, change measured over a period of ten consecutive years) is significantly related to third-party vote share in the seven federal elections examined. The effects are also in the expected direction, with the coefficient sign being positive in the case of incumbent vote and negative in the case of third-party support. And in accordance with Perrella's findings, short-term economic change has no impact on third-party vote, and long-term economic hardship has no impact on incumbent vote. It thus appears that the use of disposable income as an alternative measure of macroeconomic conditions is warranted.

Consider the substantial findings. Looking first at the effect of provincial-level income change, a 1 percentage point increase in disposable income per capita during the twelve months prior to a federal election yields an increase of 1.74 percentage points in federal incumbent support at the provincial level; a 1 percentage point increase in the same indicator over the ten years prior to an election leads to a decrease of about 0.32 percentage point in total third-party vote share. The economic effect appears to be smaller in the case of long-term income change, but one should keep in mind that this variable's range is about nine times greater than that of short-term income change, due to the much longer time span over which income change occurs.

Turning our attention next to the results obtained using national-level income indicators, we can see that their effects are slightly greater than those obtained with the provincial-level ones (2.26 percentage points compared with 1.74 percentage points for short-term effect on incumbent support and −0.41 compared with −0.32 for long-term effect on third-party support). In other words, when it comes to predicting provincial vote shares for federal incumbents and third parties, national economics appear to be slightly better than provincial economics, in both cases.

Variables other than the economy also affect aggregate federal vote patterns in Canada. As expected from the literature on regional political cultures in Canada, the Atlantic provinces display significantly less support for non-mainstream parties (between 5 and 8 percentage points less, depending on the model), whereas the western provinces provide significantly more support to them (about 17-19 percentage points more than in Ontario, our reference category in the models). The west also provides about 9 percentage points less support to the incumbent party over that period (mainly the Liberal Party). Finally, the Meech Lake constitutional crisis significantly decreased voting for the incumbent party (the Progressive Conservatives in the 1993 federal election) but had no independent impact on third-party vote share, everything else being equal. Although the western provinces variable appears to explain more variance in these models than the economic variables, a look at the standardized regression coefficients (that is, the beta weights, not shown in the table) actually indicates that the economy's impact on third-party support is comparable in size to that of the western dummy. Indeed, the beta weights for long-term income change and for the west are −0.40 and 0.54, respectively, when using provincial-level data (second column's model); they are −0.42 and 0.49, respectively, when using national-level data (fourth column's model).

It remains to be seen whether these various results hold when we estimate the effect of the economy and other variables over the much longer, sixty-six-year time period. Table 7.2 thus re-estimates our aggregate vote models for all twenty-one federal elections held in Canada between 1940 and 2006. The number of observations in this table almost triples, from 70 to 207. Federal election outcome data are missing for the province of Newfoundland and Labrador between 1940 and 1949 (three elections) since this province entered Canadian federation only in 1949.

The time-series cross-sectional regression results from Table 7.2 confirm that disposable income change significantly affects federal party vote shares in the Canadian provinces. As expected, third-party support continues to be affected by long-term income change, not by short-term income change. In other words, long-term economic hardship does explain third-party voting over the longer, sixty-six-year time period, confirming Perrella's (2005) earlier finding. The impact of long-term income change is statistically significant at the $p \leq .01$ level or better and is observed with both provincial and national income change, although the effect is almost twice as large with the latter indicator (-0.18 instead of −0.10). Put differently, each one-unit decrease in national disposable income levels results in an increase of nearly 0.2 percentage points in third-party support, compared with an increase of 0.1 percentage points due to provincial income change. Just like the results of Table 7.1, what these new results indicate is that, when it comes to estimating the impact of macroeconomic conditions on federal third-party vote shares, national-level economics are slightly better predictors than provincial-level ones. The results also suggest that, although Table 7.1's findings are broadly confirmed here, the effects of income change on third-party support over

Table 7.2

Combined effects of short-term and long-term income change on federal incumbent and third-party vote (1940-2006)

	Incumbent		Third parties		Incumbent		Third parties	
Provincial income								
Short term	0.12	(0.18)	-0.31	(0.22)				
Long term	0.01	(0.03)	-0.10**	(0.04)				
National income								
Short term					-0.03	(0.33)	-0.54	(0.37)
Long term					0.03	(0.04)	-0.18***	(0.04)
Atlantic	2.65	(1.67)	-7.75***	(1.76)	2.73	(1.67)	-8.95***	(1.80)
Quebec	2.16	(3.64)	8.45*	(3.48)	2.22	(3.64)	7.87*	(3.50)
West	-9.52***	(1.81)	17.61***	(1.95)	-9.41***	(1.83)	16.92***	(1.99)
Meech	-20.24***	(3.24)	8.68*	(3.67)	-20.34***	(3.43)	6.39*	(3.80)
Conscription	-0.64	(4.01)	14.38**	(4.54)	-1.71	(4.16)	18.29***	(4.65)
Constant	42.01***	(1.65)	23.44***	(1.72)	41.69***	(2.00)	26.97***	(2.15)
R^2	0.36		0.56		0.36		0.57	
N	207		207		207		207	

Note: Entries are unstandardized OLS coefficients with panel-corrected standard errors in parentheses.
* $p \leq .1$; ** $p \leq .01$; *** $p \leq .001$

the longer time period are a bit smaller than those found for the shorter, 1979-2000 period (a pattern that we briefly address in our concluding discussion).

Table 7.2 also reveals the continued impact of other, non-economic factors on aggregate third-party voting. All three regional variables have a statistically significant impact: the Atlantic provinces vote about 7-8 percentage points less for third parties than Ontario (the reference category), whereas Quebec and the western provinces vote about 7-8 and 16-17 percentage points more, respectively. Quebec has strongly supported some non-mainstream federal parties, such as the Bloc Populaire in the 1940s and the Social Credit in the 1960s, which accounts for the now significant impact of the Quebec dummy variable over the longer time period. Finally, the two national crisis dummy variables also have a significant impact on third-party voting. This finding confirms that the 1945 and 1993 federal elections were blips that saw third-party support rise sharply following the conscription and Meech Lake crises. Yet it is important to keep in mind that, after controlling for all these regional and political variables, long-term economic hardship does exert a statistically significant effect on non-mainstream voting, as was explained above.[8]

The one difference from our (and Perrella's [2005]) previous results is that here, in Table 7.2, incumbent party vote share is not affected by income levels at all. In fact, the only variables that are significant predictors of incumbent vote in this second table are the western region and the Meech Lake crisis, both affecting incumbent support negatively, as in our previous table. This lack of a traditional economic voting effect over the longer time period is confirmed when we compare the R-squared values of the incumbent voting models of Tables 7.1 and 7.2: they drop sharply in the second table, going from 0.47 (or 0.44 for the national economy model) to 0.36. In other words, the proportion of explained variance in incumbent support is much lower when the model is estimated over the longer, sixty-six-year time period.[9]

Conclusion

Looking at the 1940-2006 period in Canada, our study shows that long-term economic hardship partially explains the level of provincial support received by federal third parties, as Perrella (2005) and others have argued. It also indicates that, contrary to Perrella's expectation, this relationship is not necessarily a modern phenomenon that should be observed only after the economic shakeups of the 1970s, although the economic effects that we uncovered appear to be slightly smaller than those found for the shorter, twenty-year period. Our findings also suggest that disposable income levels are as good an indicator of macroeconomic conditions as the measures used in studies having previously examined the relationship between economic hardship and third-party rise. That being said, our analyses indicate that national-level income changes are related more strongly to third-party support than local (or provincial) income changes, congruent with some of the more recent findings on Canadian economic voting (Gélineau and Bélanger 2005).

In addition, our findings show that political variables are very important in accounting for third-party support in Canada. Distinct regional political cultures partly explain why non-mainstream federal parties have been more successful over time in the west and Quebec than in Ontario and the Atlantic provinces. Also, some political events have had substantial impacts on third-party voting at specific elections. Our results indicate that this has been true of the two "national crises" associated with the conscription crisis in the 1940s and the failed constitutional talks of the early 1990s. These events led to important short-term political grievances, paving the way for the electoral success of a few (often regional) third parties. Yet one should recall that the economy's impact remains significant and important in size compared with that of these various political variables.

We must note that, when reproducing Perrella's (2005) findings for the longer, sixty-six-year time period, we also observed a lack of traditional economic voting effects. That is, we did not find a significant impact of short-term economic conditions on incumbent support between 1940 and 2006. This result contrasts with the findings of Perrella (covering the period 1979-2000) and those presented by Anderson in his chapter in this volume (examining economic voting at the aggregate level between 1968 and 2006). We believe that the most compelling explanation for this lack of effect is that traditional economic voting in Canada might simply have become more prominent in recent decades. That is, it might have slowly started to emerge in the 1960s and 1970s, which explains why Perrella, Anderson, and others are able to capture this effect and why it vanishes when we extend the period of study back several more decades. Whatever the case might be, this intriguing phenomenon is beyond the scope of this chapter and warrants a separate, closer examination.[10]

Although we have been able to establish the presence of a significant and long-lasting link between long-term economic hardship and third-party voting, these conclusions must be read with two caveats in mind. First, our study has been conducted at the aggregate level of analysis, which makes it somewhat difficult to take into account the impacts of all other potential explanations of third-party support. Because factors related to value change and political party agency are difficult to operationalize systematically at the aggregate level, especially over a long period of time, we have had to focus on macroeconomic conditions, regionalism, and a few political events in the current study. Yet looking at this particular set of explanatory variables has allowed us to explore further the extent to which the economy has played a role in the success of third parties in Canadian federal elections held since 1940.

Second, two existing studies have failed to uncover a significant effect of economic grievances on federal third-party support. Michaud (1999) found no relationship between the Reform Party's district-level support and local unemployment rates at the time of the 1993 federal election. And consistent with Michaud's results, Bélanger (2004b) found that respondents to the 1993 Canadian Election Study (CES) survey who said that their personal financial situation had gotten worse in the year prior to the election, and who blamed the policies of the federal government for their situation, were not more likely to vote for either the Reform Party or the Bloc Québécois in that election. He found that support for both formations was instead linked to political grievances that rested on feelings of regional alienation exacerbated in Quebec and the west in the wake of the Meech Lake and Charlottetown constitutional debacles. These two studies looked at only one case, the 1993 election. Although this case might be exceptional in several ways, it nonetheless serves as a reminder that the economy cannot be expected to play a significant role in federal voting behaviour in all elections, all the time. But as this chapter has illustrated, we can conclude that, generally, long-term economic decline can determine third-party support in specific and predictable ways.

Acknowledgments

This study benefited from the financial support of the Social Sciences and Humanities Research Council of Canada. We thank Eugénie Dostie-Goulet, Alexandra Wilton, the editors and reviewers, and the other workshop participants for their comments, as well as Jessica Trisko and Sheena Bell for their research assistance.

Notes

1 The term "third party" originally comes from the United States, where it refers to a party other than the two major parties, the Democrats and the Republicans. This origin also explains why these parties are often referred to as "minor parties" as well. Laurent (1997) finely illustrates the degree to which a definition of "small parties" based on quantitative indicators such as votes and seats (for example, a party that "finishes" third or worse) leads to complex and often inconsistent classifications.

2 Perrella (2005) uses a logged version of third-party vote share in his analyses. We re-estimated our own models using a logged dependent variable, and our main conclusions remained unaffected. For ease of interpretation, we decided to present the results obtained with the untransformed version of the third-party vote variable.

3 Real personal disposable income per capita is the estimated income that a person has at her or his disposal for consumption after correction for inflation.

4 We calculated the weighted indicator on the basis of the following formula: $\rho = [\rho_{(t-1)} * (12-\sigma_{(t)})/12] + [\rho_{(t)} * (\sigma_{(t)}/12)]$, where "$\rho$" is the annual disposable income measure, "σ" the month of the election, and "t" the election year. For

example, if an election was held in March 1997, we would multiply the 1996 annual income measure by 9/12 and add it to the 1997 annual measure multiplied by 3/12.

5　We choose ten years as the time period for long-term economic grievances to manifest mainly because we want to remain faithful to Perrella's (2005, 347) original coding decisions. To measure long-term, as opposed to short-term, economic hardship, it is important to adopt a time period that is long enough to cover more than one government mandate; a ten-year gap seems to be a reasonably long period to capture that phenomenon. As a validation test, we re-estimated our models using a fifteen-year gap, and the results were very similar to those presented herein.

6　Atlantic provinces include Newfoundland and Labrador, Prince Edward Island, Nova Scotia, and New Brunswick. Western provinces include Manitoba, Saskatchewan, Alberta, and British Columbia.

7　This procedure is the same as the one used by Gélineau and Bélanger (2005) in their recent study of federal and provincial economic voting in Canada. The use of OLS with our time-series cross-sectional data is validated given that Fisher's test results for panel unit root reveal that our time-series are all stationary. We should also note that all of the results presented in this section have been re-estimated by including a lag of the dependent variable on the right-hand side of the equations; since our substantive results remained unaffected, we decided to leave the lagged dependent variable out of the models presented here. In his original study, Perrella (2005) also does not include a lagged measure of the dependent variable. An additional reason for not including a lagged dependent variable in OLS regression models is provided by Keele and Kelly (2006), who demonstrate that, in many circumstances, such a procedure causes the coefficients of the explanatory variables to be biased downward.

8　Again, an examination of the standardized regression coefficients (not shown) suggests that the economy's effect remains substantial compared with that of the western provinces variable, although the difference between the two variables' impacts is not as small as it was for the shorter, 1979-2000 period. The beta weights for long-term economic change and for the west are –0.17 and 0.52, respectively, with provincial-level data; they are –0.25 and 0.50, respectively, with national-level data. As a further comparison, the beta weights for the economy are similar in magnitude to those obtained for the conscription variable in these models, another important factor included here.

9　In this chapter, we have treated third-party support as a unidimensional variable. What would happen if we were to disaggregate our dependent variable according to whether third parties are ideologically from the left or the right or are regional as opposed to national in stature? Preliminary findings seem to suggest that third parties of the right benefit more from long-term economic decline than those of the left and that regional third parties benefit more from it than national ones. Such results, and the possible reasons for them, are the subject of a separate investigation that we are currently conducting.

10　Additional analyses of our data show that short-term economic voting emerges as a significant factor in incumbent support in the early 1960s. For assessments of the variation of economic voting over time in Canadian federal elections, see Guérin and Nadeau (1998) as well as Bélanger and Gélineau (2010).

References

Bélanger, Éric. 2004a. "Antipartyism and Third-Party Vote Choice: A Comparison of Canada, Britain, and Australia." *Comparative Political Studies* 37, 9: 1054-78.

–. 2004b. "The Rise of Third Parties in the 1993 Canadian Federal Election: Pinard Revisited." *Canadian Journal of Political Science* 37, 3: 581-94.

–. 2007. "Third Party Success in Canada." In *Canadian Parties in Transition*, 3rd ed., ed. Alain-G. Gagnon and A. Brian Tanguay, 83-109. Peterborough, ON: Broadview Press.

Bélanger, Éric, and Kees Aarts. 2006. "Explaining the Rise of the LPF: Issues, Discontent, and the 2002 Dutch Election." *Acta Politica* 41, 1: 4-20.

Bélanger, Éric, and François Gélineau. 2010. "Does Perceived Competence Matter? Political Parties and Economic Voting in Canadian Federal Elections." *Journal of Elections, Public Opinion, and Parties* 20, 1: 83-101.

Bélanger, Éric, and Richard Nadeau. 2005. "Political Trust and the Vote in Multiparty Elections: The Canadian Case." *European Journal of Political Research* 44, 1: 121-46.

Bell, Edward. 1993. *Social Classes and Social Credit in Alberta*. Montreal: McGill-Queen's University Press.

Blais, André. 1973. "Third Parties in Canadian Provincial Politics." *Canadian Journal of Political Science* 6, 3: 422-38.

Blais, André, and R. Kenneth Carty. 1991. "The Psychological Impact of Electoral Laws: Measuring Duverger's Elusive Factor." *British Journal of Political Science* 21, 1: 79-93.

Blais, André, and Richard Nadeau. 1996. "Measuring Strategic Voting: A Two-Step Procedure." *Electoral Studies* 15, 1: 39-52.

Brym, Robert J. 1979. "Political Conservatism in Atlantic Canada." In *Underdevelopment and Social Movements in Atlantic Canada*, ed. Robert J. Brym and R. James Sacouman, 59-79. Toronto: New Hogtown Press.

Cairns, Alan C. 1968. "The Electoral System and the Party System in Canada 1921-1965." *Canadian Journal of Political Science* 1, 1: 55-80.

Cox, Gary W. 1997. *Making Votes Count: Strategic Coordination in the World's Electoral Systems.* Cambridge, UK: Cambridge University Press.

Duverger, Maurice. 1951. *Les partis politiques.* Paris: Armand Collin.

Gagnon, Alain-G. 1981. "Third Parties: A Theoretical Framework." *American Review of Canadian Studies* 11, 1: 37-63.

Gagnon, Alain-G., and A. Brian Tanguay, eds. 2007. *Canadian Parties in Transition.* 3rd ed. Peterborough, ON: Broadview Press.

Gaines, Brian J. 1999. "Duverger's Law and the Meaning of Canadian Exceptionalism." *Comparative Political Studies* 32, 7: 835-61.

Gélineau, François, and Éric Bélanger. 2005. "Electoral Accountability in a Federal System: National and Provincial Economic Voting in Canada." *Publius: The Journal of Federalism* 35, 3: 407 24.

Gerring, John. 2005. "Minor Parties in Plurality Electoral Systems." *Party Politics* 11, 1: 79-107.

Gidengil, Elisabeth. 1990. "Centers and Peripheries: The Political Culture of Dependency." *Canadian Review of Sociology and Anthropology* 27, 1: 23-48.

Golder, Matt. 2003. "Explaining Variation in the Success of Extreme Right Parties in Western Europe." *Comparative Political Studies* 36, 4: 432-66.

Guérin, Daniel, and Richard Nadeau. 1998. "Clivage linguistique et vote économ-ique au Canada." *Canadian Journal of Political Science* 31, 3: 557-72.

Harmel, Robert, and John D. Robertson. 1985. "Formation and Success of New Parties: A Cross-National Analysis." *International Political Science Review* 6, 4: 501-23.

Hauss, Charles, and David Rayside. 1978. "The Development of New Parties in Western Democracies since 1945." In *Political Parties: Development and Decay,* ed. Louis Maisel and Joseph Cooper, 31-58. Beverly Hills: Sage.

Hetherington, Marc J. 1999. "The Effect of Political Trust on the Presidential Vote, 1968-96." *American Political Science Review* 93, 2: 311-26.

Hirano, Shigeo, and James M. Snyder Jr. 2007. "The Decline of Third-Party Voting in the United States." *Journal of Politics* 69, 1: 1-16.

Inglehart, Ronald. 1998. *Modernization and Postmodernization.* Princeton: Princeton University Press.

Jenkins, Richard W. 2002. "How Campaigns Matter in Canada: Priming and Learn-ing as Explanations for the Reform Party's 1993 Campaign Success." *Canadian Journal of Political Science* 35, 2: 383-408.

Keele, Luke, and Nathan J. Kelly. 2006. "Dynamic Models for Dynamic Theories: The Ins and Outs of Lagged Dependent Variables." *Political Analysis* 14: 186-205.

Kitschelt, Herbert. 1995. *The Radical Right in Western Europe: A Comparative Analysis.* Ann Arbor: University of Michigan Press.

Laurent, Annie. 1997. "Définir les petits partis: Le regard de l'électoraliste." In *Les petits partis: De la petitesse en politique,* ed. Annie Laurent and Bruno Villalba, 19-42. Paris: L'Harmattan.

Leuprecht, Christian. 2003. "The Tory Fragment in Canada: Endangered Species?" *Canadian Journal of Political Science* 36, 2: 401-16.

Lipset, Seymour Martin. 1959. *Political Man: The Social Bases of Politics.* Garden City, NY: Doubleday.

–. 1990. *Continental Divide: The Values and Institutions of the United States and Can-ada.* London: Routledge.

Macpherson, C.B. 1953. *Democracy in Alberta: The Theory and Practice of a Quasi-Party System.* Toronto: University of Toronto Press.

Mair, Peter, Wolfgang C. Müeller, and Fritz Plasser, eds. 2004. *Political Parties and Electoral Change: Party Responses to Electoral Markets.* Thousand Oaks, CA: Sage.

Meguid, Bonnie M. 2008. *Party Competition between Unequals: Strategies and Electoral Fortunes in Western Europe.* Cambridge, UK: Cambridge University Press.

Michaud, Denis. 1999. "L'évolution du comportement électoral fédéral entre 1984 et 1997 dans les quatre provinces de l'ouest: Une analyse des appuis au Reform Party à partir du modèle théorique de Maurice Pinard." MA thesis, Université Laval.

Perrella, Andrea M.L. 2005. "Long-Term Economic Hardship and Non-Mainstream Voting in Canada." *Canadian Journal of Political Science* 38, 2: 335-57.

Peterson, Geoff, and J. Mark Wrighton. 1998. "Expressions of Distrust: Third-Party Voting and Cynicism in Government." *Political Behaviour* 20, 1: 17-34.

Pinard, Maurice. 1971. *The Rise of a Third Party: A Study in Crisis Politics.* Englewood Cliffs, NJ: Prentice-Hall.

–. 1973. "Third Parties in Canada Revisited: A Rejoinder and Elaboration of the Theory of One-Party Dominance." *Canadian Journal of Political Science* 6, 3: 439-60.

Rosenstone, Steven J., Roy L. Behr, and Edward H. Lazarus. 1996. *Third Parties in America: Citizen Response to Major Party Failure.* 2nd ed. Princeton: Princeton University Press.

Simeon, Richard, and David J. Elkins. 1974. "Regional Political Cultures in Canada." *Canadian Journal of Political Science* 7, 3: 397-437.

Teixeira, Ruy A., and Joel Rogers. 2000. *America's Forgotten Majority: Why the White Working Class Still Matters.* New York: Basic Books.

White, Graham. 1973. "One-Party Dominance and Third Parties: The Pinard Theory Reconsidered." *Canadian Journal of Political Science* 6, 3: 399-421.

Willey, Joseph. 1998. "Institutional Arrangements and the Success of New Parties in Old Democracies." *Political Studies* 46, 3: 651-68.

Wiseman, Nelson. 1981. "The Pattern of Prairie Politics." *Queen's Quarterly* 88, 2: 298-315.

Personality Matters: The Evaluation of Party Leaders in Canadian Elections

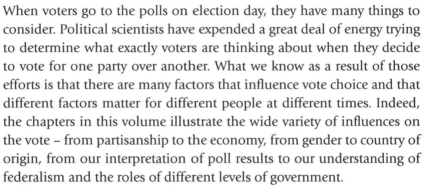

Amanda Bittner

When voters go to the polls on election day, they have many things to consider. Political scientists have expended a great deal of energy trying to determine what exactly voters are thinking about when they decide to vote for one party over another. What we know as a result of those efforts is that there are many factors that influence vote choice and that different factors matter for different people at different times. Indeed, the chapters in this volume illustrate the wide variety of influences on the vote – from partisanship to the economy, from gender to country of origin, from our interpretation of poll results to our understanding of federalism and the roles of different levels of government.

One factor that is not discussed in the other chapters, but that is a component of the Michigan (Campbell et al. 1960) and political choice (Clarke et al. 1979) models, is the impact of party leaders on vote choice. Although the impact of voters' perceptions of leaders has been examined by a number of scholars (Winham and Cunningham 1970; Brown et al. 1988; Johnston et al. 1992; Johnston 2002; Gidengil, Everitt, and Banducci 2006), the literature is not conclusive about the evaluations of party leaders and the effects of those evaluations on vote choice. Although some suggest (for example, Johnston 2002) that Canadians take the personalities of leaders into account on voting day, and that party leaders are the "superstars" of Canadian politics (Clarke et al. 1991), other studies of Canadian elections have argued that evaluations of leaders have only a weak influence on individuals' voting decisions (Blais et al. 2002). Once other factors (such as sociodemographic effects on vote choice, values, beliefs, and economic perceptions) are taken into account, leaders themselves account for very little in voters' decisions and subsequent election results.

This chapter assesses the state of the literature to date and extends and updates the analysis of the Canadian case. By examining data from the Canadian Election Studies (CES) from 1988 to 2006, the chapter assesses the evaluation of leaders' traits over time as well as the impacts of those evaluations on vote choice. Three main conclusions are drawn: first, that voters do indeed evaluate leaders' personality traits; second, that these evaluations have an impact on vote choice; and third, that these evaluations are made en masse – that is, voters do not work in a vacuum, and leaders are evaluated in comparison with one another. The chapter concludes by discussing the shortcomings in our understanding of this topic – in particular, the lack of information we have regarding the psychological mechanisms involved in leader evaluation – and suggesting directions for future research.

Theory

Is Personality Important? Why Should We Focus on Leaders?
Dating from the earliest years (Berelson, Lazarsfeld, and McPhee 1954; Campbell et al. 1960), most studies of voting behaviour have pointed to the critical role played by long-term forces: party identification, ideological beliefs, and the socioeconomic or demographic characteristics of voters. Authors suggest that who we are as people – characteristics intrinsic to socialization and personal background – affects how we vote. Thus, for example, gender affects vote choice and issue attitudes (Almond and Verba 1963; Inglehart and Norris 2000; Gidengil et al. 2003), as do partisanship (Campbell et al. 1960; Green, Palmquist, and Schickler 2002) and other sociodemographics (Conover and Feldman 1986; Bartels 1996). Contemporary scholarship continues to point to the incredible explanatory power of these variables in vote choice, issue attitudes, beliefs, and perceptions. Many of the other chapters in this volume examine variables such as religion, ethnicity, partisanship, and gender, thus contributing to a rich literature on the importance of long-term forces in elections.

Although the importance of stable and long-term forces is fundamental to understanding voting behaviour, a comprehensive look at voters' decisions must also consider "short-term" forces. Stokes, Campbell, and Miller (1958) note that short-term fluctuations in vote choice and preferences cannot really be accounted for by long-standing predispositions: gender and ethnicity do not normally change between elections, and partisanship, though it moves a little, is a fairly static and long-term identification (Green, Palmquist, and Schickler 2002; Johnston 2006) that does not really fluctuate from day to day in a campaign. Stokes, Campbell, and Miller (1958) suggest that candidates and issues can account for short-term change where long-term factors cannot. Stokes (1966) echoes these earlier comments, suggesting that party identification is not sufficient to explain shifts in vote choice, because it does not really change, whereas evaluation of leaders is constantly shifting and thus has greater potential for explaining fluctuations in the vote. Miller and Shanks (1996) support these arguments for the inclusion of short-term forces in vote models with their updated version of Campbell et al.'s (1960) "funnel of causality," the block recursive model, in which both long-term and short-term forces have their proper places in models of vote choice (see the introductory chapter for a discussion of this model).

Although all of these observations point to reasons that we ought to include evaluations of leaders in vote models, they do not necessarily explain *why* it is that voters focus on leaders in the first place. One possible reason is the media focus on party leaders and the "horse race" during election campaigns. A number of scholars have observed that media coverage of election campaigns tends to prime leaders, which has the effect of encouraging voters to base their attitudes more heavily on leaders than other factors (Mendelsohn 1993, 1994, 1996; Gidengil et al. 2000; Gidengil and Dobrzynska 2003). The idea is that since the media focus so heavily on leaders' personalities – what the leaders are doing, what they are saying, and where they are in the "race" – it is natural that, as consumers of the media, voters are also likely to focus heavily on party leaders when making their choices at the ballot box.

In addition to the effects of media priming, it has been suggested that deciding how we feel about others is a relatively "easy" process. People evaluate others regularly in everyday life: Cottrell, Neuberg, and Li (2007, 2) suggest that "humans, as discriminately social creatures, make frequent judgments about others' suitability for interdependent social relations." They suggest that, as individuals, our time is limited, and we cannot devote ourselves to being friends with everyone; therefore, we must make judgments about whether or not others are worth our time. Perhaps making judgments about party leaders is much the same thing: Rahn et al. (1990) suggest that, even for those voters who are not terribly interested or involved in politics, the formation of candidate images ought to be fairly simple, since it mirrors activities that we perform on an everyday basis. We do not need to develop an entirely new skill to be able to decide how we feel about others, so it is more likely that we will evaluate leaders and that those evaluations will factor into vote choice.

In addition to the "ease" or inevitability of the evaluation of leaders, and the fact that we are primed to think about leaders during election campaigns, it is conceivable that considering leaders might be a reliable way to make inferences about a candidate's future performance in office. Glass (1985) suggests that the evaluation of candidates and leaders might be a response to the complexity of political life. Circumstances might change, and a candidate might need to adopt new policies, but he or she is unlikely to be able to change his or her personality. Perhaps, then, personality is more reliable than platform or party as an indicator of how the individual will act in office. Rosenberg et al. (1986) put forth a complementary argument, suggesting that image and physical appearance matter because they provide clues about a candidate's character and fit- ness for public office. How a leader presents himself or herself provides us with some indication of the individual's ability to do the job.

Another possibility is that individuals use leaders as a "shortcut" to help them decide which party to vote for. That is, less informed voters, who lack the knowledge or political sophistication required to make voting decisions based on policy platforms and party stances on issues, decide whether or not they like the party's leader and vote for the party largely on that basis. Research by Sniderman, Brody, and Tetlock (1991) supports the idea that people can figure out what they oppose or support if they can simplify their options and that, among the less educated, af- fect (or how one feels about something or someone) plays a significant role in explaining policy preferences. You might not know a lot about a candidate, but with relative ease you can decide whether or not you like him or her, and you can therefore simplify your vote choice by acting on that feeling. Thus, there are many reasons that we might expect citizens to consider leaders when making decisions at the ballot box, and more research is needed for us to understand the evaluation process.

More Important than Just "Feelings": Why We Should Focus on Personality Traits
Blais et al. (2002, 165) note that "an election is not just about choosing which party will form the government, it is also about who is going to be Prime Minister." As such, it seems reasonable that Canadians will

think about leaders when deciding which party to vote for, since one of these individuals will get the job. Although the role of leaders in Canadian elections has been examined a number of times (Clarke et al. 1979; Brown et al. 1988; Johnston et al. 1992; Mendelsohn 1993, 1994, 1996; Stewart and Carty 1993; Blais and Boyer 1996; Gidengil et al. 2000; Blais et al. 2002; Johnston 2002; Gidengil and Dobrzynska 2003; Gidengil, Everitt, and Banducci 2006), the effect of voters' evaluations of the specific traits and characteristics held by leaders is still not clear.

The bulk of the discussion on the impact of leaders has focused on the impact of overall attitudes toward leaders on election outcomes: essentially, the net effect of "feeling thermometers" on vote choice. And though some scholars have looked at the role of traits themselves in the Canadian context (Johnston et al. 1992; Johnston 2002; Gidengil, Everitt, and Banducci 2006), a more systematic assessment of the role of personality traits is necessary to really understand both how people evaluate leaders' personalities and how those evaluations affect vote choice. Furthermore, a look at the evaluations of actual traits rather than feeling thermometers might help to clarify the role of leaders in elections since the thermometer is not only a very general measure but also might not be the most reliable source of information about voters' evaluations of leaders. As Johnston (2002, 174) notes, the feeling thermometer "carries too much nonpersonality freight. Even with party identification and the like controlled, it is still infused with party, group and policy judgments." By focusing solely on traits, we might get a more precise picture of what voters think about when they evaluate leaders and how those evaluations affect vote choice. Furthermore, we can gain greater insight into which traits matter most – traits relating to intelligence and strength of leadership or traits relating to honesty and trustworthiness?

There is a rich literature on "person perception" in cognitive and political psychology. Scholars in these fields have spent years assessing personality traits of individuals and leaders, and how as a society we perceive those traits in others, as part of a larger study of the human psyche and our perceptions of our environment. MacRae and Bodenhausen (2000) suggest that the perception of personality traits in others takes place as part of general "categorical thinking" by individuals. That is, to make the world ordered, meaningful, and predictable, we think categorically about others. Much of this thinking is subconscious and the result of the way in which our minds store and process information. Cognitive psychology research suggests that information is stored in our minds in what are known as "schemata" (Lau and Sears 1986). Schemata, the plural form of "schema," can be likened to a series of hierarchical storage cabinets in our minds, each cabinet essentially reflecting a different category or topic, with links between categories.

Each schema in the mind affects the way in which we gather new information as well as how we call up old information (Lodge and Hamill 1986). Scholars have suggested that schemata play an important role in how we perceive and interact with the world: they provide categories for labelling people, events, and places, they influence what information gets both stored in and recalled from memory, and they allow us to integrate what we already know into our interpretations of new circumstances where we lack a complete picture – essentially, in new situations, they allow us to "fill in the blanks" with information that we already have (Lodge and Hamill 1986; Conover and Feldman 1989).

It has been suggested that the process of evaluating political candidates and party leaders fits within the schemata framework. Kinder et al. (1980) suggest that voters agree on the traits that an ideal president should possess. They argue that voters then use this "presidential prototype" or schema as a shortcut to decision making. The idea is that voters apply existing categories (the prototype) to the leadership candidates and evaluate them based on the traits that an ideal candidate should possess. It is as if the voter opens up his or her filing cabinet, takes out the file labelled "presidential prototype," and checks to see whether the candidate's traits match those inside the file. A comparison is made between the individual candidates running in the election and the ideal model.

In the Canadian context, Brown et al. (1988) assess the extent to which the concept of schemata applies to how Canadian voters evaluated the traits possessed by party leaders during the 1984 federal election. They find that schemata or prototypes of leaders get used repeatedly, as voters consider the same types of factors when evaluating all of the leaders. This finding suggests that looking more closely at the role of trait evaluations in vote choice is a useful exercise, for it would allow us to get a deeper insight into the way in which voters think "categorically" about leaders. Rather than just looking at overall feelings toward a leader, by looking at traits we might gain a deeper understanding of how people evaluate leaders.

Early in the study of person perception and leadership candidates, Kinder et al. (1980) suggested that the presidential prototype consists of two main types of qualities: personality and performance. Since that time, a number of scholars have expended much effort determining the extent to which these dimensions of traits really are those that voters think about or whether traits more realistically fit into different dimensions. Over the years, scholars have suggested that voters evaluate traits in categories numbering anywhere from two to twelve (see, for example, Kinder et al. 1980; Kinder 1983, 1986; Glass 1985; Miller, Wattenberg, and Malanchuk 1986; Brown et al. 1988; Bean and Mughan 1989; Stewart and Clarke 1992; Bean 1993; Brettschneider and Gabriel 2002; and Johnston 2002), with the majority suggesting that traits fall into some combination of the following four main categories: *integrity, competence, leadership,* and *empathy.*

More recently, cross-national, over-time examination of trait evaluations in election studies suggests that it makes the most sense to think about traits as falling within two main "umbrella" dimensions: *competence* and *character* (see Bittner 2008 for a more complete review of the literature and detailed data analysis). A typology based on these two dimensions refines the existing literature: the competence dimension broadly includes traits falling into both the "leadership" and the "competence" dimensions listed above, and the character dimension includes traits that were previously thought to belong in both the "integrity" and the "empathy" dimensions. The labels themselves do not signify substantively different understandings of the ways in which voters perceive party leaders: they represent a collapsing of the four previous dimensions into two, based on patterns and correlations in the evaluations of party leaders of thirty-five different election studies.[1] Because the dimensions themselves do not change, even if the specific traits considered within them might differ slightly from year to year, looking at traits in this way allows us to consider evaluations of leaders' character and competence, regardless of the changes that have taken place in the question format. This operationalization of trait dimensions will allow us to gain a better understanding of evaluations and the impacts of those evaluations.

Methodology

As mentioned, though the specific traits might change from election study to election study, the *nature* of the traits within each dimension does not really change. Generally speaking, the competence category tends to be composed of traits related to intellect and strength of leadership, whereas traits in the character category relate to the individual's compassion, honesty, trustworthiness, and morality. Larger comparative analysis has revealed the strength of the connection between traits within each category, regardless of which country or year we look at (Bittner 2008). In short, the traits are related, and they are largely measuring aspects of the same thing, whether character or competence. When aggregated, the character dimension in Canada includes the following traits: honest, trustworthy, compassionate, moral, and can't be trusted; the competence dimension includes the traits intelligent, arrogant, competent, knowledgeable, strong leader, and weak leader.[2] All traits were coded on a 0-1 scale, with 1 representing the most positive evaluation of the leader for a particular trait, and 0 representing the most negative evaluation of the leader for the trait. These evaluations were then combined to create an index for each of the two trait dimensions. By doing this for each of the main party leaders in each of the elections in question, we can compare voters' perceptions of the party leaders along the two different trait dimensions.

To explore the role of evaluations of party leaders in the vote calculus, the analysis proceeds in two parts. The first includes an assessment of the overall trends in ratings of Canadian party leaders over time, and the second includes multivariate analysis of the impacts of leader evaluations on vote choice. If leaders matter in the vote calculus, then we ought to expect that (a) voters differentiate between leaders and (b) that evaluations will have an independent impact on vote choice in the multivariate analysis.

Results

Figures 8.1 and 8.2 track the evaluations of the trait dimensions of the leaders of the main parties over time. Figure 8.1 illustrates the differences in evaluations of the party leaders on the competence dimension. The zero line reflects the average of the evaluations of all leaders on this trait dimension in each election year, and thus the trend line for each party leader reflects how much better or worse he or she did in comparison with the mean.[3] Figure 8.2 illustrates the differences in evaluations of the party leaders on the character dimension, with the same reference point: the average rating for all leaders on this trait in each year.

As a glance at the trend lines suggests, there are some substantial differences in the way that respondents viewed the leaders of different parties on the two trait dimensions, and these differences change from year to year. Three main observations stem from an examination of the trend lines. First, respondents do indeed differentiate between party leaders

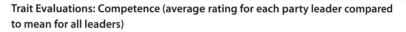

Figure 8.1

Trait Evaluations: Competence (average rating for each party leader compared to mean for all leaders)

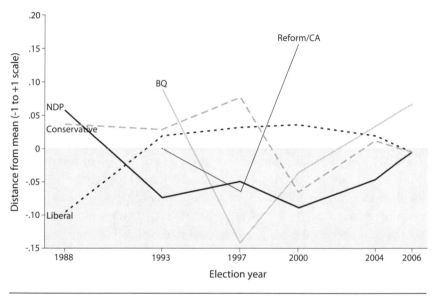

Figure 8.2

Trait Evaluations: Character (average rating for each party leader compared to mean for all leaders)

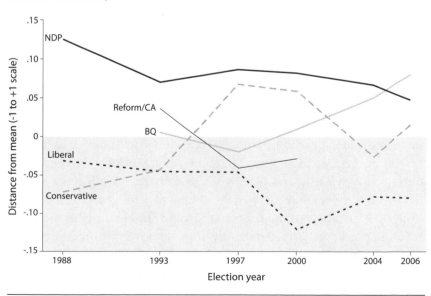

(they are not simply evaluating all Liberal leaders the same or all NDP leaders the same). Second, the data suggest that respondents differentiate between trait dimensions when they think about a particular leader: in many circumstances, a given leader was rated substantially higher or lower on one trait dimension compared with the other (respondents are not simply evaluating a particular leader positively overall). Third, the data also suggest that a single leader might be perceived differently in different election years, suggesting that perceptions can change and that, over time and in different contexts, people evaluate leaders differently.

Voters Differentiate between Party Leaders

The data suggest that respondents do a good job of differentiating between leaders and do not simply decide that all leaders of one party are the most competent or that all leaders of another party always have the most character. It does appear as though NDP leaders tend to dominate the character dimension, usually having the highest character ratings of all leaders. Even with their perceived strength in this area, it remains clear that voters do not evaluate leaders based solely on a party cue but distinguish between the individuals themselves, as in the 2006 election, when Bloc leader Gilles Duceppe had higher ratings than NDP leader Jack Layton. That voters are able to distinguish between leaders suggests that they are generally "up to the task" of leader evaluation and can make a distinction between the individual and the party as well as between one leader and the next. None of the lines is flat, and, with the exception of the NDP leaders' dominance over the character dimension (and the Liberal leaders' corresponding lack of success on this dimension), leaders generally are perceived quite differently from year to year.[4]

Tracing the Conservative leaders' ratings over time provides ample proof of the way that a leader is not simply perceived to be "a certain way" because of the party banner under which he or she is running. This party saw more leadership change over the six included in this analysis studied than any other Canadian party.[5] In 1988, Brian Mulroney was evaluated more positively on the competence dimension than John Turner, though less positively than Ed Broadbent, and he was perceived the most negatively on the character dimension. In the following election, his successor, Kim Campbell, was evaluated slightly more negatively on the competence dimension and slightly more positively on the character dimension. Jean Charest's evaluations in 1997 deviated even more substantially: Charest was evaluated the most positively among all leaders on the competence dimension, an increase of nearly 0.05 points over his predecessor, and on the character dimension he rose above the pack as well with a rating nearly 0.15 points higher than Campbell's in the previous election and fared better than all party leaders other than Alexa McDonough, leader of the NDP.

In 2000, Joe Clark's competence rating plummeted in comparison with Charest's (nearly a 0.15 point drop), placing Clark lower than almost all other leaders. His character, however, was still evaluated fairly positively, though slightly lower than that of McDonough. The year 2004 saw the emergence of the new Conservative Party, an amalgamation of the old Progressive Conservatives and the Canadian Alliance, with a new leader at its helm. Stephen Harper was evaluated more positively on the competence dimension than Clark had been, bringing his rating above the mean, though evaluations of his character were more negative than Clark's had been in the previous election. In 2006, Harper continued to lead the Conservative Party, and still we see differences in the way that he was perceived: confidence in his competence decreased, whereas the rating of his character rose since the previous election. Simply put, in each election, the leader of the Conservative Party was evaluated differently from his or her predecessor. Voters perceived differences between each individual.

Voters Differentiate between Leader Traits
In addition to being able to differentiate between individuals, voters appear to be quite capable of teasing out the different kinds of characteristics held by individual party leaders. Not a single point on a line for one of the parties in the character dimension could be superimposed over a point on a line for the same party in the competence dimension. Evaluations of the Liberal Party leaders illustrate this point.

In 1988, John Turner was evaluated more negatively on the competence dimension than he was on the character dimension (nearly a 0.07 point difference). Similarly, in 1993, Jean Chrétien received a higher than average rating on competence and a lower than average rating on character, with a spread, again, of nearly 0.07 points. The 1997 election only served to widen the gap, with a difference of nearly 0.08 points between his competence and his character ratings. In 2000, the gap widened further, with his character rating more than 0.15 points lower than his competence rating. In 2004, Paul Martin's competence rating was approximately 0.1 point higher than his character rating, and in 2006 this gap closed a bit, since even though his character rating remained similar to that of the previous election his competence rating dropped by approximately 0.03 points.

Voters do not simply decide that they either do or do not like a leader and then give him or her positive or negative ratings on both dimensions accordingly. They actually distinguish between the leader's different traits and give separate evaluations for each dimension.

Voters Evaluate the Same Leader Differently from One Election to the Next

There are a number of examples in which the same individual led a party in more than one election. The Liberals were led by Jean Chrétien in the elections of 1993, 1997, and 2000; Stephen Harper led the Conservatives in the 2004 and 2006 elections; Alexa McDonough led the NDP in the 1997 and 2000 elections; Preston Manning led the Reform Party in 1993 and 1997; and Gilles Duceppe has led the Bloc Québécois since 1997. Earlier I suggested that no line in either graph is flat. Perhaps even more interesting is that none of the segments of the lines within the reign of a single individual is flat either. The competence line for Chrétien does not move much between 1993 and 2000, and the character line for McDonough does not fluctuate much between the 1997 and 2000 elections. But even these two leaders, who received fairly similar evaluations on a single dimension from one year to the next, received wildly different evaluations from year to year on the other dimension. Evaluations of Chrétien's character plummeted between 1997 and 2000, and evaluations of McDonough's competence dropped in that same time frame.

These differences from one year to the next suggest that learning is probably taking place: voters become more familiar with the party leaders, and as they "know" them better their evaluations change accordingly. In addition to allowing voters to become more familiar with a leader, the longer the individual leads the party the more opportunities he or she has to demonstrate his or her true nature – whether we are speaking of the individual's honesty and compassion (character) or intelligence and strength of leadership (competence). Evaluations of Gilles Duceppe suggest that, as voters became more familiar with him, they saw him in a more positive light, giving him higher ratings on both trait dimensions. Similarly, as voters became more familiar with Preston Manning, they perceived him more negatively, giving him lower ratings on both dimensions. However, the bigger question is to what extent do these evaluations affect vote choice? It is to this issue that we now turn.

The Effects of Character and Competence on Vote Choice

Table 8.1 illustrates the impact of a number of variables, including evaluations of leaders' traits, on vote choice for the three main national parties, the Liberal Party, the Conservative Party, and the New Democratic Party. The table depicts odds ratios and standard errors from a logistic regression analysis, a model employed to reflect the fact that the dependent variable, vote for a particular party, is binary. The data from 1988 to 2006 were pooled, and the regression analysis was performed on all the Canadian data simultaneously rather than by year. The demographic and control variables included in the model are not shown,[6] allowing us to focus on the variables of interest.

The first column in each pair of models reflects the effect of partisanship and evaluations of the party's leader on vote choice for that party, whereas the second column also incorporates the effects of evaluations of the other two main national parties.[7] The inclusion of evaluations of the other two party leaders follows previous scholarship, which suggests that the evaluation of leaders is comparative and that we can better understand the effects of evaluations if we look at them as a group (Rahn et al. 1990; Nadeau, Niemi, and Amato 1996). A couple of key findings emerge from the analysis: first, character and competence do matter, and they matter more than a number of other variables.[8] Second, the data confirm that voters evaluate leaders as a group, comparing them with one another.

The Relative Importance of Traits and Partisanship

Table 8.1 illustrates that voters' evaluations of leaders affect vote choice, regardless of which party we look at. The first two columns present the impacts of variables on Liberal vote choice, and immediately we note the importance of ratings of the Liberal leaders' character and competence. After partisanship, evaluations of the Liberal leaders' personality traits are the most important factors influencing votes for the Liberal Party. The second column indicates that those individuals giving the Liberal leader the highest rating (a rating of 1 on the scale) on the character dimension are more than eleven times more likely to vote for the Liberal Party than those who give the leader the lowest rating (a rating of 0) on this dimension. Similarly, those giving the Liberal leader the highest rating on competence are over eight times more likely to vote for the Liberal Party than those who give the leader the lowest rating on this dimension.

Table 8.1

Effects of trait evaluations on vote choice

	Liberal vote		Conservative vote		NDP vote	
	(1)	(2)	(1)	(2)	(1)	(2)
Liberal PID	4.470 (0.305)*	4.414 (0.354)*	0.343 (0.028)*	0.509 (0.049)*	0.471 (0.046)*	0.587 (0.063)*
Conservative PID	0.319 (0.029)*	0.423 (0.047)*	4.730 (0.379)*	4.178 (0.400)*	0.180 (0.026)*	0.222 (0.034)*
NDP PID	0.352 (0.041)*	0.338 (0.045)*	0.128 (0.021)*	0.155 (0.029)*	10.622 (1.162)*	10.359 (1.212)*
Other PID	0.134 (0.021)*	0.122 (0.024)*	0.193 (0.027)*	0.155 (0.025)*	0.203 (0.044)*	0.178 (0.039)*
Liberal leader character	10.280 (1.382)*	11.675 (1.833)*		0.?3 (0.051)*		0.440 (0.089)*
Liberal leader competence	4.723 (0.647)*	8.459 (1.466)*		0.245 (0.044)*		0.472 (0.098)*
Conservative leader character		0.224 (0.035)*	9.523 (1.443)*	15.250 (2.793)*		0.342 (0.067)*
Conservative leader competence		0.632 (0.098)*	4.742 (0.748)*	11.222 (2.217)*		0.532 (0.104)*
NDP leader character		0.649 (0.109)**		0.307 (0.059)*	6.682 (1.432)*	10.881 (2.490)*
NDP leader competence		0.629 (0.102)*		0.475 (0.089)*	3.851 (0.769)*	5.158 (1.119)*
Observations	9,870	7,737	9,447	7,737	8,037	7,737
Log likelihood	-4,016.8959	-2,986.2172	-3,528.4335	-2,596.0876	-2,289.0899	-2,094.557

* significant at $p < .01$; ** significant at $p < .001$

A glance at this table might lead one to suspect that evaluations of party leaders are actually more important than partisanship, given the size of the odds ratios: in the second column, we see that Liberal partisanship has an odds ratio of 4.41, indicating that Liberal identifiers are over four times more likely to vote for the Liberal Party than non-identifiers. Contrasted with an odds ratio of 11.68 for evaluations of the Liberal leaders' character, we might think that evaluations of personality traits are more important than identification with the party. In fact, this is an artifact of the way in which the variables are coded. Party ID is a binary variable, and individuals are coded either as partisans of the party (1) or as others (0). Evaluations of character and competence are coded similarly on a 0-1 scale, but the majority of respondents evaluate the leaders somewhere in the middle, with the bulk giving ratings that fall between 0.2 and 0.7 on the 0-1 scale. Indeed, the mean Liberal leader character rating is 0.46, with a standard deviation of 0.27, whereas the mean Liberal leader competence rating is 0.57, with a standard deviation of 0.28. The comparison between those providing a rating of 0 with those providing a rating of 1, therefore, is more extreme than comparing the effects of ratings in the "real world."

To provide a more realistic idea of the relative impacts of partisanship and leader evaluations, simulations were run using Clarify.[9] With all other variables set at their means, Liberal partisans were 29 percentage points more likely to vote for the Liberal Party than were non-Liberals. In contrast, those giving the Liberal leader an evaluation on the character dimension one standard deviation above the mean were 23 percentage points more likely to vote for the Liberal Party than were those individuals giving the leader a character evaluation one standard deviation below the mean. Similarly, those giving the Liberal leader a competence evaluation one standard deviation above the mean were 20 percentage points more likely to vote for the Liberal Party than were those individuals giving the leader a rating one standard deviation below the mean.

Thus, partisanship matters, and it matters a lot. These results support over half a century of research on voting behaviour, suggesting that partisanship is the variable with the most predictive power and is most indicative of vote choice. This finding applies regardless of which party we look at, although based on Table 8.1, it appears as though partisanship has the most impact on votes for the NDP. The odds ratios are over 10 for NDP partisanship (the final two columns in Table 8.1), suggesting that partisans are more than ten times more likely to vote for the NDP than are those not claiming identification with the party.

After partisanship, evaluations of character and competence are the largest predictors of vote choice. In particular, evaluations of a given party's leader have the largest impact on vote choice for that party. If we look at each of the second columns in Table 8.1, we see that evaluations of personality traits have a substantial impact on vote choice. As mentioned, the odds ratios for evaluations of the Liberal leaders' character and competence are 11.68 and 8.46, respectively, suggesting that, even when we control for partisanship and other demographic variables, voters are between eight and twelve times more likely to vote for the Liberal Party if they rate the leader positively.

In explaining vote choice for the Conservative Party, odds ratios for evaluations of the Conservative Party leaders' character and competence are 15.25 and 11.22, respectively, suggesting that those individuals giving the Conservative leader the highest rating on character are over fifteen times likelier to vote Conservative than those individuals giving the leader the lowest rating on this dimension. In real terms, however, this means that those giving Conservative leaders a character rating one standard deviation above the mean are nearly 20 percentage points more likely to vote for the Conservative Party than those giving the leaders a rating one standard deviation below the mean. Similarly, those giving the leader a competence rating one standard deviation above the mean are nearly 19 percentage points more likely to vote for the Conservative Party than those giving the leader a rating one standard deviation below the mean on this dimension (in contrast, Conservative partisans are 25 percentage points more likely than non-Conservatives to vote Conservative).

In understanding vote choice for the NDP, it is notable that the odds ratios for partisanship are the largest, whereas the odds ratios for evaluations of the NDP leaders' character and competence are smaller than those for the evaluations of other party leaders. The odds ratios for evaluations of the NDP leaders' character and competence are 10.88 and 5.16, respectively, and running these numbers through Clarify suggests that those giving the leader a character rating one standard deviation above the mean are 8 percentage points more likely to vote NDP than those giving the leader a rating one standard deviation below the mean. Similarly, those giving the leader a competence rating one standard deviation above the mean are 6 percentage points more likely to vote NDP than those giving the leader a rating one standard deviation below the mean. In contrast, with all other variables set at their means, partisans are 35 percentage points more likely than non-NDPers to vote NDP.

Thus, partisanship is a larger indicator of vote choice than evaluations of leaders, for all three major parties, but evaluations have a discernible and substantial impact on vote choice.

In terms of vote choice, one interesting result from the above is that the impact of the leaders' traits is more substantial for both the Liberal and the Conservative Party than it is for the NDP. That the odds ratios for the NDP leaders' trait evaluations are lower in the NDP vote choice model than the Liberal or Conservative leaders' evaluations in their respective vote models points to the importance of comparison: not all leaders matter in the same way.[10] Furthermore, the odds ratios presented indicate that not all traits matter in the same way: the data indicate that evaluations of *character* affect vote choice more than evaluations of *competence*. This finding might disappoint those who would have voters consider nobler factors such as policy stances and platforms when deciding which party to vote for. It is perhaps problematic that leaders' personalities appear to matter more than issues,[11] but surely a leader's competence ought to have a larger effect on vote choice than his or her character. These data do confirm earlier results in Canada based on both fewer election studies (Johnston 2002) and comparative analysis (Bittner 2008), suggesting that character is more important than competence. Johnston et al. (1992) also find that character evaluations influence overall "feelings" toward a leader more than competence evaluations. What is not yet clear is why. It is possible that character traits are more important since they are less likely to change, whereas an individual's competence can change (through learning or experience, for example).[12] More research is needed to determine the mechanisms by which individuals evaluate leaders – it might shed some light on the issue of the relative importance of the two trait dimensions.

Voters Evaluate Leaders as a Group

Perhaps most interesting are the dynamics that we see in the transition from one column to the next for each vote model presented in Table 8.1 – that including the evaluations of the leaders of the other two major parties has an important effect on the size of the odds ratios. For all three parties, including evaluations of the other leaders has the effect of *boosting* the size of the odds ratios of the evaluations of the party's leader. Thus, in the Liberal vote model, by including evaluations of the Conservative and NDP leaders, the odds ratios of the Liberal leader evaluations increase. As the first column indicates, the odds of voting for the

Liberal Party are over ten times greater among those giving the Liberal leader a positive evaluation on character compared with those giving the leader a negative evaluation on character. When we control for evaluations of the other two leaders (the second column), the odds of voting for the Liberal Party are nearly twelve times greater among those giving the leader a positive evaluation on character compared with those giving the leader a negative evaluation on character. This result is even more pronounced when we look at evaluations of the Liberal leaders' competence, with the odds ratios nearly doubling in size when the evaluations of the other leaders are included in the model.

The same occurs for Conservative and NDP leaders in their respective vote models. In the Conservative vote model, controlling for evaluations of the Liberal and NDP leaders' personality traits boosts the size of the odds ratios of evaluations of the Conservative leaders' character and competence from 9.5 to 15.3 and 4.7 to 11.2 respectively. Similarly, controlling for Liberal and Conservative leaders' personality trait evaluations has the effect of boosting the odds ratios of evaluations of the NDP leaders' character and competence from 6.7 to 10.9 and 3.9 to 5.2 respectively. These results indicate that people consider leaders en masse: that the model is improved by the inclusion of other leaders' evaluations provides support for the idea that voters evaluate leaders in comparison with one another and that leaders are not evaluated in a vacuum.

Conclusion

Based on the data analysis presented, a number of conclusions about the role of leaders in Canadian elections can be made. First, we have observed that the evaluation of leaders' traits is an important factor incorporated into vote choice – less important than partisanship but substantially more important than sociodemographics or attitudes toward policy issues. Second, a leader's character is apparently more important than his or her competence in influencing the vote for his or her party. Third, voters evaluate leaders' traits in comparison with one another: we do not really get the full picture of how evaluations of Jean Chrétien influenced the Liberal vote in 1993, 1997, or 2000 until we consider evaluations of the other party leaders in those elections.

But do we really know all there is to know about the evaluation and impact of leaders' traits? Although the purpose of this chapter was to present the state of the literature and the current understanding of the impact of leaders in Canadian elections, there are certainly more questions that ought to be raised. This chapter set out by listing a number of potential reasons that voters evaluate leaders, none of which was actually investigated. We know that Canadian voters evaluate and consider leaders when they go to the ballot box, but we still do not really know why. Is it because they lack information about "more important" things, such as policy platforms and the state of the economy? Or is it something else? What role does voters' knowledge of politics play? Do the more knowledgeable focus more on policy issues than the less knowledgeable? Do they focus more on the leaders' competence than character? Do they perceive leaders in the same way as those who are less knowledgeable? There is substantial reason to expect that political knowledge is likely to influence evaluations of leaders as well as the impacts of those evaluations: generally, those who are more knowledgeable have been found to behave differently and hold vastly different attitudes and opinions from those who are less knowledgeable (Campbell et al. 1960; Converse 1964; Bartels 1996; Bittner 2007b; Roy 2007). An examination of the role of political knowledge would provide us with a deeper understanding of voters' evaluations of party leaders. Elsewhere (Bittner 2008), I began this process and made some headway into the impact of voters' knowledge levels on evaluations, but more research is still needed.

By exploring the role of political knowledge, we can also address the question of why individuals evaluate leaders as part of the voting process: is evaluation the result of media priming, greater "reliability" or insight gained by focusing on leaders, or a "shortcut" in decision making, because it is an "easy" process? These are very different explanations that might manifest themselves in different ways. We might expect that, if people are evaluating leaders to overcome a lack of information about policy platforms, or because doing so is simply easy, then the less informed or less knowledgeable should incorporate evaluations of leaders more substantially into their vote choices, whereas the more knowledgeable would not need to rely so heavily on leaders to make their decisions. In contrast, if voters evaluate leaders as a result of media priming or because they can gain greater insight into future performance in office, then the most knowledgeable (who, presumably, are both more exposed to the media and better positioned to use the "greater insights" gained) would incorporate the evaluations of leaders more substantially into their vote choices.

Although comparative scholarship on the evaluation of party leaders has explored the issue of political knowledge to some extent, the results remain inconclusive, and more research is needed to understand the mechanisms involved. Miller, Wattenberg, and Malanchuk (1986) find that those with higher levels of education are more likely than less informed voters to consider a candidate's personality. Cutler (2002) and Glass (1985) reach similar conclusions, suggesting that it is not only the least informed who respond to leaders' characteristics. These findings coincide with Sniderman, Brody, and Tetlock's (1991) detailed assessment of the considerations made by voters with differing levels of political sophistication. They note that affect *does* function as a shortcut for less informed voters and that, though all voters incorporate how they feel when making choices, the most informed/sophisticated do so most of all. Taken as a whole, these findings suggest that the evaluation of leaders might act as a shortcut, helping the less informed to compensate for their lack of information. However, this might not be the only explanation for why people evaluate leaders – the "media priming" and "greater insight" explanations are also supported by the results, perhaps even more so than the "shortcut" explanation. Indeed, recent work investigating these questions (Bittner 2008) suggests that this is the case, leaving room for further investigation in the future.

This chapter has provided a number of insights into the evaluation of leaders in Canada and the impact of these evaluations on vote choice. We know that voters consider and evaluate party leaders' personality traits and that they distinguish one leader from the next, both across parties and within parties over time. We also know that voters do not simply evaluate each party leader in isolation but evaluate leaders in comparison with one another. Furthermore, we know that these evaluations affect vote choice more than either sociodemographics or attitudes toward issues. Finally, it appears that a leader's character affects vote choice more than his or her competence – Canadians are giving the leader the biggest job in the country, and whether they can trust that leader to do the job really matters.

Notes
1 Organizing and conceptualizing traits into overarching dimensions is particularly valuable in that doing so facilitates longitudinal assessment of the evaluation of leaders' traits where it otherwise would not be possible. One of the main difficulties with assessing voters' evaluations of leaders' traits over time is the extent to

which surveys change over time. These changes are characteristic not only of Canadian Election Studies but also of all election studies. Question formats change, the types of traits that respondents are asked to evaluate change, and (obviously) leaders change, all of which make isolating and examining patterns in evaluations a real challenge. Although previous research suggests that question format does have an effect on our understanding of the effects of trait evaluations (Bittner 2007a), these effects are not so substantial as to preclude longitudinal analysis of traits even with the changes in question format over time.

2 As a group, these are the eleven traits included in the closed-ended trait evaluations of at least one of the Canadian Election Studies included in this analysis, and they are grouped together to form each of the dimensions.

3 Means presented are based on the average of evaluations made by all respondents, regardless of the respondent's region of residence. This means that, in the figure, the Bloc leader rating is compared with the ratings of other leaders made by respondents in all provinces, even though usually the Bloc leader was evaluated only by respondents in Quebec. Interestingly, when the same charts are generated only for Quebec, the lines do not change substantially. Although evaluations of the Bloc leader do not change (not surprising since the ratings presented are based mainly on Quebec respondents), small differences do exist for the other party leaders: the NDP and Liberal Party leaders are viewed more negatively in Quebec, on both dimensions, and the Conservative Party leader is generally viewed more positively in Quebec. The Reform Party leaders were also evaluated more positively in Quebec, on both dimensions, with one exception: Stockwell Day was seen as less competent among the Québécois than in the rest of Canada (a difference of 0.1 on the 0-1 scale).

4 It might be argued that differences in perceptions of leaders over time are the result of how the dimensions are constructed. If the specific traits included in the character and competence dimensions change, then should ratings not be expected to change as well? Perhaps, except that the dimensions are quite cohesive, even if the specific traits in the dimensions change from year to year. Furthermore, this concern overstates the extent to which traits are different in each election study. Between 1988 and 2000 in particular, there was a high degree of consistency in the traits incorporated into the CES. Sixty percent of the traits incorporated in the surveys for each year are identical, indicating that, where we see changes in the mean evaluations, they likely reflect "real" changes from year to year. Furthermore, when we track evaluations of a specific trait over time, for example, the extent to which the Liberal leader is perceived to be compassionate, ratings vary substantially, ranging from 0.17 to 0.57 (results not shown). These results support the notion that leaders are indeed perceived quite differently from year to year.

5 Brian Mulroney, Kim Campbell, Jean Charest, Joe Clark, and later Stephen Harper all led the Conservative Party over this time period.

6 Demographic and control variables include dummy variables for sex, religion, income, education, native French speakers, ethnicity, and employment status. In addition, dummies for each election year are included to control for variation in leader effects. All coding decisions are available from the author on request. The influence of these variables is substantially smaller than the impacts of the variables displayed in Table 8.1. Their odds ratios, usually statistically significant, range from 0.6 to 3.8.

7   The reader will note the exclusion of either partisanship or evaluations of the Bloc Québécois and Reform/Alliance leaders. This was done to maximize the number of elections examined and included in the model. If we were to include partisanship and evaluations of these leaders in the model, then the analysis would apply only to the 1997 and 2000 elections, because identification with the Bloc was not included in the CES until 1997, and evaluations of and identification with Reform and Alliance leaders were no longer a part of the CES after 2000 and 2004 respectively. Furthermore, when these questions were included in the CES, they often applied only to segments of the population (that is, either inside or outside Quebec), thus reducing the number of respondents included in the pooled analysis even further. When models are run including identification with the Bloc and Reform Parties, the impact of the evaluations of leaders' personality traits as presented remains nearly identical (with odds ratios only slightly smaller than those presented in Table 8.1), although the number of respondents included in the analysis is reduced dramatically.

8   Earlier analyses of the data also incorporated perceptions of the economy and attitudes toward a number of prominent issues as independent variables in the model. These analyses indicated that the impacts of these variables on vote choice, when statistically significant, were substantially smaller than the impact of either partisanship or leader evaluation, and the effect was about the same as (or smaller than) the impact of demographic variables. These variables were therefore removed from the model because their presence did not improve the fit or the explanatory power of the model, although they reduced the number of respondents included in the model.

9   See Tomz, Wittenberg, and King (2003) for more information.

10   Indeed, these results confirm the findings of others. Johnston (2002) and Bittner (2008) find that leaders have a larger impact on vote choice for "main" parties and less of an impact for third or smaller parties. Similar vote models run for other small parties either on the right or on the centre-right have equally small (and even smaller) predicted probabilities for evaluations of leaders' traits (Bittner 2008), suggesting that the leaders of larger parties may matter more.

11   Readers will recall that issues are not included in the present model but that preliminary research suggested that issues had a substantially smaller impact on vote choice than evaluations of leaders.

12   I thank one of the anonymous reviewers for offering this theory.

References

Almond, Gabriel, and Sidney Verba. 1963. *The Civic Culture: Political Attitudes and Democracy in Five Nations.* Princeton: Princeton University Press.

Bartels, Larry M. 1996. "Uninformed Votes: Information Effects in Presidential Elections." *American Journal of Political Science* 40, 1: 194-230.

Bean, Clive. 1993. "The Electoral Influence of Party Leader Images in Australia and New Zealand." *Comparative Political Studies* 26, 1: 111-32.

Bean, Clive, and Anthony Mughan. 1989. "Leadership Effects in Parliamentary Elections in Australia and Britain." *American Political Science Review* 83, 4: 1165-79.

Berelson, Bernard, Paul Lazarsfeld, and William McPhee. 1954. *Voting.* Cambridge, MA: Harvard University Press.

Bittner, Amanda. 2007a. "Competence or Charisma? The Effects of Measurement on Why Some Leaders' Traits Matter More Than Others." Paper presented at the annual meeting of the Canadian Political Science Association, Saskatoon, SK.

–. 2007b. "The Effects of Information and Social Cleavages: Explaining Issue Attitudes and Vote Choice in Canada." *Canadian Journal of Political Science* 40, 4: 935-68.

–. 2008. "Platform or Personality? Understanding the Role of Leaders in Electoral Outcomes." PhD diss., University of British Columbia.

Blais, André, and M. Martin Boyer. 1996. "Assessing the Impact of Televised Debates: The Case of the 1988 Canadian Election." *British Journal of Political Science* 26, 2: 143-64.

Blais, André, Elisabeth Gidengil, Richard Nadeau, and Neil Nevitte. 2002. *Anatomy of a Liberal Victory: Making Sense of the Vote in the 2000 Canadian Election.* Peterborough, ON: Broadview Press.

Brettschneider, Frank, and Oscar W. Gabriel. 2002. "The Nonpersonalization of Voting Behaviour in Germany." In *Leaders' Personalities and the Outcomes of Democratic Elections,* ed. Anthony King, 127-57. Oxford: Oxford University Press.

Brown, Steven D., Ronald D. Lambert, Barry J. Kay, and James E. Curtis. 1988. "In the Eye of the Beholder: Leader Images in Canada." *Canadian Journal of Political Science* 21, 4: 729-55.

Campbell, Angus, Philip E. Converse, Warren E. Miller, and Donald E. Stokes. 1960. *The American Voter.* Chicago: John Wiley and Sons.

Clarke, Harold, Jane Jenson, Lawrence LeDuc, and Jon H. Pammett. 1979. *Political Choice in Canada.* Toronto: McGraw-Hill Ryerson.

–. 1991. *Absent Mandate: Interpreting Change in Canadian Elections.* 2nd ed. Agincourt, ON: Gage Publishing.

Conover, Pamela Johnston, and Stanley Feldman. 1986. "The Role of Inference in the Perception of Political Candidates." In *Political Cognition,* ed. Richard R. Lau and David O. Sears, 127-58. Hillsdale, NJ: Lawrence Erlbaum Associates.

Conover, Pamela J., and Stanley Feldman. 1989. "Candidate Perception in an Ambiguous World: Campaigns, Cues, and Inference Processes." *American Journal of Political Science* 33, 4: 912-40.

Converse, Philip E. 1964. "The Nature of Belief Systems in Mass Publics." In *Ideology and Discontent,* ed. David E. Apter, 206-61. New York: Free Press.

Cottrell, Catherine A., Steven L. Neuberg, and Norman P. Li. 2007. "What Do People Desire in Others? A Sociofunctional Perspective on the Importance of Different Valued Characteristics." *Journal of Personality and Social Psychology* 9, 2: 208-31.

Cutler, Fred. 2002. "The Simplest Shortcut of All: Sociodemographic Characteristics and Electoral Choice." *Journal of Politics* 64, 2: 466-90.

Gidengil, Elisabeth, André Blais, Richard Nadeau, and Neil Nevitte. 2000. "Are Party Leaders Becoming More Important to Vote Choice in Canada?" Paper presented at the annual meeting of the American Political Science Association, Washington, DC.

–. 2003. "Women to the Left? Gender Differences in Political Beliefs and Policy Preferences." In *Women and Electoral Politics in Canada,* ed. Manon Tremblay and Linda Trimble, 140-59. Oxford: Oxford University Press.

Gidengil, Elisabeth, and Agnieszka Dobrzynska. 2003. "Using a Rolling Cross-Section Design to Model Media Effects: The Case of Leader Evaluations in the

1997 Canadian Election." Paper presented at the annual meeting of the American Political Science Association, Philadelphia, PA.

Gidengil, Elisabeth, Joanna Everitt, and Susan A. Banducci. 2006. "Gender and Perceptions of Leader Traits: Evidence from the 1993 Canadian and 1999 New Zealand Elections." Paper presented at the Conference on Women and Leadership, Toronto, ON.

Glass, David P. 1985. "Evaluating Presidential Candidates: Who Focuses on Their Personal Attributes?" *Public Opinion Quarterly* 49, 4: 517-34.

Green, Donald, Bradley Palmquist, and Eric Schickler. 2002. *Partisan Hearts and Minds: Political Parties and the Social Identities of Voters.* New Haven: Yale University Press.

Inglehart, Ronald, and Pippa Norris. 2000. "The Developmental Theory of the Gender Gap: Women's and Men's Voting Behaviour in Global Perspective." *International Political Science Review* 21, 4: 441-63.

Johnston, Richard. 2002. "Prime Ministerial Contenders in Canada." In *Leaders' Personalities and the Outcomes of Democratic Elections,* ed. Anthony King, 158-83. New York: Oxford University Press.

–. 2006. "Party Identification: Unmoved Mover or Sum of Preferences?" *Annual Review of Political Science* 9: 329-51.

Johnston, Richard, André Blais, Henry E. Brady, and Jean Crête. 1992. *Letting the People Decide: Dynamics of a Canadian Election.* Stanford: Stanford University Press.

Kinder, Donald R. 1983. "Presidential Traits." Pilot Study Report to the 1984 NES Planning Committee and NES Board.

–. 1986. "Presidential Character Revisited." In *Political Cognition,* ed. Richard R. Lau and David O. Sears, 233-56. Hillsdale, NJ: Lawrence Erlbaum Associates.

Kinder, Donald R., Mark D. Peters, Robert P. Abelson, and Susan T. Fiske. 1980. "Presidential Prototypes." *Political Behaviour* 2, 4: 315-37.

Lau, Richard R., and David O. Sears. 1986. "Social Cognition and Political Cognition: The Past, the Present, and the Future." In *Political Cognition,* ed. Richard R. Lau and David O. Sears, 347-66. Hillsdale, NJ: Lawrence Erlbaum Associates.

Lodge, Milton, and Ruth Hamill. 1986. "A Partisan Schema for Political Information Processing." *American Political Science Review* 80, 2: 505-20.

MacRae, C. Neil, and Galen V. Bodenhausen. 2000. "Social Cognition: Thinking Categorically about Others." *Annual Review of Psychology* 51: 93-120.

Mendelsohn, Matthew. 1993. "Television's Frames in the 1988 Canadian Election." *Canadian Journal of Communication* 19, 2: 149-71.

–. 1994. "The Media's Persuasive Effects: The Priming of Leadership in the 1988 Canadian Election." *Canadian Journal of Political Science* 27, 1: 81-97.

–. 1996. "The Media and Interpersonal Communications: The Priming of Issues, Leaders, and Party Identification." *Journal of Politics* 58, 1: 112-25.

Miller, Arthur H., Martin P. Wattenberg, and Oksana Malanchuk. 1986. "Schematic Assessment of Presidential Candidates." *American Political Science Review* 80, 2: 521-40.

Miller, Warren E., and J. Merrill Shanks. 1996. *The New American Voter.* Cambridge, MA: Harvard University Press.

Nadeau, Richard, Richard G. Niemi, and Timothy Amato. 1996. "Prospective and Comparative or Retrospective and Individual? Party Leaders and Party Support in Great Britain." *British Journal of Political Science* 26, 2: 245-58.

Rahn, Wendy M., John H. Aldrich, Eugene Borgida, and John L. Sullivan. 1990. "A Social-Cognitive Model of Candidate Appraisal." In *Information and Democratic Processes*, ed. John A. Ferejohn and James H. Kuklinski, 136-59. Urbana: University of Illinois Press.

Rosenberg, Shawn W., Lisa Bohan, Patrick McCafferty, and Kevin Harris. 1986. "The Image and the Vote: The Effect of Candidate Presentation on Voter Preference." *American Journal of Political Science* 30, 1: 108-27.

Roy, Jason. 2007. "When Less Is More: No Information versus Low Information and the Application of Heuristics in Canadian Context." Paper presented at the annual meeting of the Canadian Political Science Association, Saskatoon, SK, 30 May-1 June.

Sniderman, Paul, Richard Brody, and Philip Tetlock. 1991. *Reasoning and Choice: Explorations in Political Psychology*. New York: Cambridge University Press.

Stewart, David K., and R.K. Carty. 1993. "Does Changing the Party Leader Provide an Electoral Boost? A Study of Canadian Provincial Parties: 1960-1992." *Canadian Journal of Political Science* 26, 2: 313-30.

Stewart, Marianne C., and Harold D. Clarke. 1992. "The (Un)Importance of Party Leaders: Leader Images and Party Choice in the 1987 British Election." *Journal of Politics* 54, 2: 447-70.

Stokes, Donald E. 1966. "Some Dynamic Elements of Contests for the Presidency." *American Political Science Review* 60, 1: 19-28.

Stokes, Donald E., Angus Campbell, and Warren E. Miller. 1958. "Components of Electoral Decision." *American Political Science Review* 52, 2: 367-87.

Tomz, Michael, Jason Wittenberg, and Gary King. 2003. "Clarify: Software for Interpreting and Presenting Statistical Results." *Journal of Statistical Software* 8, 1: 1-30.

Winham, Gilbert R., and Robert B. Cunningham. 1970. "Party Leader Images in the 1968 Federal Election." *Canadian Journal of Political Science* 3, 1: 37-55.1.

Part 3

Proximate Considerations in Vote Choice

Enlightenment, Equalization, or What? Campaigns, Learning, and the Economy in Canadian Elections

J. Scott Matthews

There is no shortage of political science research and commentary on the origins, nature, and consequences of political ignorance in the mass public. The state of mass political knowledge is perhaps best summarized by the seminal contributor to this line of research, Philip Converse, who once observed that political knowledge is a variable with a low mean and a high variance (1990). By this, Converse meant that the general level of knowledge about public policy and political affairs is low but that some groups in society – the educated, the politically attentive, and so forth – clearly possess more knowledge than others.[1] For representative democracy, the implications seem to be dire. How can democratic institutions properly reflect the preferences of the electorate if most voters lack the ability and motivation to form – and express and act on – meaningful preferences among political alternatives? The question embodies what the field has come to know as the "problem of citizen competence" (Kuklinski and Quirk 2001).

It is easy to imagine that election campaigns, and the onslaught of political information that they generate, offset this problem. The intuition, articulated eloquently by Gelman and King (1993) (see also Markus 1988, 1992; Bartels 1992, 2006; Finkel 1993; Andersen, Tilley, and Heath 2005; and Arceneaux 2006), is that the contestation and noise of the campaign supply voters with both the motivation and the resources to make better-informed vote choices. The dissemination of party platforms, the extensive political reporting in the mass media, the torrent of political advertisements, the direct mobilization efforts of the parties, the conflict and information exchange of candidates' debates, the emotional excitement of the race itself – collectively, features of campaigns are expected to fire voter interest in politics while simultaneously providing voters with informational resources far greater than those available outside the campaign period. Put simply, from this view, the campaign increases both the demand for and the supply of political information. In this way, the campaign might be said to facilitate the *enlightenment* of the voter (Gelman and King 1993).

Although plausible on its face, the empirical case for this "enlightenment thesis" is uneven at best. The most convincing work is confined to US presidential elections, and there the evidence is mixed (see, especially, Bartels 2006). Results for elections outside the – possibly peculiar – US setting are still more inconsistent and are largely indirect in any case (Stevenson and Vavreck 2000; Arceneaux 2006). Furthermore, key elements of the enlightenment perspective, including critical claims concerning the quality of political perceptions, have been insufficiently tested.

This chapter, accordingly, presents a systematic treatment of the enlightenment thesis, focusing on political learning in the domain of the economy. A focus on the economy is apt in this context for a host of reasons. Most obviously, economic issues are invariably central to political conflict – a fact reflected in the massive literature on economic voting (see Anderson, this volume; also see Lewis-Beck and Stegmaier 2000). Moreover, in contrast to most ingredients in the typical vote decision, economic perceptions are, in principle, correctable: the state of the national economy is objectively measurable, and a steady diet of such measures is supplied by the media (see Haller and Norpoth 1997). In an important sense, then, learning on the economy is a "most likely case" (Eckstein 1975) for the enlightenment thesis.

In addition to effecting an important test of the campaign enlightenment claim, the chapter extends existing work by considering a closely related yet largely unexamined[2] theoretical possibility: that the campaign not only enlightens but also *equalizes*. Indeed, as Converse's (1990) "low mean, high variance" conclusion emphasizes, political knowledge is not just thin on the ground but also highly unequal in distribution. Thus, a truly enlightening campaign would concentrate political learning among the political knowledge laggards – those who are chronically inattentive to and uninformed about political matters. In this way, to borrow from Converse, the campaign would not only raise the mean of political knowledge but also lower its variance.

The chapter's empirical claims rest on a pooled analysis of rolling cross-sectional (RCS) survey data collected during five recent Canadian elections (1988-2004). RCS survey methodology essentially produces a random sample of respondents for each day of the survey period (typically the length of the campaign), permitting analysis of subtle dynamics in voter cognition as the campaign unfolds (Johnston and Brady 2002). Deploying these data thus affords a uniquely direct examination of the campaign dynamics of political learning. To preview my findings, the result of this examination upsets much in the standing view of election campaigns as enlightening experiences for voters.

The Enlightenment Thesis
Gelman and King (1993) are not so much motivated by the problem of political learning – or "citizen competence" (Kuklinski and Quirk 2001) – as they are by an apparent paradox in the literature on US presidential elections. The paradox is summarized in the title of their seminal paper, "Why Are American Presidential Election Campaign Polls So Variable When Votes Are So Predictable?" Gelman and King seek to explain why aggregate vote intentions move around erratically in the weeks and months before election day, even though the final outcome can be reliably forecast on the basis of variables (such as economic conditions and presidential performance evaluations) measured months before voters go to the polls. The puzzle is that the former suggests that the ultimate outcome might be the result of a random or quasi-random process, whereas the latter suggests that the outcome is highly structured and turns on "rational" and easily observable forces.

The solution to the paradox, according to Gelman and King (1993), is that the progress of the election campaign informs voters about and focuses their attention on these rational and easily observable forces – what they term "the fundamentals." The fundamentals include the policy positions of the candidates, their partisan and ideological affiliations, assessments of past government performance, and the state of the national economy. By election day, Gelman and King contend, the voter has learned a great deal about the levels of these variables, along with the appropriate weights to accord them in the vote calculus. With respect to the economy, for instance, this means that the voter has, first, become informed about the state of the economy and, second, made the "proper" connection between this consideration and vote choice: that is, the voter knows when conditions are objectively good (poor) and rewards (punishes) governments accordingly (see Key 1968; Kramer 1971; Fiorina 1981; Lewis-Beck and Stegmaier 2000; Anderson, this volume; and

Bélanger and Nadeau, this volume). From this perspective, then, what appears to be random movement in vote intention instead reflects the unfolding of a learning process, albeit an uneven one.

Gelman and King (1993) supply mostly indirect evidence for the enlightenment claim, and, notably, they provide no evidence at all that the campaign increases knowledge about and attention to the national economy. Their principal exhibits concern the increasing impacts of ideology and race on vote choice in the 1988 presidential election campaign – by their rendering, the impacts of both variables grew by roughly 50 percent in that year. The best evidence for the enlightenment hypothesis is in Bartels (2006), and that evidence is mixed. Pooling survey data from two decades of US presidential elections, Bartels finds that the impacts of party identification, issue attitudes, candidate evaluations, and economic perceptions increase with the approach of election day, albeit in varying degrees. The biggest shift is in the impact of issues – effects generally double over the fall campaign. Regarding economic perceptions, the effect of the campaign is typically to increase their weight by roughly 90 percent.[3] At the same time, however, Bartels uncovers only modest evidence that the campaign moves the fundamentals themselves – that is, that the campaign increases knowledge of key considerations, such as candidates' positions and the state of the economy. Significant movement is confined to perceptions of candidates – such as judgments of character and competence – and, excepting closely fought contests, would have only modest substantive effects on electoral outcomes (see Bittner, this volume, for a discussion of leader evaluation effects on vote choice).

These key contributions aside, evidence for the enlightenment claim is largely focused on over-time changes in the impacts of – rather than changes in knowledge about – the fundamentals. Work on the US case uncovers evidence of moderate to strong election year increases in the effects of partisanship, ideology, and economic perception (Finkel 1993; Campbell 2000; Bafumi, Gelman, and Park 2004). On the other hand, the most direct test of the enlightenment thesis on record, reported in Johnston, Hagen, and Jamieson's (2004) analysis of the 2004 presidential election, finds a more equivocal pattern, at least regarding economic effects: the impact of the economy bumps around unsystematically across the fall campaign, with its ultimate effect weaker on election day than on Labour Day. Outside the United States, a handful of cross-national studies depicts campaign-period increases in the impact of the economy, although the evidence is modest and, in any case, indirect (Stevenson and Vavreck 2000; Arceneaux 2006; but see Sekhon 2004).[4] Finally, regarding dynamics in knowledge of the fundamentals, a handful of studies shows increases in a variety of forms of political knowledge (such as knowledge of the policy commitments of candidates and parties) over the campaign (Mendelsohn and Cutler 2000; Jenkins 2002; Andersen, Tilley, and Heath 2005; Cutler et al. 2008), in rough accord with enlightenment expectations. None of these studies, however, speaks to knowledge of economic conditions – an important goad for the present research.

In general, then, evidence of campaign learning is modest at best. Existing work is undermined, in part, by its typically indirect implications for enlightenment claims, generally weak or inconsistent effects, and, as suggested above, a disproportionate emphasis on dynamics in the weights – rather than the levels – of key variables. This chapter aims to respond to these shortcomings, at least regarding learning in the economic domain. In particular, the analysis considers the question of dynamics in economic perceptions in far greater depth than earlier investigations of campaign learning. The chapter also employs a much higher level of "temporal measurement" than that used in earlier research (excepting Johnston, Hagen, and Jamieson 2004), benefiting from the uniquely time-sensitive design of the rolling cross-section election studies. And, as noted above, the analysis extends the enlightenment argument by considering the possibility of equalization in political knowledge across the electorate over the campaign.

Campaign Learning and the Economy

Complications and Assumptions

The *enlightenment thesis* has two major implications for political learning in the economic domain: first, the progress of the campaign improves voter knowledge of economic conditions; second, the progress of the campaign increases the impact of perceptions of economic conditions on vote choice. What we might term the *equalization thesis* has just one pivotal implication: the progress of the campaign reduces gaps across the electorate in the quality of voter knowledge of economic conditions and in the impact of perceptions of economic conditions on vote choice. These expectations immediately raise complications for empirical research.

The basic theoretical problem concerns the claim that the campaign "improves" voter knowledge of economic conditions. Leaving aside scientific uncertainty about the way in which the economy works, the level and the form of knowledge that the voter requires to make a reasonable judgment about the performance of political incumbents are unclear (Kuklinski and Quirk 2001). Another problem concerns the relevance of different plausible units of economic evaluation. Is it the national economy that matters? Or is one's personal economic situation most important? What about the economic well-being of the social groups with which one identifies?

A critical assumption for the present analysis is that *it is perceptions of national economic conditions that matter.* That is, the focus is on voters' evaluations of the state of the national economy and the link between these evaluations and vote choice. This assumption fits the current conventional wisdom in political science (see Kiewiet 1983; Lewis-Beck and Stegmaier 2000; Sears 1993; and Mutz 1998; but see Downs 1957; Key 1968; Kramer 1971; and Gomez and Wilson 2003). Indeed, it is national economic perceptions that typically matter to vote choice (Lewis-Beck and Stegmaier 2000; Anderson, this volume). Furthermore, whatever other economic considerations might plausibly and properly be involved in political evaluation, the question of the quality of national economic perceptions and the link between these perceptions and vote choice is crucial.

Two further critical assumptions concern the evaluation of the quality of economic perceptions. The first, what we might term the *low variance condition,* holds that *whatever the "correct" perception of national economic conditions, everyone should share it.* No particular, substantive benchmark of economic perception (change in unemployment or GDP, for instance) is assumed. What is assumed is that there *is* a single valid perception of economic conditions and that, consequently, a fully informed electorate would be unanimous in its economic judgments (compare Kramer 1971 and Page and Shapiro 1992). This might seem to be a heroic standard, yet any substantive standard of economic perception must assume at least this much.[5]

The final critical assumption, what we might term the *low bias condition,* holds that *variance in national economic perceptions should not be systematically related to politically important individual-level characteristics.* In particular, judgments about national economic conditions should not be subject to politically consequential forms of perceptual bias. A raft of studies supports the view that evaluations of the national economy are generally subject to two forms of bias: partisan and personal (Weatherford 1983; Conover, Feldman, and Knight 1986, 1987; Mutz 1992, 1994, 1998; Duch, Palmer, and Anderson 2000; Johnston, Hagen, and Jamieson 2004). Partisan bias refers to the tendency of those who identify with the party of the incumbent to evaluate the economy more favourably than others. Personal bias, on the other hand, occurs when individuals simply generalize from the personal to the national economic domain – for instance, when the recently unemployed are more likely than others to perceive national conditions as souring. By distorting perceptions of economic conditions, partisan and personal bias can vitiate economic voting as a mechanism of democratic accountability.

It is important to note here that these assumptions embody what might be termed a "formal" standard for the evaluation of national economic perceptions. There are at least two arguments in favour of such an approach over the alternative, more substantive, approach. The first argument is that the choice of any substantive benchmark of economic performance, or even a combination of such benchmarks, is effectively arbitrary and thus problematic as a relevant datum for economic evaluation. A more serious concern relates to the mapping of substantive benchmarks of economic performance onto survey measures of economic perceptions. When economic conditions are clearly negative or positive, this seems to be simple enough: a crude, if adequate, analytical strategy would examine the ratio of negative to positive evaluations (or vice versa). Things are not so straightforward when economic conditions are middling (as seems to have been the case in almost all of the elections in the analysis[6]). If the economy has improved a little, for instance, are economic conditions the "same" or "better"? And would that be "somewhat better" or "much better"? It is in view of these complications, then, that this chapter adopts the formal evaluative standard described above. If nothing else, the standard seems to constitute a set of necessary, although not sufficient, conditions for sound economic judgment.

Hypotheses

In light of these critical assumptions, a series of formal hypotheses can now be derived. The following hypotheses formalize the *enlightenment thesis.*

1   H_1: The progress of the campaign reduces non-response in national economic perceptions.
2   H_2: The progress of the campaign reduces variance in national economic perceptions.
3   H_3: The progress of the campaign reduces partisan bias in national economic perceptions.
4   H_4: The progress of the campaign reduces personal bias in national economic perceptions.
5   H_5: The progress of the campaign increases the impact of national economic perceptions on vote choice.

H_1 stipulates simply that those who are unable to form or express perceptions of the national economy (those who respond "don't know" on queries about national economic perceptions) at the beginning of the campaign are more likely to be able to do so by election day. Formation of evaluations of economic conditions is a necessary, though not sufficient, condition for voter knowledge of the national economy. Consequently, H_1 functions as a kind of evaluative baseline. Operationally, the chapter assesses this hypothesis by examining over-time dynamics in rates of non-response on queries about national economic perceptions.

H_2 reflects the low variance condition, expressed above. The hypothesis implies that economic judgments become more alike as election day approaches – that the variance in national economic perceptions declines over time in the campaign. H_2 is assessed through an examination of over-time dynamics in the variance (operationally, standard deviation) of national economic perceptions.

H_3 and H_4 embody the low bias condition. The hypotheses imply that the impact on national economic perceptions of indicators of partisanship and personal economic conditions[7] declines over time in the campaign. In comparison with H_1 and H_2, H_3 and H_4 represent a rather stringent test for voter knowledge of economic conditions.

H_5 implies that the relationship between national economic perceptions and vote choice strengthens as election day approaches. The chapter approaches this question by examining dynamics in the impact of economic judgment on incumbent vote intention, an approach that parallels existing work (Gelman and King 1993; Johnston, Hagen, and Jamieson 2004; Arceneaux 2006; Bartels 2006).

The *equalization thesis* is evaluated by conditioning the analysis of H_1, H_3, H_4, and H_5 on a measure of political knowledge.[8] The details are presented below. Suffice it to note that in these analyses the question is: Does the progress of the campaign reduce the gap across the electorate in the quality of voter knowledge of economic conditions and in the impact of perceptions of economic conditions on vote choice?

Data and Measurement

The data consist of the Canadian Election Studies (CES) from 1988 to 2004.[9] The peak daily sample size in the rolling cross-sectional component of each study is roughly 100. Pooling the data thus yields as many as 15,000 respondents for some analyses or roughly 500 respondents per day.[10] Regarding measurement issues, the critical quantities in the analysis are the following: *national economic perceptions, party identification, employment status, vote intention, political knowledge,* and, of course, *campaign time* itself.

Economic effects on vote choice have been widely studied, so survey instrumentation concerning *national economic perceptions* is nearly standardized internationally. There has been some variation in the CES wording over the years, but the item from 1997 to 2004 is representative: "Now, I want to ask you about the economy. Over the *past year,* has *Canada's* economy *gotten better, gotten worse,* or *stayed about the same?"*

The items for 1988 and 1993 differ mainly in the number of response levels – in those years, respondents could moderate their impressions by adding a "much" or "somewhat" qualifier to their responses. Otherwise, the items are essentially identical. In the analysis, all items have been recoded to vary along the $(0,1)$ interval.

Similarly, *party identification* is measured generically across surveys. The typical item is some minor variation on the following (from the 2004 CES): "In federal politics, do you usually think of yourself as a Liberal, Conservative, NDP, Bloc Québécois, or none of these?" In the models, incumbent partisans and those expressing no party identification are separated from all others – that is, those identified with some party other than the government party. The setup is obviously a simplification. But the incumbent partisans versus other partisans contrast does go to the heart of arguments about partisan bias: all other things being equal, incumbent partisans should take a more positive view of the economy than everyone else. Non-partisans are isolated to clarify the perceptual contrast between the voters who matter: that is, those who possess live identification with a political party.

The standard approach to the measurement of personal economic perceptions is to rely on items styled after the standard measure of national economic perceptions.[11] The problem with these measures, as I have argued elsewhere (Matthews 2006), is that they are suspiciously "close" to measures of national economic perceptions, especially when the items are asked successively during the same survey interview.[12] In other words, any analysis that models national economic perceptions in terms of subjective measures of personal economic status faces the threat of endogeneity bias. Consequently, this chapter pursues an alternative measurement strategy and relies on a measure of personal economic status that is clearly exogenous to national economic perceptions: *employment status*. In the analysis, this concept is represented by a dummy variable (unemployed versus others). The virtue of this approach is that it should produce a consistent estimate of the effect of interest, but this estimate comes at the cost of a certain degree of slippage between the theoretical concept and its operational indicator.[13]

Measurement of *vote intention* is fairly standard across the surveys. The item from 2004 is typical: "Which party do you think you will vote for: the Liberal Party, the Conservative Party, the New Democratic Party, (the Bloc Québécois,) or another party?" In the analysis, vote choice is collapsed into a dichotomy between support for the incumbent and support for non-incumbents. This is obviously a simplification. Economic effects are not generally confined to incumbents, and indeed economic effects on support for non-incumbents are present in the sample of elections examined here (see, for example, Blais et al. 2002). Still, these effects are typically complementary to the effects on incumbent support – that is, these relationships are typically negative. Thus, operationalizing vote choice as a dichotomy, where 1 indicates support for the incumbent party and 0 indicates support for non-incumbent parties, is a useful simplifying assumption that does little violence to reality. The operationalization is also true to the pith and substance of the economic voting model – reward and punishment of incumbent governments for their economic performances (Key 1968; Fiorina 1981).[14]

Relative to the other critical variables in the analysis, the measurement of *political knowledge* poses some challenges. The conventional wisdom is that direct measures of general, factual political knowledge work best for this purpose (Price and Zaller 1993; Delli Carpini and Keeter 1996).

Alas, such measures are available only for the three most recent election studies, and, even so, their comparability is debatable. Consequently, to standardize measurement across the surveys, a plausible surrogate is substituted: education. In the analysis, those holding at least an undergraduate university degree are separated from all others. This measurement approach is appropriate since the correlation between education and political knowledge – to say nothing of its correlation with political knowledge cognates such as political interest and attention – is irrefutable (Luskin 1991; Fournier 2002).

The final variable of theoretical interest, the measure of *campaign time,* is simply the day of the campaign. The variable is a counter that starts on the first day of the campaign period and reaches its maximum (which varies across elections[15]) on the day before election day. To simplify interpretation of the model results, the maximum value of the counter is zero, and the minimum value for each election is equal to the additive inverse of the length of the campaign minus one. For instance, for the longest campaign in the analysis, the election of 1988, the counter runs from –47 to 0.

The remaining variables in the analysis serve mainly as controls and are standard in Canadian voting research. These variables are *ethnicity* (non-Europeans versus others), *religion* (Catholics and non-religious versus others), *language* (French speakers versus others), *income,*[16] *union membership* (members versus others), and *region* (Atlantic, Quebec, and west versus Ontario).

Enlightenment, Equalization, or What?
Prior to evaluating the specific expectations derived from the enlightenment and equalization theses above, a useful first step is to consider the distribution of national economic perceptions across the five elections, as reported in Table 9.1. On the whole, economic evaluations are fair to middling across these elections – excepting 1993, a year when economic conditions were sour indeed. Otherwise, the modal perception each year corresponds to the view that economic conditions had "stayed about the same" as those of the previous year, and the mean of economic perceptions across the five elections, appropriately enough, is 0.50.

More critical for this analysis is the pattern of economic perceptions over time. Regressing national economic perceptions on campaign time and a set of fixed effects for the survey years reveals a statistically significant, although exceedingly shallow, positive trend (analysis unreported).

Table 9.1

National economic perceptions by election							
Year	0	.25	.5	.75	1	DK	N
1988	2.46	10.39	53.32	28.64	5.19	5.42	3,582
1993	28.45	34.36	30.17	6.60	0.42	1.85	3,775
1997	21.09	–	47.83	–	31.07	4.30	3,949
2000	14.16	–	45.88	–	39.96	3.81	3,651
2004	26.76	–	52.05	–	21.19	3.98	4,323

Note: Cell entries are percentages; data are not weighted.

Across the five elections, the typical campaign day improved economic judgments by less than one hundredth of the range of the national economic perceptions measure; across the length of the modal Canadian campaign of thirty-six days, this would mean an increase of slightly more than 0.02 units. Interacting the passage of time with education suggests that this movement is largely confined to the politically informed and attentive: the model indicates that the trend in economic perceptions is roughly sixteen times greater among degree holders. Even in this group, however, the typical campaign's impact is modest: a thirty-six-day campaign would produce a positive increment in economic perceptions of just 0.09 units on the measure.

Overall, then, the crucial fact is that campaign-period movement in national economic perceptions seems, on the whole, to be trivial. If election campaigns facilitate political learning, it is not reflected in significant baseline shifts in national economic perceptions.

Non-Response and Variance

Of course, stability in the valence of economic perceptions might disguise other important dynamics in the quality of economic judgments. H_1 focuses our attention on changes in the level of non-response to queries about national economic perceptions over the campaign period. The expectation is that, as election day approaches, non-response should fall. At the same time, the equalization thesis suggests that the gap in non-response across levels of political knowledge should narrow across the campaign.

Consider first the general pattern of non-response (see Table 9.1). Significantly, although varying some at the election level, non-response in economic evaluation is, on average, modest across the studies – roughly

4 percent. The highest percentage of non-response is just 5.42 percent (1988); the lowest percentage is a minuscule 1.85 percent (1993). Appropriately, non-response also varies a great deal by political knowledge, as indexed by education: averaging across the elections, degree holders are significantly less likely than others to reply "don't know" when asked for their assessments of economic conditions ($p < .001$; analysis unreported). Among other things, this finding validates non-response as an indicator of political learning. It also neatly sets up a central question in the analysis: Can the campaign close the non-response gap? The answer, in short, is no.

The pivotal analysis involves a logit regression of non-response on campaign time; also included in the model are, once again, fixed effects for the survey years. Considering first the overall pattern – that is, *not* conditioning on education – the model estimates suggest that levels of non-response are, in general, unmoved by the progress of the campaign.[17] The trend in non-response over the campaign period is vanishingly small, statistically insignificant, and, perversely, *positive*. Taken at face value, the model implies that, over the length of a thirty-six-day campaign, the probability of non-response increases by just over half a point. Interacting campaign time with education reveals that the pattern of stability is generic across levels of political knowledge: the (non-)effect of the campaign is statistically indistinguishable between degree holders and others. Clearly, the "non-response gap" is not closed by the approach of election day. Thus, by this standard, there is not a hint of enlightenment, much less equalization, across the campaign.

Stability in levels of non-response in national economic evaluation could, however, coexist with significant shifts in the content of these evaluations, at least among those prepared to express them. The progress of the campaign might, for instance, lead to declining variance in national economic perceptions as voters home in on a common assessment of conditions, as countenanced in H_2. Regressing the daily standard deviation of national economic perceptions on campaign time, along with fixed effects for the survey years, reveals no detectable movement (analysis not reported). That is, the variance of national economic perceptions is stable over time – *contra* enlightenment expectations, economic judgments are no more alike on the last day than they are on the first day of the campaign. H_2, then, meets a similar fate as H_1. By these "formal" criteria of sound economic judgment, there is no sign that election campaigns either enlighten or equalize.

Bias

The above obviously narrows the scope for campaign learning regarding the state of the national economy. Significant developments in the nature of economic evaluations must consist of some combination of opinion mobilization and conversion, and this combination, presumably, would be reflected in changes in levels of non-response, variance in perceptions, and aggregate perception itself. Even so, aggregate stability in these critical parameters of national economic perception might conceal significant dynamics in the magnitude of perceptual bias.

This important possibility is the focus here. H_3 and H_4 draw our attention to the impact of partisan and personal bias on national economic perceptions. The crucial question is this: Does the campaign erode bias in national economic perceptions? A further possibility, entertained by the equalization thesis, is that the campaign narrows the gap in the magnitude of bias (if any) across levels of political knowledge.

The analysis proceeds by estimating ordinary least-squares regressions that model temporal dynamics in partisan and personal effects on economic judgment. Two equations are central. The first simply models temporal dynamics in the impact of partisanship and employment status on national economic perceptions with a pair of two-way interactions. The equation is as follows:

$$NEP = f(\beta_0 + \beta_1 PID + \beta_2 PID^*DAY + \beta_3 NOPID + \beta_4 UNEMP + \beta_5 UNEMP^*DAY + \beta_6 DAY + \Sigma\beta_k SD_k + \Sigma\beta_l YR_l + u), \tag{1}$$

where

NEP = national economic perceptions;
PID = incumbent party identification (dummy);
$NOPID$ = no party identification (dummy);
$UNEMP$ = unemployed (dummy);
DAY = day of campaign;
SD_k = k sociodemographic variables, described above;
YR_l – l survey year indicator variables (excluded year is 1988); and
u = random error.

The critical parameters are β_2 and β_5, which quantify the linear, over-time trends (if any) in the impacts of party identification and unemployment on national economic perceptions. A negative, statistically significant estimate for β_2, on the one hand, and a positive, statistically significant estimate for β_5, on the other, would indicate that the progress of the campaign erodes bias in national economic perceptions.

The second equation permits an analysis of campaign dynamics within education levels by adding to the mix a pair of three-way interactions, along with appropriate lower-order interactions:

$$NEP = f(\beta_0 + \beta_1 PID + \beta_2 PID*DAY + \beta_3 PID*DEG +$$
$$\beta_4 PID*DAY*DEG + \beta_5 NOPID + \beta_6 UNEMP + \beta_7 UNEMP*DAY$$
$$+ \beta_8 UNEMP*DEG + \beta_9 UNEMP*DAY*DEG + \beta_{10}DAY$$
$$+ \beta_{11}DAY*DEG + \Sigma\beta_k SD_k + \Sigma\beta_l YR_l + u), \tag{2}$$

where *DEG* is a dummy indicating degree-holder status, and all other terms are defined as above. The interesting parameters here are β_4 and β_9, which model variation between degree holders and others in the campaign's impact on partisan and personal bias. If the campaign narrows any gaps in the magnitude of bias across levels of political knowledge (at least as indexed by education), these parameters should turn up as statistically significant.

Table 9.2 reports coefficient estimates for these models. Looking first at results for equation (1), the "main effects"[18] of partisanship and unemployment appear to be roughly as they should be: that is, on average, incumbent partisans perceive the national economy to be doing better than opposition partisans perceive it to be doing, and the unemployed perceive the economy to be doing worse than the employed perceive it to be doing. The model suggests that, by the end of the campaign, incumbent and opposition partisans find themselves roughly one-tenth of a unit apart on the national economic perceptions measure. Similarly, just over one-tenth of a unit separates the economic judgments of the employed and unemployed on the last day of the campaign. Thus, in keeping with standard findings, there is evidence of both partisan and personal bias in national economic perceptions across these elections.

The critical question for the enlightenment thesis, of course, concerns dynamics in these effects. Does the campaign erode partisan and personal bias in national economic perceptions? The answer, in short, is no. Indeed, it is likely that the opposite is true. With respect to partisan bias, the model estimates suggest that the campaign's impact is essentially neutral – that is, partisan effects in economic judgment are roughly as large on the first day as on the last day of the campaign. The coefficient

Table 9.2

Modelling partisan and personal bias in economic perceptions (OLS regression estimates)

	Equation			
	(1)		(2)	
PID	0.097***	(0.010)	0.097***	(0.008)
NOPID	-0.001	(0.006)	-0.000	(0.006)
PID*DAY	0.001	(0.000)	0.001*	(0.000)
PID*DEG			-0.006	(0.021)
PID*DAY*DEG			-0.001	(0.001)
UNEMP	-0.109***	(0.019)	-0.094***	(0.021)
UNEMP*DAY	-0.003***	(0.001)	-0.002***	(0.001)
UNEMP*DEG			-0.101*	(0.052)
UNEMP*DAY*DEG			-0.004	(0.003)
Constant	0.518***	(0.008)	0.509***	(0.009)
Observations	15,539		15,539	
R^2	0.175		0.176	

Note: Results for sociodemographics and survey years are not reported. Robust standard errors are in parentheses.

* significant at $p \le .1$, ** significant at $p \le .01$, *** significant at $p \le .001$

estimate of the interaction between partisanship and day of campaign is substantively small, statistically insignificant, and – perversely from the standpoint of the enlightenment thesis – positively signed (that is, implying increasing bias over the campaign). The story regarding personal bias is equally upsetting to the enlightenment view, if not more so. The interaction between unemployment and day of campaign is highly significant ($p < .001$) and clearly negative, implying that personal bias in national economic perceptions grows significantly across the campaign. Indeed, the model suggests that the impact of unemployment is nine times greater on the last day than on the first day of the campaign period (the impact of a unit shift grows from –0.012 to –0.109). Far from enlightening voters, then, the campaign seems to aggravate their predicament. H_3 and H_4 clearly fail.

It is imaginable, however, that equation (1), which aggregates the campaign's effect over the whole population, disguises a pattern of impact that varies across population subgroups, especially subgroups defined by education level. This is a critical premise, of course, of the equalization

Figure 9.1

Partisan bias in national economic perceptions by day by education, Canada, 1988-2004

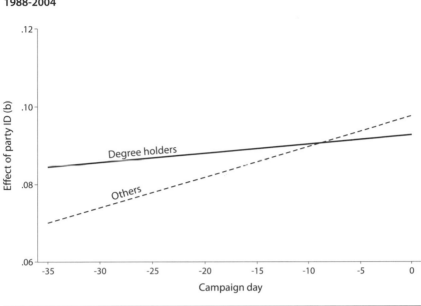

thesis, which suggests that any "enlightening" impact of the campaign might be concentrated among those who need it the most – the political knowledge laggards, typically the less educated. And the estimates for equation (2) reveal that the impact of the campaign *is* conditioned by education – but not in an "equalizing" way. The relevant results are reported in Table 9.2 and, to facilitate interpretation, represented graphically in Figures 9.1 and 9.2.

Consider first Figure 9.1, which depicts the impact of party identification on national economic perceptions, among degree holders and others, over the typical thirty-six-day Canadian election campaign. The figure suggests that, whatever impact the campaign has on partisan bias, it is largely confined to non-degree holders: partisan effects seem to trend steadily upward in this group, whereas effects for degree holders are essentially flat. Note, however, that these effects are indistinguishable, at least in a statistical sense: the p-value associated with the estimate for the three-way interaction between party identification, day of campaign, and degree holding is 0.569. Furthermore, these dynamics are substantively minuscule, as even for non-degree holders partisan effects increase by

Figure 9.2

Personal bias in national economic perceptions by day by education, Canada, 1988-2004

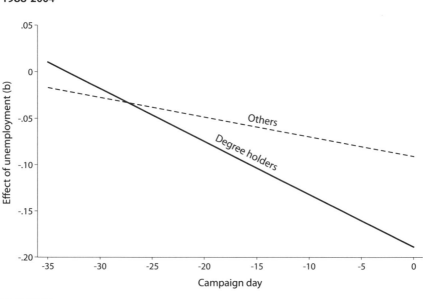

just 0.02 units (on the scale of national economic perceptions). In short, then, partisan bias is essentially undisturbed by the campaign, irrespective of political knowledge.

Figure 9.2 tells a rather different story. The plot suggests that the massive growth in personal bias reflected in the estimates for equation (1) is strongly conditioned by education. To be sure, the campaign magnifies personal bias in national economic perceptions across the electorate. But the trend is, at least substantively,[19] much steeper for degree holders than non-degree holders. Indeed, whereas effects for non-degree holders increase more than threefold across a thirty-six-day campaign (from −.024 to −.094 units), effects for degree holders increase from essentially nullity to roughly −0.2 units. By election day, the educated-employed and educated-unemployed are far apart in their perceptions of economic conditions, separated by one-fifth of the range of the national economic perceptions measure.

This is hardly the pattern imagined in the equalization thesis, which would imply, at a minimum, that the magnitude of partisan and personal bias in economic judgment becomes more similar across levels of education as the campaign proceeds. If anything, however, the empirical pattern suggests that degree holders and non-degree holders become *less* similar with the approach of election day. Indeed, regarding personal bias, the two groups are scarcely distinguishable thirty-six days out, but they are separated by roughly a tenth of a unit on the measure of economic perceptions at the end of the campaign.

The central points are these. First, there is no evidence that the campaign erodes either partisan or personal bias in economic judgment. On the contrary, the impact of the campaign – insofar as it has one – seems to be to magnify bias in national economic perceptions. Second, there is no sign that the campaign equalizes levels of perceptual bias across levels of political knowledge (as indexed by education). In short, there is not a hint of campaign enlightenment or equalization in these results.

Impact

The foregoing speaks rather loudly against the enlightenment and equalization theses, at least as they bear on the quality of national economic perceptions. The final component of the analysis concerns the campaign's impact on the link between these perceptions and the vote itself. H_5 implies that the link strengthens as the campaign progresses.

As above, analysis proceeds by estimating regressions that incorporate interactions with campaign time and education. The first equation parallels equation (1) in that it models temporal dynamics across the population as a whole:

$$INCVOTE = f(\beta_0 + \beta_1 NEP + \beta_2 NEP*DAY + \beta_3 PID + \beta_4 NOPID + \beta_5 DAY + \Sigma\beta_k SD_k + \Sigma\beta_l YR_l + u), \qquad (3)$$

where *INCVOTE* is incumbent vote intention, and all other terms are defined as above.[20] β_2 is the crucial parameter in this model. The coefficient quantifies the linear trend in the impact of national economic perceptions on support for the incumbent. A positive, statistically significant estimate here would imply an "enlightening campaign," in the Gelman-King sense.

The second equation parallels equation (2), incorporating a three-way interaction between campaign time and education, along with lower-order interactions:

$$INCVOTE = f(\beta_0 + \beta_1 NEP + \beta_2 NEP^*DAY + \beta_3 NEP^*DEG +$$
$$\beta_4 NEP^*DAY^*DEG + \beta_5 PID + \beta_6 NOPID + \beta_7 DAY +$$
$$\beta_8 DAY^*DEG + \Sigma\beta_k SD_k + \Sigma\beta_l YR_l + u), \tag{4}$$

where all terms are defined as above. β_4 is the critical quantity in this equation: it models variation in the impact of the campaign on the magnitude of economic effects among degree holders and others.

Table 9.3 reports the coefficient estimates of interest from equations (3) and (4). Sensibly, the impact of the economy is substantively large across these elections. The equation (3) estimate for national economic perceptions implies that, by the end of the campaign, the marginal effect of economic judgments is an 11.3 point shift in the probability of voting for the incumbent. This finding neatly and predictably fits the existing literature (see Anderson, this volume). More awkward for the existing literature is the estimate for the interaction between national economic perceptions and campaign day, which is statistically indistinguishable from zero. That is, *contra* H_5, the model estimates imply that the impact of the economy on support for Canadian incumbents is unmoved by the campaign. The coefficient, though appropriately positive, is tiny in substantive terms and dwarfed by its standard error ($p = .654$). This is a striking result considering previous findings (especially Arceneaux 2006 and Bartels 2006). Economic considerations, it seems, are invariably important in Canadian elections – and in a very strong sense: their impact neither grows nor shrinks amid the noise and activity of campaigning.

Of course, as in the case of personal bias in economic perceptions, the campaign's impact might vary significantly by level of education. Furthermore, whatever the direction of the campaign's impact, the approach of election day might level asymmetries in economic effects across the electorate. Figure 9.3, which renders graphically the estimates of equation (4) (reported in Table 9.3), reveals that, indeed, the campaign's impact on economic effects *is* differentiated by level of education. But, as the scissor-like plot suggests, the result is hardly equalizing. *Per* enlightenment expectations, economic effects increase massively as the campaign progresses *but only among degree holders:* the marginal effect of national economic perceptions in this group grows almost threefold over a thirty-six-day campaign, from just over six to more than seventeen points in the probability of an incumbent vote. Among non-degree holders, however, the impact of the economy is effectively stable. The three-way

Table 9.3

Modelling economic effects on incumbent support (logit regression estimates)

	Equation			
	(3)		(4)	
NEP	0.919***	(0.150)	0.785***	(0.142)
*NEP*DAY*	0.004	(0.008)	-0.003	(0.007)
*NEP*DEG*			0.464	(0.291)
*NEP*DAY*DEG*			0.023	(0.014)
Constant	-3.063***	(0.128)	-3.013***	(0.130)
Observations	15,595		15,595	
Pseudo R^2	0.308		0.308	

Note: Results for sociodemographics and survey years are not reported. Robust standard errors are in parentheses.

* significant at $p \le .1$, ** significant at $p \le .01$, *** significant at $p \le .001$

interaction between national economic perceptions, campaign day, and degree holding, which quantifies the difference in effects, just misses the conventional statistical significance threshold ($p = .119$) – and this amid a high level of collinearity.[21] The implication is that, far from equalizing the magnitude of economic effects across levels of education, the campaign in fact engenders them. By election day, the marginal effect of national economic perceptions on the probability of incumbent support is almost twice as great among degree holders (0.173) as among non-degree holders (0.091). In short, the campaign does not equalize – it simply makes the information rich richer (compare Holbrook 2002).[22]

Conclusion

This chapter has evaluated a two-part argument concerning political learning during election campaigns. The argument is that election campaigns *enlighten* voters in general – that is, enable all voters to make better-informed, higher-quality vote choices – while simultaneously *equalizing* the capacity of voters to engage in high-quality political decision making across levels of *ex ante* political knowledge. In this way, as suggested in the introduction, election campaigns might raise the mean and lower the variance of political knowledge. The title of the chapter frames the empirical problem of campaign learning as an answer to the question "enlightenment, equalization, or what?"

Figure 9.3

Economic effects on support for incumbents by day by education, Canada, 1988-2004

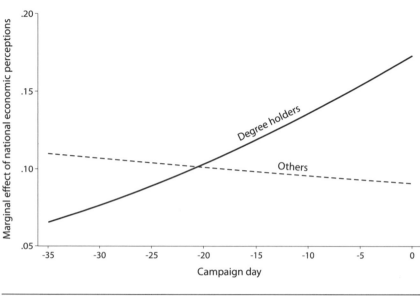

The empirical results suggest that the appropriate response is certainly "what?" That is, in the domain of the economy, there is precious little evidence of enlightenment or equalization across these five recent Canadian elections, much less a happy coincidence of both. On the contrary, the campaign seems (1) to have little effect on the ability of voters to form and express perceptions of economic conditions; (2) more likely to increase than decrease perceptual bias in economic judgments; and (3) to magnify the gap between the politically informed and politically uninformed in the impact of these perceptions on vote choice. In short, far from enhancing the quality and *equality* of mass political decision making, election campaigns seem as likely to make things worse as to have any effect at all.

How might we make sense of these results? A useful approach is to interrogate several important, if largely unstated, assumptions of the enlightenment thesis. Indeed, several of these implicit claims are problematic on their face.

One set of assumptions concerns the campaign as an information generator. The notion here is that the campaign reliably supplies useful information regarding the "fundamentals" of the vote decision. However, the campaign may not always, or with much intensity, supply real and digestible economic information. No doubt the political information level rises during the campaign, but economic information must compete with countless other considerations vying for voters' attention, and it is far from obvious that economic considerations will necessarily, or even generally, triumph in this contest. Indeed, the dominant view of the campaign's informational output emphasizes the prominence of "horse race journalism" – journalism that focuses on poll results and campaign gaffes rather than on, for instance, substantive treatment of election issues (Patterson and McClure 1976; Trimble and Sampert 2004). Furthermore, those bits of information that do get through might vary a great deal in terms of their economic positivity, especially when economic conditions are neither clearly negative nor clearly positive (as across four of the five elections in the analysis). Put differently, the economic message of the campaign might be quite equivocal. Thus, economic information may be less plentiful and more diverse than campaign enlightenment requires, resulting in, as observed above, over-time stability in levels of non-response and variability in national economic perceptions and only incidental movement in the aggregate perception itself.

A second set of potentially problematic assumptions in the enlightenment account focuses on characteristics of the voters themselves. One such assumption concerns the campaign's motivational power and, in particular, the manner in which the campaign motivates intensive or "effortful" cognition about politics (Petty and Cacioppo 1986). Implicit in the enlightenment thesis, and related "campaign learning" arguments, is the claim that political interest and attention, which the campaign presumably elevates, motivate voters to pursue accuracy in their political judgments – to make judicious use of the information that the campaign provides to form judgments that are at least approximately "rational." It seems unlikely, however, that this is generally so. Indeed, the earliest systematic work on elections and voting behaviour emphasized the campaign's potential to motivate biased political judgment, where the motivation is to avoid the psychic stress associated with cognitive dissonance (Lazarsfeld, Berelson, and Gaudet 1944; Berelson, Lazarsfeld, and McPhee 1954; Festinger 1957; for a more contemporary view, see Redlawsk 2002).[23] This might help to explain the finding that the campaign actually inflates personal bias in economic judgment (Figure 9.2): heightened attention to economic evaluations might encourage the voter to bring these into line with other salient economic cognitions, such as those concerning her or his personal economic situation.

Furthermore, the informative power of the campaign might be more constrained than commonly realized. In particular, the campaign's attractive force might be conditional on prior interest in and attention to the campaign. That is, the increased political noise level of the election period might disproportionately excite the interest of those who are politically informed and attentive anyway. This makes intuitive sense: the likelihood of exposure to campaign stimuli is a function of prior motivation, so the unique inducements of the campaign period should redound to the already motivated. Accordingly, we observe asymmetry between degree holders and others in the campaign's impact on personal bias (see Figure 9.2) and economic effects (see Figure 9.3).

A wrinkle in all this concerns the campaign's impact on partisan bias in economic judgment (see Figure 9.1). If the campaign motivates biased political judgment, and if the campaign oversupplies motivation to the already motivated (that is, the politically interested and attentive), then Figure 9.1 should mirror Figure 9.2: partisan bias should increase for all, though most steeply among degree holders. But recall that the typical Canadian campaign of thirty-six days increases the impact of party identification on national economic perceptions by just two one hundredths of the range of the measure and that, statistically speaking, the effect is undifferentiated by education. One possible explanation is that, even on the first day of the campaign, partisan perception of the national economy is suffused with bias: partisan thinking might be *so* partisan that it is difficult for it to be *more* partisan. The fact that partisan bias is roughly as large for degree holders as for non-degree holders lends some credence to this supposition: it might be that what matters to the magnitude of partisan bias is the *fact* – and perhaps the intensity – of partisanship, not the partisan's level of political information and interest.[24]

However one explains the particular pattern of results in this chapter, the critical finding is that, in contrast to much of the received wisdom, political learning during election campaigns seems, at best, to be incidental. The notable exception is the growth in economic effects over the campaign among degree holders. But then this is political learning where it can do the least good – among that group in the population that is likely to recognize the significance of the economy on its own. The implication is a campaign that reinforces inequalities – a deeply ironic conclusion given enlightenment expectations.

A constraint on all this, of course, is that the analysis is confined to the economic domain; as they say, the findings might not travel well. Evidence of campaign-period increases in knowledge of candidates and policies, much of it concerning Canadian samples, reinforces this point (Mendelsohn and Cutler 2000; Jenkins 2002; Andersen, Tilley, and Heath 2005; Cutler et al. 2008). Yet this possibility only enhances the interest of this chapter. A question for future research is what distinguishes economic evaluations from other political perceptions? An answer here may help to define the conditions of possibility for political learning during election campaigns.

Acknowledgments

The original version of this chapter was prepared for presentation at the Canadian Political Behaviour Workshop, London, ON, 2-4 November 2007. Much of the analysis arises out of my dissertation research, which was funded, in the form of a doctoral fellowship, by the Social Sciences and Humanities Research Council of Canada. For comments on the chapter, I would like to thank the participants in the aforementioned workshop, in particular Mark Pickup and the volume's editors, Cameron Anderson and Laura Stephenson, and the anonymous reviewers of this volume. And, for advice, comments, and criticism on the dissertation, I thank Richard Johnston, Fred Cutler, and Paul Quirk.

Notes

1 The conclusion has been widely reproduced and applies equally well to a range of closely associated variables, including political sophistication, political attention, and political interest (see Campbell et al. 1960; Converse 1964; Butler and Stokes 1969; Luskin 1991; Sniderman, Brody, and Tetlock 1991; Zaller 1992; Delli Carpini and Keeter 1996; and Fournier 2002).
2 Two exceptions are Mendelsohn and Cutler (2000) and Holbrook (2002).
3 This is the average impact of the campaign on the magnitude of economic effects in presidential vote choice from 1980 to 1996. Bartels drops the 2000 election from the analysis as economic effects actually decline over the course of that campaign, a finding reproduced in Johnston, Hagen, and Jamieson (2004).
4 In particular, neither Stevenson and Vavreck (2000) nor Arceneaux (2006) examines campaign dynamics in economic effects directly: the former consider variation in economic effects at the aggregate level by campaign length, whereas the latter examines variation in economic effects at the individual level by time to election day.
5 This assumption is also implicit in Gelman and King (1993), insofar as the election forecasting models that they have in mind include representations of national economic conditions as key terms. In principle, meeting this standard requires only that some (more or less) consensual opinion on economic performance is formed at an elite level and that this opinion is then mediated, through whatever means, to the mass of voters. Given the dominant view of the relationship between elite discourse and mass opinion (Zaller 1992), this hardly seems to be an implausible test of political learning.

6 For instance, unemployment rates were moderate in most of these elections (mean unemployment rate of 8.5 percent), and only the rate for 1993 enters the double digits (11.3 percent). Regarding year-over-year change in unemployment rates, all are negative, if generally minuscule – that is, unemployment seems to have been dropping during these elections (OECD 2005).

7 As discussed below, employment status proxies for personal economic perceptions in the analysis.

8 Note here that H_2 does not appear in this set. The reason is that reduction in the variance of national economic perceptions within political knowledge levels has, at best, ambiguous implications for both the enlightenment and the equalization hypotheses. For instance, declining variance within knowledge levels is consistent with the equalization hypothesis if variance across knowledge levels declines simultaneously, but it is inconsistent with the hypothesis otherwise.

9 Data for the 1988 Canadian Election Study, funded by the Social Sciences and Humanities Research Council (SSHRC), were collected by the Institute for Social Research (ISR), York University, for Richard Johnston, André Blais, Henry E. Brady, and Jean Crête. Data for the 1993 Canadian Election Study were provided by the ISR. The survey was funded by the SSHRC and was completed for the 1992-93 Canadian Election Team of Richard Johnston, André Blais, Henry E. Brady, Elisabeth Gidengil, and Neil Nevitte. Data for the 1997 Canadian Election Study were provided by the ISR. The survey was funded by the SSHRC and was completed for the 1997 Canadian Election Team of André Blais, Elisabeth Gidengil, Richard Nadeau, and Neil Nevitte. Data for the 2000 Canadian Election Study were collected by the ISR and Jolicoeur and Associates for André Blais, Elisabeth Gidengil, Richard Nadeau, and Neil Nevitte. The survey was funded by the SSHRC, Elections Canada, and the Institute for Research on Public Policy. The 2004 Canadian Election Study was funded by the SSHRC in partnership with Elections Canada and the Institute for Research on Public Policy. The principal co-investigators of the study were André Blais, Elisabeth Gidengil, Neil Nevitte, Joanna Everitt, and Patrick Fournier.

10 Strictly speaking, the latter figure applies only to the last thirty-four days of the campaign period – the length of the shortest campaign in the analysis and, consequently, the shortest period of CES fieldwork.

11 For instance, in the Canadian Election Studies of 2000 and 2004, the item is this: "Financially, are you *better* off, *worse* off, or about the same as a year ago?"

12 This is clearly the case in the election studies examined here. Indeed, across the studies, temporal variation in personal economic perceptions is largely explicable in terms of changes in national economic perceptions (Matthews 2006, 54-57). Moreover, any systematic movement in personal economic perceptions over the campaign period is somewhat puzzling. If personal economic perceptions reflect real conditions, then the campaign should have no particular impact on them, on the following reasoning: voters have roughly as much information about their personal economic circumstances on the first day as on the last day of the campaign. In the aggregate, this reasoning implies that personal economic perceptions are essentially unmoved by the campaign.

13 Another approach would be to estimate the model by the method of two-stage least squares (2SLS) regression. Unfortunately, the most plausible instruments available across these election studies produce highly imprecise estimates of the effects of interest (analysis unreported).

14 One complication with this approach concerns the partisan identities of Canadian governments over time: across these five elections, the Liberal Party was incumbent three times, whereas the Progressive Conservative Party was incumbent just twice. Consequently, it is necessary to control for some of the standard determinants of (party) vote choice in Canadian elections – ethnicity, language, region, and so forth – even though there is no theoretical reason to expect them to be implicated in support for incumbents, as such.

15 Following convention, and in view of data limitations, the start of the campaigns is set to the day on which Parliament is dissolved – or "writ day." Campaign lengths (days): 1988: 48; 1993: 45; 1997: 36; 2000: 34; 2004: 36.

16 This variable consists of a ten-level scale, where the bottom-most category includes all those earning less than $20,000 per year, the topmost category includes all those earning $100,000 per year or more, and in-between categories are bounded at $10,000 intervals. In the analysis, the variable is rescaled to the $(0,1)$ interval.

17 Analysis unreported. Full results are available on request from the author.

18 Note that, given the coding of *DAY*, the main effect of *PID* and *UNEMP* should be interpreted as each variable's impact on the last day of the campaign period.

19 The coefficient estimate for *UNEMP*DAY*DEG* does not rise to conventional levels of statistical significance. Note, however, that the model estimate, understandably, suffers from non-trivial collinearity: the variance inflation factor for this term is 4.20.

20 Note that religion is excluded as a control in equations (3) and (4) since it did not exert significant effects, controlling for the remainder of the model.

21 The variance inflation factor for *NEP*DAY*DEG* is 14.61.

22 Note that this pattern of results is robust to the inclusion of the full set of campaign time and education interactions of equation (2). A possible alternative explanation for this pattern of results bears noting. The point of departure is recent work that has questioned the assumption of the strict exogeneity of national economic perceptions with respect to vote intention (Evans and Andersen 2006; Evans and Pickup 2007). The argument, in short, is that economic evaluations are strongly conditioned by vote intention; consequently, recursive economic voting models (such as those estimated in this chapter) greatly overstate the macroeconomy's impact on electoral outcomes. If this is so, then increasing economic effects among degree holders over the campaign, far from indicating "enlightenment," might reflect increasing pressures to rationalize economic perceptions in light of vote intention as election day approaches. Alas, it is not possible to evaluate this argument with the present data: plausible instruments for economic perceptions are not available, so the imaginable correctives, such as 2SLS regression, are not possible. Furthermore, the claim that economic perceptions are endogenous to the vote is vigorously disputed (Lewis-Beck 2006; Lewis-Beck, Nadeau, and Elias 2008), and strict exogeneity remains the dominant assumption (Anderson, this volume). Finally, if national economic perceptions were, indeed, wholly endogenous to vote intention, then it would hardly upset this chapter's skeptical conclusions about the enlightenment thesis. Indeed, vote intention would then constitute a source of bias in economic judgments, much like partisanship and personal economic status.

23 Among other things, this assumption is a critical component of the "minimal effects thesis" (see the discussion in Anderson and Stephenson, this volume) that has motivated much of the work on campaign effects.

24 The chapter by Bélanger and Stephenson in this volume contains a discussion of the import of partisanship for voting. The chapter demonstrates that committed partisans vary in loyalty by intensity of partisanship.

References

Andersen, Robert, James Tilley, and Anthony Heath. 2005. "Political Knowledge and Enlightened Preferences: Party Choice through the Electoral Cycle." *British Journal of Political Science* 35, 2: 285-302.

Arceneaux, Kevin. 2006. "Do Campaigns Help Voters Learn? A Cross-National Analysis." *British Journal of Political Science* 36, 1: 159-73.

Bafumi, Joseph, Andrew Gelman, and David Park. 2004. "What Does 'Do Campaigns Matter?' Mean?" Unpublished manuscript, Columbia University.

Bartels, Larry. 1992. "The Impact of Electioneering in the United States." In *Electioneering: A Comparative Study of Continuity and Change*, ed. David Butler and Austin Ranney, 244-77. Oxford: Clarendon Press.

–. 2006. "Priming and Persuasion in Presidential Campaigns." In *Capturing Campaign Effects*, ed. Henry Brady and Richard Johnston, 78-112. Ann Arbor: University of Michigan Press.

Berelson, Bernard, Paul Lazarsfeld, and William McPhee. 1954. *Voting*. Cambridge, MA: Harvard University Press.

Blais, André, Richard Nadeau, Elisabeth Gidengil, and Neil Nevitte. 2002. *Anatomy of a Liberal Victory: Making Sense of the Vote in the 2000 Canadian Election*. Peterborough, ON: Broadview Press.

Butler, David, and Donald Stokes. 1969. *Political Change in Britain: Forces Shaping Electoral Choice*. London: Macmillan.

Campbell, Angus, Philip E. Converse, Warren E. Miller, and Donald E. Stokes. 1960. *The American Voter*. Chicago: John Wiley and Sons.

Campbell, James. 2000. *The American Campaign: U.S. Presidential Campaigns and the National Vote*. College Station: Texas A&M Press.

Conover, Pamela Johnston, Stanley Feldman, and Kathleen Knight. 1986. "Judging Inflation and Unemployment: The Origins of Retrospective Evaluations." *Journal of Politics* 48, 3: 565-88.

–. 1987. "The Personal and Political Underpinnings of Economic Forecasts." *American Journal of Political Science* 31, 3: 559-83.

Converse, Philip E. 1964. "The Nature of Belief Systems in Mass Publics." In *Ideology and Discontent*, ed. David E. Apter, 206-61. New York: Free Press.

–. 1990. "Popular Representation and the Distribution of Information." In *Information and Democratic Processes*, ed. John Ferejohn and James Kuklinski, 369-88. Chicago: University of Illinois Press.

Cutler, Fred, Richard Johnston, R.K. Carty, André Blais, and Patrick Fournier. 2008. "Deliberation, Information, and Trust: The BC Citizens' Assembly as Agenda Setter." In *Designing Deliberative Democracy: The British Columbia Citizens' Assembly*, ed. Mark Warren and Hilary Pearse, 166-91. Cambridge, UK: Cambridge University Press.

Delli Carpini, Michael, and Scott Keeter. 1996. *What Americans Know about Politics and Why It Matters*. New Haven: Yale University Press.

Downs, Anthony. 1957. *An Economic Theory of Democracy*. New York: HarperCollins.

Duch, Raymond M., Harvey D. Palmer, and Christopher J. Anderson. 2000. "Heterogeneity in Perceptions of National Economic Conditions." *American Journal of Political Science* 44, 4: 635-52.

Eckstein, Harry. 1975. "Case Study and Theory in Political Science." In *Handbook of Political Science: Strategies of Inquiry*, vol. 7, ed. Fred Greenstein and Nelson Polsby, 79-137. Reading, MA: Addison-Wesley.

Evans, Geoffrey, and Robert Andersen. 2006. "The Political Conditioning of Economic Perceptions." *Journal of Politics* 68, 1: 194-207.

Evans, Geoffrey, and Mark Pickup. 2007. "The Political Conditioning of Economic Perceptions in the 2004 Presidential Election." Paper presented at the annual meeting of the Midwest Political Science Association, Chicago, 12 April.

Festinger, Leon. 1957. *A Theory of Cognitive Dissonance*. Evanston, IL: Row, Peterson.

Finkel, Steven. 1993. "Reexamining the Minimal Effects Model in Recent Presidential Campaigns." *Journal of Politics* 55, 1: 1-21.

Fiorina, Morris P. 1981. *Retrospective Voting in American National Elections*. New Haven: Yale University Press.

Fournier, Patrick. 2002. "The Uninformed Canadian Voter." In *Citizen Politics: Research and Theory in Canadian Political Behaviour*, ed. Joanna Everitt and Brenda O'Neill, 92-109. Don Mills, ON: Oxford University Press.

Gelman, Andrew, and Gary King. 1993. "Why Are American Presidential Election Campaign Polls So Variable When Votes Are So Predictable?" *British Journal of Political Science* 23, 4: 409-51.

Gomez, Brad T., and J. Matthew Wilson. 2003. "Causal Attribution and Economic Voting in American Congressional Elections." *Political Research Quarterly* 56, 3: 271-82.

Haller, H. Brandon, and Helmut Norpoth. 1997. "Reality Bites: News Exposure and Economic Opinion." *Public Opinion Quarterly* 61, 4: 555-76.

Holbrook, Thomas. 2002. "Presidential Campaigns and the Knowledge Gap." *Political Communication* 19, 4: 437-54.

Jenkins, Richard. 2002. "How Campaigns Matter in Canada: Priming and Learning as Explanations for the Reform Party's 1993 Campaign Success." *Canadian Journal of Political Science* 35, 2: 383-408.

Johnston, Richard, and Henry Brady. 2002. "The Rolling Cross-Section Design." *Electoral Studies* 21, 2: 283-95.

Johnston, Richard, Michael Hagen, and Kathleen Hall Jamieson. 2004. *The 2000 Presidential Election and the Foundations of Party Politics*. Cambridge, UK: Cambridge University Press.

Key, V.O. 1968. *The Responsible Electorate: Rationality in Presidential Voting, 1936-1960*. New York: Vintage Books.

Kiewiet, D. Roderick. 1983. *Macroeconomics and Micropolitics: The Electoral Effects of Economic Issues*. Chicago: University of Chicago Press.

Kramer, Gerald H. 1971. "Short-Term Fluctuations in U.S. Voting Behaviour, 1896-1964." *American Political Science Review* 65, 1: 131-43.

Kuklinski, James, and Paul Quirk. 2001. "Conceptual Foundations of Citizen Competence." *Political Behaviour* 23, 3: 285-311.

Lazarsfeld, Paul, Bernard Berelson, and Hazel Gaudet. 1944. *The People's Choice*. New York: Columbia University Press.

Lewis-Beck, Michael. 2006. "Does Economics Still Matter? Econometrics and the Vote." *Journal of Politics* 68, 1: 208-12.

Lewis-Beck, Michael, Richard Nadeau, and Angelo Elias. 2008. "Economics, Party, and the Vote: Causality Issues and Panel Data." *American Journal of Political Science* 52, 1: 84-95.

Lewis-Beck, Michael, and Mary Stegmaier. 2000. "Economic Determinants of Election Outcomes." *Annual Review of Political Science* 3: 183-219.

Luskin, Robert C. 1991. "Explaining Political Sophistication." *Political Behaviour* 12, 4: 331-61.

Markus, Gregory. 1988. "The Impact of Personal and National Economic Conditions on the Presidential Vote: A Pooled Cross-Sectional Analysis." *American Journal of Political Science* 32, 1: 137-54.

–. 1992. "The Impact of Personal and National Economic Conditions on Presidential Voting, 1956-1988." *American Journal of Political Science* 36, 3: 829-34.

Matthews, J. Scott. 2006. "Campaign Learning and the Economy." PhD diss., University of British Columbia.

Mendelsohn, Matthew, and Fred Cutler. 2000. "The Effect of Referendums on Democratic Citizens: Information, Politicization, Efficacy, and Tolerance." *British Journal of Political Science* 30, 4: 685-99.

Mutz, Diana C. 1992. "Mass Media and the Depoliticization of Personal Experience." *American Journal of Political Science* 36, 2: 483-509.

–. 1994. "Contextualizing Personal Experience: The Role of Mass Media." *Journal of Politics* 56, 3: 689-714.

–. 1998. *Impersonal Influence: How Perceptions of Mass Collectives Affect Political Attitudes.* New York: Cambridge University Press.

Organization for Economic Cooperation and Development (OECD). 2005. *Economic Outlook No. 77.* Paris: OECD.

Page, Benjamin I., and Robert Y. Shapiro. 1992. *The Rational Public: Fifty Years of Trends in Americans' Policy Preferences.* Chicago: University of Chicago Press.

Patterson, Thomas, and Robert McClure. 1976. *The Unseeing Eye: The Myth of Television Power in National Politics.* New York: Putnam.

Petty, Richard, and John Cacioppo. 1986. *Communication and Persuasion: Central and Peripheral Routes to Attitude Change.* New York: Springer-Verlag.

Price, Vincent, and John Zaller. 1993. "Who Gets the News? Alternative Measures of News Reception and Their Implications for Research." *Public Opinion Quarterly* 57, 2: 133-64.

Redlawsk, David. 2002. "Hot Cognition or Cool Consideration? Testing the Effects of Motivated Reasoning on Political Decision Making." *Journal of Politics* 54, 4: 1021-44.

Sears, David. 1993. "Symbolic Politics: A Socio-Psychological Theory." In S. Iyengar and W. J. McGuire (eds.), *Explorations in Political Psychology.* Durham, NC: Duke University Press.

Sekhon, Jasjeet. 2004. "The Varying Role of Voter Information across Democratic Societies." Unpublished manuscript, Harvard University.

Sniderman, Paul, Richard Brody, and Philip Tetlock. 1991. *Reasoning and Choice: Explorations in Political Psychology.* New York: Cambridge University Press.

Stevenson, Randolph, and Lynn Vavreck. 2000. "Does Campaign Length Matter? Testing for Cross-National Effects." *British Journal of Political Science* 30, 2: 217-35.

Trimble, Linda, and Shannon Sampert. 2004. "Who's in the Game? The Framing of the Canadian Election 2000 by the *Globe and Mail* and the *National Post.*" *Canadian Journal of Political Science* 37, 1: 51-71.

Weatherford, M. Stephen. 1983. "Economic Voting and the 'Symbolic Politics' Argument: A Reinterpretation and Synthesis." *American Political Science Review* 77, 1: 158-74.

Zaller, John. 1992. *The Nature and Origins of Mass Opinion.* New York: Cambridge University Press.

Election Campaign Polls and Democracy in Canada: Examining the Evidence behind the Common Claims

Mark Pickup

Political information is a key component of democratic elections; accurate political information is required for an effective democracy; and an increasing amount of the available information during election campaigns is based on poll results.[1] Beliefs such as these and concerns raised in public hearings about the accuracy of published opinion polls prompted the Royal Commission on Electoral Reform and Party Financing to commission a study to consider which processes should be put in place to regulate campaign polls (Lachapelle 1991). In response, an amendment was made to the Canada Elections Act in 1993 that included regulations on the publication of election polls. Elements of the poll regulations were struck down by the Supreme Court of Canada in 1998, being found to violate the Canadian Charter of Rights and Freedoms. The Canada Elections Act was again amended in 2000 to include further regulations for poll publication (Ferguson and de Clercy 2005). The controversy surrounding polls has only intensified since, particularly after "the failure of the polls" in the 2004 Canadian election.[2]

Concerns have been voiced about the systemic bias in published election polls, the use of poll information by the media in their election coverage, and the ultimate effect of polls on electoral outcomes. Unfortunately, not enough is known about the effect of poll information on voters or about the polls themselves to conduct this debate properly. This is particularly unfortunate as the possible effect of polls on election outcomes has normative implications for democracy in Canada. This chapter considers these implications and examines the evidence behind the common claims that (1) an increasing amount of the media coverage of election campaigns is dominated by poll information; (2) polls published during an election can be systematically biased; (3) the treatment of polls by the media will exacerbate any errors in the polls; and (4) members of the electorate use the information that originates from polls in their vote decisions.

Theory

Arguments over the key components of an ideal democracy have raged on for thousands of years. However, most classic conceptions of democracy require a (somewhat) informed electorate. As clearly stated by Downs (1957, 258), "political information is valuable because it helps citizens make the best possible decisions." And, although some limited forms of democracy only require an informed elite, the need for an informed electorate has become unavoidable in modern Western democracies with the expansion of the franchise. Delli Carpini and Keeter (1996, 57) put it starkly: "The less informed citizens are, the more likely that [election] campaigns will develop into sensationalism and demagoguery, as the media and political leaders play to the public's baser instincts or seek to capitalize on their inability to distinguish between fact and fiction."

The importance of an informed electorate to electoral democracy has caused many to worry about the apparent political ignorance and apathy of most individuals. This concern has led to suggestions that members of the electorate can make informed choices even with limited information. There are various methods by which voters are proposed to be able to turn limited information into informed decisions – such as elite cue taking and information shortcuts (Sniderman, Brody, and Tetlock 1991; Popkin 1994). Matthews' chapter in this volume discusses how political institutions might assist the voter to make an informed choice. In each of the methods, the primary source of information used is that published by the media, particularly during election campaigns. If the polls dominate the information published by the media during election campaigns, as is commonly believed, then they are likely to provide much of the information used by voters. In this way, published election campaign polls might play an important role in electoral democracy. As a large component of the information that is so key to electoral democracy, polls have a real chance of influencing voters and electoral outcomes. Conceptually, this is relatively straightforward. The normative implications are much less clear since they depend greatly on the actual effects of published polls. The current literature suggests a number of possibilities, which are reviewed here.

Studies of poll effects on public opinion often categorize possible effects into "bandwagon" and "underdog," where any psychological process that results in a positive poll result increasing a candidate's popularity is classified as a bandwagon effect (Kenney and Rice 1994). The types of processes that might fall under this category are varied and have different implications for the normative interpretation of the effect of polls. This is also true of the types of processes that produce what is traditionally called an underdog effect – an increase in the popularity of a candidate who is falling behind in the polls. By refining the definitions of bandwagon and underdog effects and considering other psychological processes that others might include under these categories as separate types of effects, we can identify six types of poll effects: strategic, bandwagon, underdog, cue taking, cognitive response, and behavioural response. I turn now to describing these six types of effects.

A *strategic voting effect* refers to the phenomenon of voting for one's second choice to prevent one's third or lower choice from winning an election.[3] Polls can provide information about each candidate's chances of winning an election. If the voter's first choice is clearly unlikely to win, then he or she might consider the second choice. Strategic voting is particularly likely to occur when the voter's second choice is in a tight race with some less preferred candidate. This is a calculation made at the constituency level, so a degree of political sophistication is required for a voter to combine poll information with other political knowledge to assess the choice to vote strategically. Studies have found evidence of strategic voting in Canada in past elections (Johnston et al. 1992; Blais, Gidengil, and Nevitte 2006; Merolla and Stephenson 2007). In the last two Canadian federal elections (2004 and 2006), claims were made regarding the importance of strategic voting in Ontario. Many voters with NDP as their first choice perhaps voted Liberal (their second choice) to prevent a Conservative victory in their constituency (*Winnipeg Free Press*, 29 June 2004; *Toronto Star*, 30 June 2004). Presumably, the incentive to vote strategically increased as polls reported the increased probability of a Conservative win.

An alternative form of strategic voting was also suggested to have occurred in the 2004 election. According to some pollsters (e.g., Adams 2004), many voters wished to penalize the Liberals by returning them as a minority but did not wish to penalize them to the extent of producing a Conservative government. The voters, therefore, used the polls to coordinate their votes to produce the desired outcome. This is not what is traditionally meant by strategic voting, but it is essentially equivalent in terms of how poll information is used to inform one's vote – using information regarding the intended votes of others to optimize the effect of one's own vote choice.

A more traditionally identified poll effect is the *bandwagon effect*, which is affective. It can be a contagion effect in which candidates who are moving up in the polls tend to look more attractive. Or, even if a candidate's qualities do not seem to have improved, a bandwagon effect can occur simply through a desire to be associated with a winner. Generally, some people prefer winners to losers (Bartels 1988; Kenney and Rice 1994).

The *underdog effect* is also affective. Some individuals might sympathize or identify with a party or candidate that is struggling to come from behind. They might even enjoy being identified with the less popular alternative, belonging to the minority, and rejecting majority opinion. Note that the bandwagon and underdog effects are alternative responses to the same event. The same piece of poll information might produce a bandwagon effect in some and an underdog effect in others.

Another possibility is that voters interpret a swing in the polls toward a party as information about the competence of that party, as indicated by the judgment of other voters (a *cue-taking effect*). In this way, poll information is used as a proxy for information that the poll respondents are presumed to have taken the trouble to acquire (Ansolabehere and Iyengar 1994). Cue taking is based on the psychological phenomenon of using heuristics to simplify a complex decision, where heuristics are a loosely defined, simple set of judgmental rules (Kahneman, Slovic, and Tversky 1982) – for example, "if an object is blurry, then it must be far away," or "if more and more people are supporting a party, then that party must have desirable qualities." Bittner's chapter in this volume discusses the use of another type of heuristic, leader evaluations.

A fifth possibility is that polls induce a *cognitive response* (Petty and Cacioppo 1996). When the polls indicate increasing support for a particular party, a voter might ask, "is this possible, and why might this be occurring?" In response, she or he might generate a mental list of the party's positive attributes that could explain the increased popularity and in the process become more likely to support that party (Mutz 1997, 1998). Alternatively, when considering the possible reasons for a party's increasing support in the polls, an individual who is strongly committed to a different party might mentally list counterarguments. Doing so reduces the cognitive dissonance created by being committed to a party that is declining in the polls. This mental resistance to being influenced by the polls is hypothesized to make the individual ultimately less likely to support the party rising in the polls.[4] Although it has been argued (Mutz 1997, 1998) that it is the most sophisticated who will exhibit this type of resistance effect, my reading of cognitive response theory is that it is those with opinions in opposition to that being suggested by the poll information who will exhibit an oppositional reaction. As for sophistication, since cognitive response requires that voters already have available a number of facts or beliefs about the candidates to be listed mentally, the most sophisticated are the most likely to exhibit cognitive response effects in either direction.[5] Unlike the cue-taking effect but like the affective bandwagon/underdog effects, the cognitive response effect accounts for the possibility that the same piece of information can have a different or even opposite effect on different individuals.

The sixth and final possibility is that polls induce a *behavioural response.*[6] It is similar to a cognitive response in the sense that a voter responds to the increased support for a party in the polls by asking why and/or how. It is different in that the voter goes beyond listing what he or she already knows, either to explain the poll or to reduce dissonance, and seeks out new information. The nature of the information sought is likely to be conditioned by previous inclinations, just as with cognitive response. Those inclined to support the party are likely to seek out what the party has done well to deserve an increase in popularity. Those inclined to support an alternative party are likely to seek out information that confirms their position. The ultimate effect on vote intention is likely to be similar to that from a cognitive response, but a real increase in information occurs only for the behavioural response. The latter response also differs in the time scale at which it operates. A single poll alone, unless it suggests a truly surprising result, is unlikely to motivate someone to seek out new information. A sustained change in the polls might, though, so a behavioural response might occur but only after a period of time.

What are the implications of each of these six effects for democracy? Political information, if it is accurate, plays a key role in democracy by allowing voters to make the "correct" choice on election day. A choice is correct when it maximizes the probability that the outcome of the election is optimal from the perspective of the voter making the choice. Defining the optimal outcome for a particular voter is a contentious point of debate. Fortunately, it is not necessary to resolve this debate to assess the value of poll results as political information.

Beginning with strategic voting, if poll information can help voters to understand that their first choice has no chance of winning and that they can best use their vote to choose between their second and third choices, then this information is of benefit to democracy. It is beneficial in that it reduces the likelihood of a commonly identified problem with plurality electoral systems – wasted votes.[7]

Cue taking might also be a benefit to democracy, at least to the extent that the cue operates properly. At best, it allows voters who are disinclined to spend a great deal of time gathering other political information to make a more informed choice than they would otherwise. Given the disinclination of democratic electorates (Canadian and otherwise) to invest in information gathering,[8] poll information used as a cue can be very beneficial. Of course, cues do not always operate properly. Because they are shortcuts, they can cause voters to make incorrect inferences.

The behavioural response results in voters seeking out new information. They can acquire information that they might not have otherwise considered. From the perspective that more information is better than less when making an electoral choice, the behavioural response to poll information benefits the democratic process.

The cognitive response causes voters to sift through the information that they already have and selectively emphasize key items. Individuals are most likely to select those pieces of information that favour the party that they are most inclined to support. In this way, cognitive response reinforces the positions of those who already have inclinations. Poll information then acts to solidify positions, reduce indecision, and polarize the electorate. In terms of its democratic effects, cognitive response motivates voters to clarify their opinions but does not in itself add any new information to the choice.

As affective responses, both the bandwagon and the underdog effects provide no assistance to voters in making the correct choice. The appeal of a party and candidate will increase whether or not they are the correct choice. If either of these responses leads to the voter making the correct electoral choice, it is only by coincidence. Therefore, bandwagon and underdog effects are not only of no benefit but also potentially harmful to democracy.

Clearly, the normative implications of poll effects on Canadian democracy depend on the exact mechanism or mechanisms at work. So what types of poll effects are seen in Canada? No piece of research on polls in Canada has been able to distinguish between each type. A large part of the difficulty is due to two subtle distinctions that have been glossed over in the previous six descriptions of poll effects. First, some of these effects are depicted as the consequences of polls indicating an increase (or decrease) in the popularity of a party, regardless of its popularity relative to other parties. Other effects require not only increased (or decreased) popularity in the polls for a party but also that the party leads (or trails) the other parties. Cognitive response, behavioural response, and cue taking, for example, are produced by movement in the polls, independent of which party is ahead or behind. Compare these responses with a bandwagon effect that can only occur for a party in the lead or an underdog effect that can only occur for a party trailing behind. Different again, strategic voting can only occur when the polls indicate a specific ordering of party support.

A second distinction is that some effects suggest that a party will be rewarded for upward movement in the polls, and some effects suggest that a party will be rewarded for downward movement in the polls, whereas other effects suggest that the same piece of poll information can have two different effects – with some individuals moving toward and other individuals moving away from an increasingly popular party.

These distinctions require that models of poll effects must account for individual-level and contextual differences. Different individuals might respond differently to the same movement in polls depending on their previous preferences, and the same individual might respond differently to the same movement depending on the relative aggregate support for the parties at the time. Moreover, some of the mechanisms are more likely among low-information individuals (for example, cue taking), whereas others are more likely among high-information individuals (for example, cognitive response). The ability to distinguish between different mechanisms of poll effects is vital to determining the normative implications of polls on democracy in Canada. Unfortunately, this ability is just beyond the current reach of observational studies of poll effects in Canada and elsewhere, although some experimental studies are making important headway in the United States (Ansolabehere and Iyengar 1994).

It is important to note, though, that (1) any of the suggested mechanisms could be detrimental to democratic elections if they are based on biased poll information, but (2) it is not at all clear that Canadians even use information from polls in their vote decisions.[9] We will turn our attention to these issues after first considering the availability of poll information in the media during election campaigns.

Analyses

Canadian Election Campaign Polls and Media Coverage

As indicated in the introduction, this chapter examines four common claims regarding the role of polls in Canadian elections. The first claim examined is that an increasing amount of the media coverage of election campaigns is dominated by poll information. This is euphemistically called "horse race journalism."[10] Claims of this sort were raised in Canada after the 1984 election (Wagenberg et al. 1988). There is some evidence that this claim of poll dominance has become true in the United States (Frankovic 2005). But is this true in Canada? Public opinion polling began in Canada with the 1941 poll by the Canadian Institute of Public Opinion – also known as Gallup Canada – and Canadian parties began to use polling by the 1960s (Carty, Cross, and Young 2000). However, published election polls really did not take off until the 1980s. Prior to the 1984 election, Gallup was virtually the only house producing published election polls. Each party had its own pollsters working for it, but of course the results of these polls were not made public. Published polls not originating with Gallup were few and far between. Gallup itself published only a limited number of polls in a given election campaign. For each of the 1965 and 1979 elections, Gallup produced and published three polls. During the 1968, 1972, and 1974 elections, Gallup produced only two polls per election. The 1980 election saw four published polls from Gallup.[11] Table 10.1 provides a summary of polls published during federal elections since the 1980 election.

The first two columns of Table 10.1 indicate the length of each election campaign and the number of independent polls published.[12] The column indicating the number of independent polls suggests that there has been a steady increase, with 1988 as an outlier. It is an outlier in that the number of polls published (twenty-two) is even greater than one would expect from a simple election-by-election increase. It was not until the 2000 election that the equivalent number of polls was published (twenty-three). The 2000 level was then nearly tripled in 2006 with sixty-six independent polls. As the number of polls published is potentially a function of the length of the campaign period, the third column contains the average number of polls published per campaign day. Again, there has been a clear increase. The 1984 election saw an average of 0.18 polls per campaign day. By 2004, the equivalent statistic is 0.72 polls per day. The 2006 campaign represents the first time that there were more polls

Table 10.1

Summary of published federal election polls, 1984-2006

Election		Length of campaign period	Number of independent polls	Polls/days	Number of polling organizations	Last poll – days before end	First poll – days before beginning	Proportion of newspaper election coverage
08 September	1984	57	10	0.18	6	6	0	0.11
21 November	1988	51	22	0.43	5	4	0	0.25
25 October	1993	47	13	0.28	6	4	0	0.27
02 June	1997	36	13	0.36	7	5	4	0.30
27 November	2000	36	23	0.64	7	3	0	0.30
28 June	2004	36	26	0.72	6	3	0	0.32
23 January	2006	55	66	1.2	8	1	0	0.27

Sources: (for all but newspaper coverage data): 1984 data (Frizzell and Westell 1985); 1988 data (Johnston et al. 1992, Table 4-1); 1993 data (Blais, Gidengil, and Nevitte 2006); 1997 data (Andersen and Fox 2001); 2000 data (elections website maintained by Andrew Heard, Simon Fraser University, http://www.sfu.ca/); 2004 and 2006 data (Pickup and Johnston 2007). *Sources* for newspaper coverage data: for 1993 through 2006, the statistics are based on a calculation of all election campaign stories in two national and four regional newspapers that mentioned election polls.[1] These papers are the *Globe and Mail,* the *National Post,* the *Vancouver Sun,* the *Calgary Herald,* the *Toronto Star,* and the Montreal *Gazette.* The data for 1984 and 1988 are from Frizzell and Westell (1985) and Frizzell, Pammett, and Westell (1989) respectively. this analysis were provided by Stuart Soroka and Lori Young. The results for 1984 and 1988 are from Frizzell and Westell (1985) and Frizzell, Pammett, and Westell (1989) respectively.

Note: The polling houses included in the count of polls are Gallup, CROP, Carlton, Sorecom, Angus Reid, Environics, Insight Canada Research, Canada Facts, Comquest Research, Leger, Ekos, SES, Ipsos Reid, Decima, Pollara, Strategic Counsel, Zogby, Compas, and unidentified houses that conducted polls for CTV and CBC in 1984.

1 This was done simply by counting every story that included the word poll or some derivative (polls, polling, etc.). Further analysis examined the average number of times that the word poll and its derivatives appeared and the average position of the mention of polls relative to the beginning of the media story. This analysis also revealed no significant change over the 1953-2006 period.

than there were campaign days, with an average of 1.2 polls being published per day. This is particularly remarkable given that this campaign period includes the Christmas and New Year breaks, during which no polls were published.

Clearly, coverage of election campaigns by polls has increased in terms of their sheer number. This has also resulted in a greater proportion of the campaign being covered by polls in the field. For example, polling has extended further and further to the end of the campaign. Polls have generally always been in the field during the first days of the campaign but historically not during the last days – at least not published polls. As the number of polls has increased, the period between the last poll in the field and election day has shrunk till, in 2006, published polls were in the field right until the day before. This increased coverage has occurred even though the Canada Elections Act prohibits polls from being published within twenty-four hours of election day.[13] Consequently, the last poll in the field in 2006 was not published until after the election.

Interestingly, this increased coverage of the campaign by polls has not really been matched by an increase in the number of polling houses. In 2006, there were eight houses producing published polls compared with six houses in 1984.[14] This essentially means that increased poll coverage is a product of each polling house producing a greater number of polls than in previous elections.

Has the increased coverage of the election campaign by polls both in terms of the number of polls published and the proportion of the campaign period covered meant an increase in the proportion of campaign media coverage using poll information? This is the common wisdom in Canada and the empirical evidence in the United States (Frankovic 2005). As it turns out, this is an instance in which political patterns in Canada have not reflected those in the United States, and the common wisdom is incorrect. In terms of election campaign media coverage (measured through newspaper articles), the proportion that uses poll information has not increased substantially since 1988. This can be seen in the final column of Table 10.1, which presents the proportion of newspaper election coverage that refers to polls.[15]

There was a clear increase in media coverage of polls between the 1984 and 1988 elections. The proportion of newspaper campaign stories referring to polls increased from 11 to 25 percent. The level of media coverage of polls in 1984 was itself an increase over the levels of previous elections. During the 1979 election, only 5.7 percent of newspaper campaign stories referred to polls (Soderlund et al. 1984). This finding is consistent with the trend suggested by Wagenberg et al. (1988). Since 1988, though, the proportion of newspaper election coverage referencing polls has remained relatively steady, with a high of 32 percent in 2004. The 2006 election saw levels similar to that of the 1993 election – 27 percent. Despite the much larger number of polls in 2006 relative to those of 1988, the proportion of media coverage dedicated to polls is basically the same.

The evidence suggests that concerns about poll information increasingly dominating election media coverage are premature if not unfounded. However, the statistics clearly indicate that a substantial part of media coverage does use poll information and engage in horse race journalism (Andersen 2000). What are the consequences? One of the clearest concerns regarding polls published during an election campaign is that they can be systemically biased. Even if polls are used in such a way as to produce an information gain (through cue taking, a behavioural response, or strategic voting), this gain could be negated by a systemic bias in the polls. Worse yet, systemically biased poll information could produce a misinformed electorate. The potential for a systemic bias in Canadian election campaign polls is the second claim that I examine in this chapter.

Canadian Election Campaign Polls and Systemic Bias

Published campaign polls were a matter of controversy in the 2004 and 2006 Canadian elections (Pickup and Johnston 2007). The Canadian debate echoed controversy elsewhere, notably in the United States, the United Kingdom, Germany, and France.[16] Due to the controversy surrounding them, the performance of campaign polls was headline news. For 2004, the press largely agreed that predictions missed their target. Jeffrey Simpson in the *Globe and Mail* (29 June 2004) suggested that election "night's biggest losers were pollsters, none of whom had accurately predicted the size of the Liberal popular vote." In 2006, according to a Montreal *Gazette* headline the day after election day, "pollsters missed their mark again: Liberal support again underestimated as most firms misread Canadian voters."[17]

The concern regarding poll accuracy[18] in Canada, as well as elsewhere, goes well beyond issues of random sampling error and focuses on issues of bias. It is common for measures, such as vote intention, to contain a systemic error (bias) as well as random sampling error (Zeller and Carmines 1980; Marks 2007). It is common to think of the systematic error as being fixed or at least non-random, but more generally it is a random error with a non-zero mean. Although sampling error is a well-understood phenomenon, bias is not. It is not a conscious misrepresentation of reality but the product of the methodological practices of the individual survey firms (Traugott 2001, 2005), and it is systemic in the sense that the errors have a non-zero mean. This non-zero mean distinguishes it from sampling error, which has a mean of zero, and it results in the individual firms producing vote intention results for the parties that are *on average* too high or too low. The magnitude and direction of this average over- or underestimation for a given firm is called its "house bias." It is the average direction as well as the distance of a polling firm from the target (the true vote intention), excluding inaccuracy due to random sources of error, such as from sampling.

Methodological choices made by houses that may (or may not) result in a systemic error include how they convert a general commitment to equal probability of selection into a specific set of fieldwork choices – for instance, the method of choosing telephone numbers (the sampling frame), persistence in clearance of the numbers once chosen, selection of respondents within households, and post-stratification weighting of data;[19] method of interview – telephone, online, face to face, or mail out; whether or not and how to employ "likely voter" screens;[20] how to frame the vote intention question; and how to treat "undecided" respondents. Other methodological decisions include the number of days that the poll is in the field, polling on weekdays versus weekends, interviewer training, procedures for coping with refusals, and the use of tracking polls and/or panels.[21] The collection of choices for a given house will produce a systemic bias to the extent that each choice produces a consistent error in the polls. Consequently, a given house might consistently under- or overestimate the support for a given party. Moreover, just as individual houses might exhibit systemic errors, the industry as a whole might also exhibit a bias. This "industry bias" is the average bias of all the houses engaged in polling. This bias can occur simply because individual house biases do not average out to zero or because of methodological problems in polling that affect all houses in an equivalent manner. An example is universally low response rates leading to sample bias (Lau 1994).

In terms of the potential effect of campaign polls on democracy, both house and industry effects are troublesome. Even if the house effects average out to a zero industry bias, depending on the treatment of polls by the media, house bias might also be a source of concern – for example, if the media disproportionately report polls from a house with a bias (more on this in the next section). Surprisingly, then, the bulk of the work on poll accuracy fails to separate sampling error from bias and simply focuses on how well the last polls predicted the election outcome (Buchanan 1986; Crespi 1988; Shelley and Hwang 1991; Worcester 1996; Mitofsky 1998; Traugott 2001, 2005).

Fortunately, there are a few key pieces of work that centre on the issue of bias. Pickup and Johnston (2008), Wlezien and Erikson (2002), Erikson and Wlezien (1999), and Lau (1994) examine the biases of polling houses in US presidential elections, finding significant individual biases. Erikson and Sigelman (1995) demonstrate that the polling industry contains an incumbent bias in US midterm congressional elections. Jackman (2005) demonstrates that a number of polling houses produced biased polls in the 2004 Australian federal election, consistently underestimating Coalition support. The estimates of house and industry bias are varied and sometimes complex – for a comparison of methods, see Pickup and Johnston (2008) – but they generally all agree that such biases can and do exist.

In the Canadian context, Pickup and Johnston (2007) demonstrated that in 2004 and 2006 individual houses exhibited biases, as did the industry as a whole. There was less industry bias in 2006 than in 2004 – but only marginally so. In each election, the industry underestimated the Liberal share and overestimated the NDP one. On average, it underestimated Liberal support by 3.8 and 3.6 percentage points in the 2004 and 2006 elections, respectively. It overestimated NDP support by 2.9 and 1.6 percentage points.[22]

Correcting for the house and industry biases in the 2004 and 2006 Canadian federal elections produces a very different picture for each election campaign relative to the raw polls. The 2004 case can be seen in Figures 10.1 through 10.3. Figure 10.1 is an illustration of the raw poll results (each day that a poll was in the field is represented by a separate point, so each poll appears as a series of identical values over consecutive days). Figure 10.1 also provides the "poll of polls" – the average reading for all polls in the field on a given day weighted by sample size (which

Figure 10.1

Poll of polls for vote intention share (2004) (with raw polls)

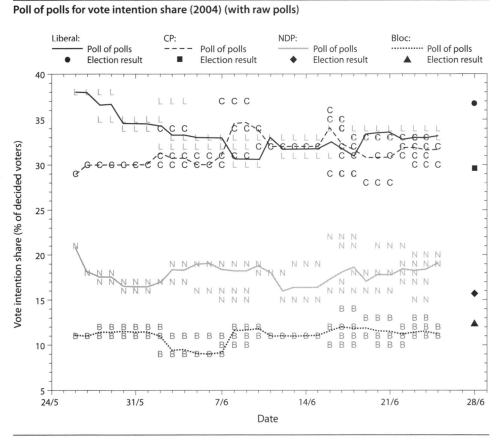

Note: Scatterplot points are results from the raw polls, replicated for each day that the poll was in the field.

for any published poll is its total size divided by the number of days in the field). Together the raw data and the poll of polls tell a story similar to that presented in the media. After an initial loss in support by the Liberals to the Conservatives, the support for each party swung back and forth, with some polls suggesting that the Conservatives could win the election with a strong minority and the Liberals trailing far behind (*National Post*, 12 June 2004). One election postmortem even suggested that at one point the Conservatives were about 20 percentage points ahead of the Liberals ("How the Race was Won," *Globe and Mail*, 14 July 2004). Figure 10.1 also suggests a fair bit of movement in support for the NDP and Bloc Québécois.

Figure 10.2

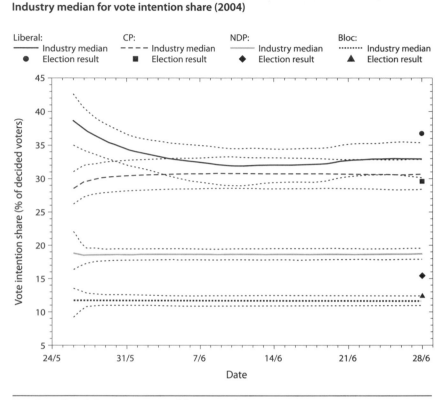

Industry median for vote intention share (2004)

Liberal:	CP:	NDP:	Bloc:
—— Industry median	– – – Industry median	—— Industry median	⋯⋯ Industry median
● Election result	■ Election result	◆ Election result	▲ Election result

Note: Dotted lines indicate 95 percent confidence intervals.

Figure 10.2 presents estimates of party support correcting for measurement error and with individual house biases averaged out. The method of estimating the house biases is described elsewhere (Pickup and Johnston 2007), but in short they are estimated by allowing the errors in vote intention estimates to have firm specific non-zero means.[23] These means are the house biases. The daily estimates of support for each party can be adjusted up or down to have the same average systemic error as the house with the median bias. This represents the estimated level of support according to the house with the median house bias. This is the best estimate of party support from the industry as a whole. In some ways, the story is similar to that of Figure 10.1. Once the Liberals lost support to the Conservatives, it was difficult to tell whether either party was ahead. However, contrary to Figure 10.1 and the media's reporting of events

Figure 10.3

Bias-corrected estimate for vote intention share (2004)

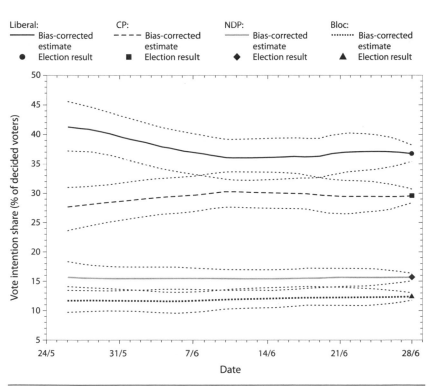

Note: Dotted lines indicate 95 percent confidence intervals.

(which roughly approximated the raw polls), the results from the industry as a whole suggest that the Conservatives were never actually ahead of the Liberals and certainly were not in a position to form a strong minority. Figure 10.2 also demonstrates how little movement there really was in NDP or Bloc support. Moreover, the discrepancy between the industry's estimate of Liberal and NDP support and the actual electoral outcome is clear. The industry overestimated NDP support and underestimated Liberal support.

Figure 10.3 presents estimates of party support in the 2004 election, this time correcting for industry bias. This is done by adjusting the daily estimates of support for each party up or down to have zero systematic error. The election result itself is used to identify the point of zero error – again see Pickup and Johnston (2007, 2008) for details. The story now

Figure 10.4

Poll of polls for vote intention share (2006) (with raw polls)

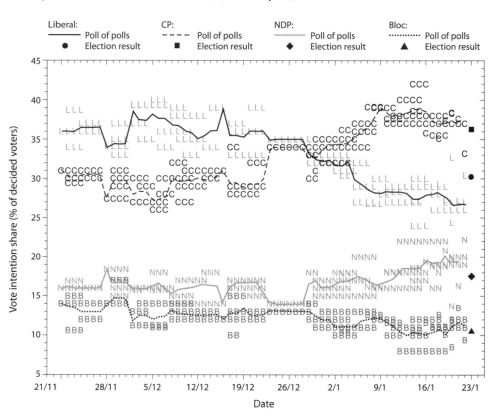

Note: Scatterplot points are results from the raw polls, replicated for each day that the poll was in the field.

is quite a bit different. At no point in the campaign was it unclear that Liberal support was greater than Conservative support. Whether the Liberals would form a minority or majority government was certainly a point of debate, but whether they would win was not. And there certainly was no question of the Conservatives winning a strong minority.

As the above demonstrates, the polls described a very different race than the one that occurred. The results of correcting for house and industry bias in the 2006 election also produce differing pictures of the campaign, although the difference is less dramatic due to the greater magnitude of the actual movement in party support (see Figures 10.4 to

Figure 10.5

Industry median for vote intention share (2006)

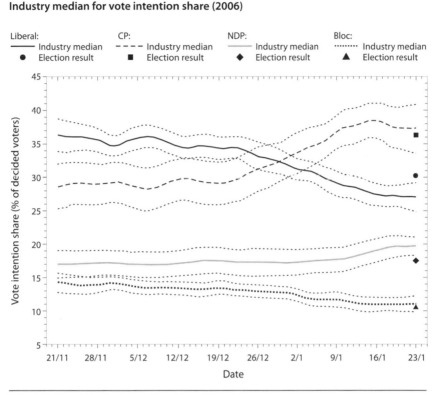

Liberal:
— Industry median
● Election result

CP:
--- Industry median
■ Election result

NDP:
— Industry median
◆ Election result

Bloc:
········ Industry median
▲ Election result

Note: Dotted lines indicate 95 percent confidence intervals.

10.6). In 2006, the real loss of Liberal support to the Conservatives was much more extensive than in 2004. Consequently, the Conservative advantage suggested by the raw polls was not purely an artifact of poll bias (Figure 10.4).

However, a comparison of the industry estimate of support and the industry bias corrected estimate of support makes it clear that the polls greatly overestimated the Conservative advantage (Figures 10.5 and 10.6). The media overestimated the success of the Conservatives and incorrectly suggested the possibility (cautiously this time) of a Conservative majority.

In these accounts of the 2004 and 2006 Canadian federal elections, references to mistakes in media coverage are connected to biases in polling. These are anecdotal examples and leave open the question of whether

Figure 10.6

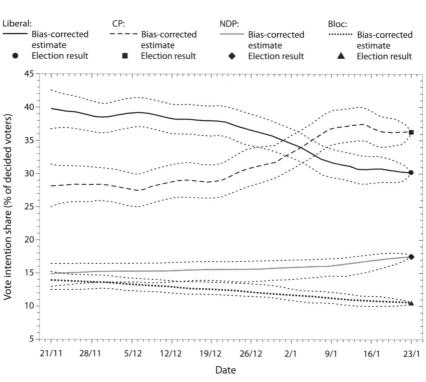

Bias-corrected estimate for vote intention share (2006)

Note: Dotted lines indicate 95 percent confidence intervals.

systemic errors in polls will be reflected in their treatment by the media. This question is of key importance if polls are to have an effect on public opinion, electoral outcome, and ultimately democracy in Canada.

Canadian Election Campaign Polls and Media Exacerbation of Bias

We can now examine the third claim: treatment of polls by the media will exacerbate any errors in the polls. This belief stems in part from the concern that those reporting polls do not properly understand statistical concepts such as measurement error (Soderlund et al. 1984). It is also partly a concern about the fact that certain news outlets have arrangements with certain polling houses, and the results from certain polling houses are disproportionately covered by the news media. If these houses are afflicted with bias, then the reported poll results might be biased even if the results from the industry as a whole are not. These concerns, however, might be unfounded. The converse might hold. The media's treatment of polls could mitigate any errors. The media might focus on results that are unbiased even if the results from the industry as a whole are biased. Moreover, if a large enough range of results is reported by the media, then discrepancies produced by problems such as measurement error might simply be averaged out.

One of the simplest ways to get at the truth is to examine exactly which polls the media report and how often they do so. I do this here for the 2006 election by examining all stories reporting election poll results found in the front sections of two national (*National Post* and *Globe and Mail*) and four regional (*Vancouver Sun, Calgary Herald, Toronto Star,* Montreal *Gazette*) papers during the period of the election campaign. Of all the stories mentioning polls, 151 made specific reference to vote intention results.[24] For each of these stories, the poll(s) reported as a measure of current party support were identified. As a summary of the poll information reported, a daily "media signal" statistic was calculated. This is the mean reported support for a given party over all stories mentioning polls on a given day.[25]

The media signal for the Liberals and Conservatives is presented in Figure 10.7. It also presents the average support for the Liberals and Conservatives calculated over all polls released on a given day. The difference represents the discrepancy between the average released poll (uncorrected for measurement error or bias) and the average media report of polls – in short, the difference between the polls released and the polls covered in the media. It is immediately evident that, for the first part of the campaign, the media were more likely to report stories that indicated lower support for the Liberals than did the average poll. This "media bias" is particularly interesting as the polls themselves underestimated Liberal support (on average 3.6 percentage points, as discussed earlier). In this way, the media exacerbated the bias already present in the polls.

For the remainder of the campaign and for the Conservative Party throughout, the media signal generally lined up with that from the polls. Therefore, during the post-New Year portion of the campaign, the bias in the polls (underestimating Liberal support) was faithfully reflected in the media coverage – being neither exacerbated nor mitigated. This is true, at least, in terms of the levels of support reported. As for the volatility, the media's coverage exaggerated this aspect of party support.[26] This is particularly evident in the final days of the campaign. The polls

Figure 10.7

Media signal: Liberal and Conservative vote intention share (2006)

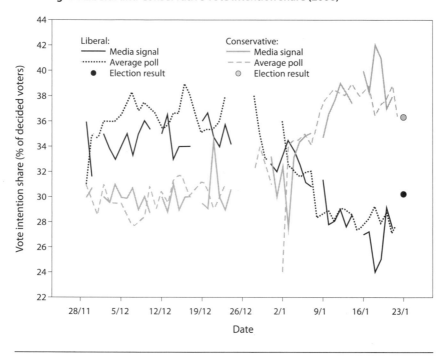

themselves, due to measurement error, indicated greater volatility than likely existed.[27] So the media also exacerbated this element of inaccuracy in poll measures of support. For example, on 21 January – three days before the election – SES released a poll suggesting that Liberal support was at 29.4 percent, Strategic Counsel released a poll suggesting that Liberal support was at 27 percent, and Ekos released a poll suggesting that Liberal support was at 24.4 percent. The average of these results – 27 percent – is consistent with polls estimating public opinion before and after that day. On average, however, the media put much greater focus on the lower (more interesting) Ekos poll than on the Strategic Counsel or SES poll. Consequently, the media signal suggested a rather substantial drop in Liberal support and exaggerated the volatility in party support in the final days of the campaign.

As for the Bloc Québécois and the NDP, the media signal was similar to the released polls in terms of both level and volatility of support. There is some indication that the media were more likely to report polls that

Figure 10.8

Media signal: NDP and Bloc vote intention share (2006)

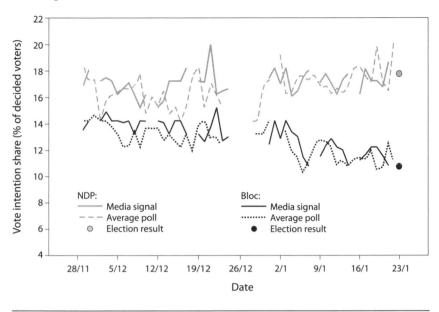

indicated higher support for the Bloc than did the average poll, introducing a bias that did not already exist in the polls. This effect, however, is relatively minor.

Overall, the evidence certainly suggests that the media's treatment of election campaign polls in no way mitigated the measurement error or bias inherent in the polls. In some instances, the media exacerbated the problems presented both by bias and by measurement error. This is bad news for the media, but what does it mean for public opinion and/or democracy? Does the electorate actually use the information provided by the media in its vote decisions? This commonly claimed possibility is the focus of the next and penultimate section of this chapter.

Canadian Election Campaign Polls and Their Effects on the Electorate

The bulk of the literature examining the effects of polls does so for presidential primaries (Marshall 1983; Bartels 1988; Sigelman 1989), and it is generally argued that poll effects should be relatively smaller for national elections (Hickman 1991).[28] However, plenty of evidence (much of it from experimental work) suggests that poll effects do occur during national elections: during US presidential elections (Fleitas 1971; Ceci and Kain 1982; Skalaban 1988; Ansolabehere and Iyengar 1994); during UK general elections (Marsh 1985; McAllister and Studlar 1991); during Dutch national elections (Irwin and van Holsteyn 2002); during New Zealand national elections (Vowles 2002); and during Canadian federal elections (Blais, Gidengil, and Nevitte 2006).

Finding empirical evidence of poll effects using observational studies is complicated by what is known as an endogeneity issue. Published election polls are a measure of public opinion. Analysts measure the effect of polls on public opinion with another poll. If a published election poll suggests that support for the Liberals has increased just a day or two before the analyst's poll suggests that support for the Liberals has increased, then one must ask, is this a function of polls affecting public opinion, or are both polls simply capturing the same upward swing in support produced by any number of other potential campaign effects? As the solution to this issue is technically complicated, I relegate its description to the appendix of this chapter. In summary, the vote model that solves this thorny issue is presented in Figure 10.9.

The first line of the model describes the probability of voter i intending to vote for the party of interest (coded $IVOTE_{it} = 1$) at a particular time t given the polls published at time t. This probability is represented by V_{it}. It states that this is a non-linear function, which is based on a logistic model of vote intention.[29] The probability of an individual voting for the party of interest at a given time t is a non-linear function of an equilibrium to which public opinion reverts in the absence of campaign activity (γ_{00}), published polls (γ_{01}), and other campaign events (μ_{0t}). The effect of these other events is the usual residuals in a poll effects model. Here they are modelled as an autoregressive process in the final line, so that the residuals are v_t.[30] The crux of the solution to the endogeneity problem is to specify the model in such a way as to prevent the residuals,

Figure 10.9

Poll effects vote model

$$PR\,(IVOTE_{it} = 1|poll_t) = V_{it} = \frac{1}{1 + \exp\,[-(\gamma_{00} + \gamma_{01}poll_t + \mu_{0t})]}$$

$$\mu_{0t} = \rho\mu_{0,t-1} + v_t$$

---

the product of other campaign events, in such a way as to prevent them from being correlated with the published polls.[31] Specifying the model in this way removes the potential for the estimated poll effect to be biased.[32]

This is an overly simple model in that it does not allow for the fact that poll effects might vary by individual.[33] (The appendix describes how this added complexity can be included in such a model.) There is plenty of evidence that the influence of political information varies across individuals (Zaller 1991, 1992) and preliminary evidence that this is true for information from political polls (Pickup 2007). Due to the multiplicity of mechanisms through which polls can have their effect on voters, as described at the beginning of this chapter, determining individual-level differences in poll effects is important in understanding fully the implications of polls for the health of democracy in Canada. Specific models that capture each of the possible mechanisms are beyond the scope of this chapter or the literature on poll effects as it currently stands. However, it is still useful to estimate a baseline model to get a sense of what the average poll effect is for a given party. This is the net effect of polls after the cross-cutting consequences of different individuals being moved in different directions cancel each other out. This effect is not without interest since it represents the potential for polls to change the outcome of an election and since evidence of any poll effects in Canadian elections is still rather limited. It is particularly interesting for the 2006 election given the evidence of industry bias in the published polls.

An analysis using this model was run using individual-level vote intention data from the 2006 Canadian Election Study and the media report of poll results as calculated in the previous section.[34] Undecided voters were excluded from the analysis. The results are presented in Table 10.2. Poll effects are positive and significant for the Liberal and Conservative Parties. They are insignificant for the NDP and Bloc Québécois.[35] Individuals do use information from polls in their vote decisions. Determining the magnitude of a poll effect is a little tricky as any change in popularity due to poll information might be reflected in the next poll, which would in turn produce an additional change, and so on. Given the magnitude of the estimated coefficients, each subsequent change would be smaller than the previous one (as demonstrated below), so poll effects do not increase indefinitely, but their full effect is not necessarily felt immediately. Some examples might be useful.

Table 10.2

Estimated poll effects, 2006 election

		Poll effect	Constant	Residuals Q-test	
Liberals	Log odds	0.043**	-2.092	Q statistic	19.090
	SD	(0.014)	(0.472)	p value	0.793
Conservatives	Log odds	0.039***	-1.956	Q statistic	18.900
	SD	(0.010)	(0.341)	p value	0.802
NDP	Log odds	-0.013	-1.363	Q statistic	18.980
	SD	(0.048)	(0.816)	p value	0.798
Bloc	Log odds	0.013	-2.265	Q statistic	18.410
	SD	(0.090)	(1.196)	p value	0.824

Note: ** two-tailed *p* value < .01, *** two-tailed *p* value < .001

To start, assume that Liberal popularity is at 30.2 percent. This was the Liberals' electoral vote percentage. Also assume that there has not been any new poll information in quite some time. If a poll is published that accurately reports the Liberals' popularity, then it will result in an additional 0.94 of a percentage point boost for the Liberals. If this popularity boost is not picked up in subsequent polls, then Liberal popularity will remain at the new 31 percent. If the gain in popularity is reflected in subsequent polls, then the Liberals will receive an additional 0.88 of a percentage point in popularity.[36] If the next published poll reports the Liberals' new popularity (about 32 percent), the party will gain 0.83 of a percentage point, bringing it to 32.8 percent. It is in this way that increased popularity can build momentum. Each additional gain reflected in the polls produces an additional (but gradually decreasing) boost.

Now assume that Liberal popularity increases by 1 percent to 33.8 percent. Part of this increase might be due to momentum, and part might be due to campaign events. As before, news of this increase in popularity will gain the Liberals a boost (0.76 of a percentage point), taking their popularity to a high of 34.6 percent. However, consider a scenario where Liberal popularity does not increase and remains at 32.8 percent but where a poll reports the Liberals' popularity as 33.8 percent simply because of measurement error. Media-reported increases will still gain the Liberals support. The gain will be 0.78 of a percentage point, bringing Liberal popularity to 33.6 percent. Obviously, this is not as good a scenario for the Liberals as that in which the reported gain is real, but note that the error in the poll is almost self-fulfilling. A 1 percent over-estimation of support results in a popularity gain of almost 0.8 of a percentage point. The reporting of this increase in popularity, even though it is due to measurement error, will result in a subsequent gain. Therefore, popularity can build momentum off an inaccurate poll, even in the absence of real movement.

Figure 10.7 suggests that the media-reported polls underrepresented Liberal support at the start of the campaign but caught up with public opinion (minus the 3.6 percent poll bias) by Christmas 2005. An alternative interpretation suggested by these estimated poll effects is that it was public opinion that adjusted to match media reports of support. That is, the underrepresentation of Liberal support in the media became self-fulfilling. Further work is required to adjudicate between these two alternatives.

The estimated poll effect for the Conservatives is a little smaller. Assuming that Conservative popularity is at 36.3 percent (the Conservative electoral vote percentage) and a poll is published, inaccurately reporting Conservative support a percentage point higher (37.3 percent), then the Conservatives would receive an additional 0.42 of a percentage point boost in popularity. If this gain were accurately reflected in the next poll, then it would produce an additional gain of 0.39 of a percentage point. The magnitudes of these poll effects suggest that momentum would build up more slowly for the Conservatives than the Liberals.[37]

Now consider the consequences of poll bias. If the polls are continuously biased against the Liberals, then their support is constantly suppressed. This bias would stifle any chances of building momentum. A 3.6 percent bias against the Liberals (the average bias estimated by Pickup and Johnston 2007) would, in fact, more than suppress the Liberals' chances of gaining momentum. Returning to the scenario in which Liberal popularity is 30.2 percent, a poll report with a bias of –3.6 percent would bring Liberal popularity down to 28 percent. If the next poll report is similarly biased, then Liberal support will continue to be drawn downward. In the absence of any other campaign event or poll inaccuracy, this descent would continue until Liberal support reached some minimum value (in this scenario calculated to be roughly 20 percent). There is no evidence of a sustained Conservative poll bias that might have artificially inflated or suppressed Conservative support. Therefore, only the Liberals' potential poll-induced momentum was suppressed.

It is useful to compare these results to earlier work done on the 1988 Canadian federal election (Blais, Gidengil, and Nevitte 2006). This work determined the effect of a change in the difference between the Liberals and Conservatives and the Liberals and NDP in the polls. The estimated effect of a one percentage point change in the difference between the Liberals and the Progressive Conservatives was a 0.52 percentage point difference in the vote. The estimated effect of a one percentage point change in the difference between the Liberals and NDP was a 0.77 percentage point difference in the vote.[38] The magnitude of these effects is roughly that of those found here. In both cases, there is a bigger potential effect for the Liberal Party relative to the Conservative/Progressive Conservative Party. The difference in the results is that those here suggest that the reporting of the change in support would produce an additional change (momentum), whereas the work on the 1988 election does not address this possibility.

In the 2006 election, neither the NDP nor the Bloc Québécois was in a position to develop momentum from poll results (Table 10.2 shows that the poll effect was insignificant). Movement in the polls for these parties did not result in subsequent additional movement when this information was published. As a consequence of the poll bias against the Liberals, only the Conservatives were in a position to receive positive momentum from published poll results. Moreover, the 3.6 percent industry bias against the Liberals would have consistently dampened Liberal support considerably. Therefore, polls did have a substantive effect on public opinion and most likely the outcome of the election.

Conclusion

This chapter began by considering the normative implications of election campaign polls in Canada. Some worry that a heavy emphasis on poll standings conditions the electorate to evaluate candidates in terms of their aggregate popularity rather than their specific policy stances. An electorate that evaluates candidates in this way might produce an election result based on affective responses to limited information rather than reasoned and informed decisions. Others suggest that poll results communicate important information to those with little political information by providing the opinions of voters who have presumably spent the time to collect the necessary political information to make an informed decision. Still others suggest that polls might benefit voters by triggering them to question their previous opinions and/or seek out new information. And some suggest that poll information allows voters to make strategic choices. Importantly, any of the suggested poll effects could be detrimental to democratic elections if they are based on biased poll information. Accordingly, this chapter set out to examine the evidence behind the claims that (1) an increasing amount of the media coverage of election campaigns is dominated by poll information; (2) polls published during an election can be systematically biased; (3) the treatment of polls by the media will exacerbate any errors in the polls; and (4) members of the electorate use the information that originates from polls in their vote decisions.

The collected evidence to date suggests that a significant but not necessarily increasing amount of the media coverage of election campaigns is dominated by poll information. Analyses of the 2004 and 2006 elections confirms that polls published during an election can be systematically biased. Analysis of the 2006 election confirms that the treatment of polls by the media can exacerbate errors in the polls. Finally, the evidence confirms that at least some members of the electorate do use the information that originates from polls in their vote decisions. The jury is still out on the normative implications of poll effects and awaits the type of sophisticated analysis that can distinguish between the many mechanisms by which polls influence public opinion, electoral outcomes, and democracy. Chances are that more than one mechanism is in effect. In the meantime, however, it is clear that work needs to be done on reducing the bias in both polls and their media coverage. These biases are clearly problematic for democracy in Canada, contaminating the information that voters rely on when making electoral decisions.

Acknowledgments
A previous version of this chapter was presented to the Perspectives on the Canadian Voter: Puzzles of Influence and Choice workshop, 3-4 November 2007, in London, Ontario. I am grateful to Laura Stephenson and Cameron Anderson for their efforts in organizing the workshop. The comments made at the workshop were extremely helpful, particularly those provided by Blake Andrew. I would also like to acknowledge that important aspects of this chapter have been informed by extensive conversations with my research partners Fred Cutler and Scott Matthews. Furthermore, this chapter benefited greatly from data provided by Stuart Soroka and data coding performed by Thees Spreckelson. However, all responsibility for errors remains mine.

Appendix: Derivation of Multilevel Poll Effects Vote Model

I start with a linear poll effects model and then move on to the logistic model used in the body of this chapter. $AVOTE_t$ is the aggregate vote for the candidate of interest on day t. $AVOTE_t$ is a function of an equilibrium to which public opinion reverts in the absence of external shocks (γ_{00}), the effect of polls published on day t, and other campaign effects on that day (see Figure 1).

$$AVOTE_t = \gamma_{00} + \gamma_{01} \, poll_t + \mu_{0t}$$
$$\mu_{0t} = \rho\mu_{0,t-1} + v_t \tag{1}$$

The term μ_{0t} captures campaign effects other than polls. The effects of these other events are the residuals in the usual poll effects model. Here they are modelled as autoregressive since events on previous days might continue to have effects on subsequent days. The term $\mu_{0,t-1}$ is that part of the movement in public opinion away from its equilibrium on day $= t$ that remains from forces acting on the previous day (t-1). By modelling μ_{0t} as an autoregressive process, the residuals in this model are v_t.

As the aggregate vote on day t, $AVOTE_t$ is equivalent to the probability of the average individual voting for the candidate of interest on day t. $poll_t$ is the percentage of the population reported to be in support of the candidate of interest based on polls published on day $= t$. γ_{01} is the effect of these polls on the probability of the average individual voting for the candidate of interest on day t.

$IVOTE_{it}$ is the observed intention of individual i to vote for the candidate of interest at time t (coded 1 = yes, 0 = no). The probability of $IVOTE_{it} = 1$ is presented in Figure 2.

$$PR(IVOTE_{it} = 1) = AVOTE_t + \beta_{1t} \text{ (individual effect 1)} +$$
$$\beta_{2t} \text{ (individual effect 2)} + \dots \beta_{nt} \text{ (individual effect n)} + \varepsilon_{it}$$
$$AVOTE_t = \gamma_{00} + \gamma_{01} \, poll_t + \mu_{0t} \tag{2}$$
$$\mu_{0t} = \rho\mu_{0,t-1} + v_t$$

As stated before, $AVOTE_t$ is the probability of the average individual voting for the candidate of interest on day t. The probability of a particular individual i voting for the candidate of interest on day t is this average plus the effects of individual characteristics that make that individual more or less likely than the average to vote for the candidate of interest (such as political values, knowledge, and so on). This includes random unmodelled individual characteristics that are captured by ε_{it}.

The effect of polls on the probability of individual i voting for the candidate of interest on day t is through its effect on the probability of the average individual voting for the candidate of interest on day t. The challenge is to find a way to estimate the effect of these polls, controlling for the fact that published polls are highly correlated with other campaign events affecting the average vote and are therefore endogenous if μ_{0t} are the residuals, as they are in the usual voting model. This correlation/endogeneity must be accounted for since it will otherwise produce biased results for poll effects.[39]

Because polls are published at least one or two days after they are in the field, $poll_t$ is not affected by events that occur on day t and is therefore not contemporaneously correlated with μ_{0t}. It is what is called predetermined. $poll_t$ is correlated, however, with μ_{0t} in that events that occurred when the poll was conducted (say on day t-1) influenced *poll*$_t$ and, due to the autoregressive nature of public opinion, are captured in μ_{0t} as $\rho\mu_{0,t-1}$. Another way to state this is that both *poll*$_t$ and μ_{0t} are functions of $\mu_{0,t-1}$ and are therefore correlated. It is necessary, then, to control for that movement in public opinion that remains from events in previous time points. Explicitly modelling $\rho\mu_{0,t-1}$ does so by removing it from the residuals. Consequently, the residuals of the model used in this chapter (v_t) are not correlated with *poll*$_t$, so the model provides an unbiased estimate of poll effects.

Figure 2 is a linear poll effects model. As the dependent variable is the probability of an individual voting for a particular candidate, a logistic rather than a linear model is appropriate. Combining these considerations, the appropriate logistic model (leaving aside explicit individual effects for the moment) is presented in Figure 3.

$$IVOTE_{it} \sim bern(V_t)$$
$$logit(V_{it}) = logit\,(AVOTE_t)$$
$$logit\,(AVOTE_t) = \gamma_{00} + \gamma_{01}\,poll_t + \mu_{0t} \qquad (3)$$
$$\mu_{0t} = \rho\mu_{0,t-1} + v_t$$

The first line of the model describes an individual's intended vote for the party of interest at a particular time (coded 1 = yes, 0 = no) as having a Bernoulli distribution. This distribution has a single parameter V_{it}, which is the individual's probability of voting for that party at that time. As described by the second line, the logit of that probability is a linear function of the logit of the probability of the average individual voting for the party of interest at that time ($AVOTE_t$).[40] The third line describes how the logit of the probability of the average voter voting for the party of interest at time t is a function of an equilibrium, published polls, and other campaign events (μ_{0t}). These other events are described as an autoregressive process in the final line. The equilibrium and μ_{0t} are now expressed in log-odds units. *poll*$_t$ could also be converted to log-odds, but for the purposes of this chapter it was not.

As the second line in Figure 3 is redundant, this model can be expressed in the simpler form presented in the body of this chapter, with the first line relegated to a footnote (see Figure 4).

$$V_{it} = PR(IVOTE_{it} = 1|poll_t) = \frac{1}{1 + exp\,[-(\gamma_{00} + \gamma_{01}poll_t + \mu_{0t})]} \qquad (4)$$
$$\mu_{0t} = \rho\mu_{0,t-1} + v_t$$

The model of $IVOTE_{it}$ (Figure 3) was used in the analyses presented in this chapter. It can be extended to include equations describing how individual characteristics interact with polls so that different individuals are influenced by polls differently. For example, if β_{1t} is a measure of the effect of political ideology (*values*$_i$) on $IVOTE_{it}$, then the effect of *poll*$_t$ on $IVOTE_{it}$ contingent on the individual's political values can be estimated in the following way (see Figure 5).

$$IVOTE_{it} \sim bern\,(V_{it})$$
$$logit(V_{it}) = \beta_{0t} + \beta_{1t}\,values_i$$
$$\beta_{0t} = \gamma_{00} + \gamma_{01}poll_t + \mu_{0t}$$
$$\beta_{0t} = \gamma_{10} + \gamma_{11}poll_t + \mu_{1t} \qquad (5)$$
$$\mu_{0t} = \rho\mu_{0,t-1} + v_t$$
$$\mu_{1t} = \rho\mu_{1,t-1} + v_t$$

Here *AVOTE*$_t$ has been replaced by the more conventional notation β_{0t}. This more complex model is not used in this chapter.

Notes

1   See Delli Carpini and Keeter (1996) for a useful discussion on the first two of these assertions.
2   The term "failure of the polls" was popularized by Jowell et al. (1993) in their paper on the poor performance of polls in the 1992 UK general election. The performance of the polls was poor in terms of the surprising discrepancy between their measured support for the parties and the actual election outcome. Similarly, poll failure has been suggested to have occurred in a series of elections: US, 1948, 1980, and 1996; France, 2002; Germany, 2005; and Canada, 2004 and 2006.
3   The utility function for such a vote has been outlined for some time. For the Canadian case, see Black (1978). For the UK case, see Cain (1978). Strategic voting is also known as tactical voting.
4   This type of effect is consistent with the empirical results that Ceci and Kain (1982) use oppositional reactivity theory to explain.
5   The chapters in this volume by Bittner, Matthews, and Stephenson examine how political sophistication conditions political behaviour.
6   I am indebted to Fred Cutler for proposing this effect.
7   A wasted vote is commonly conceived as one that has little chance of changing the outcome of the election, such as a vote for a candidate who has very little chance of winning. Of course, even a vote for a top candidate in a close race has a low probability of changing the outcome, so one could say that just about every vote is "wasted." This is what underlies the paradox of voting.
8   See the chapter by Matthews in this volume for a discussion of this well-established finding.
9   There is some limited evidence that voters do use poll information in their vote decisions, most of which relates to strategic voting (Black 1978; Blais et al. 2001; Blais, Gidengil, and Nevitte 2006; Merolla and Stephenson 2007).
10   This term comes from the reference to vote intention polls as "horse race polls." The imagery of an election race between candidates as a horse race is also reflected in the reference to the single-member plurality electoral system as the "first-past-the-post" system.
11   Data collected from *Gallup Report*, 1963-87 (Toronto: Canadian Institute of Public Opinion).
12   It is necessary to explain what is meant by "independent" polls. In the 2004 and 2006 elections, some polling houses were in the field virtually every day. Each day they would publish the results from the last three days of polling. This means that two-thirds of the respondents from a given published poll are the same as those included in the previously published poll. In calculating the number of polls, it would be inaccurate to count these as two separate polls. The number of polls published by such polling houses was instead calculated as the total number of non-overlapping (or independent) polls.
13   For the 1993 and 1997 elections, the poll blackout period was seventy-two hours.
14   However, there was at least one additional house running only Internet polls in 2006 that is not included in this statistic.

15 Details on the sources of this data are provided below Table 10.1. Although there has been a shift toward media consumption through television and away from newspapers, the content of television coverage of polls tends to reflect closely that in newspapers. Moreover, there are data limitations on TV coverage prior to 1993 (Soroka 2002). Therefore, I use newspaper coverage in this chapter as it provides a consistent measure of media content that is likely made no less accurate by the trend toward greater television media consumption.

16 Particularly controversial were the 1948 US presidential election, the 1992 British general election, the 2005 German Bundestag election, and the first round of the 2002 French presidential vote. Many other elections have also been accompanied by debates regarding the accuracy of election polls, most recently the 2008 New Hampshire Democratic Party Primaries.

17 Much of the media coverage attributed the error to a misreading of Ontario voters in both the 2004 and the 2006 elections.

18 By *accuracy* is meant the distance of a given poll prediction from its target (the election result) measured as an absolute value (Martin, Traugott, and Kennedy 2005).

19 For useful reviews of such choices and their implications, see Voss, Gelman, and King (1995) and Groves (2004).

20 On this, Erikson et al. (2004) offer an especially chilling cautionary note from the US case.

21 The literature discussing the potential consequences of each of these decisions is substantial and includes Perry (1979); Converse and Traugott (1986); Crespi (1988); and Lau (1994).

22 The polling houses were inconsistent in terms of reporting results for the Green Party during the 2004 and 2006 elections. Consequently, they were left out of the analysis of poll bias. Subsequent to the 2006 election, results for the Green Party are much more consistently reported. An analysis of poll bias for or against the Green Party is possible for the 2008 election and can be found on the *Polling Observatory* website, http://pollob.politics.ox.ac.uk/.

23 The standard deviation of the error is allowed to be a function of the number of respondents in each poll. As discussed in Pickup and Johnston (2008), the form of that function is important.

24 I determined this simply by examining each story mentioning polls and identifying the exact horse race polls (if any) reported.

25 I calculated this both for all six papers and for just the two national papers. The differences in the resulting estimated media signal were minor. Therefore, Figures 10.7 and 10.8 present the results from the calculation using all six papers. The media signal for a given party at given time t was calculated as

$$\mu_t = \frac{\Sigma_i^m(n_{it} * poll_i)}{\Sigma_i^m n_{it,}}$$

where $poll_i$ is the level of party support indicated by poll; n_{it} is the number of stories at time t reporting $poll_i$ as the current level of party support; and m is the number of different polls reported at time t.

26 The exaggerated volatility exists in the aggregated media signal. Any individual media outlet might have had much lower variance in the poll results that it chose to report.

27 Again, this occurs after aggregating across polls.

28 The basis of this argument is that a candidate's popularity in the primary is an important indication of his or her ability to win the presidency and is therefore a strong factor in the party faithful's consideration of a candidate's attractiveness.

29 The probability of expressing a vote intention for the party of interest is mapped onto an observed expression of vote intention by a Bernoulli distribution: $IVOTE_{it} \sim bern(V_{it})$. The probabilistic nature of this mapping incorporates random differences between individuals, making them more or less likely than the average individual to express a vote intention for the party of interest.

30 The equilibrium and the residuals will be in log-odds units.

31 Strictly speaking, the objective is to ensure that the residuals are *independent* of the published polls.

32 Work using simulations is currently being done to demonstrate that this does in fact work in practice.

33 The model is also simplistic in that it assumes that a given reported poll result will have the same effect regardless of whether the result suggests an increase, a decrease, or no movement in party/candidate popularity. This is corrected easily by estimating separate effects for each of these possibilities. This was done in the following analysis, but the results were not substantially different from those produced by the simpler model and are therefore not reported.

34 The 2006 Canadian Election Study consists of a rolling cross-section campaign survey and a post-election survey. Only the rolling cross-section component was used in this analysis. Interviews of 4,058 eligible voters were conducted by telephone. The response rate was 57 percent. The fieldwork was conducted by the Institute for Social Research at York University, and the study was funded by Elections Canada.

35 The purpose of the model used to estimate poll effects is to control for unmeasured events that could produce endogeneity. As described in the appendix, these unmeasured events would exhibit themselves as autoregression in the error term. If the model has served its purpose, then its residuals should be white noise. That this has occurred can be tested with a Q-test. The results from this test are included in Table 10.2. The P-value for each Q-test indicates that we cannot reject the null hypothesis that the residuals are a white noise process, as we would expect if the model is properly specified.

36 These effects are produced by using the estimated coefficients in Table 10.1 to calculate the probability of an individual voting for the Liberals under the given circumstances. As described in the appendix, this is interpreted to be equivalent to the proportion of the aggregate voting population that would vote for the Liberals under the same circumstances.

37 As the Liberal and Conservative poll models are estimated separately, these results are based on the unlikely assumption that the poll effect from one party is independent of that from the others. This is a problem that needs to be addressed in further work.

38 From Table 2 in Blais, Gidengil, and Nevitte (2006, 269). The effect for the difference between the Conservatives and Liberals was not significant at the 0.05 level.

39 Strictly speaking, it is not just correlation that is a problem but also any violation of independence.

40 Note that, in the logistic model, the random effects of individual characteristics (ε_{it}) that make an individual more or less likely than the average to vote for the party of interest do not appear explicitly. Instead, this randomness is captured in the mapping of a vote probability onto an observed vote through a Bernoulli distribution.

References

Adams, Michael. 2004. "The Pollsters Did Not Blow It." *Environics* http://erg.environics.net/media_room/default.asp?aID=558.

Andersen, Robert. 2000. "Reporting Public Opinion Polls: The Media and the 1997 Canadian Election." *International Journal of Public Opinion Research* 12, 3: 285-98.

Andersen, Robert, and John Fox. 2001. "Pre-Election Polls and the Dynamics of the 1997 Canadian Federal Election." *Electoral Studies* 20, 1: 87-108.

Ansolabehere, Stephen, and Shanto Iyengar. 1994. "Of Horseshoes and Horse Races: Experimental Studies of the Impact of Poll Results on Electoral Behaviour." *Political Communication* 11, 4: 413-30.

Bartels, Larry M. 1988. *Presidential Primaries and the Dynamics of Public Choice.* Princeton: Princeton University Press.

Black, Jerome H. 1978. "The Multicandidate Calculus of Voting: Application to Canadian Federal Elections." *American Journal of Political Science* 22, 2: 610-38.

Blais, André, Elisabeth Gidengil, and Neil Nevitte. 2006. "Do Polls Influence the Vote?" In *Capturing Campaign Effects,* ed. Henry Brady and Richard Johnston, 263-79. Michigan: University of Michigan Press.

Blais, André, Richard Nadeau, Elisabeth Gidengil, and Neil Nevitte. 2001. "Measuring Strategic Voting in Multiparty Plurality Elections." *Electoral Studies* 20, 4: 343-52.

Buchanan, William. 1986. "Election Predictions: An Empirical Assessment." *Public Opinion Quarterly* 50, 2: 222-27.

Cain, Bruce. 1978. "Strategic Voting in Britain." *American Journal of Political Science* 22, 2: 639-55.

Carty, R. Kenneth, William Cross, and Lisa Young. 2000. *Rebuilding Canadian Party Politics.* Vancouver: UBC Press.

Ceci, Stephen J., and Edward L. Kain. 1982. "Jumping on the Bandwagon with the Underdog: The Impact of Attitude Polls on Polling Behaviour." *Public Opinion Quarterly* 46, 2: 228-42.

Converse, Philip E., and Michael W. Traugott. 1986. "Assessing the Accuracy of Polls and Surveys." *Science* 234, 4780: 1094-98.

Crespi, Irving. 1988. *Pre-Election Polling: Sources of Accuracy and Error.* New York: Russell Sage.

Delli Carpini, Michael X., and Scott Keeter. 1996. *What Americans Know about Politics and Why It Matters.* London: Yale University Press.

Downs, Anthony. 1957. *An Economic Theory of Democracy.* New York: Harper and Row.

Erikson, Robert S., and Lee Sigelman. 1995. "A Review: Poll-Based Forecasts of Mid-Term Congressional Election Outcomes: Do the Pollsters Get It Right?" *Public Opinion Quarterly* 59, 4: 589-605.

Erikson, Robert S., Costas Panagopoulos, and Christopher Wlezien. 2004. "Likely (and Unlikely) Voters and the Assessment of Campaign Dynamics." *Public Opinion Quarterly* 68, 4: 588-601.

Erikson, Robert S., and Christopher Wlezien. 1999. "Presidential Polls as a Timeseries: The Case of 1996." *Public Opinion Quarterly* 63, 2: 163-77.

Ferguson, Peter A., and Cristine de Clercy. 2005. "Regulatory Compliance in Opinion Poll Reporting during the 2004 Canadian Election." *Canadian Public Policy* 31, 3: 243-57.

Fleitas, Daniel W. 1971. "Bandwagon and Underdog Effects in Minimal-Information Elections." *American Political Science Review* 65, 2: 434-38.

Frankovic, Kathleen. 2005. "Reporting 'the Polls' in 2004." *Public Opinion Quarterly* 69, 5: 682-97.

Frizzell, Alan, Jon H. Pammett, and Anthony Westell. 1989. *The Canadian General Election of 1988*. Ottawa: Carleton University Press.

Frizzell, Alan, and Anthony Westell. 1985. *The Canadian General Election of 1984: Politicians, Parties, Press, and Polls*. Ottawa: Carleton University Press.

Groves, Robert M. 2004. *Survey Errors and Survey Costs*. New York: John Wiley.

Hickman, Harrison. 1991. "Public Polls and Election Participants." In *Polling and Presidential Election Coverage*, ed. Paul J. Lavrakas and Jack K. Holley, 100-33. London: Sage Publications.

Irwin, Galen, and Joop J.M. van Holsteyn. 2002. "According to the Polls: The Influence of Opinion Polls on Expectations." *Public Opinion Quarterly* 66, 1: 92-104.

Jackman, Simon. 2005. "Pooling the Polls over an Election Campaign." *Australian Journal of Political Science* 40, 4: 499-517.

Johnston, Richard, André Blais, Henry E. Brady, and Jean Crête. 1992. *Letting the People Decide: Dynamics of a Canadian Election*. Montreal: McGill-Queen's University Press; Stanford, CA: Stanford University Press.

Jowell, Roger, Barry Hedges, Peter Lynn, Graham Farrant, and Anthony Heath. 1993. "Review: The 1992 British Election – The Failure of the Polls." *Public Opinion Quarterly* 57, 2: 238-63.

Kahneman, Daniel, Daniel Slovic, and Amos Tversky. 1982. *Judgment under Uncertainty: Heuristics and Biases*. Cambridge, UK: Cambridge University Press.

Kenney, Patrick J., and Tom W. Rice. 1994. "The Psychology of Political Momentum." *Political Research Quarterly* 47, 4: 923-38.

Lachapelle, Guy. 1991. *Polls and the Media in Canadian Elections: Taking the Pulse*. Research study of the Royal Commission on Electoral Reform and Party Financing. Toronto: Dundurn Press.

Lau, Richard R. 1994. "An Analysis of the Accuracy of 'Trial Heat' Polls during the 1992 Presidential Election." *Public Opinion Quarterly* 58, 1: 2-20.

Marks, Gary. 2007. "Introduction: Triangulation and the Square-Root Law." *Electoral Studies* 26, 1: 1-10.

Marsh, Catherine. 1985. "Back on the Bandwagon: The Effect of Opinion Polls on Public Opinion." *British Journal of Political Science* 15, 1: 51-74.

Marshall, Thomas R. 1983. "The News Verdict and Public Opinion during the Primaries." In *Television Coverage of the 1980 Presidential Campaign*, ed. William C. Adams, 49-67. Norwood, NJ: Ablex.

Martin, Elizabeth A., Michael W. Traugott, and Courtney Kennedy. 2005. "A Review and Proposal for a New Measure of Poll Accuracy." *Public Opinion Quarterly* 69, 3: 342-69.

McAllister, Ian, and Donley T. Studlar. 1991. "Bandwagon, Underdog, or Projection? Opinion Polls and Electoral Choice in Britain, 1979-1987." *Journal of Politics* 53, 3: 720-41.

Merolla, Jennifer L., and Laura B. Stephenson. 2007. "Strategic Voting in Canada: A Cross Time Analysis." *Electoral Studies* 26, 2: 235-46.

Mitofsky, Warren J. 1998. "Review: Was 1996 a Worse Year for Polls than 1948?" *Public Opinion Quarterly* 62, 2: 230-49.

Mutz, Diana C. 1997. "Mechanisms of Momentum: Does Thinking Make It So?" *Journal of Politics* 59, 1: 104-25.

–. 1998. *Impersonal Influence: How Perceptions of Mass Collectives Affect Political Attitudes.* New York: Cambridge University Press.

Perry, Paul. 1979. "Certain Problems in Election Survey Methodology." *Public Opinion Quarterly* 43, 3: 312-25.

Petty, Richard E., and John T. Cacioppo. 1996. *Attitudes and Persuasion: Classic and Contemporary Approaches.* 2nd ed. Boulder, CO: Westview Press.

Pickup, Mark. 2007. "A Receive-Accept Model of Poll Effects." Paper presented at the 2007 European Consortium of Political Research, Pisa, September.

Pickup, Mark, and Richard Johnston. 2007. "Campaign Trial Heats as Electoral Information: Evidence from the 2004 and 2006 Canadian Federal Elections." *Electoral Studies* 26, 2: 460-76.

–. 2008. Campaign Trial Heats as Election Forecasts: Measurement Error and Bias in 2004 Presidential Campaign Polls." *International Journal of Forecasting* 24, 2: 272-84.

Popkin, Samuel L. 1994. *The Reasoning Voter: Communication and Persuasion in Presidential Campaigns.* Chicago: University of Chicago Press.

Shelley, Mack C. II, and Hwarng-du Hwang. 1991. "The Mass Media and Public Opinion Polls in the 1988 Presidential Election." *American Politics Research* 19, 1: 59-79.

Sigelman, Lee. 1989. "The 1988 Presidential Nominations: Whatever Happened to Momentum?" *PS: Political Science and Politics* 22, 1: 35-39.

Skalaban, Andrew. 1988. "Do the Polls Affect Elections? Some 1980 Evidence." *Political Behaviour* 10, 2: 136-50.

Sniderman, Paul M., Richard A. Brody, and Philip E. Tetlock. 1991. *Reasoning and Choice: Explorations in Political Psychology.* New York: Cambridge University Press.

Soderlund, Walter C., Walter Romanow, E. Donald Briggs, and Ronald H. Wagenberg. 1984. *Media and Elections in Canada.* Toronto: Holt, Rinehart, and Winston.

Soroka, Stuart. 2002. *Agenda-Setting Dynamics in Canada.* Vancouver: UBC Press.

Traugott, Michael W. 2001. "Trends: Assessing Poll Performance in the 2000 Campaign." *Public Opinion Quarterly* 65, 2: 389-419.

–. 2005. "The Accuracy of the National Preelection Polls in the 2004 Presidential Election." *Public Opinion Quarterly* 69, 5: 642-54.

Voss, D. Stephen, Andrew Gelman, and Gary King. 1995. "A Review: Preelection Survey Methodology – Details from Eight Polling Organizations, 1988 and 1992." *Public Opinion Quarterly* 59, 1: 98-132.

Vowles, Jack. 2002. "Did the Polls Influence the Vote? A Case Study of the 1999 New Zealand Election." *Political Science* 54, 1: 67-77.

Wagenberg, R.H., W.C. Soderlund, W.I. Romanow, and E.D. Briggs. 1988. "Campaigns, Images, and Polls: Mass Media Coverage of the 1984 Canadian Election." *Canadian Journal of Political Science* 21, 1: 117-29.

Wlezien, Christopher, and Robert S. Erikson. 2002. "The Timeline of Presidential Election Campaigns." *Journal of Politics* 64, 4: 969-93.

Worcester, Robert. 1996. "Political Polling: 95% Expertise and 5% Luck." *Journal of the Royal Statistical Society, Series A (Statistics in Society)* 159, 1: 5-20.

Zaller, John R. 1991. "Information, Values, and Opinion." *American Political Science Review* 85, 4: 1215-38.

–. 1992. *The Nature and Origins of Mass Opinions.* Cambridge, UK: Cambridge University Press.

Zeller, Richard A., and Edward G. Carmines. 1980. *Measurement in the Social Sciences: The Link between Theory and Data.* Cambridge, UK: Cambridge University Press.

Reflecting on Lessons from the Canadian Voter

Cameron D. Anderson and Laura B. Stephenson

11

In the introduction to this volume, we suggested the analogy of a puzzle as a way to understand the study of voting behaviour in Canada. There are two important aspects of a puzzle: the individual pieces and the overall picture that the pieces make. Identifying the salient pieces of the voting behaviour puzzle has come a long way since the scholarly treatment of voting behaviour first began in the middle of the twentieth century. Political scientists have produced a large body of literature that both identifies the important pieces and provides an overall picture of how the pieces fit together. The Canadian voter is not an enigma. There exists a rich collection of sources that scholars and the informed public can turn to in order to understand election outcomes.

In this vein, it is important to recognize that the current literature paints a much more complex picture of voting than did the early studies of voting behaviour, which almost universally used the logic of the Columbia model to examine socioeconomic categories as the sources of voting preferences. Researchers today pursue a variety of approaches to understand either the whole picture or (more commonly) one of the puzzle pieces in detail, such as looking at individual characteristics of voters, examining trends in the general population, assessing variation in political and economic context, considering differential reactions of subsets of the electorate, and focusing on the effects of campaigns, media, and political information. The chapters in this volume have considered many of the major factors in the study of voting behaviour and have made original contributions to our knowledge of them.

What has become clear, and what is readily evident if one considers other recent publications on voting behaviour, is that trying to understand the dynamics of a single election can overlook many of the fascinating nuances of the vote decision process. That is, to know that a particular issue did or did not matter in a single election – say the economy in 1997 (Blais et al. 2002b) or the same-sex marriage issue in 2004 (Dostie-Goulet 2006) – gives us an interesting piece of information about aggregate voting in a single context, but it does not give us particulars about the effects of those issue considerations across time or on individual voters. If nothing else, the chapters in this volume reinforce the fact that the many potential voting factors matter at different times for different people. Not all voters or situations are alike, and until we look more closely at the potential influences individually, our understanding of voting behaviour, apart from the outcomes of specific elections, will be limited.

To conclude this volume, we would like to comment on three themes arising from the collective insights of the research contained in the previous chapters. Each chapter could stand on its own as a scholarly contribution to the literature, but as a whole, we believe, they present a unique snapshot of the voting behaviour literature and insights into the direction of future research.

First, and most clearly, the study of voting behaviour in Canada is focused on assessing how and when known correlates of electoral choice influence the decisions of voters. Although we know the main parameters of influences on vote choice, many of the chapters in this volume explore the importance of identifying variation (at the individual level as well as between parties or elections) in *how* these factors influence vote choice.

Second, some of the chapters present null or partially null findings. Despite sound logical foundations, Canadian voters do not always act according to theoretical expectations. These sorts of findings, though unexpected, remain informative. Indeed, questions arising from such findings might include the following. What are the implications when the data do not confirm what logic has predicted? How do these non-findings contribute to the study of voting behaviour? As reflected in the discussions in many of the chapters, the presence of null or unexpected findings denotes an important lesson in the conduct of voting behaviour research and demonstrates the challenge of finding theories that are borne out in reality.

Third, it is appropriate to take stock of what the chapters in this volume contribute to our understanding of *Canadian* elections and voting as well as to the broader *comparative* literature on voting behaviour. Although the chapters here do not exhaust the breadth of voting behaviour work in Canada, they do provide a representative sample of current research agendas in the field. As such, they also provide a good example of the state of the literature – not only what is known from previous work but also what is still to be investigated.

Heterogeneity in Canadian Voting

A central contribution of the key models of voting behaviour (such as Columbia or Michigan) to the study of voting in Canada has been to highlight the importance of regularities and consistencies in human behaviour. For example, were it not for the Columbia model's emphasis on religious background, Meisel (1975) and others might not have discovered the tendency of Catholic Canadians to vote for the Liberal Party. Similarly, the importance of region was found only by considering how where one lives impacts his or her voting preferences (Gidengil et al. 1999). These findings suggest general expectations that should apply to all Canadian voters, as these regularities were found among many voters who share the same characteristic.

However, despite the summary evidence, looking for the same effect among all voters might not provide the most accurate picture of voting behaviour. Important differences between voters might be obscured. For instance, though we know that Catholics are more likely to vote for the Liberal Party, it may be that not all Catholics support the Liberal Party. Perhaps it is only those who hold certain attitudes, beliefs, or experiences. By having the same expectations for all voters, and treating them equally in our analyses, we run the risk of distorting the true effects of particular variables by averaging them out over the population. Some voters might be swayed in one direction and other voters in the opposite direction. These sources of heterogeneity in voting behaviour might be masked unless researchers probe deeply.

This type of differentiation among voters is similar to what Clarke et al. (1979) proposed when they developed the flexible and durable categories of partisans. In their 1996 book, they demonstrate that issues, leader evaluations, and long-term allegiances contributed to vote choice in 1993 in different proportions depending on one's type of partisanship. Although the nature of partisanship remains contested (see, for example, Gidengil et al. 2006), the idea that different people will respond to voting factors in different ways has been gaining currency and support for many years.

Exemplifying the theme of individual-level heterogeneity in voting behaviour are the effects of partisanship considered in a few of the preceding chapters. Specifically, the evidence presented suggests that all partisans are not the same. One's personal characteristics, or the party that one supports, might make a difference to the effect that partisanship has on vote behaviour. Bilodeau and Kanji observe differentiation on the basis of immigrant experience. They find that Liberal partisans are not all alike – if a partisan is an immigrant, then he or she is likely to be more stable and loyal to the Liberal Party than Canadian-born partisans. Furthermore, Bilodeau and Kanji suggest that this finding has implications for the future of the party. As a party that relies on its relatively larger number of partisans for electoral success (Blais et al. 2002a), the Liberals might consider strategically targeting or maintaining their appeal to immigrants in order to boost their committed constituency.

These findings mesh well with those of Bélanger and Stephenson, who point out differences in the nature of partisanship across parties. In their study, they propose that the ideological clarity of a party might influence the strength, loyalty, and commitment of partisans. Except with respect to stability, these expectations hold – the NDP, BQ, former Reform and Alliance Parties, and Conservative Party have the most committed partisans, whereas the Liberals have the least. However, the Liberal supporters are (unexpectedly) stable – perhaps due to the number of immigrants in the group. These differences are the kind that can be overlooked in vote models if partisanship is included as a variable and expected to have a uniform influence on all vote decisions. By looking at the issue more closely, these authors have provided us with a more nuanced way of understanding why and when partisanship matters for vote choice.

Another well-documented case of heterogeneity within the electorate comes from research on the effects of political information. Since the work of Sniderman, Brody, and Tetlock (1991) and Zaller (1992), it has become popular (and in many senses necessary) to consider how information accentuates, distorts, or clarifies effects in traditional vote models. Earlier studies, such as Fiorina's (1981) retrospective voting work, noted that those high in political information (or sophistication, as it is sometimes called) were able to vote retrospectively, whereas those low in political information behaved differently. Studies that examine the use of heuristics (such as party labels, candidate traits, and so on) also confirm the importance of political information (see, for example, Lau and Redlawsk 2001), and recent work in Canadian political behaviour has addressed the effects of information on various aspects of voter behaviour (Roy 2009). It is thus important to consider how one's personal characteristics might or might not interact to diminish or magnify influences on voting.

In this volume, consideration of the differentiating effects of information and sophistication is present in the chapters by Stephenson, Bittner, and Matthews. Not all voters are equally influenced by the long-term, short-term, and proximate factors that make up the voting "funnel of causality" (see Figure 1.1). For instance, Stephenson's chapter on the tendency of Catholics to vote for the Liberal Party finds that the impact of the sponsorship scandal on the decision to vote Liberal was most pronounced for high sophisticates and that sophisticated Catholics' long-standing attachment to the Liberal Party is most vulnerable to being overcome by their issue preferences. If the electorate is examined as a whole, without investigating differences in sophistication, then these results are not evident. Similarly, Bittner speculates that information might influence the use of candidate evaluations in vote decisions such that low-information voters might be more likely to draw on leader evaluations. She finds that leader evaluations do influence Canadian voters, but she recognizes that factoring such evaluations into one's vote decision might be a cognitive shortcut – and thus most likely to be used by those in need of a shortcut to avoid having to gather additional information to cast an informed ballot. Finally, Matthews' chapter considers whether campaigns work as equalizers to increase the information of low sophisticates and, in so doing, level the impact of economic considerations on the vote decision. Although his findings mostly run opposite to his expectations (which we discuss below), he does find that campaigns have a differential effect on those with university degrees compared to those without degrees. Degree holders demonstrate an increase in the effect of economic evaluations on their vote decisions by the end of the campaign.

Although empirical generalizations provide useful traction for understanding voting behaviour in the aggregate, one of the central insights of this volume is the intellectual value of identifying and understanding nuance and differentiation. As demonstrated by many of the chapters here, focusing our analytical lens on distinctions within the electorate is a promising direction of study and can add much to our collective understanding of voting behaviour in Canada. By examining heterogeneity within core findings about Canadian voters, we can sharpen our election models and improve their explanatory and predictive capabilities.

The Usefulness of Null Findings

The second issue that we see emerging from the chapters in this volume is that voters do not always behave as theories, and possibly even extant research, indicate they should. The voting models, as initially developed, do not discriminate between national contexts, and thus the regularities found through voting models are assumed to apply to all voters everywhere. However, research into Canadian elections has long found that voting models developed in the United States are not always directly applicable in Canada. Consider, for example, the null findings for the influence of class found by Alford (1963) and others. When a theory is refuted, what are the implications for the research?

Null findings do not inherently indicate that a model should be discarded in a specific context. Rather, negative findings can point to a need to understand how the context in which a voting model is applied affects the elements of the model. Are there underlying assumptions of the model that have not been acknowledged? Does the model's success depend on a particular type of voter, or party, or issue? For instance, it is important to account for specific long-term, short-term, and proximate factors that are particular to a country. One example is the effect of race in the United States. Race is an important predictor of vote choice in the United States in that African Americans are much more likely to vote for the Democratic Party. Although this observation is central to American voting, there might be no or very little effect of race on voting patterns in other countries. Indeed, including race in a model of Canadian voting behaviour is likely to be inconsequential. At the same time, within Canada, language is a central predictor of vote choice, particularly within Quebec, so the inclusion of whether or not the respondent speaks French is much more important in Canada (although not in the American context). Thus, understanding when and why theories "fail" provides researchers with important information about the potential limits of theoretic generalizability. Furthermore, such "failures" help to push research agendas forward with amendments or adaptations that more fully specify the causal processes at play.

The chapters in this volume go beyond pointing out country-specific exceptions to demonstrate that there are instances when voters do not fulfill the expectations of political scientists for how they cast their ballots.

The chapter on campaign effects by Matthews is an excellent example. As developed in his chapter, there is ample theoretical reason to expect that one's sophistication will amplify the importance of campaign events for a voter, and evidence of this effect exists in other national contexts. However, Matthews finds almost no evidence for the theorized effects of an election campaign. What do such findings mean? Is there something wrong with the theories that have been applied? Are the data inappropriate to answer the question? How should a researcher proceed?

First and foremost, it is important to recognize that null findings, even though they tend to be underreported in academic journals, can tell us a great deal about political phenomena. Finding that a theory is not supported by data can open up new avenues of investigation. In the case of campaign effects, null findings inevitably raise further questions, such as whether there was anything about specific elections that might have eliminated or undermined the observation of campaign effects. For example, were the campaign messages of each major party salient and well publicized? Were there specific events in the campaign that might have served to obscure the observation of campaign effects? Did any aspects of the election campaigns violate fundamental assumptions of the theoretical propositions?

Other chapters also demonstrate the incidence of null findings and constructive responses to them. For instance, Anderson's chapter produces some surprising, if not completely null, findings. Anderson addresses the influence of economic conditions on vote choice by demonstrating that sociotropic prospective economic evaluations have the greatest effect on federal incumbent support in the elections under consideration. This finding contradicts much existing work in the field that points to retrospective evaluations as generally being more important. Attempting to respond to this surprising finding, Anderson speculates that, consistent with other work on economic voting, the specific political context of each election under consideration might contribute to these findings. Thus, this response opens up the possibility of incorporating contextual variables into the study of economic voting in Canada. This represents a step forward in our theoretical understanding of how economic conditions impact Canadian voters.

The chapter by Goodyear-Grant also includes null findings. She tests whether a sex-based affinity exists for voting for female candidates and finds that men are more likely to vote for female candidates than women – a finding that is opposite to expectations. Goodyear-Grant uses the null finding as an opportunity to examine the attitudinal characteristics of who *does* vote for women candidates, exploring a multitude of potential arguments that have been put forth by other researchers. She finds two factors apart from partisanship that influence the decision to vote for a female candidate. Once again, null findings provide the spark for further research that provides a more nuanced picture of voting behaviour, and null findings in Canada with respect to theories that have been supported in the American case open up an additional avenue of research into contextual differences that might matter.

As some of the chapters in this book demonstrate, null findings can be theoretically useful. The fact that a well-developed theory (particularly if it has empirical support elsewhere) fails to be confirmed with Canadian data opens up many possibilities for future research and for improving existing theory. Understanding the Canadian case in this way, "importing" theories from other countries or political contexts can be an extremely rewarding endeavour for both Canadian researchers and the larger community of voting behaviour researchers around the world.

Contributions of This Volume

The final theme that we wish to highlight is what we believe to be the collective contribution that this volume makes to our understanding of voting behaviour in Canada as well as the broader comparative literature on elections and voting. The chapters here serve as an update, reassessment, and reinvigoration of the major theories of voting behaviour. Drawing on the initial insights of the Columbia model of voting, the chapters assessing the role of gender, religion, and ethnicity elaborate on these influences in Canadian voting. Together they demonstrate the continued salience of core sociodemographic characteristics in voting. Other chapters comment on the application of the Michigan model in Canadian voting. Whether through a consideration of partisanship or through the role of issues (such as economic conditions) and leaders on vote choice, many of the chapters reassess some of the core applications of the sociopsychological model of voting and push our understanding of how these influences manifest themselves within the Canadian case.

Beyond focusing on vote choice and updating theoretical applications in Canada, the chapters here make a novel contribution by isolating the sustained impacts of specific variables on vote choice. Each chapter gives prime theoretical attention to the effects on vote choice of one type of independent variable (be it religion, partisanship, campaign effects, or campaign poll effects). This feature allows the authors to explore in depth how their particular independent variable shapes vote choice in Canada. In this sense, the chapters have been written and the analyses developed with a great degree of parsimony and theoretical clarity.

Although many chapters are deeply rooted in an existing literature and theoretical tradition in understanding Canadian voting and elections, some of them embark on new directions of study. For instance, the chapter by Goodyear-Grant on sex-based affinities for female candidates is the first of its kind in the Canadian case. By exploring who votes for women candidates and why, the chapter uncovers a new angle of research into the relationships between electoral choice and gender in Canada. Similarly, the chapter by Pickup on the effects of poll bias in election campaigns contributes to a recently developed research agenda in the study of election campaigns. The field of voting behaviour in Canada still contains significant unmapped terrain, and research such as that contained in these chapters helps us to understand better the full range of factors that influence voting.

Many of the chapters also provide speculation on directions for future research in the study of voting behaviour in Canada. Each chapter closes its discussion of findings and implications with fresh ideas for research into voting behaviour in Canada. As a result, not only do these chapters collectively update and renew our understanding of electoral choice in Canada, but they also contribute myriad directions for where voting research can and should go in the future. It is our hope that current and future scholars will pursue many of these research directions and that the field of Canadian voting behaviour will grow both in depth (through further analysis of existing research areas) and breadth (through the study of new research topics).

Finally, and perhaps most importantly, we believe that this volume contributes to the broader comparative literature on voting and elections. Many of the central theoretical statements about voting and elections were originally developed to understand and explain electoral phenomena in the United States. The application of these theoretical contributions in other democratic countries has been fruitful since it allows for a consideration of how well these theories "travel": that is, whether they can be considered accurate for democratic political behaviour in general. Consider, for example, the study of party identification. The original development of the term in the United States sparked great interest elsewhere and led scholars not only in Canada but also in Great Britain and France (among other places) to apply the concept. The findings demonstrated that the concept could not be understood the same way in each country.[1] When findings from other countries contradict or challenge the accepted wisdom, comparative theory is compelled to account for these varying observations. Indeed, in the case of partisanship, the literature has developed significantly because of these findings. In this sense, the study of elections and voting as undertaken in this volume can be viewed as contributing to the comparative conversation among scholars about influences on vote decisions and when they are most likely to operate. Through testing, retesting, and proposing new theories and amending existing hypotheses developed to explain voting behaviour, each chapter adds to our understanding of how citizens arrive at vote decisions.

The findings in this volume also make clear that Canada has particular cultural and institutional features that facilitate as well as mitigate the applicability of comparative theory in Canada. The collective exercise of researching and writing the chapters that comprise this book depended on an awareness of which findings and theories exist elsewhere and how (and how well) they apply to the Canadian case. Discovering and comprehending the implications of this uniqueness better enables researchers to understand not only the Canadian voter but also the mechanisms by which many voting factors operate. This is a contribution to the study of political behaviour writ large, and thus we see the insights of each chapter as important and original contributions to the comparative literature on elections and voting in democratic states.

Just as each chapter closes by looking to the future, so too does our discussion here. The study of voting behaviour is important because it is through the act of voting that democracy operates. Knowing how and why voters act provides keen insight into the nature and health of the democratic process in Canada. It also provides us with an understanding of where the country is headed. As population demographics change and as issues rise and fall in importance, voting patterns and influences on vote choice might change as well. As a result, keeping abreast of changes within the Canadian electorate as well as considering the implications of changes for the vote decision itself provide an important indication of what shape Canadian democracy will take in the twenty-first century.

Note

1 More detail on this topic is provided in the first chapter of this volume.

References

Alford, Robert R. 1963. *Party and Society: The Anglo-American Democracies.* Chicago: Rand McNally.

Blais, André, Richard Nadeau, Elisabeth Gidengil, and Neil Nevitte. 2002a. *Anatomy of a Liberal Victory: Making Sense of the Vote in the 2000 Canadian Election.* Peterborough, ON: Broadview Press.

–. 2002b. "The Impact of Issues and the Economy in the 1997 Canadian Federal Election." *Canadian Journal of Political Science* 35, 2: 409-21.

Clarke, Harold D., Lawrence LeDuc, Jane Jenson, and Jon H. Pammett. 1979. *Political Choice in Canada.* Toronto: McGraw-Hill Ryerson.

–. 1996. *Absent Mandate: Canadian Electoral Politics in an Era of Restructuring.* 3rd ed. Toronto: Gage.

Dostie-Goulet, Eugénie. 2006. "Le mariage homosexuel et le vote au Canada." *Politique et sociétés* 25, 1: 129-44.

Fiorina, M. 1981. *Retrospective Voting in American National Elections.* New Haven: Yale University Press.

Gidengil, Elisabeth, André Blais, Joanna Everitt, Patrick Fournier, and Neil Nevitte. 2006. "Is the Concept of Party Identification Applicable in Canada? A Panel-Based Analysis." Paper presented at the ECPR 34th Joint Sessions of Workshops, Nicosia, Cyprus, 25-30 April.

Gidengil, Elisabeth, André Blais, Neil Nevitte, and Richard Nadeau. 1999. "Making Sense of Regional Voting in the 1997 Federal Election: Liberal and Reform Support Outside Quebec." *Canadian Journal of Political Science* 32, 2: 247-72.

Lau, Richard R., and David P. Redlawsk. 2001. "Advantages and Disadvantages of Cognitive Heuristics in Political Decision Making." *American Journal of Political Science* 45, 4: 951-71.

Meisel, John. 1975. *Working Papers on Canadian Politics.* 2nd ed. Montreal: McGill-Queen's University Press.

Roy, Jason. 2009. "Voter Heterogeneity: Informational Differences and Voting." *Canadian Journal of Political Science* 42, 1: 117-38.

Sniderman, Paul, Richard Brody, and Philip Tetlock. 1991. *Reasoning and Choice: Explorations in Political Psychology.* New York: Cambridge University Press.

Zaller, John. 1992. *The Nature and Origins of Mass Opinion.* New York: Cambridge University Press.

Contributors

Cameron D. Anderson is an assistant professor of political science at the University of Western Ontario. His research interests include elections, voting, and public opinion. His work has appeared in the *American Journal of Political Science*, the *Canadian Journal of Political Science*, *Electoral Studies*, and *Acta Politica*.

Éric Bélanger is an assistant professor in the Department of Political Science at McGill University and is a member of the Centre for the Study of Democratic Citizenship. His research interests include Quebec and Canadian politics, political parties and party systems, and public opinion and voting behaviour. His research has been published in a number of scholarly journals, including *Comparative Political Studies*, *Political Research Quarterly*, *Electoral Studies*, *Publius: The Journal of Federalism*, *European Journal of Political Research*, and the *Canadian Journal of Political Science*. He is also the co-author of a book on Quebec politics, *Le comportement électoral des Québécois* (2009).

Antoine Bilodeau is an assistant professor of political science at Concordia University. His research focuses on the political integration of immigrants in Canada and other Western democracies in terms of political participation and values. He has published work in the *International Migration Review*, the *Journal of Ethnic and Migration Studies*, the *International Political Science Review*, *PS: Political Science and Politics*, the *Canadian Journal of Political Science*, and the *Australian Journal of Political Science*.

Amanda Bittner is an assistant professor in the Department of Political Science at Memorial University. She is interested in the study of public opinion and voting, including the effects of knowledge and information on voter decision making and the institutional and structural incentives affecting voting behaviour in both Canadian and comparative contexts. Her work has appeared in the *Canadian Journal of Political Science* and *Electoral Studies.*

Elizabeth Goodyear-Grant is an assistant professor in the Department of Political Studies at Queen's University. Her research interests include political behaviour, elections, media and politics, and women and politics. Her work appears in the *Canadian Journal of Political Science, Canadian Public Administration,* and *Electoral Studies.*

Mebs Kanji is an assistant professor of political science at Concordia University. His research interests include the correlates and consequences of value diversity between different value communities in Canada and across other advanced industrial states. His most recent publications can be found in the *Journal of Comparative Policy Analysis,* the *American Review of Canadian Studies,* and the *Journal of Parliamentary and Political Law.*

J. Scott Matthews is an assistant professor of political studies at Queen's University. His research specializes in the study of elections, voting, and public opinion. His work has been published in the *Canadian Journal of Political Science, Electoral Studies,* the *European Journal of Political Research,* and the *Canadian Review of Sociology and Anthropology.*

Richard Nadeau is a professor in the Department of Political Science at Université de Montréal and is a member of the Centre for the Study of Democratic Citizenship. He is also a research director of the Chaire d'études politiques et économiques américaines at the Centre d'études et de recherches internationales at his university, and he was a member of the Canadian Election Studies team for many years. A specialist in elections, electoral behaviour, opinion polls, public opinion, media and politics, and methodology, he has had work published in many journals, such as the *American Political Science Review, American Journal of Political Science, Journal of Politics,* and *British Journal of Political Science.* He is also a co-author of several books on Canadian electoral politics, including *Citizens* (2004), *Anatomy of a Liberal Victory* (2002), *Unsteady State* (2000), and *Le comportement électoral des Québécois* (2009).

Mark Pickup is an assistant professor in the Department of Political Science at Simon Fraser University and runs the Oxford Polling Observatory website. He is a specialist in comparative politics, with a particular interest in North American and European countries, focusing on election campaigns, political behaviour, and polling methodology. His work has appeared in several venues, including *Electoral Studies,* the *Canadian Journal of Political Science,* the *British Journal of Political Science,* and the *International Journal of Forecasting.*

Laura B. Stephenson is an assistant professor in the Department of Political Science at the University of Western Ontario. Her research interests include studying the links between electoral systems, party strategies, and voting behaviour; the effects of party label cues on cross-national voting behaviour; and partisanship in Canada. Her work has appeared in several journals, such as *Electoral Studies, Political Psychology,* and the *Canadian Journal of Political Science.*

Index

Printed and bound in Canada by Friesens

Set in Myriad, Giovanni, and Garamond Condensed
by Artegraphica Design Co. Ltd.

Copy editor: Dallas Harrison

Proofreader and indexer: Dianne Tiefensee